13537

364.1
Vog   Vogel, Steve

REASONABLE DOUBT

DATE DUE			
JAN. 1 6 1990	SEP. 2 0 1990	JUL. 0 8 1992	APR 0 2 1992
JAN. 1 8 1990	NOV. 2 1990 R	MAR 2 9 1996	
FEB 1 6 1990	DEC. 0 8 1990	APR 1 5 1996	
MAR. 0 5 1990	DEC. 2 4 1990	DEC 0 5 1998	
MAR. 1 5 1990	JAN 0 9 1991	APR 2 7 2000	
MAR. 2 8 1990	JAN 2 1 1991	DEC 0 5 2003	
APR. 1 6 1990	FEB 0 2 1991	AUG 0 8 2008	
MAY 1 0 1990	APR. 2 3 1991	SEP 2 2 2010	
MAY 3 1 1990	JUL. 1 0 1991		
JUN 2 1 1990	JUL. 2 4 1991		
JUN 2 8 1990	MAR. 1 9 1992		

D0948921

REASONABLE
DOUBT

REASONABLE DOUBT

STEVE VOGEL

CB
CONTEMPORARY
BOOKS
CHICAGO · NEW YORK

Library of Congress Cataloging-in-Publication Data

Vogel, Steve.
    Reasonable doubt : a true story of lust and murder
in the American heartland / Steve Vogel.
       p.   cm.
    ISBN 0-8092-4321-0 : $19.95
    1. Murder—Illinois—Bloomington—Case studies.
2. Hendricks, David.   I. Title.
HV6534.B56V64   1989
364.1′523′09772255—dc20   89-15889
                                             CIP

Material from *Lake Wobegon Days* by Garrison Keillor. Copyright © 1985
by Garrison Keillor. All rights reserved. Reprinted by permission of Viking
Penguin, a division of Penguin Books USA, Inc.

Material from *The Implosion Conspiracy* by Louis Nizer (NY: Doubleday,
1973). Copyright © 1973 by Louis Nizer. Reprinted by permission of the
author.

Copyright © 1989 by Steve Vogel
All rights reserved
Published by Contemporary Books, Inc.
180 North Michigan Avenue, Chicago, Illinois 60601
Manufactured in the United States of America
International Standard Book Number: 0-8092-4321-0

Published simultaneously in Canada by Beaverbooks, Ltd.
195 Allstate Parkway, Valleywood Business Park
Markham, Ontario L3R 4T8 Canada

To my parents,
James and Hazel Vogel,
who sacrificed so often
so I could have so much

Acknowledgments

Much of what is in this book I personally observed. Much of it is from the official record. None of it is invented. Assertions about what people said, thought, or did are based on the memories of dozens of people. Their names are contained in these pages. But I particularly want to thank Ron Dozier, Laverne Hendricks, Hal Jennings, and John Long for their help, cooperation, understanding, and patience with me during repeated and lengthy interview sessions.

Without the early encouragement and advice of my late friend and bestselling author Charles Merrill Smith, this book would not even have been started. Thanks, too, to his widow, poet Betty Lore Smith, for her early encouragement.

My thanks to my friend, Stew Salowitz, who was the first to read the manuscript as it neared completion, when I needed still more encouragement. He provided it, along with helpful suggestions. And to another friend, Garrett Scott, who cheered me on.

Thanks to my agent, Clyde Taylor, for four years of handholding during this process; to my editors, Nicholas Bakalar and Karin Evans; to photographers Lori Ann Cook and Bob Handley; and to many of my colleagues at WJBC-WBNQ Radio, especially Ron Romine. If Ron had not introduced me to the world of word processing, guided me through it, and answered my panicked phone calls for help, I'm not sure the words to follow would ever have seen ink.

And finally my gratitude and love to my wife, Mary, and to Rob, Eric, and Krista for their full support, encouragement, and understanding.

—SV

Introduction

As the large garage door curled upward, two uniformed policemen held high a wide yellow ribbon that fenced off the entire property known as 313 Carl Drive in Bloomington, Illinois. Two hearses, each carrying two bodies in bright orange body bags, pulled out of the garage, under the streamer, onto the street, and past the maze of television news cameras and curious townspeople.

Nadine Palmer was in that maze of cameras and curious. She used a crumpled tissue to wipe tears from her eyes at this first tangible evidence that what she had been told was true: her thirty-year-old daughter, Susan, and Susan's three young children were dead.

Mrs. Palmer, wrapped in a winter coat to protect her from the chilly November morning, turned to a reporter standing nearby. "I'll tell you one thing. There's just no way David could kill those children or Susie. He loves them. They're a perfect family."

Her verbs were in the present tense. She couldn't think of her daughter and grandchildren as now existing only in the past.

Nadine Palmer's comment was the first hint outside police and family circles that David Hendricks was a suspect in the murders of his wife and children.

Neighbors, friends, and relatives knew David Hendricks as a loving father who was never known to physically discipline his children and who had been hoping to adopt a child.

They saw an affectionate and considerate husband who had just taken his wife on a tenth wedding anniversary trip to England. They saw a successful businessman who gave tens of thousands of dollars to the needy.

And they saw a deeply religious person.

But police and prosecutors saw a different person in David Hendricks.

They believed Hendricks's marriage had gone stale and that his newfound wealth had given him a taste for a more exciting lifestyle.

They saw Hendricks as a person who had wanted to dispose of his wife, yet preserve his prominent standing in an obscure religious group that forbade divorce except in cases of adultery.

To them, Hendricks was a very intelligent person who had plotted to kill his family in a way that left no physical evidence against him and in a fashion so savage that observers would consider it improbable—unthinkable—that a father and a husband could be responsible.

Another thought lingered in the minds of police, prosecutors, and the public: if Hendricks wasn't responsible, then who was?

And, finally, the presiding judge in a lengthy and highly publicized trial, about to impose a sentence on this man, made an incredible statement: "Based upon the *evidence* admitted on trial against the defendant, I am not *personally* convinced that he has been proven guilty beyond a reasonable doubt."

What is presented in this book is true. I was the reporter Nadine Palmer turned to as the twin hearses carried the bodies of her daughter and three grandchildren from 313 Carl Drive. As a reporter who also covered the investigation and every moment of a two-month-long trial, I have made every effort to sift fact from fiction. Where transcripts are available, as in the trial and police recordings, exact words are used with editing for clarity and brevity. Where no written or recorded description is available, conversations are reconstructed based upon the best recollections of those involved.

One

Like his father and grandfather, Mike Hibbens was a Bloomington, Illinois, policeman. Nothing in the youngest Hibbens's eleven years as a patrolman (or anything his dad or grandpa had taught him) would prepare him for what he would see the night of November 8, 1983.

Hibbens was only a half hour away from ending his 3 to 11 P.M. shift in a roving squad car on the city's east side. Already he was technically outside his patrol area, just minutes away from driving back to police headquarters, filling out some routine paperwork, and calling it a night.

Election results were being broadcast over the squad car's AM radio as he drove past Evergreen Cemetery on the city's near south side. If it had been daylight, he might have been able to spot the large stone that marks the grave of Bloomington's most famous citizen, Adlai Stevenson II. But Mike Hibbens wasn't thinking about the former United Nations ambassador and unsuccessful presidential candidate, or about tombstones. He was ready to end what had been a quiet and boring shift.

"Two-adam-three." The female radio dispatcher's voice was almost as crisp as the air outside. Damn, Hibbens thought to himself. He hoped it wasn't some assignment that would add to tonight's paperwork. He responded with his call number, hoping that it wouldn't become apparent that he was outside his assigned patrol area a full half hour before shift-change time.

"Two-adam-three, go to 313 Carl Drive. See if you can make contact with the people there. Some relatives haven't been able to reach the mother and children there. The husband's out of town."

The dispatcher's tone was neutral, but Hibbens knew what she was thinking. He'd been on dozens of calls like this. Sometimes a phone was out of order. Sometimes a traveling husband was simply having the police check up on his errant wife. Very rarely was there anything even approaching a problem.

Hibbens had to think for a moment. Carl Drive? Oh yes. Short street, nice neighborhood. Near the edge of town.

"Adam-three, ten-four," he responded. He wouldn't waste any time getting across Veterans Parkway back into his assigned area and onto Carl Drive. It was nearly quitting time.

Detective Dennis O'Brien, already traveling Veterans Parkway, heard the call. His interest was stirred. He had been at police headquarters four hours earlier and vaguely remembered hearing some conversation then about someone concerned about the well-being of some people on Carl Drive.

Now O'Brien radioed headquarters, asking whether any of the Carl Drive neighbors had a key to the house. The answer was negative. O'Brien messaged Hibbens that he'd meet him at the address.

Hibbens pulled onto Carl Drive, only then remembering that this was the street the city manager lived on. He watched for 313. There it was, a new two-story, right across the street from the city manager's house.

Hibbens turned off his squad car's lights as he pulled into the driveway leading to the two-car garage.

"Adam-three, ten-twenty-three." He let headquarters know he had arrived. And in decent time. The dispatcher acknowledged.

As he stepped out of the squad and into the chilly night, Hibbens sized up the big brown house, grabbed his portable police radio, zipped his jacket, positioned his holster, and flipped on his flashlight.

He stepped toward the front door. Through a window he could see the gentle glow of a light. Night-light, probably. He walked to his left around the house, shining his light on windows. Everything seemed okay. He stepped onto a screened-in porch at the rear of the house. Astroturf on the porch floor led to a sliding door to the house. He tested it. Hibbens involuntarily sucked in his breath. The door was unlocked.

It was a double gasp. He caught the ray of another flashlight. Two men had just appeared at the porch. They sensed they had startled the policeman. One of them spoke.

"My sister lives here, and this is my brother-in-law. We're worried there might be something wrong."

"Okay." Hibbens hoped the slight quiver in his voice wasn't too apparent. "Since you're relatives, you can go in with me." Just then, O'Brien's voice sounded over Hibbens's radio. The detective had arrived.

"I'm around back," Hibbens answered. When O'Brien stepped onto the porch, Hibbens explained who the two strangers were and that he had found the sliding door closed but unlocked.

O'Brien turned toward the two men. He had an off feeling. "You wait here in case there's something you don't want to see."

The detective sergeant stepped through the door first. His flashlight lit the dining half of a kitchen area. Hibbens, a step behind, flashed his light to the left, illuminating a large family room. Some cabinets and drawers on either side of a fireplace were partly open.

The two policemen walked to their right into the kitchen. It was a bulb in the hood over the kitchen stove that provided some light. O'Brien continued straight into a dining room. Hibbens turned left into a short hallway. He shined his light into a small bathroom. Cabinet doors were open there, too. Hibbens continued toward the front door and foyer where he met O'Brien.

"Some things are kind of messed up back here," Hibbens said. His tones were hushed. More than once he had entered people's homes to check on their safety, only to find them asleep in their beds. He was hoping to avoid the day that someone awoke and put a shotgun in his face.

"Back here, too," O'Brien said softly. In the dining room and living room, O'Brien had seen some cabinet doors open, a few things out of place. Not so much like a burglary as a hurried effort to locate something.

Both men turned toward the carpeted staircase. Hibbens, the beam from his flashlight preceding him by only a step or two, started his ascent. Suddenly an overhead light flashed on. In the moment it took for Hibbens's eyes to adjust, he presumed a resident at the top of the stairs had flicked on the light to see who was invading the house. He quickly realized O'Brien had turned it on.

Hibbens secretly wished he hadn't. Hibbens would rather check the family's safety and quietly exit the house as he had done at other times. A hallway light was certain to wake the family. But O'Brien was the senior officer on the scene and Hibbens wasn't about to express his regrets. Besides, the light was on.

At the top of the stairs, a door to a large bedroom was halfway open. Without entering the room, Hibbens could see a form in the bed. "Somebody's asleep in there," Hibbens said. As O'Brien stepped into that room, Hibbens walked to his left, down a hallway. At the end of it, he shined his light into what was obviously a child's room. It was messy. Toys on the floor, along with some rolls of wallpaper. The drawers in a bureau were all pulled out, the weight causing the bureau to tip forward off its back legs. The bed was unmade, but there was no one in it.

Hibbens turned his attention to another bedroom on the right. The hallway light was enough for him to see twin beds with figures in them. He moved his flashlight's beam along the floor up to the foot of the far bed, being careful not to shine the light directly into the faces of any sleeping persons. The white bedspread reflected the light, and then he noticed it. Blood. Just a few specks at the foot of the bed. But as he moved the beam toward the head of the bed, there was more. And then he could see a girl, perhaps nine years old, her long, dark hair tied in pigtails. Hibbens quickly moved his light to the closer bed.

Two more children in a blood-soaked bed. On the right side, another girl, this one about seven years old. She lay in a sleeping position, too. Her face was a bloody fright. And to her right, a younger boy. Even more horrible. Hibbens tried to find his voice.

"Got a problem down here." Hibbens didn't sound like himself. His voice cracked. "There's something you ought to see."

O'Brien walked down the hall, and Hibbens used his flashlight to scan the room.

"Jesus Christ!" O'Brien faced Hibbens. Hibbens's look told O'Brien that he wanted to know what O'Brien had found in the other bedroom but was afraid to ask. "She's dead."

O'Brien used the butt end of his flashlight to turn on the bedroom light. And then and only then did the absolute gore of the situation become apparent. The flashlight had illuminated only small sections of the scene at a time. But now under a full light, the macabre scene swept over the seasoned policemen like a foul wind.

The white walls were spattered in red. The beds were soaked with blood. And the children. Hibbens and O'Brien, even with sidelong glances, had to swallow hard when they looked at them. They thought of their own young children and worried about their safety.

The boy was the worst. His face looked like it had been attacked by an animal. The whole lower left side hung open, as if it had a second mouth. A cut tongue and smashed teeth were visible through the wide, bloody opening. The damage was almost as great on the other side of his face, where a pair of deep and wide gashes stretched from his eye to his ear and to his mouth. His neck had been sliced open.

And while each of the two girls appeared to be in a peaceful sleeping position, the boy was on his back, his head touching his sister's, his right leg hanging off the bed at the knee, offering the stunned policemen a full frontal view of the boy's wounds. The boy's position made O'Brien think the child had seen his attacker.

The younger girl, much of her face pressed into a pillow, was also horribly lacerated. A blow to the left side of her face had left a deep indentation from the corner of her eye to her ear, and had opened up a hole in her skull the size of a quarter. Her throat had also been slashed open, from ear to ear. Her pigtails were saturated with blood.

The older girl had only a single gash, stretching from her left eye into her hairline. Her neck was intact.

When Hibbens and O'Brien finally were able to unlock their eyes from the bloodied corpses—there was no doubt the children were dead—they caught sight of two objects, every bit as repulsive and repelling as the butchered bodies of the three children.

There, lying horizontally across the middle of the closer bed, were an ax and a large butcher knife.

It was Detective O'Brien's turn to try to find his voice.

He spoke into his portable radio. "This is ida-twenty-seven. We're going to need the coroner and a lot of extra help out here on Carl Drive."

At that moment, the husband and father of the four murder victims, twenty-nine-year-old David Hendricks, was traveling south on U.S. Route 51, hurrying home from a Wisconsin business trip.

For months and years afterward, people would wonder what Hendricks expected to find when he arrived home.

Two

David Hendricks, the second of seven children, grew up in the Chicago suburbs. Always big for his age, David was a bit of a loner and had few close friends. He was obviously bright. But his unwillingness to apply himself during his early schooling frustrated his teachers and parents.

During most of Dave's formative years, the large and generally happy Hendricks family lived in an imposing three-story home in Oak Park, Illinois, just one door away from a home designed by Frank Lloyd Wright. Most would describe David's mother, Laverne, as loving, outgoing, and matronly. She was also very supportive of the head of the house, Charles. And there was no doubt that Charles Hendricks was head of his household. His perfectionist attitude made him particularly well-suited for his job as an electrical engineer in charge of quality assurance. He would also be described as strict. Charles firmly believed that order was necessary in a houseful of children surrounded by worldly temptations that seemed more evident with each passing day.

A fundamentalist Christian faith was clearly at the center of the Hendrickses' family life. And at the center of that faith was the Bible. "Wives, submit yourselves unto your own husbands, as unto the Lord," reads Ephesians. "For the husband is the head of the wife, even as Christ is the head of the church; and he is the saviour of the body. Therefore as the church is subject unto Christ, so let the wives be to their own husbands in every thing."

In the Hendricks family, the Bible was not only meant to be read, as it was several times each day. It was meant to be followed. in all things.

And so it was with their own religious gatherings. Because Matthew reads, "For where two or three are gathered together in my name, there am I in the midst of them," certain fundamentalist Christians who frequently met together refused to give their group any name at all, preferring simply to think of themselves as gathering together in the Lord's name.

Outsiders, of course, insisted on a name, and these fundamentalists were known as the Plymouth Brethren, dating back to the early 1800s in Plymouth, England, where a former Anglican priest, disillusioned with existing organized religions, established a "meeting" of people of like minds. These people held to a fundamentalist interpretation of the Bible and a philosophy that all Christians should be united in a common belief but that each group should also be autonomous.

The Brethren spread around the world, but still they remain relatively few. They have no ordained clergy, no churches, no specific organization. Instead they choose to meet in homes or sometimes meeting halls, usually in small numbers. Most of the Brethren meetings (groups) hold a Sunday morning worship service in which "Breaking of the Bread" occurs, a type of communion ritual that the Brethren believe recalls Christ's suffering on the cross and symbolizes Christian unity. Adult males lead the service. Women are not allowed to speak.

In addition to the Sunday morning services, most Brethren meetings gather on Sunday afternoons for Sunday School, on Sunday evenings for Gospel readings and hymn singing, and on one or two weeknights for Bible study and prayer.

The Plymouth Brethren apply New Testament texts to every element of their lives. Divorce, for example, is forbidden except in the case of adultery because in Matthew it is written, "I tell you that anyone who divorces his wife, except for marital unfaithfulness, and marries another woman commits adultery."

The Brethren are discouraged from mixing with unbelievers and from joining organizations, even those whose aims are philanthropic or religious in nature.

In short, the Plymouth Brethren go beyond being a fundamentalist Christian faith. They try to duplicate the most primitive Christian Church based on personal knowledge of Christ and the New Testament, which Brethren must be prepared to teach.

The closest thing the Plymouth Brethren have to an organized ministry are "the laboring brothers," men who feel inspired to occasionally travel from meeting to meeting to help spread God's word and help his faithful look forward to the day that they'll join Jesus in heaven.*

And so it was in this deeply conservative religious environment that Hendricks grew up. The family would have dinner together each night. There would be Bible reading after dinner and a family prayer before bed. The Hendricks home had no television because it would subject the family to evil outside influences.

On some Friday nights, David accompanied his father to Chicago's skid row, where David would hand out gospel literature while Charles preached to the passing parade of drunks, druggies, prostitutes, pimps, and police.

David would also carry Bible tracts to school. But he wasn't always serious. In fact, he enjoyed playing an occasional practical joke.

One of his favorites was to drop a fake dollar bill into the school hallway debris in the path of a custodian who was sweeping up and then watch as the janitor casually swept it around the corner and went for the bogus bill. David and his friends would be guffawing in the background.

Ralph Dear was one of David's best friends and the only other member of the Brethren in the high school of forty-five hundred students. David delighted in putting his friend's books on a school

---

*In *Lake Wobegon Days* Garrison Keillor wrote about his youthful days in a slightly different sect of the Brethren:

> We met in Uncle Al's and Aunt Flo's bare living room with plain folding chairs arranged facing in toward the middle. No clergyman in a black smock. No organ or piano, for that would make one person too prominent. No upholstery, it would lead to complacency. No picture of Jesus, He was in our hearts. The faithful sat down at the appointed hour and waited for the Spirit to move one of them to speak or to pray or to give out a hymn from our Little Flock hymnal. No musical notation, for music must come from the heart and not off a page. We sang the texts to a tune that fit the meter, of the many tunes we all knew. The idea of reading a prayer was sacrilege to us—"if a man can't remember what he wants to say to God, let him sit down and think a little harder," Grandpa said.

For a humorous glimpse of Brethren worship and lifestyle, see the chapter "Protestant" in Keillor's *Lake Wobegon Days* (New York: Viking Penguin, Inc., 1985).

cafeteria tray and watching a conveyor belt carry them toward the dishwasher. It was also David's relationship with Ralph that took them both and two others to the dean's office for a stern lecture after a hallway confrontation. David had gone to Ralph's defense when another boy bullied Ralph.

There was, of course, time for David's swimming and backyard basketball, an occasional bike ride or tennis game with his father, and a paper route. Charles Hendricks had been a good college athlete and encouraged his sons to participate in sports. On many Saturdays, a group of the older boys and young men from the meeting would play football at a city park. Family activities outside their home generally consisted of picnics or potluck dinners with other members of the meeting or a trip in the family station wagon to a weekend Bible conference. Hymns would be sung en route to the conference site, frequently in a neighboring state.

At one of these conferences in Des Moines in the late 1960s, the Hendricks family became acquainted with the Palmers of Delavan, near Peoria in central Illinois. They had much in common, including their faith and the fact that each family contained seven children.

Because of their aversion toward mingling with unbelievers, the Brethren took pains to provide their young with social opportunities with believers from other meetings. Such a gathering of some twenty young people took place one weekend at the Palmers' large home on Fourth Street in Delavan, a small town populated by factory workers and retired farmers. It was at this gathering that David Hendricks, age fifteen, first became aware of Susan Palmer.

Susan, a year older than David, was small and shy. Pictures would seldom do her justice. She was prettiest when she smiled. David liked her from the start and spent time with Susan's younger sister, Liz, just to be near Susan. But Susan wasn't paying much attention. In fact, years later she wouldn't even remember the first time she met David.

As she ended her junior year at Delavan High School, Susan played first clarinet in the small school band and was a member of the honor society, achieving straight-A grades, save for one B in math.

It was the summer before her senior year when she was offered a vacation job at Bible Truth Publishers, an Oak Park firm with loose connections to the Brethren. With little hesitancy from her parents, Susan accepted the summer position, arranging to live with the Hendricks family until other housing could be found. Her stay in the Hendricks home was short, but David was pleased.

As the summer ended, the people at Bible Truth were so impressed with Susan's shorthand, filing, and record-keeping work that they asked her if she would like to stay on full-time.

This decision was not easy. Susan had not completed her high school work. She was still a bit young to be completely untying the apron strings. "If it were for any other type of job, absolutely not," Susan's mother said as she gave her consent. Arrangements were made for Susan to get her Delavan High School diploma by taking only a couple of needed courses in Oak Park. But after only three days at Oak Park–River Forest High School, Susan was determined not to return there. It was about twenty times the size of her school in Delavan and markedly ahead academically. She disliked the fact that she had to turn to David, a year behind her in school, for help in math. She dropped out of school and was not unhappy about it. She had dreaded the thought of possibly having to give a valedictory speech at the Delavan graduation.

There were vicious small-town rumors about why Susan Palmer had moved to Oak Park and not returned for her senior year, but they were untrue. She had found a job that helped her spread God's word. She shared an apartment with two other young Brethren women employed at Bible Truth, worked full-time during the day, and studied high school correspondence courses at night. Within a few months, she had earned her high school diploma, long before her former Delavan classmates.

David Hendricks, now a high school junior, worked part-time at Bible Truth Publishing and continued to court Susan's attention. He got it by leaving poems on her desk; once he recorded a tape of his efforts at a piano keyboard and left it for her. Before long Susan and David were taking hand-in-hand walks over their lunch hour— a practice not endorsed by their boss.

Susan was the first and only girl David ever dated. Susan, however, had gone out with about seven other boys—all but one of them, remarkably, were named David.

Within a few months Susan Palmer and David Hendricks were secretly engaged, planning to get married just as soon as David could support them. David had always taken extra classes, including summer school. In a written test with about five hundred other high school students, he had been the top scorer in a competition for a scholarship in computer programming. But because of the desperate financial need of the girl who had placed second, the scholarship was given to her.

David might have pursued computer work anyway had it not been for a visit to a family friend in Wisconsin, Heinz Brinkmann. David was intrigued by Brinkmann's prosthetics and orthotics business, which fabricated and fitted artificial limbs and braces.

Brinkmann had known the Hendricks family for years, first meeting Charles and Laverne when he emigrated from Germany. They had just joined a Chicago-area Brethren group, and Brinkmann knew virtually no English. But he learned the language through Bible verses and discussions with the Hendricks family and others. Brinkmann urged David to consider a career in prosthetics and suggested that if David would agree to work for him after his schooling, Brinkmann would help cover David's education costs. David accepted the offer. It was an important decision.

By July of 1971, just before his high school senior year, David had already earned enough credits to graduate. He appeared before the Oak Park School Board to ask for his diploma, explaining that he was anxious to get on with his career in prosthetics.

"You show signs of success by knowing so clearly what you want to do," a school board member said. David Hendricks became the first student to be allowed to graduate from Oak Park–River Forest High School after three years of classes.

David and Susan were very pleased. It meant that they could be married a year earlier.

David lived at home as he continued his education. First there was a year at a Chicago public college, Olive-Harvey—a year he found less challenging than his junior year at Oak Park. Then there was a follow-up year of rigorous study of prosthetics at Northwestern University's medical school. On the side he earned money by doing wallpapering and painting work.

In June of 1973, at the age of eighteen, Hendricks completed his professional education. He had a job and a fiancée awaiting him. He and Susan Palmer would be married a month later.

Three

The late summer of 1973 was busy for Charles and Nadine Palmer. Two of their seven children would be married in a week's time. Their oldest son, Jonathan, was getting married in Oregon on August 4. Their daughter Susan's wedding would be just a week earlier in Delavan.

Because the Brethren have no church buildings or ordained clergy, the American Legion hall in Delavan was chosen as Susan's wedding site, and a minister from a nearby Mennonite church was asked to officiate at the ceremony.

About 125 people, most of them members of the Brethren, gathered to witness the marriage of Susan and David. Susan wore the traditional white dress and veil she and her mother had purchased in Oak Park. The wedding party reflected just how close-knit Brethren families tend to be. Susan's younger sister Liz, who years before had had a secret crush on Dave, was maid of honor. Vernon Buchanan, who married Dave's older sister Bonnie, was best man. Vernon's brother, Jerry, would later marry Liz.

A reception followed in the same building. Susan's grandmother had made the mints, and a friend made the wedding cake as a gift. With two hundred dollars in borrowed money, Mr. and Mrs. David Hendricks soon were off on a week-long honeymoon.

They spent their first night as a married couple at the Holiday Inn in Olney, a small southern Illinois community known for its albino squirrels. Aware of their financial limitations, the newlyweds had resisted the temptation of reserving the honeymoon suite. But then the desk clerk learned that Susan and David had been married only hours earlier. Susan and David Hendricks surrendered their virginity to each other that night in the special honeymoon suite made available to them at no extra charge.

They spent several delightful days and nights in Indiana state parks, played perfectly the role of giddy newlyweds at a Chicago Bible conference, and concluded their honeymoon with Susan's orthodontist appointment near Delavan. Susan would wear braces for the first two years of their marriage.

David had already begun work for Heinz Brinkmann in Mosinee, Wisconsin, just a short distance south of Wausau. For only eighty-five dollars a month the newlyweds rented an unused parsonage. It was conveniently located just across an alley from Dave's work.

By spring, Susan learned she was pregnant and the couple had plans to buy their first home. The house, located along the Wisconsin River, was a wreck—even at its $11,000 price. But for David, it was a labor of love as Susan worked alongside him, teaching and learning from each other, as they repaired and redecorated the home. All the while they attended frequent meetings of the area Brethren.

The young couple felt proud that they had been able to save the 10 percent down payment for their new home. David's $3.20 per hour salary was supplemented by a side business of buying and reselling used cars. David had found he had quite a talent and taste for sales a couple of years earlier when he bought a 1967 Volkswagen "bug" for $650, put twenty thousand miles on it, and sold it for a $300 profit.

In later years David said that if Susan was the patient Job of the Bible, he then was the scheming Jacob. Susan refused to accompany him whenever he bought a different car. She couldn't stand his quibbling and bargaining. He relished the challenge of getting the best possible deal.

David quickly became a valuable employee in Brinkmann's business. He was friendly and personable. The customers liked him. But more important, Hendricks's fresh education energized Brinkmann's firm with state-of-the-art techniques and technology. Hendricks did more and more of the company's brace and prosthesis fabrication and handled some of the hospital patient care business.

On the morning of September 24, at Wausau South Hospital, the Hendricks family grew in size and joy. Rebekah, a pretty baby girl with an abundance of dark hair, was born. She was Nadine Palmer's first grandchild. Nadine and Uncle Nate, Susan's brother, were Rebekah's first visitors.

About a year later, Susan was again pregnant and David had plans to set out on a business of his own. Ambitious and bright, his relationship with Brinkmann somewhat strained over business practices, Hendricks had been investigating communities of any respectable size in the northern half of Illinois that had no prosthetist or orthotist. Hendricks had been with Brinkmann full-time for nearly three years when he learned of an opportunity connected with a hospital in Galesburg, in downstate Illinois, only about an hour's drive from Susan's parents.

Hendricks didn't expect Brinkmann to be pleased with his relocation plans. But he was sincerely grateful for the start Brinkmann had given him and felt obligated to give his boss more than the usual notice.

Hendricks's announcement that he planned to set out on his own in two months enraged Brinkmann, who had recently released another employee who had been with him longer than David. He felt betrayed and thought that Hendricks was unappreciative and ill-prepared to go into business for himself. Brinkmann, who had hoped David would stay with him at least until Brinkmann's son was ready to join the business, spoke of loyalty. He warned David that Galesburg's population was too small to support a prosthetist, that at age twenty-two he was too young to inspire patient confidence, that he had no business experience. Hard feelings erupted and Brinkmann fired Hendricks on the spot.

So two weeks after Grace Hendricks was born on April 30, 1976, David Hendricks left Mosinee, driving a U-Haul truck filled with the family possessions. His daughter Becky sat beside him. Susan followed in the family car with their new daughter. They had been on welfare their final few weeks in Mosinee but did manage to turn a tidy profit on their home, selling it for $22,000— twice what they paid for it.

The newly expanded Hendricks family first lived in an apartment in a poor part of Galesburg. They promptly moved into a nicer home and then into the upstairs apartment of a two-story home. They later bought the structure and quickly learned they could make good money by using their combined talents to renovate a house and resell it. They accomplished it six times in two years.

David also found a new love—flying. A mail offer of a free flying lesson took him to Galesburg's airport with a promise to his wife that he'd be home by 4 P.M. Hours after his free lesson, he was still at the airport, watching and asking questions, when his beeper sounded a familiar voice. It was Susan. "You *said* that you'd be home by four o'clock!" David was hooked.

His original arrangement with Galesburg's Cottage Hospital had him working as a self-employed orthotist who contracted for space at the hospital. But after just a few months on the job, David realized he had little free time for his family, his work within the Brethren, and his home-renovation projects.

With no resistance from the hospital, David negotiated a package by which the hospital bought Hendricks's business and he became a hospital employee. Within weeks there was a pay dispute between Hendricks and the hospital. Hendricks was told he could quit or be fired. The hospital said he resigned. Hendricks said he was fired and deserved unemployment compensation—a battle he eventually won a year later.

For a time Hendricks concentrated on his house-renovation projects, some car buying and selling, and some missionary work on behalf of the Brethren. He made a short trip to Bolivia and Peru, later returning to Bolivia with his whole family for a month of missionary work. Susan and the girls stayed in Santa Cruz with the family of a missionary while David and his host traveled through the altiplano. While the missionary work seemed to agree with David, the water did not agree with Susan, who was sick much of the time they were in South America. She was more than happy to return to the comforts of central Illinois.

By now, Hendricks had begun work on his idea for a new type of orthotic brace for people who suffered compression fractures. He was convinced it had possibilities, and he especially wanted his next move to be permanent. Not only was his older daughter just a year away from starting school, but Susan was now pregnant with their third child.

After some careful research, Hendricks found opportunity in Bloomington-Normal, some seventy miles southeast of Galesburg and even a bit closer to Susan's family. He and Susan had considered the community of seventy-five thousand people even before their move to Galesburg, but had crossed it off their list because Susan was not comfortable with the Brethren meeting there—a feeling she would find hard to recall three years later.

Hendricks established a firm that fitted and sold braces and artificial limbs and also provided wheelchairs, crutches, and other health-care appliances. He chose a rather grandiose name for his new company, especially since Illinois Orthopedic Appliances was located in a rather run-down, one-story building near the downtown area.

He and Susan also picked out a modest, split-level home on the city's east side. Four months after their move to Bloomington, Benjamin Hendricks was born. David finally had the son he wanted. The Hendrickses believed God had blessed their family, even though Benjy's nearly constant crying in his early infancy—a problem traced to a stomach condition—tested Susan's motherly disposition.

David's new business was certainly blessed with success. In October of 1979, with several workers on his payroll, he moved it to more modern quarters on the city's busy east side. Religious pamphlets lay on tables in the waiting room.

Flying lessons became a regular part of Hendricks's schedule. His expanding patient-care business in hospitals fifty miles from Bloomington was all he needed to justify buying a plane of his own. Even before he had obtained his pilot's license, Hendricks bought a new Cessna 172 for $31,000. He paid cash.

All the while he was refining his idea for a new back brace. And even after he had his rather simple but effective invention in its final form, he was reluctant to invest the money it would take to patent and market it. After long discussions with his wife and parents, Hendricks applied for and received U.S. patent 4,173,973 for his hyperextension back brace on November 13, 1979.

Susan Hendricks had been troubled by unusual vaginal and uterine bleeding for several years. The problem grew worse, and on the day before Valentine's Day 1980, she was admitted to Bloomington's St. Joseph's Hospital for a scheduled hysterectomy. Because a routine test found Susan six weeks pregnant, the surgery was abandoned. She was released from the hospital and didn't appear for a routine follow-up appointment at her doctor's the next day. Seven weeks later, Susan had a miscarriage. An infection had developed. Later she did have the hysterectomy that had been planned for fifteen weeks earlier.

Anxious to return to the small-town life they had learned to appreciate in Mosinee, David and Susan bought a home in Stanford, a rural community closer still to Susan's parents and less than a half hour's drive from David's business. They extensively remodeled the home's interior (the exterior's pink paint annoyed some neighbors) and had a large garden that yielded enough produce for Susan to preserve for use throughout the year.

David developed a production and marketing plan for his new brace, which he labeled the CASH Brace. CASH stood for "cruciform anterior spinal hyperextension."

Susan helped her husband launch CASH Manufacturing by mailing fliers describing the brace to twenty-four thousand orthopedic surgeons, physical therapists, and orthotists.

David and Susan were elated with the response. They obviously had found a need. The brace couldn't be manufactured quickly enough. In what was left of calendar year 1981, CASH Manufacturing cleared nearly $14,000 on net sales of $65,000.

It quickly became apparent that Hendricks wasn't going to have time to operate his patient-care business and still develop his promising CASH Brace enterprise. So he sold Illinois Orthopedic Appliances in November of 1981 to a Chicago orthotist, Ed Roman, on a contract basis. Hendricks had quizzed Roman about his religious background, wondering if he was Jewish. Roman suspected Hendricks wouldn't have sold him the business if he was.

Hendricks moved CASH Manufacturing back to the more modest structure near the downtown area where he had begun. He distributed calendars which included a Bible verse from the third chapter of John: "For God so loved the world, that he gave his only begotten Son, that whosoever believeth in him should not perish, but have everlasting life."

He advertised for a secretary-bookkeeper, and when Beverly Crutcher applied for the position Hendricks told her that he wanted a nonsmoker, and that he didn't want to ever hear any off-color jokes. Mrs. Crutcher was hired as Hendricks's only full-time employee at a wage of five dollars per hour with the agreement that if she did well, her pay would be increased to six dollars per hour after ninety days. She began work at a card table set up in the small building's front room, and her pay was increased to the six-dollar level after only a month on the job. The business was doing well. The first three months' profit in 1982 doubled all of the previous year's.

Although the Hendricks family enjoyed the small-town life Stanford offered, David found the amount of time it took to commute to and from work increasingly frustrating. With his new business booming, Hendricks contracted to have a large, two-story home built in a developing area of Bloomington. The family moved into 313 Carl Drive in July and within two months had paid cash for the $92,000 house.

By now Becky and Grace were full-time students at Stevenson School, a short bus ride away from their new home. Most of the enforcement of the conservative Plymouth Brethren attitudes and practices was left to Susan.

The children had very few playthings, and toy guns were forbidden. They were usually required to eat everything on their plates at meals, and between-meals snacks were discouraged, although there was often a bedtime snack of popcorn or hot chocolate. When there were visitors, a special treat like ice cream or cheese was served.

The home contained no radios or televisions. A stereo phonograph frequently played religious records. The Hendricks family received no daily newspaper.

The children enjoyed playing board games like Sorry, Monopoly, and checkers with their parents. Family trips would take them to a zoo, park, hobby show, shopping mall, or fast-food restaurant.

At Halloween, the children weren't allowed to go trick-or-treating like most of their school friends. They instead made caramel corn at home and passed out small religious pamphlets to the young goblins who rang their doorbell. If there was to be a Halloween parade at school, Susan would pick up the children at school before the costume event began. Grace once told her teacher that her mom was mean because she wouldn't let her do things other children did.

Christmas was not observed in the Hendricks home either, as is the case in most Brethren families. Christmas has no biblical authorization, they say, and they trace its celebration to a pagan holiday. Susan, on at least one occasion, expressed disappointment that some Brethren friends had begun celebrating Christmas for their children's sake.

Susan used little makeup, wore her hair long with little curl, and made most of her own clothing. She tried to make religion the centerpiece of her family's life. She would read to her children from the Bible after breakfast. David would read to them before bed. There were frequent Bible-study sessions in their home. And all of this was in addition to frequent meetings of the Plymouth Brethren in Bloomington. The Bloomington meeting included perhaps a dozen families (many of them related) who gathered in a meeting hall on the city's north side.

David was one of the leaders of the group and, like his parents, frequently attended Bible conferences—sometimes several hundred miles away. He often would combine a business trip with a Bible conference, and his family frequently accompanied him.

It was at about this time that the Charles Hendricks family was facing a crisis.

Jim Hendricks was five years younger than his brother David, and like David, he was raised in the strict Brethren faith. Many years before, as a young man, their father had gone through a period of serious religious unsettlement. The result was Charles Hendricks's conversion to the Plymouth Brethren. Now it was his son Jim who was having doubts about where and how he wanted to worship. The difference was that this time a young Hendricks was inside the Brethren, looking out.

Jim was concerned about the Brethren's exclusive nature, its members' isolation from other people, its legalistic approach, and what he viewed as an intolerance toward fresh ideas.

And there was a compounding problem.

Jim, good-looking, unmarried, and twenty-one years old, had recently had a sexual encounter with a young woman. Fornication was a sin. It was also reason to be expelled from the Brethren. An "unclean" person was not to be allowed to break bread with the Brethren. It would be sacrilegious. Jim knew what had to be done. He would have to tell his father.

It wasn't easy. Jim considered his father a good parent, very loving, but unlikely to express that love. There was very little said. The course was set. Charles, one of the leaders of the Brethren group, took his son's confession to the Brethren assembly. It was difficult and embarrassing. The assembly had no choice. It was bound to "set aside" Jim. He would not be allowed to participate in Brethren meetings and he would be shunned by other members of the meeting, theoretically even by his family.

Jim continued to live at home, and he was allowed to eat meals with the rest of the family, although strict adherence to Brethren rules would have barred him from even that. The only way Jim could be "placed back at the Lord's table," as the Brethren put it, was for Jim to express remorse for his sin. Several members of the assembly were appointed to visit Jim to determine whether he was sorry for what had occurred.

Yes, he was sorry, Jim told them, but he wasn't going back to the meeting. He had determined that he preferred to worship elsewhere. Events of the past couple of months had helped him make his decision.

Charles Hendricks was angry, almost beside himself. While the rest of the family was dismayed, they were more tolerant. But it became increasingly uncomfortable for Jim to live at home. A solution presented itself when Charles decided to retire and move his family to the tiny town of Allendale in southeastern Illinois, far away from the worrisome big city, close to where his oldest daughter lived, and no farther from where David lived. Jim did not go with them. He moved instead to an apartment in another Chicago suburb.

Of all the family members, Jim viewed his brother Dave as the most understanding. In visits with Jim, Dave would express his concern for Jim's personal and spiritual welfare and encourage him to rethink his decision not to return to the Brethren. But David was much more open-minded than his father.

Jim was visited once by both his father and brother. David did most of the talking. "I know that Dad would say we have to accept these things as matters of faith, but that's not what I think you should necessarily do," David told him as their father solemnly listened. David simply wanted his younger brother to think things through, to consider the alternatives and the meaning of his decision. But he didn't want him to return to the Brethren if Jim didn't feel right about it.

Jim greatly appreciated his brother's attitude. His esteem for his brother increased. He grew closer to David, while his relationship with his father remained strained.

Only one vague reference to the situation occurs in Susan Hendricks's diary. On May 30, 1982, she wrote "Sad circumstances with Jim."

With her marriage to David, who was outgoing, almost extroverted, Susan overcame some of her shyness. But even in her diary, she remained a very private person.

It reflects a very busy, family-oriented life filled with sewing, baking, religious meetings, and keeping her children in check and her home in perfect order. One of the many wall plaques in their home quoted Proverbs 31: "A good wife . . . looks well to the ways of her household, and does not eat the bread of idleness."

Here are some typical entries as they appeared in the white, five-year diary, written in a tiny, somewhat cramped hand:

Jan. 3, 1982—Lord's Day. Our kids performed poorly.

Jan. 23, 1982—Saturday. David got home from New Orleans about 1 P.M. So good to have him back.

April 8, 1982—Thursday. Becky's 1st grade had spring program, finished spring cleaned [sic] and then cleaned house. More snow! David took me out to eat. David surprised me at dinner (restaurant) by saying he signed contract for our new house!!

May 2, 1982—Lord's Day. Tea mtg. Grandmother Brown went home to heaven last night! 108 years old. Dad–Mom came to Bloomington.

June 1, 1982—Tuesday. Took gift to Martha Brown. David called—he's lonely and so am I. Did some sewing, decorated cake for Mrs. Ruston.

July 28, 1982—Wednesday. David surprised me for our 9th anniv.—arranged for J & L to take kids. We went to Jumer's for night and supper.

Oct. 13, 1982—Wednesday. Had Dr. appt. To begin 1000 calorie diet. David & I are working on it together.

Oct. 18, 1982—Monday. Laundry. Went to David's office to get instructions.

Oct. 19, 1982—Tuesday. David & Bev & Troy left for Houston early A.M. I went to the office and only 3 CASH sold today.

Nov. 19, 1982—Friday. Visited school. Watched Grace's class do a skit. David surprised me & took me to Jumer's. Ate there & spent night. David gave me nightie!

Dec. 25, 1982—Saturday. At Sackville conf. John & April there. John did a lot of cooking.

Feb. 12, 1983— Saturday. Left Galesburg. Had lunch in Peoria at Hunt's. Stopped to see Grandma. David took pictures of model with braces on in basement for brochures.

June 11, 1983—Saturday. Got back home from camping at noon. David put up new clothes line. Went to Macy's for supper & saw their slides of Europe.

July 28, 1983—Thursday. Our 10th anniversary. Angie babysat & we went out for afternoon & evening. David gave me a camera.

Sept. 15, 1983—Thursday. David ordered flowers for me! We went out to eat at Grand Cafe.

Oct. 7, 1983—Friday. Dr. app't. took Becky to Glenna's for weekend. David & I ate late candlelight supper together.

Nov. 1, 1983—Tuesday. Not feeling well. Martha babysat. We went to Bennigan's & browsed thru mall.

Nov. 2, 1983—Wednesday. Dr. appt. He wants me to get thyroid scan. Pr. mtg.

Nov. 3, 1983—Thursday. Teacher conferences. All doing fine in school. We left at suppertime, went to Knoxville for pr. mtg. Stayed at hotel in Galesburg.

Nov. 4, 1983—Friday. Drove on to Quad Cities. David did some business. Stayed at Jumer's. Kids swam. Ate there for supper. Relaxed.

Nov. 5, 1983—Saturday. Left Jumer's. Stopped at Bishop Hill. Ate lunch at Hunt's in Peoria. Went to see Gr. Monroe, came home & got food ready for tea meeting.

Nov. 6, 1983—Lord's Day. Tea mtg. Nunniklovens, Jean Engberg, Bob & Eleanor Brimlow (Mr. Lunden's daughter) came over for mtg. & evening.

That was the last entry in Susan Hendricks's diary.

With his business doing well (he sold nearly $50,000 in braces in January of 1983 alone), Hendricks established what he called the Bloomington Fellowship Fund. His company made contributions to it, simultaneously giving CASH Manufacturing a charitable deduction and giving Hendricks a way to channel money to fellow Christians who found themselves in need.

In December of 1982, Hendricks put $14,000 into the Fellowship Fund account. Another $12,000 was deposited three months later. A month after that, Hendricks withdrew $7,100 and returned it to CASH Manufacturing. Much of the money went to individuals David knew only in passing or to persons recommended by his father. In April of 1983, David sent a check to his father-in-law, along with a letter that was surprisingly formal considering the "young couple" he referred to was Susan's sister and her husband:

Dear Brother Palmer:

Please find enclosed a check for $1,000. It is from the Bloomington Fellowship Fund, which is a non-profit corporation for the purpose of helping those in need and supplying good Gospel literature to those who will benifit [*sic*] from it.

In your case, the included gift is to help with the expenses of keeping the young couple, Martha and Jon Lewis, who have no job and no money at the present time. Use the money any way you see fit in connection with the expenses of helping them or to replenish some of the funds that have been used up to help them. . . .

Your Brother in Christ,

David Hendricks

At about the same time, Hendricks sent a smaller Fellowship Fund check to an area woman and concluded with a postscript:

I don't want to broadcast that I have this fund, especially in this area where I am well-known, so I will appreciate your not telling anyone about it. Thank you.

One of the larger contributions Hendricks made was to an Iowa family that distributed religious literature. A check for three thousand dollars accompanied the following letter:

Dear Brother Ron:

I hope this letter finds you well. I have long thought that the work you are doing in writing, publishing, and distributing good literature is an excellent work. I operate the Bloomington Fellowship Fund whose purpose is to provide funding for such efforts. Therefore it is with great pleasure that I am able to send you these funds in connection with Joy Gospel Distributors.

Excuse the brevity of this letter, but I have been very pressed for time lately. My wife and I leave for England in the morning and I am trying to get all the loose ends tied up.

Your Brother in Christ,

David Hendricks

The summer of 1983 was indeed a busy time for the Hendricks

family. David was wrapped up in refining a hinged modification for the CASH Brace. He was anxious to have it ready for distribution at a major trade show in Phoenix in October. There was regular business to take care of, too, plus trade conferences in Ohio and Wisconsin.

Susan quietly complained about the amount of time his work was taking. And she considered the family's new wealth almost a nuisance. But she tolerated what she considered to be David's toys, a motorcycle and a new airplane—the third that he had owned.

David may have been feeling a little guilty. He purchased a used van, and on July 8, the whole family set out on a vacation that would include camping out in the Rocky Mountains, visits with friends, and some business sidetrips for David. Even during trips to distant states, the family would find Brethren meetings they could attend.

A day after the family's return on July 24, David flew his plane on an overnight business trip to Minneapolis. Four days after that, the whole family and Susan's parents went to a three-day Bible conference near Chicago. The day after they returned, David's parents came to Bloomington for a five-day visit. And then on the following weekend David flew Susan and the children to spend the day swimming and waterskiing at a relative's cabin in northern Illinois.

That was two weeks before the big trip. David and Susan were going to England.

Susan had visited there as a teenager, and in 1981, when David was busy trying to get CASH Manufacturing off the ground, he had promised her that if they were ever financially able, they would travel to England together. David's mother, Laverne, and his sister, Bonnie Buchanan, shared baby-sitting duties in Bloomington while David fulfilled that promise with a three-week vacation. It would mix business with pleasure and a religious conference.

Religion came first. Upon arrival in London, Susan and David went directly to the Bournemouth Conference, a three-day meeting held in the small city on the English Channel, about one hundred miles east of where the Plymouth Brethren got their name.

Then David and Susan drove northwest into Wales, staying at bed-and-breakfasts for five nights. On September 5 they made their way into London, just in time for David to attend an international conference on orthotics and prosthetics. While her husband attended those sessions, Susan shopped at Harrods and along

Brompton Road and visited the Victoria and Albert Museum.

In the late afternoons and evenings, Susan and David walked through Hyde Park and Kensington Gardens together. They enjoyed a day tour of London, visiting St. Paul's Cathedral, the Tower of London, and Westminster Abbey, and seeing the changing of the guard at Buckingham Palace. That evening they took the underground to a prayer meeting.

David's conference wrapped up on September 9. They managed a quick visit to Madame Tussaud's Wax Museum shortly before they took a train out of London to Wokingham, where they spent the night with friends.

David and Susan arrived home on September 12. "So good to see kids though they were asleep" was Susan's diary notation.

Susan tended to be the disciplinarian of the family. When David would take one of the children aside for a serious talking-to, he would end up laughing with them. The children caused so much of a ruckus, racing to see which one of them would sit next to their dad at a meeting of the Brethren, that Susan made up a schedule so the kids could take turns in an orderly fashion.

In a rather uncharacteristic moment, Susan once confided to David's secretary–office manager, Bev, that she felt worthless at times. She wanted to have a large family, but she could have no more children. And her religious upbringing largely prevented her from working outside the home, except to help out as needed in her husband's business.

She also felt overweight and unattractive and found her husband facing a similar weight problem. When Dave asked her what she wanted for her birthday, she told him that she would like him to lose 40 pounds. He had ballooned to 255 pounds, 75 pounds more than what he had weighed when they were married a decade earlier. So he established a rigid diet-and-exercise routine. Three months later he was down 18 pounds and losing more. His success encouraged Susan, who wanted to drop 15 pounds from her 135-pound frame. She began wearing her hair in a somewhat more stylish fashion. And she also tried to put a little more style into the clothes she made and the few she bought.

School was well underway by the time Susan and David got back from England. Benjy started half-day kindergarten. He went to afternoon sessions at the same school his sisters attended.

A week after their return from Britain, Hendricks ordered two new cars: a Pontiac station wagon for his wife and a Buick

Century sedan for himself. The total cost would be $22,300. Susan's diary makes mention only of the station wagon. Five days later David called the car dealership to cancel the Buick and order a Pontiac 6000 STE instead. It cost $2,800 more.

On October 11th, David sent roses to Susan. A few days later he left for another trade show in Phoenix. His only full-time employee, Bev, attended it with him, just as she had helped out at the same show in Houston a year earlier. The idea, Hendricks said, was to train Bev so that she could attend most of the convention shows on behalf of the CASH Brace and he could stay home.

Susan held down the office the few days they were away. If she had checked the financial records, she would have seen that CASH Manufacturing had a net profit of $158,000 on sales of $282,000 over the last seven months.

Four

D avid and Bev returned from Phoenix late in the week. The Hendrickses were quickly off on another weekend trip, this time to Bettendorf, Iowa, where they visited friends and stayed at a rather elegant motel-lodge. The children loved it.

The following Monday, November 7, was cool and damp. Many people who had been talking about the terrorist truckbombing of the U.S. Marine compound in Beirut now had a fresh matter of international consequence to consider: the American invasion of Grenada.

For Susan Hendricks, it was a day for a doctor's appointment.

About two months earlier she had noticed a tenderness in her neck. During a regular visit to her gynecologist, he had recommended some tests. She was now about to get a second opinion from a local family practitioner, Dr. Grant Zehr. It would be her first visit to him. The Hendrickses' previous general physician had moved out of town, and Dr. Zehr, whose office was across the hall, had taken the medical records. If Susan liked Dr. Zehr, she would probably take the children to him.

With Becky and Grace in school, Susan dropped off Benjy at Dave's office en route to her late-morning appointment. Dave apparently forgot that he'd be baby-sitting. He wasn't there when

Susan arrived, but Benjy was content to stay with Bev until his dad arrived a short time later. Susan had packed her son a lunch, which he ate at his dad's desk before he was dropped off at kindergarten.

Dr. Zehr's examination of Susan found a nodule on her thyroid gland. "One centimeter, smooth, minimally tender," his notes would read. He discussed the problem with her and suggested that she undergo an ultrasound scan at a local hospital in an effort to determine whether the nodule was benign or cancerous. It was the second time Susan had heard that recommendation, so she agreed to an appointment for the next afternoon. Before she left the doctor's office, a nurse drew blood from Susan's arm for a test that would determine how well her thyroid was functioning.

Susan was home by the time Dave stopped off for lunch. They talked about her potential thyroid problem and agreed that Susan wouldn't make dinner that night. She would be off to a baby shower near Delavan. Dave and the children would eat out at one of the kids' favorite spots.

Back at his office, David was making last-minute preparations for his Wisconsin trip. These included a visit to the Bloomington Public Library, where Hendricks looked through the yellow pages of cities he planned to visit, preparing a list of orthotists and physical therapists he'd want to see.

When he returned home at four o'clock, all three children were playing outside. He joined them for a short time and then did some minor maintenance on his motorcycle, which he was about to store for the winter. A neighbor, Sara Kater, was taking her garbage out to the curb. Tuesday morning was garbage pickup time on Carl Drive, and she found that a mouse had invaded her garbage can. She detested mice, and her husband was out of town, so she asked Hendricks to remove the mouse, which had attracted quite a group of neighborhood children.

"What do you want me to do with it?" he asked. "Do you want me to kill it or let it go?"

"Oh, don't kill it in front of all these kids. Just let it go." So Hendricks turned the garbage can upside down, shook it, and the mouse scampered free.

A few minutes later he changed into his jogging clothes, which included, on this rather cool evening, a blue stocking cap. As David left the house, Susan and the children were snacking on cake at the kitchen table. Hendricks rode his two-wheeler the two miles to his rented hangar at the Bloomington-Normal Airport, where he would store the cycle. He jogged back home and cooled down from his run by tossing a football around with the kids.

At 5:50 Susan, gift in hand, left for the baby shower. She kissed the children good-bye and explained she would be driving to Sharon Zwanig's home and that they'd take Sharon's car to the shower near Delavan, picking up another woman along the way.

Within a few minutes, Hendricks called the children into the house. He showered and changed clothes. Becky, Grace, and Benjy were quickly in the car, ready for what promised to be a fun-filled night.

The first stop was at the nearby Eastland Shopping Center where school artwork was on display. Becky's poster had won a prize, and she proudly pointed it out to her father, sister, and brother. Grace and Benjy were interested but eager to move on to their next stop: the Chuck E. Cheese Pizza Time Theater.

They had been there several times before. The Hendricks children liked pizza, but pizza was secondary at Chuck E. Cheese. The main attraction was the playland atmosphere with its large, animated characters, and, better still, its video games, scaled-down mechanical rides, and the play area set aside for the smaller kids with its rope swing, a large air cushion for jumping, and a swimming pool–like area filled with colorful plastic balls the size of oranges. Children loved to plunge into the balls, cover themselves, and "swim" through them. The Hendricks children were no different.

David and the children arrived at 6:30 and ordered a medium-size vegetarian pizza.

The kids, with tokens for the rides and games in hand, headed off to the play area. Hendricks paid the $10.55 bill, and, with a pitcher of root beer and four paper cups, he retreated to a quieter part of the restaurant, which had a large-screen television.

Within a few minutes, the pizza arrived, cut into ten pieces and ready to eat. Hendricks summoned the children, who quickly ate and returned to their play. David continued to watch TV and occasionally checked on the children. They were enjoying themselves, especially when they knew their dad was watching and could show off for him.

By 7:30, David thought it was time to go. The children didn't. They pleaded for more playtime. Their father relented. He told them he needed to get the car filled with gasoline. He would do that and be back in a few minutes. Then it *would* be time to go.

Hendricks drove his current car, a '77 Buick, nearly a mile to the nearest gas station and pumped his own fuel. The receipt, stamped at 7:36 P.M. was for 14.4 gallons at seventeen dollars.

Now it became clear that in order to catch the Bloomington Public Library's bookmobile on its regularly scheduled stop only a block from the Hendricks home, he'd have to hurry. Grace and Becky were bookmobile regulars and had some books that were due.

Back at Chuck E. Cheese, Dave quickly collared the kids. Thinking that the bookmobile left at 8 P.M., Hendricks hastened home. He pulled up the driveway of his home, partially into the garage, and Becky raced inside to collect the books that were stacked in the kitchen. Within a moment, Hendricks's car was parked down the block near the huge library van. He grimaced when he learned that the rush had been unnecessary. The bookmobile wasn't scheduled to depart until 8:15. The children had a full fifteen minutes to return their books and make new selections.

While the children looked over the possibilities, David chatted with the librarian, Lavonda Nichols. The two girls' library cards needed to be renewed, and Benjy was getting his first card. As the librarian completed the paperwork, David complimented the bookmobile service, remarking that the mobile library selection was larger than the entire library's in Stanford.

At 8:10, the Hendricks family left the bookmobile. The children had checked out several books. One of them was *The Three Sillies* by Paul Galdone, in which the three characters are concerned that an ax will hit them in the head.

Susan Hendricks returned home from the baby shower at about 10:30. Sometime after that, David Hendricks left for Wisconsin.

Five

By eight o'clock the next morning, Hendricks was already in Wausau, Wisconsin, more than three hundred miles north of Bloomington, making the first of perhaps a dozen sales calls on behalf of his CASH Brace.

All of the calls were without appointment, but that was not particularly unusual under the circumstances. Hendricks mainly wanted to make sure that the orthotic appliance dealers were familiar with his product and that they knew they could buy directly from him, thereby saving themselves some money (and increasing his profit), and to tell them that he was about to introduce a modification to the brace.

By 9:30 he was already thirty miles to the south (and closer to home), in Stevens Point, where he called on Charlene Dineen, a physical therapist in St. Michael's Hospital. She hadn't seen Hendricks since he worked for Brinkmann, but had no trouble recognizing him. She saw the hinge brace modification as a major improvement and immediately ordered some.

Shortly after eleven, Hendricks was making calls in Portage, another seventy miles to the south. At 12:05 P.M., after traveling forty more miles south, Hendricks checked into the Red Roof Inn in

Madison. He made five more sales calls and then returned to his motel room. At 3:01 he called home. There was no answer.

He drove across the street to a Perkins Restaurant, had something to eat, and returned to the Red Roof Inn. Shortly after four o'clock he called his office. Bev Crutcher sometimes suspected that David called late in the day when he was gone just to see if she had skipped out early.

Hendricks gave Bev the name and phone number of the motel he was staying at and asked her whether she had talked with Susan. He hadn't been able to reach her, he said, and he wanted Susan to know where he was staying.

"Do you want me to try to call her?" Bev asked.

"Yeah, because she and the kids are supposed to go over to Nate and Maryanne's for dinner tonight. I don't want Susie to worry because she hasn't heard from me. Just keep trying."

David said he was ready to go to sleep because he hadn't slept since Monday night.

At 5:31 Hendricks called his home. His first effort was a misdial, dialing a *7* instead of a *6* for the first number. A moment later he dialed the correct number. There was no answer.

Then he called Bev Crutcher's home. Bev's sister-in-law, Maralee, answered. Hendricks asked if Bev was home yet.

"No," Maralee answered. "She might be at the baby-sitter's picking up the kids. Do you want that number?"

"No thanks," Hendricks responded. The call lasted only forty-five seconds.

Next he phoned Nate and Maryanne's. Maryanne answered.

"Hi, this is Dave. Is Susie there yet?"

"No. Where are you? Aren't you coming for dinner tonight?"

"No, didn't anybody tell you? I'm up in Wisconsin on business."

"Oh." Maryanne looked across the dining room at Nadine Palmer. Nate's mom, dad, and youngest brother, Seth, had arrived a few minutes earlier. "Well, Susie and the kids aren't here yet. We were just starting to get a little worried because you all were supposed to be here at 5:30." Maryanne looked at the clock on the kitchen wall. It read 5:40.

"That's strange," David said. "I've been trying to reach her all day and haven't had any luck. Have Susie call me when she gets there, and if she isn't there in a half hour, call me back, would you?"

David gave Maryanne the Red Roof Inn's phone number.

"It's not like her to run late," Maryanne said as she wrote down the number.

"She was probably running some errands and got tied up," David responded.

After Maryanne hung up, Nadine apologized to her daughter-in-law. Nadine hadn't told Maryanne that Dave wouldn't be joining them for dinner because of his trip to Wisconsin.

Nate dialed the Hendricks home. There was no answer.

Nate, his wife, parents, and brother stood around the dining room table, wondering what to do next. And then Nadine remembered that Susie was planning to stop at her sister's to deliver some clothing Grace had outgrown. A quick call to Liz and Jerry Buchanan's found that Susan and the children hadn't been there. Nadine Palmer was getting worried about her daughter and grandchildren. She flashed back to the night before, as she and Susan were leaving the baby shower.

"Now, Mom, I'm going to tell you something," Susan had said. "But don't tell anybody because it's probably nothing. I have an appointment tomorrow to have an ultrasound scan of my thyroid. I went to the doctor's today and he said I've got a little growth on it."

Susan's mother, a registered nurse, had tried to sound reassuring at the time. She knew it probably wouldn't be a problem, but it was also nothing to be ignored.

Now, standing across the table from her daughter-in-law, Nadine silently wondered whether Susie had received bad news and had gone somewhere to be alone with the children to think things out. Or maybe she just had had car trouble.

In the meantime, Hendricks had called the Cramer residence, three doors away from the Hendricks home. John and Karen Cramer were the Hendrickses' best friends in the neighborhood. They exchanged baby-sitting, studied the Bible together, and had dinner in each other's homes.

Karen answered. Hendricks explained he was calling from Wisconsin.

"Have you seen Susie today?"

Karen thought for a moment. "No, I haven't seen her since yesterday when she watched Andrew for a while. Why? Is something wrong?"

"Well, I just haven't been able to get her on the telephone all day, and she was supposed to be at Nate and Maryanne's for dinner and she hasn't shown up there yet. I thought maybe our phone is out of order. Would you mind walking down there to see if they're home?"

Karen said she didn't mind at all. They agreed that Hendricks would call her back in a few minutes.

Back in Delavan, the Palmers were becoming more concerned. They had called the Buchanans again, hoping Susie and the children had arrived there, but they hadn't. Maryanne put off calling David at the end of a half hour, as she had promised to do if Susan hadn't shown up by then. She was sure their car would pull up at their house at any moment. There would be a logical, even comical, explanation.

Finally, after thirty-five minutes, Maryanne's husband, Nate, called Dave to tell him that Susie and the kids hadn't arrived. Nate became more concerned when Dave told him that Susie had mentioned she would be calling Maryanne that morning to see if they were still having dinner that night. Maryanne hadn't received any such call.

"Well, call me if you hear anything," David told Nate. "And I'll call you when I track them down."

David hung up the phone and dialed the Cramers.

No, there was nobody home, Karen told him. She volunteered to check the house once more and call him back.

Again Karen Cramer slipped on her jacket, walked down the street, and rang the doorbell at 313 Carl Drive. She knocked on the door. No one responded.

When she got home, Karen called some neighbors to see if Becky, Grace, and Benjy had been in school that day. Nobody seemed to remember whether they had been on the bus. She called Hendricks and told him what she knew. As she dialed the number, she regretted that her information wouldn't be very reassuring.

Hendricks asked if she could check her phone book for the Bloomington Police Department's number. Karen volunteered to call the police for him, but Hendricks said he would rather do it. She gave the number to Hendricks and pledged to watch for Susan and call him at the moment she found out anything.

At 6:34 P.M., David called the Bloomington Police Department, where incoming calls are automatically recorded. He talked with the radio dispatcher.

"Yeah, this is David Hendricks calling from, I'm in Madison, Wisconsin. I live in Bloomington and I'm on a business trip right now. I'm a little concerned about my wife and kids because I've been trying to call them all day and haven't . . ." The dispatcher interrupted.

"Where do you live?"

"I live at 313 Carl Drive. Now here are the circumstances. I've tried to call them periodically through the day and haven't gotten them. I'm sure it's no big deal, no big emergency, but, uh, they're supposed to be at a dinner date tonight at five-thirty, so I called there to talk to her there and, uh, they never showed up there."

"What's your wife's name?"

"Susan Hendricks and they're not at home 'cause I called a neighbor who's gone over to the house and knocked, so I think they might have been in an accident between Bloomington and Delavan. Probably took Stringtown Road."

The dispatcher suggested the police could check the home.

"Well, the neighbor's been here. They're not home."

The dispatcher said that Hendricks should call the McLean County Sheriff's Department to see if an accident had occurred in the rural area. When Hendricks reminded her that he was calling from Wisconsin, she summoned the desk sergeant, Roger Aikin, to the phone. Hendricks repeated what he had told the dispatcher and added that the neighbors' children didn't remember seeing his children on the school bus earlier that day.

Sergeant Aikin checked accident reports from both the city and the county sheriff's department and found nothing involving a Hendricks. Aikin suggested Hendricks call the Illinois State Police District that included the Delavan area. Aikin gave Hendricks the state police phone number and took Hendricks's phone number in Wisconsin along with his local address and phone number. Hendricks asked that Sergeant Aikin call him in case something should turn up.

"Okay, what kind of car would your wife be driving?"

"A yellow Cadillac. '72 Cadillac with a green top."

"Okay, I'll do that."

"Thank you for your assistance."

"All right. Bye-bye."

Hendricks immediately dialed the state police headquarters, where Corporal Tom Siron told him no accidents had been reported.

"In fact, we haven't even had a report of a car broke down tonight. Of course, I'm not saying that she's not broke down somewhere."

As Hendricks waited on the phone, the state police corporal radioed the Tazewell County Sheriff's Department. It reported no accidents in the rural areas it covered. Siron relayed that information to Hendricks, who gave the state policeman the phone number at the Red Roof Inn.

"Okay. If I hear anything, I'll give you a call then."

"Please. Thank you, sir."

At 7 P.M., Hendricks used a VISA charge card to pay his $24.93 bill and checked out of room 110, telling clerk Sandy Smith that he had to leave because of an emergency.

Meanwhile, back in Delavan, Nate and Maryanne's three young children were hungry, so after another conversation with Liz Buchanan—Liz had called them this time to see if Susie had arrived—the eight Palmers ate dinner at a table that originally had been set for thirteen.

After dinner, Nadine Palmer called the Red Roof Inn. Her son-in-law had checked out. After a joint prayer for the safety of Susan and the children, Nadine and her husband went home. Seth had a date. Nadine and Maryanne promised to call one another when they heard anything.

Once home, Nadine called the Bloomington police. She wanted authorities to call the school principal to determine whether the children had been in school that day.

The dispatcher resisted the idea. It was too late in the day, she said, to ask a principal to go to school to check attendance records. Besides, Mrs. Palmer was uncertain about which school the children attended. But Mrs. Palmer was insistent. "Well, this is an emergency," she said.

"Just a minute. I'll let you talk to the sergeant."

Mrs. Palmer turned to her husband. "I bet David is upset. He's probably driving down a hundred miles an hour. Unless he flew in. I don't know."

Lieutenant Tim Linskey picked up the phone.

"Hello, I'm Nadine Palmer, Mrs. Charles Palmer of Delavan, and I was just talking to the lady there. My daughter is missing. We don't know where she is. This is a very, very unusual thing."

"How old is your daughter?" Linskey was wondering if this was a routine teenaged-runaway situation.

"Oh, let me think. She's thirty."

"Where's she missing from?"

"From home."

"Where does she live?"

"She lives in Bloomington on Carl Drive and her name is Susan Hendricks and she has her three children."

"We had a phone call from her husband earlier, ma'am."

"Right. From David. He is on his way home. He's checked out of the motel."

"Where was he?"

"A business trip to Madison. He is at the Red Roof Inn at Madison, Wisconsin. So it'll be another at least three hours or so 'til he gets to Bloomington. In the meantime, my son and son-in-law, who live here, are driving toward Bloomington. Now she often takes Stringtown Road. She's supposed to be at my son's house with us for supper tonight, and we've been trying to reach her all this time and have not been able to reach her at all. And anyway my son and son-in-law are on their way to Bloomington, taking the Stringtown Road 'cause that's the usual way she would come to our place, checking to see if maybe she has car trouble or something or whatever."

A tone of deep concern had entered Mrs. Palmer's voice.

Lieutenant Linskey said he was dispatching a squad car to the Hendricks home and that an officer would search the house with Hendricks when he returned home.

"And if they're still not there, if there's no note left or he still thinks they're missing, we'll take a missing-person report from him." Before ending the conversation, Linskey thought to ask a routine question.

"Have they ever had any problems in the past, ma'am?"

"Never."

"No marital problems at all?"

"Never."

"How long have they been married?"

"Ten, eleven years."

"All right. We'll give you a call if we hear anything. But as soon as your son-in-law gets back in town, have him call us."

"Okay. Thank you very much."

"Yes ma'am. Bye now."

By now, David Hendricks was well on his way home. He stopped at a pay phone at a gas station near the tiny town of Compton, Illinois—about ninety miles north of Bloomington. Once again he called the Cramers.

No, nobody had seen them, John Cramer told Hendricks.

"Well, there's probably a reasonable explanation," Hendricks said. "I'm on my way back now. I'll be there in about an hour and a half."

Cramer told David that he would pray for his family's safety. He hung up the phone, walked down to 313 Carl Drive, and rang the doorbell. There was no answer.

Meanwhile Nate and Liz's husband, Jerry, were in Jerry's van on the 45-mile drive to Bloomington. In Stanford, about ten miles out of Bloomington, they had stopped at a pay phone to call Jerry's home and the Hendricks house to see if the family had been located. The pay phone was out of order.

They continued their drive into Bloomington, pulling up in front of 313 Carl Drive at 10:10 P.M. The house was mostly dark, except for a faint glow that seemed to come from near the back of the house, probably from the kitchen.

The two men walked to the front door. Nate rang the bell. They waited and rang it again. They rapped on the door. There was no answer.

They walked across the front of the garage, turned the corner of the house, and tried to look inside the garage window to determine whether Susie's car was inside. It was no use. The window was completely covered by a curtain. They walked back out front and saw a woman hurrying toward them from down the street.

"Are you looking for Susan?" the woman asked.

It was Karen Cramer. Jerry Buchanan had met her before, but he reintroduced himself and Nate and explained how they had looked for Susan's car.

"Dave's on his way back," Karen said. "He just called. My husband talked to him. He wanted to know if we'd seen Susie and the kids."

Based on Nadine Palmer's earlier call to the Red Roof Inn, Nate and Jerry had assumed that Hendricks was en route home. They used the Cramers' phone to call the Palmer family home. Nadine was even more anxious when she learned that Nate and Jerry hadn't found Susie's car. She told them she was glad she had asked the Bloomington police to check the house.

It was about then that the Cramers and their two visitors saw a squad car pull into the Hendricks driveway. Nate and Jerry left the Cramer house just as the policeman walked around the side of the Hendricks house. They could see the beam of his flashlight as he checked the windows. They'd meet up with the patrolman at the rear of the home.

Six

Nate and Jerry patiently waited on the screened-in porch for the two policemen to come back outside. After about five minutes, the uniformed officer, Hibbens, stepped through the curtains and the sliding door first. His silence prompted Nate.

"Is everything all right?"

Hibbens was grateful he could defer to his senior officer, O'Brien, who had followed him out.

"Men, I'm sorry to have to tell you. They're all in there, but they're all dead."

Nate and Jerry looked at each other in the darkness. Nate staggered backward.

Jerry's usually thin voice sounded even more frail than usual. "Was it natural gas?"

"We can't answer any questions right now," O'Brien responded.

The detective told Hibbens to stand guard at the door while he went across the street to the city manager's house to telephone headquarters. Further use of the regular police radio now would alert the news media and every busybody in town with a scanner to what had occurred on Carl Drive.

Hibbens thought about what he had seen inside and about his present responsibility. Obviously, he was to prevent any unauthorized person, including Nate and Jerry, from going inside. And then it occurred to him. Might he also have to prevent someone from leaving the house? It seemed clear that the children had been dead for some time. And the same appeared to be true of the mother when he and O'Brien had together surveyed the master bedroom. But that didn't necessarily mean that the killer wasn't still inside. Hibbens shuddered as he asked himself whether he had checked behind the shower curtain in the hallway bath. Certainly there were large parts of the house, including the entire basement, that hadn't been searched.

Voices interrupted Hibbens's thoughts. Nate and Jerry were wondering whether they should call their families.

Hibbens suggested they wait for a while.

The two men agreed there was not much use calling home when they had no answers to the many questions they knew would be asked. They walked around to the front of the house, where they found Karen Cramer asking what was happening. Already a third and fourth squad car were parked in front of 313 Carl Drive.

As O'Brien, Hibbens, and three other policemen conducted a more thorough search of the house, being careful not to touch or disturb anything, Nate, Jerry, and the Cramers knelt in the Cramers' living room, praying for strength for David Hendricks. Jerry, distressed at the thought of having to break the bad news to his wife, swallowed two overflowing tablespoons of an antacid offered by Karen. She mopped a spill from the kitchen floor.

By now Dan Brady, a mortician who worked part-time as a deputy coroner, had surveyed the crime scene. As he emerged from the house, Nate and Jerry were standing out front, aware that David could be arriving home at any moment. Although they knew it would be an unpleasant duty to tell Hendricks that his family was dead, better he hear it from them than some stranger.

What happened next is open to dispute. It's also pivotal in Hendricks's immediately becoming a prime suspect. Here is the way Nate and Jerry remember it.

At 11:15 Nate and Jerry recognized Hendricks's blue Buick as it rapidly approached the house. It abruptly halted a couple of houses away from 313 Carl Drive, since police cars made it impossible to get any closer. Hendricks emerged from his car. Nate and Jerry walked toward him.

"What's wrong? Something's wrong," he said.

Nate answered. "David, your family's gone."

Jerry spoke. "They're with the Lord."

Hendricks looked at them both. "What do you mean?"

"They're dead," Nate said, repeating what he had now been told. "They've been murdered."

Hendricks's knees seemed to buckle as he let out an almost animal-like groan. Nate and Jerry supported him at the elbows.

"Even Benjy? Even little Benjy?" Hendricks asked as Detective O'Brien stepped forward.

But O'Brien and Brady, the deputy coroner, don't remember it that way. Here is how they recall it:

O'Brien had been talking with several other policemen outside the house when he heard someone say, "That's him. Here comes David."

O'Brien was aware that Hendricks was en route from Madison but surprised he had arrived so soon. He made a mental note to check to see how hot Hendricks's car engine was. The only surviving family member, in this case the husband and father, would automatically be on an early list of suspects, and O'Brien wanted to see Hendricks's reactions when he was told the news. In fact, if O'Brien had it his way, he would be the one to tell him.

So when Hendricks got out of his car, O'Brien moved quickly toward him. He was only a few feet away when Nate and Jerry took Hendricks by the arms but heard no words exchanged. O'Brien had his badge out.

"Are you Mr. Hendricks?"

"Yes, what's wrong?"

"Mr. Hendricks, your family is inside the house. They've been murdered."

Hendricks's head dropped as he let out a groan and said, "Oh, no. Did they suffer?"

"The scene was violent," the detective answered.

"They're with the Lord now," O'Brien heard Hendricks respond.

Hendricks's response wasn't what he expected from a man who had just learned that his wife and three children were dead. As far as O'Brien was concerned, Hendricks definitely belonged on his list of suspects.

Brady, who had been standing back, stepped forward, introduced himself, and offered his hand to shake.

"I'm sorry," Hendricks said. "I'm shaking too bad right now to shake anybody's hand. Are they all dead?"

"Yes, I'm afraid so," Brady said. Hendricks put his hand to his head. "Oh, my God."

Brady confirmed the names and ages of Hendricks's wife and children with Hendricks, who then asked if he could go inside the house. Someone told him that he couldn't at the moment, but that police might want him to go inside later to help determine whether anything was missing.

Karen Cramer, who had watched Hendricks's arrival at a distance, stepped up and suggested that David come to her house to sit down.

Nate and Jerry helped Hendricks to the Cramer home, where Hendricks sat in a rocking chair in the living room. He said he was cold and asked for something to wrap around him. Karen gave him an afghan and asked if he wanted something hot to drink.

A moment later, as Karen handed Hendricks a cup of hot coffee, Detective Charles Crowe stepped through the front door.

Seven

In his twelve years as a Bloomington police detective, Charlie Crowe had developed a reputation as a tenacious digger of facts. And anyone who had felt the sting of his derisive wit knew that his deliberate, sometimes ponderous speech belied his intelligence.

His tact was sometimes as thin as his hair, his inelegance about as thick as his bushy mustache. But he had been the principal investigator on most of the thirty murders that Bloomington had experienced since Crowe became a detective only five years after joining the police force. But none of those cases had been multiple homicides.

Crowe was at his home, about ten blocks from the murder scene, when the shift commander called him at 10:30 P.M. At 313 Carl Drive, the man temporarily in charge of the detective division, Sergeant Gene Irvin, briefed Crowe on what had been seen inside the house and sent him to the Cramer home to interview Hendricks.

When Crowe arrived there, Hendricks was sitting in the living room, surrounded by the Cramers, Nate Palmer, Jerry Buchanan, and rookie Detective Michael Scott. Without introducing himself, Crowe asked John Cramer whether there was someplace in the house he could talk privately with Hendricks. John Cramer volunteered the master bedroom. It was then 11:30. Crowe conferred briefly with Detective Scott before the three men went upstairs to the large bedroom and sat around a circular glass-topped table. Crowe asked few questions and recorded Hendricks's lengthy, calm answers on a legal notepad. Detective Scott listened.

Hendricks said he had left home at about midnight the night before, stopping at the Perkins Restaurant on his way out of town to get a cup of coffee to go. He recounted his business calls the next morning, saying he had tried to call his wife from the Portage hospital at about 11:30 and gotten no answer. He said he had driven on to Madison, where he had checked into the motel before calling on clients in Madison. Hendricks said he had returned to the Red Roof Inn at about 3 P.M. and tried to telephone his wife then because he had been sure she would be there when the kids got home from school. He told Crowe about the subsequent calls to his secretary and to his in-laws. He said that when he found that his family wasn't at the Palmers', he had called Karen Cramer, asking her to go down to his house, tell Susie their phone wasn't working, and have her call him.

There were long delays between Hendricks's answers and Crowe's next question while Crowe tried to write down both his question and Hendricks's response.

"How did you know the phone wasn't working?" Crowe wanted to know.

"Because it was ringing in my ear," Hendricks explained. "I was sure Susie was there, but I figured the phone was just out of order and she didn't know I was trying to call her."

A pause.

"Did you ask Karen to see if your wife's car was there?"

"It wouldn't have done any good. Susie always put the car in the garage every time she uses it. The first time I called Karen, I didn't even ask her to call me back."

Hendricks stopped, a blank look taking hold of his face as he stared at nothing. After a moment, he continued.

"I was concerned, but I just *knew* they would be home. I was in my motel room. I was trying to get some sleep, so time doesn't mean anything to me. I called Karen back at around six-thirty. Actually I never asked Karen to go down before. I just asked her if she had seen Susan around and she volunteered to go down and check. On the second call she volunteered to go down and check again. Karen was concerned. I tried to settle her down because I wasn't that concerned. She went down and checked with one of the neighbor girls to see if she had played with my kids. I might have called her three times. Karen told me she had to go out for an hour but John would look out for them."

Hendricks recounted how he had called the Bloomington police, then the Illinois State Police, to see if an accident had been reported.

"I really wasn't satisfied with the answers the police gave me. They told me there wasn't any accident, so I started home. Susie's just so . . ."

Hendricks paused, again the vacant look shading his face. "She just doesn't . . ." Another short pause. "She's always on time. If you can't reach her all day, you know something is wrong."

Hendricks went on to explain how his wife had had a doctor's appointment that morning, how he had left Madison at 7:10 P.M. and driven directly back to Bloomington, save for one stop to call Karen Cramer to determine if she had seen Susan. It was now 12:22 A.M. and Sergeant Irvin stepped into the bedroom. The crime-scene technician from the state crime lab had arrived and needed written permission to search Hendricks's house and car. A form was completely filled out already, except for the time of day, the year of car, and the signatures of Hendricks and witnesses.

Irvin slid the form in front of Crowe and Hendricks. Hendricks asked its purpose.

"Just a matter of routine," Irvin answered. "The state wants us to get written permission before we search a crime scene."

Hendricks read the form and signed it. Irvin, Crowe, and Scott also signed it as witnesses.

Irvin left. Crowe asked Hendricks about what his family was doing when he left them late the night before.

"My wife was in bed, in her nightgown, in the master bedroom. The girls were sleeping in their bedroom, in separate beds, and Benjy had crawled in bed with Grace."

Did he lock the doors when he left?

"I think I remember latching the back patio door. The front door was locked. I think it was locked. I always check. I didn't lock the door that leads from the garage to the house."

Hendricks told the detectives that it wasn't unusual for him to leave late at night on a business trip.

"I work through the night about once a week or ten days," he said. "Usually when I go on sales trips I leave at two or three in the morning. I have my own plane and I usually fly."

"When did you first become concerned about not reaching Susie?" Crowe wanted to know.

"Probably not until . . . well, that's hard to say. Probably when I called Maryanne and she said Susan wasn't there."

Crowe repeated the same question in different fashions several times. Hendricks's answer remained the same.

"Okay, tell me again about your trip up north."

"I stopped at Perkins at about midnight and got a cup of coffee to go from the girl at the front counter."

"What were you wearing?"

"I was wearing these blue pants and this shirt. I might have had this camel shirt over my blue one. I would have had my black shoes on. The rest of my clothes are in the car. I changed my clothes on the way up at a rest stop about halfway between Portage and Madison on I-90. I changed into my suit, my gray suit. It's in the garment bag."

"Why didn't you just wear your suit all the way up there?"

"Because I don't like getting it all wrinkled on the long drive up there."

There was a tap on the bedroom door. It was Irvin again. He motioned Crowe into an adjacent bathroom. Crime-scene technician Rodney Wamsley had asked Irvin to find out if an ax was kept in Hendricks's house and, if so, where. Crowe returned to the table.

"Mr. Hendricks, do you have any of these items in your house. Any guns?"

"No."

"Any hatchets?"

"An old ax in the garage."

"Knives?"

"Just the usual kitchen knives."

"Any hunting knives?"

"No. There are some crowbars and carpenter and ball peen hammers in the garage."

It was now 12:45 A.M. Crowe had Hendricks sign another search consent form, this time for his business office, airplane hangar, and the airplane and motorcycle stored in it. Crowe told Hendricks that either he or his secretary could be present when the office was searched.

"David, we'd like to continue this interview down at the police station. Is that all right with you?"

Hendricks agreed.

As the three men walked downstairs, Crowe told those gathered in the living room that they were going downtown. Jerry Buchanan suggested that Hendricks looked pale.

"I'll be okay," Hendricks said.

Seth Palmer, who had arrived from Delavan only a few minutes earlier, thought David looked like he had been crying. As Hendricks and the detectives were about to walk out the Cramers' front door, Seth asked, "Why are you taking Dave?"

Seth says that Crowe wheeled around and put his finger on Seth's chest. "We have our reasons."

Crowe says that event never happened.

A few moments later, Detectives O'Brien and Scott drove away with Hendricks in an unmarked police car. Crowe stood on the sidewalk, reflecting on the past hour. He was bothered. Crowe thought Hendricks seemed too prepared, too guarded, perhaps too helpful. But most of all Crowe was puzzled by Hendricks's composure. If I was in his place, Crowe thought to himself, the police wouldn't be talking to me until after I came out from under sedation in the hospital. Crowe turned to Sergeant Irvin and said, "He's dirty."

The Bloomington Police Department was deceptively quiet at 2 A.M. A couple of extra detectives had been called in. The chief and his assistant had been there and left. A single copy of a late edition of that morning's *Daily Pantagraph* lay on a desk, its ink slightly wet. There was a front-page picture of the Hendricks home with a single-line headline, "Multiple Deaths Probed." Behind a closed door inside the detective division, Hendricks sat alone with a Styrofoam cup of coffee in hand.

Detective O'Brien was listening to the tape of Hendricks's call to the police department switchboard that had occurred eight hours earlier. At 2:30 A.M., Crowe and O'Brien conferred. O'Brien nodded toward the room that held Hendricks. "That son of a bitch did it. I know he did," O'Brien said. "We're going to have to give him his Miranda rights." Crowe was resistant, thought it was too soon, that it might put Hendricks on the defensive.

"I'm not going into that room and I'm not going into court without reading him his rights," O'Brien insisted. Crowe relented and the two detectives mapped their strategy.

A few moments later they entered the room where Hendricks waited.

The interrogation room was small. A standard steel office desk and three chairs was all it could handle. With its door closed, it would quickly become uncomfortably close. It had been decided that O'Brien would take the lead.

"Mr. Hendricks, we want to talk with you some more, and before we do that, we're going to advise you of your rights, so please pay attention to what I'm about to read," O'Brien already had the printed card he carried in his wallet in hand.

"You have the right to remain silent. Anything you say can and will be used against you in a court of law."

Crowe glanced at Hendricks to measure his reaction. O'Brien read on.

"You have the right to talk to a lawyer and have him present with you while you are being questioned. If you cannot afford to hire a lawyer, one will be appointed to represent you before any questioning if you wish. You can decide at any time to exercise these rights and not answer any questions or make any statements."

Hendricks's gaze was locked on the floor. O'Brien turned over the card and continued reading.

"Do you understand each of these rights that I have explained to you?"

Hendricks answered yes.

"Having these rights in mind, do you wish to talk to us now?"

"Yes, but why am I being advised of my rights?"

"Well, because at this point in our investigation we don't know who committed the murders, and because neither Detective Crowe nor myself know you, and from what we've found out so far in our investigation, you could be the last person to see your family alive. It's really for your own protection in the investigation and for our protection, too."

Hendricks appeared to accept the explanation. Crowe and O'Brien both breathed an inner sigh of relief. They had hoped he would be willing to talk now. They began. Both detectives would ask questions. Crowe would record Hendricks's answers on paper.

"David, was your wife awake when you left home?" Crowe asked.

"Yes, she was. I kissed her and gave her a hug good-bye."

"Was she covered with a blanket at the time?" Crowe's manner was casual yet deliberate.

"Yes. We were in bed together for about an hour before I got up to leave for Wisconsin."

"When was the last time you had sex with Susan?" Crowe was still asking the questions.

"I think it was Sunday morning, before we went to church."

"What church is that?"

"It's really not a church. Just a group of Christians that meet together."

"What are the ages of your kids, and where were they when you left?"

"Rebekah Caleb is nine. Grace Esther is seven. Benjamin Caleb is five." Hendricks swallowed hard. "Becky and Grace were in their beds, and Benjy had crawled into bed with Grace. I kissed them good-bye."

It was O'Brien's turn. "Do you remember checking the doors to see if they were locked before you left?"

"I don't specifically remember checking, but it's usually my habit to check the doors to make sure the vertical locks are in place and the wooden bar is in place on the patio door. I made that bar myself."

"What about the garage door?"

"It has an automatic opener, and there's a controller in each car."

"Can you physically open the garage door by pulling up on it?"

"No."

"Was your wife paranoid about burglars?"

"No."

"Do you think your wife would have let someone in after you left?"

"She could have. I don't think she would open the door to a stranger. But I was more careful than Susan. I really had to get on her at night to lock the doors because she comes from the country where they're not used to it."

"Were you and Susan having any kind of troubles whatsoever?"

"No, we were very happy. As a matter of fact, we were talking about adopting a boy in the last hour we were together. That's why I was trying to call her today, to give her some thoughts on that. Susan had a hysterectomy and couldn't have any more children."

The detectives quizzed Hendricks about his business, his business trips, his airplane and motorcycle. They asked whether there was anybody connected with Hendricks's business or with the religious group who might seek revenge.

"As far as I know, I don't have any enemies."

"Is there anything of particular value in your home that might have been taken?" Crowe wrote down the question as he asked it.

"Nothing much. Maybe a couple hundred dollars. We don't own a TV."

Crowe asked again about where Hendricks had changed into his suit en route to Wisconsin.

"At a rest area between Portage and Madison on Interstate 90."

"Did it have bathroom facilities?"

"Yes, but it was dark outside, so I just changed my clothes by the car."

Crowe carefully recorded the answer and without missing a stroke asked, "David, did you kill your wife and kids?"

And without missing a stroke in return and without emotion, Hendricks answered, "No."

O'Brien quickly followed up. "Would you take a polygraph test for us?"

"Why?"

"Because it's a tool we use in our investigations, and if you passed it, we'd be able to concentrate our efforts elsewhere. At this stage of our investigation, everyone's a suspect, and we'd like to eliminate you from the list."

"Who would give the test? How would it work?"

"It would be administered by a state examiner either in Morton or here in Bloomington. It measures your body's reaction to questions, and your responses would be determined to be truthful, untruthful, or inconclusive."

"I don't trust them. What would you do if I failed it?"

"We'd probably focus more of our investigation on you," Crowe said.

"I don't know. I had a friend who worked in a department store. He was required to take a polygraph exam and he failed it. It was wrong about him. Anyway, I'd want to talk to an attorney before I decided to take the test."

It was now 3 A.M. O'Brien and Crowe glanced at each other. They knew it was time to put the heat on Hendricks. Crowe moved from his chair and sat on the desk, only inches from Hendricks's face. Crowe wouldn't be taking any notes now. The questions would be rapid-fire. O'Brien began.

"You know what, David? The reason you don't want to take the polygraph is because you're the one who killed your family. That's the reason!"

O'Brien, who had been troubled, almost annoyed, by Hendricks's lack of emotion, was certain this would get a rise out of him.

It didn't.

"No, I didn't kill my family. Why would I kill my family? I loved my family."

Hendricks's voice remained calm. The only change was that he no longer looked directly at the detectives. His focal point was now the wall.

"How could a person as religious as you profess to be kill your family? That's what I'd like to know."

"I didn't kill them."

"What do you think the Lord will do, what do you think will happen to a person who did something like this?"

"I hope there would be forgiveness. Whoever did this, I think the Lord will forgive them if they seek forgiveness."

"I can understand how a husband might kill his wife, but his children, too?" O'Brien half expected Hendricks to come up out of his chair after him. Hendricks didn't move, except to shake his head.

Crowe jumped in. "You now what, David? If some fat detective jumped up in my face and told me that I killed my wife and kids, I'd be fighting him all over the room. And you just sit there!"

"You're wrong. I didn't kill them. I had no reason to kill them."

"What was it? Were you after some life insurance? Was your business going down the tubes and you need some quick cash?"

"We don't have any insurance. The business is doing well. In fact, we paid cash for the house."

"Are you some kind of religious fanatic or something? How could anyone kill his own kids?"

Hendricks just shook his head.

"What, do you have some girlfriend and you wanted to get rid of your wife?" It was O'Brien again.

"No, I loved my wife."

"She probably had a boyfriend. That was it, wasn't it?"

"No. We just celebrated our tenth anniversary. I took her to England."

Crowe again. "What's the license number on your car?"

"XA 7803."

"Then why did you list your license number as PJ 2030 when you checked into the motel up in Madison?"

"That's just a number that came to mind. I didn't look at the license number on my car. I think I used to have a license number like that. I think I've been using that number for two or three years."

O'Brien left the room to call the motel. He wanted to make sure Hendricks's room hadn't been cleaned. It hadn't.

While he called the Madison Police Department, asking them to seal off the room, Crowe continued to question Hendricks in a calmer manner. He had Hendricks repeat the information about baby-sitting the children while his wife attended a baby shower and then leaving for Wisconsin when she got home.

O'Brien reentered the interrogation room. He would give it one more try. A bluff.

"David, we know you did it. Just admit it now and save all of us a lot of trouble."

Hendricks said nothing. He simply lowered his chin to his chest.

Crowe stood up. "We're going to get you. Sooner or later, we'll get you."

O'Brien stormed out of the room again, unable to shake the image of what he had seen inside 313 Carl Drive some five hours earlier. He informed Sergeant Irvin about what had occurred during the interrogation. Irvin told O'Brien to head for Madison to check out the motel. O'Brien, simultaneously tired and provoked, began the long drive north almost immediately. But not before a stop at his home to check the safety of his own children.

Crowe had told Hendricks that they were going to want the clothes he was wearing and the clothing out of his car as evidence. Crowe offered to take Hendricks back to the Cramer home where he might be able to borrow some pajamas to wear temporarily.

Hendricks said he'd rather wait at the police department until he could get some fresh clothing out of the house.

Hendricks remained in the interrogation room. A few minutes later, Crowe returned.

"I've got another question for you. You said you made all these phone calls from the motel up there in Wisconsin, so why is there only one call on your hotel bill?"

"All the Red Roof Inns are the same. You pay a flat rate of

thirty cents and you can make as many calls as you want. My long distance calls were charged to my credit card."

In a nearby room, another detective was interviewing Nate Palmer. Palmer wasn't read his rights. Still another team of detectives was interviewing Hendricks's in-laws near Delavan.

At 4 A.M. Hendricks opened the door to the interrogation room and asked Sergeant Irvin for some more coffee. Irvin handed him a fresh cup.

"Was there anything in your home that was particularly valuable?"

"No, not really. There's not much there except maybe for the microwave oven and maybe a couple hundred dollars. We don't have a safe."

"Any idea who might have done this?"

"No, I don't."

A team of uniformed officers was making the rounds of homes within several blocks of 313 Carl Drive. The purpose was twofold: to make sure there were no other murders in the neighborhood and to see if any neighbors had seen or heard anything.

One doorbell they rang was that of McLean County State's Attorney Ron Dozier. The policemen told him what had been discovered five and a half hours earlier just one and a half blocks from his home.

Dozier was miffed. He wondered just when he would have learned about the murders if he hadn't happened to live within the door-to-door canvas area. He got dressed, carefully locked his wife and four young boys inside his home, and went to Carl Drive.

County Coroner Bill Anderson was there. He described the crime scene to Dozier. Despite the fact that Dozier had been the county's chief prosecutor for seven years and an assistant prosecutor for four years before that, he had never viewed a murder scene with the bodies still present. He braced himself as he entered the home but was surprised by his reaction. He felt no instant revulsion. He was prepared for bright red blood, but it had dried to a dirty brown. The bodies looked like displays in a wax museum.

At 5:25 A.M., Detective Crowe was back in the interrogation room with Hendricks.

"What color is the ax that you keep in the garage?"

"It has a red handle. They didn't use an ax on them, did they?"

Crowe didn't respond and instead asked Hendricks to sign another search consent form, this one for Hendricks's body. They would look for any telltale blood. Hendricks agreed. Crowe gave Hendricks some clean clothes, obtained from Hendricks's home, to change into. Hendricks wanted to change in private. He was told that wouldn't be possible.

With Hendricks stripped to the waist, Crowe took a couple of instant photographs of Hendricks that would be used by police as they checked out his story. Two other detectives, Scott and Dan Katz, carefully scanned Hendricks's body, paying special attention to his fingernails. Then they had him bend over so they could direct an overhead light onto his head, deep into his hairline. They told Hendricks he could get dressed.

Outside the interrogation room, Crowe asked the detectives what they found.

"No blood."

Coroner Anderson and his deputy, Brady, had arrived at the police department to ask Hendricks some routine questions.

"Is there any medical history we should know about?"

"No, everyone was in relatively good health, except that Susan had a nodule on her thyroid gland and Dr. Zehr was checking into it."

Hendricks told the coroner that he didn't know yet which funeral home he wanted his family sent to. He wasn't familiar with any of them, except for one he passed when he drove from his home to his office. It was decided the bodies would be sent there, to Metzler Memorial Home.

Anderson also received Hendricks's permission to release the names of the children and his wife to the news media.

When Anderson returned to Carl Drive, a single reporter from a local radio station, WJBC, was there. At 6:05 A.M. Anderson was interviewed live on the air. He listed the names of the dead and their ages but would disclose nothing more, except to say that a joint investigation between the police department and his office was underway.

Inside 313 Carl Drive, the state crime-scene technicians, Dennis Dodwell and Rodney Wamsley, were already in their fifth hour of investigation. Using high-intensity lights, they had spent much of that time on their hands and knees, closely examining the pathway from the back door they had all entered up the stairs and into the two bedrooms where the four bodies still lay. The purpose was to clear a path so that the corpses could be removed without disturbing any evidence. Photographs followed. Now Dodwell was in the master bedroom. The high-intensity lights illuminated the bed where Susan Hendricks's body lay on its right side, head on a pillow, mostly covered by a heavy, blue bedspread. Its corner was so neatly turned back to reveal the body that Dodwell had accused some members of the city police department of disturbing the crime scene. O'Brien confirmed that the spread had been found that way. Daylight was just entering the bedroom window as Dodwell leaned over the bed, inches from the pale body, for a closer examination. Without warning, a piercing sound broke the stillness. Dodwell jumped. An electric alarm clock, set to go off at 6:30, was doing its job.

Outside the Hendricks home, a young man approached a reporter to learn as much as he could about what had happened at 313 Carl Drive. It was Jon Lewis, the husband of Susan Hendricks's sister Martha. He had just reported to his job as an orderly at Brokaw Hospital when a fellow worker showed him the newspaper article. He would later ask for permission to be present at the autopsies in the hospital's morgue. Permission would be denied.

At about 7 A.M. Beverly Crutcher, summoned by police to Bloomington from her home about thirty miles away, unlocked the front door to CASH Manufacturing and allowed Detectives Crowe and Scott inside for their search. They looked for anything that might link Hendricks to the crime, particularly any bloodied clothing or cleaning materials. They found nothing. As they were leaving the small building, another squad car pulled up and delivered Hendricks to his business.

About an hour before, Bev had seen David at the police department, but only for a moment. They had said very little to each other. Bev had thought Hendricks looked lost. Now, here at his office, he still looked lost. He asked her if she was going to work today.

"Of course." Her tone was sympathetic. "Have you talked to your parents yet?"

"No."

"Do you want me to call them for you?"

"Yes, go ahead." Then he changed his mind. "No, I think I can do it."

Beverly still had to deliver her children to their baby-sitter. Before she left, she suggested to Hendricks that he should talk to his attorney, Mercer Turner.

Laverne Hendricks, David's mother, was dazed and unbelieving when her son told her that his wife and children were all murdered. Upon hearing the news, she could manage to talk on the telephone with him for only a few moments. She told David she would call him back. She prayed, tried to telephone her husband, who was evangelizing in Canada, and then called her son back.

Lawrence Macy, a leading member of the local Plymouth Brethren, learned of the murders when he opened his morning newspaper. He had known Hendricks since David was twelve years old but had come to know him much better since he moved to Bloomington.

Macy rushed to the Bloomington Police Department, only to find that David had just been taken to his office. There the two men fell into each other's arms. Hendricks was sobbing as Macy and his wife tried to comfort David by telling him that Susan and the children were safe and happy with Jesus now. Hendricks would nod but then break down again. When Macy asked Hendricks if there was anything he could do for David, Hendricks said he needed to find his mother-in-law to start making funeral arrangements. Macy said he would find Nadine Palmer and tell her that David was looking for her. The Macys also told Hendricks that he should plan on spending the night at their home.

When Ed Roman, who two years earlier had purchased Hendricks's orthotics business, heard the news, he turned to his wife and said, "My God, Susie went into a religious frenzy and killed her kids and herself."

At that moment, the two hearses which had been backed into the Hendricks garage to collect the bodies were well on their way to the morgue at Brokaw Hospital. Nadine Palmer was standing on Carl Drive, surrounded now by the flock of reporters and camera crews from Bloomington and surrounding communities that had descended on the normally quiet street. They had found police and neighbors tight-lipped and were pleased when they discovered that she was the mother and grandmother of the four victims and willing to talk about them.

"Just a perfect family," she said, "no drinking, no smoking, a religious family." And she said that somehow this tragedy must be God's will.

"We know that at this time they're with the Lord. They're with Him, they're safe and there's no more pain or sorrow for them. At all. And Dave is the one who has the pain right now. And the rest of the family."

Ralph Storrs was preparing to go to work at his manufacturing plant in Kankakee, about eighty miles northeast of Bloomington, when he heard a radio news broadcast about the horrible crime. Uncertain that he had heard it correctly, Storrs waited for a second newscast and then called the Bloomington Police Department to confirm what he had heard.

Storrs, a past president of the American Orthotic and Prosthetic Association, first met Hendricks when David was a student at Northwestern University. Late in 1981, Storrs's company began making Hendricks's CASH Brace. Now it accounted for about 20 percent of Storrs's manufacturing business. In mid-1982 Storrs had begun talks with Hendricks about David's joining Storrs's firm. Those discussions continued.

Now Storrs and his office manager hurried to Bloomington, certain that Hendricks would need help. When they arrived at the CASH office, they joined a small stream of relatives and friends who had gone to Hendricks's office to comfort him and share their shock.

With Hendricks's cars impounded by police, Storrs lent Hendricks his car and remained at the CASH office to greet visitors and mind the business.

By 9:30 Hendricks's business attorney, Turner, had made an appointment for Hendricks to see Bloomington's best-known and most successful criminal defense lawyer, Harold Jennings. Jennings, whose snow-white hair and full beard belied his age but not his experience, gave Hendricks the usual basic, early advice to keep quiet, particularly to the police and the media, not to do anything foolish, and to keep Jennings apprised of any developments. In the meantime Jennings would try to determine exactly how seriously police considered Hendricks to be a suspect.

By midmorning both major wire services, both Chicago daily newspapers and at least one Chicago television station had representatives at Bloomington's police department. The pressure for more information increased substantially. The local media had seemed less willing to press for information that might jeopardize the investigation. But at 10:30 Police Chief Louis Devault and Coroner Anderson went before the press in the city council chambers.

Devault said his department had no suspects. When asked about Hendricks, the chief responded, "There have been many people interviewed. The investigative process is continuing at this time with complete cooperation of all law-enforcement agencies in McLean County."

He said that Hendricks's alibi had been "partially confirmed" and that "robbery is not necessarily ruled out as a motive." But he deflected most questions "because of the sensitive nature of the investigation."

The news conference, which was broadcast live on a local radio station, revealed virtually nothing that hadn't already been reported. After the news conference, a local reporter cornered Devault.

"Chief, you've got to say something about whether this is an isolated incident or whether we've got some nut on the loose in this town. Otherwise, you've got a big problem. People are going to go crazy."

"We really don't know what we've got yet, but we're pretty sure this is an isolated thing."

By the time the news conference ended, every locksmith in the community was fully engaged for the rest of the day, and well into the night, installing dead-bolt locks on sliding patio doors. A lot of Bloomington people, particularly those in the Carl Drive area, weren't inclined to take chances.

Hendricks was on the telephone to Metzler Memorial Home.

"Hello. My name is David Hendricks and I have tremendous problems. You probably read the paper or heard the radio."

August "Bud" Metzler assured Hendricks that he knew of the tragedy and expressed his condolences.

"I have to make arrangements, and I don't know what to do," Hendricks said.

"Are your parents with you?"

"No, they live in the southern part of the state, and it will be quite a while before they get here."

"How about your wife's parents?"

"I haven't seen them, but I think they're in town."

Metzler suggested that Hendricks and his in-laws meet at the funeral home.

Nadine Palmer, her daughter Liz Buchanan, and Liz's husband, Jerry, were at the all-brick funeral home only a few blocks from the CASH office when Hendricks arrived alone. Nadine and Liz, who hadn't seen David since he returned from Wisconsin, embraced him and cried. Jerry, who had been on Carl Drive when Hendricks returned home, stood by, his head bowed. Together they tried to comfort Dave.

"I know they're happy with the Lord now," Hendricks said, "but I still wish they were back with me here, now."

The family agreed that a visitation would be held Friday evening with the funeral at the funeral home Saturday morning.

When Metzler took the family into a large room where various caskets were on display for selection, Hendricks bawled. For a short time he seemed inconsolable.

Mrs. Palmer suggested that her daughter and grandchildren be buried in Delavan, near her home.

"I think I would rather have them buried here, where I am," Hendricks said, as he wiped away tears. "But I'm not from around here. I don't know anything about the cemeteries."

Metzler made some telephone calls, knowing that cemeteries sometimes make financial concessions in tragic situations. When he returned, he suggested the city-owned Evergreen Cemetery.

"It's the city's oldest cemetery. It's where Adlai Stevenson is interred. It's well kept."

Hendricks thought it sounded like an acceptable place. Hendricks, his in-laws, and Metzler drove to the cemetery and selected lots. But before they left, Metzler had to settle the question of burial clothing.

"Can you tell me what the condition of the bodies is?"

"I've never been inside the house since I returned from my trip. I don't know."

Doug Haas, the sales manager at Rebbec Motors, was paged to the phone. David Hendricks was calling.

"Due to what has happened, I'd like to cancel the order for my wife's car. But I still want my car. I'll still need it."

Reporters had been in and out of the CASH office throughout the day, hoping to interview Hendricks. The husband and father of the murder victims hadn't been there much, but when he was, Ralph Storrs shielded him from the press. As the day wore on, though, Storrs said he was convinced that Hendricks might as well talk briefly with the reporters, who might then leave Hendricks alone.

"I'll be happy to run interference for you," he told David. "But I can't be here tomorrow."

With Hendricks's agreement, Storrs telephoned the *Daily Pantagraph*, which quickly dispatched a reporter and a photographer to Hendricks's office. An Associated Press reporter accompanied them. It was about 2:30 P.M.

Hendricks sat at his desk, holding his head, apparently fighting back tears as reporters Scott Richardson of the *Pantagraph* and Bob Springer of AP asked a few questions. There were few usable quotes.

He told the reporters that the last time he saw his family alive was when he left home at eleven o'clock Monday night.

After a couple of minutes, Hendricks realized who the photographer was. It was Marc Featherly, who had purchased Hendricks's home in Stanford about two years earlier. Hendricks apologized for not immediately recognizing Featherly and asked how the Featherlys liked the house.

WJBC Radio officials had decided not to attempt to interview Hendricks unless it became clear that other media had already talked with him. As the anchor for the 4:30 P.M. news was putting the final touches on the day's lead story, the AP wire reported that Hendricks had been interviewed. A quick call to the CASH office determined that Hendricks was there and would go on the air. There were about twenty seconds before airtime.

"I don't listen to the radio, but I understand your station is the main station in town," Hendricks told the anchor before the newscast began.

After an update on the murder investigation, the anchor asked Hendricks why he was willing to be interviewed under these circumstances. The anchor was sensitive to the public criticism that would certainly erupt if it appeared that the radio station had badgered Hendricks into a live interview.

"I thank you for giving me the chance," was Hendricks's reply. "I mainly wanted to say to the people of this community that I love ya, and I thank you very much for all of the support that has come my way. It's been absolutely fabulous. All of the people that I didn't even realize I knew that have called in here with offers for help and support. I just want to say at a time like this, the love and generosity of people is . . ." He paused. "Tremendous."

"Mr. Hendricks, are you able to tell us about the circumstances of the last time you saw your family and of your trip to Wisconsin?"

"Oh Steve, I . . . I think to do that, I would break down completely."

"Okay. I understand that. One more question and we'll let you go. Do you have any reason to suspect any person or persons? Do you have any ideas at all about what might have happened?"

"No, no, I really don't, and I really think it's best for me to consciously try not to form ideas like this. I need to think about brighter things. I would like to make just one more comment. I want to let the community know that the people who are gone, the four that were part of my family are the most wonderful people . . ."—Hendricks's voice seemed to break—". . . that ever touched my life. They're great."

As the anchor wrapped up that part of the newscast, he swallowed hard to maintain his composure. He thought of his own wife and three children. He had been following the story since 2 A.M., but up until that moment it had been little more than a major news story that demanded his total attention. Now he thought of the children.

In a television interview a few minutes later, Hendricks said that he knew "that Susie and my three children are much better off, and I wish them back for me as a selfish thing, but I know that they are with the Lord Jesus in heaven, and I am satisfied now in knowing that."

"Dave, you are a fairly religious person," a TV reporter said. "If they find the person who did this, do you believe in the death penalty? What would you like to see happen?"

"I would like to see him get saved. It would be worth it if one person found their way to heaven, don't you think?"

At that moment the autopsies on the bodies of Susan, Becky, Grace, and Benjy Hendricks were well underway.

Detective O'Brien was back from Wisconsin. He had found that, as requested, Madison police had sealed off Room 110 at the Red Roof Inn off Interstate 90, leaving it just as Hendricks apparently had left it.

O'Brien had taken fifteen photos of the motel room and collected the room's towels, bed linens, and wastebasket contents as evidence.

Because Hendricks had volunteered that he had changed clothes at a rest stop along I-90 between Madison and Portage, Bloomington police had asked Wisconsin authorities to be on the lookout for any discarded clothing in that area.

On his way back to Bloomington, O'Brien stopped at the Rock County, Wisconsin, Sheriff's Department to pick up what had been found along I-90 just across the Illinois–Wisconsin border: a knapsack containing some clothing, a Bible, and jar of peanut butter. None of the items belonged to Hendricks.

The mood inside 313 Carl Drive was less subdued now that the four bodies had been removed.

Crime-scene technicians, who had entered the home in midnight darkness and pored over the house in darkness and daylight, now noticed that night was again upon them. They had been on the job for eighteen straight hours, but there was more to be done.

They took special care collecting certain articles they felt could yield important fingerprints or other evidence: a dirty cup, saucer, and tea bag found on the kitchen counter; the plastic sleeves inside Susan Hendricks's blue wallet, discovered dumped out of her purse on the family room floor; numerous door handles; fibers from where carpeting appeared stained; and, of course, the ax and thirteen-inch-long knife found on one of the girls' beds. The detectives noticed that the wooden block in the kitchen that held several kitchen knives had one vacant slot.

By 7:30 P.M., in the Brokaw Hospital morgue, pathologist Dr. Antonie Romyn was beginning the autopsy on the fourth body of a member of the Hendricks family.

Assisted by Deputy Coroner Ed Books, Dr. Romyn had begun six hours earlier with Susan Hendricks's body, which had been clothed only in a blue nightgown.

Romyn found a small, encapsulated nodule in her thyroid and a gallstone measuring 2.2 centimeters. He found no evidence of recent sexual contact. Her stomach, he noted, contained about twenty milliliters of "cloudy, mucoid, slightly greenish material."

The pathologist's work included taking an impression of the area around Susan's left ear, where she had been struck savagely.

Next Romyn moved to Grace's body, clothed in a blue and white nightgown, pink floral underpants, and dark green knee socks. The doctor described "three large gaping cuts on the left side of the head and neck, one abrasion on the left forehead, and one superficial cut on the upper right chest." In her stomach Romyn found about seventy milliliters of "partially-digested food which is brown-gray in color with particles identifiable as pizza."

Benjamin Hendricks's stomach contained about sixty milliliters of "dark gray material with food particles identifiable as pizza."

Each of those autopsies had taken at least ninety minutes. And now Rebekah's body lay open in front of the pathologist. Her stomach, he found, contained about one hundred milliliters of a "thick brown material with food particles identifiable as pizza."

As Romyn ladled part of the contents from the stomach into a Styrofoam cup held by Books, neither man knew how important what they were saving would be in the Hendricks case.

One by one the bodies were delivered to Metzler Memorial Home, where Bud Metzler and his associate Claude Miller prepared them for burial. It wasn't until months later, when they learned that police and prosecution believed that the murders occurred late on the night of November 7, that a revelation hit both men. Metzler, a mortician for forty years, and his younger colleague had independently arrived at the same startling conclusion: that the bodies' circulation was much too good; there was too little decomposition for the deaths to have occurred within the prosecution's time-of-death estimate.

It was a belief that Bud Metzler took to his own grave two years later. It's a belief that Claude Miller holds today.

The Bloomington patrolman assigned to stand watch over the

interior of the Hendricks home that night was startled when, at 1:02 A.M., the telephone rang.

"Mr. Hendricks?" The voice sounded like that of a white female, about seventeen years old. "I know the two people who did this. They went to Chicago. I'm sorry I can't say any more."

The caller hung up.

It was too late to trace the call.

Eight

The next morning, acting Chief of Detectives Irvin called together the little-rested members of his division to discuss their findings, share their suspicions, and outline the day's assignments.

A thorough canvas of the neighborhood had found that no one had heard or seen anything out of the ordinary the night of the murders. And the most unusual people seen in the neighborhood over the past couple of days were those collecting signatures on a petition against toxic waste and someone distributing fliers offering residents a chance to have their house number painted on their curb.

One neighbor, noting Hendricks's cars, airplane, motorcycle, collapsible bicycle, and Walkman radio, told police that Hendricks "obviously was living life in the fast lane." The same neighbor said she had once believed that Susan Hendricks was David's mother rather than his wife.

The detectives were evenly divided on whether Hendricks was their prime suspect. Some wanted to check out some local hoods and weirdos they believed capable of such a crime. There were suspicions about some relatives and neighbors. There was a chance that the killings were simply random, possibly linked to a burglary or drugs. There was even the suggestion of there being a mistake, that the killer (or killers) had intended to enter the home of the state's attorney a short distance away.

Charlie Crowe was among those convinced that Hendricks was their man. Why had Hendricks seemed so calm, so alert, so prepared, even rehearsed, under intense interrogation? Wasn't it unusual for a person to have such a detailed memory of when and the order in which he made a series of phone calls, particularly under the circumstances? Didn't Hendricks seem fairly polite, impossible to anger, yet very guarded? And if Hendricks was so security-conscious that he even built his own locking device for the patio door, why would he be so careless as to leave it unlocked when he left his family behind that night? It even bothered Crowe that Hendricks was cooperative to the point that Hendricks had called police the previous afternoon to tell them that he would be staying with the Lawrence Macy family.

Crowe's thoughts were broken when Irvin announced that a total of nineteen officers would be working on the case virtually full-time, a dozen from the Bloomington department and the rest from the state, county, and neighboring town of Normal police departments.

They would fan out, checking Hendricks's account of his Monday night outing with his children and his trip to Wisconsin. They would continue interviews with relatives, friends, and neighbors. Because Tuesday had been garbage pickup day in the Carl Drive neighborhood, men were assigned to the local landfill in an effort to locate the neighborhood's garbage and sift through it on the off chance that the killer or killers discarded something in a trash can at the curb. The state crime lab technicians would continue their work in and around the house.

Crowe was assigned to go to Chicago with Deputy Coroner Brady to deliver blood and gastric samples to the state crime lab for toxicology tests.

Hendricks was driven to the Delavan home of Susan's parents, where other family members had gathered. Hendricks appeared inconsolable. He drifted from stony silence to convulsive crying. At one point he took one of his young nieces onto his lap and broke into tears. He ate virtually nothing.

With little help from Hendricks, family members tried to decide which elder from the Brethren would speak at the funeral, now two days away. David's father, Chuck, said he didn't think he would be able to handle it emotionally. Lawrence Macy also declined to lead the funeral service but agreed to say a few words at the burial. Finally they made a request of a laboring brother from Kentucky, Paul Geveden, who had spoken when Susan's sister Liz and Jerry Buchanan were married. He agreed.

That night at Bloomington's city hall, about a hundred Carl Drive area residents met behind closed doors with police officials. The police hoped to gather more information. So did the neighbors, particularly about whether there was any truth to rumors that some sort of religious cult might be responsible for the killings. They also received promises of increased police patrol of the area, complained about the heavy sightseer traffic through Carl Drive (one neighbor counted fifty cars a minute at one point), and objected to the intense media coverage of their normally unnoticed neighborhood.

With little new to report that day, local media had resorted to telling information-hungry townspeople that police were receiving many more prowler reports than usual and that gun sales had increased 30 percent.

Later there would be a grim consequence of the general anxiety. A handgun that had been kept unloaded until the Hendricks murders discharged accidentally, killing a young boy.

By the next day police had interviewed people who remembered seeing Hendricks at the pizza restaurant, gas station, and bookmobile in Bloomington or at various health-care organizations in Wisconsin. They had checked Hendricks's police background. The most damaging information they could find was a total of four speeding tickets—two in 1979, two in 1981.

Police searched the Hendricks home's basement, an attic area above the garage, and a crawl space under the family room. Nothing turned up except that a door to a freezer in the basement had been left open an inch.

They scoured the Buick Electra 225 that Hendricks had taken to Wisconsin.

And they began a meticulous inventory of the two hundred books in the home. The vast majority of them were religious in nature. A few were in Spanish, a holdover from the family's missionary work in South America. There were also some travel, diet, and do-it-yourself books. Notes taken about three of the books found in the master bedroom reveal that police were looking for anything strange or curious:

King Saul, the Man After the Flesh, bookmarked to Chapter XVI which begins "David is now an outcast and fugitive."
The Act of Marriage/The Beauty of Sexual Love, bookmarked to Chapter 8 entitled "The Unfulfilled Woman."
Lay up Your Treasures in Heaven, subtitled "How a family faced the tragic deaths of three of their children."

Hendricks had visited attorney Hal Jennings several times by now. When he returned to the CASH Manufacturing office after one such visit, two detectives were waiting for him. They said they wanted to ask Hendricks just a few questions. Hendricks was prepared, but not for questions.

"Well, after I was accused by the police the other night, I went out and hired an attorney," Hendricks told them. "He has told me not to cooperate with someone who's trying to put me away. He advised me to have you leave a list of questions and then we'll answer them and get back with you. He said that he's sure we'd be able to answer them.

"I know my attorney wouldn't agree that I talk with you like this, but I just want you to know that there's nothing I would rather do than to get the persons responsible for this and I don't see anything wrong with answering these questions."

Still, Hendricks agreed to answer questions only if they were submitted in writing. The detectives left.

Visitation was that evening at the funeral home. Even though nearly three full days had passed since the murders were discovered, time enough to at least grasp the idea that the murders had occurred, some were still startled at the sight of the four white caskets lined up end to end.

For about two hours Hendricks, supported by family, stood by the closed caskets as other relatives, friends, and a handful of the curious filed by. Outside, police watched. Inside, family members noticed an unfamiliar man sitting in a corner, smoking. Bud Metzler wrote down the car license number as the man drove away. He would later give the number to police.

Hendricks's parents and in-laws were concerned about his well-being. At seven o'clock, an hour before the visitation was to end, they persuaded him to leave and get some rest. The funeral was tomorrow.

Saturday, November 12, was cloudy and crisp. By the time the funeral began that morning, at least 250 people had crowded into the memorial home. Thirty-one close family members sat in a special area. When Nate Palmer hung up his young son's hand-me-down coat, David Hendricks's loud sobs broke the quiet. It was the same black Pittsburgh Steelers jacket that Benjy had worn and cherished a year earlier.

Hendricks's sobbing returned when strains of the children's song "Jesus Loves Me" were heard. Benjy had chosen the song to be sung at Sunday School less than a week earlier.

Paul Geveden, the laboring brother from Arlington, Kentucky, began his remarks by saying, "Today heaven was made four times richer." At one point he seemed to address the community about the rumors that the Brethren were a cult. He recalled a time decades before when a young man found Jesus in Bloomington, became part of the Plymouth Brethren, and later moved on to Kentucky. Geveden said he was that young man, and that many respected people, including lawyers, doctors, and nurses, considered themselves part of the Brethren.

Geveden's last thought, one of hope and anticipation of the day when all believers would be joined with God in heaven, led graciously into a hymn. The first phrase was sung only by Geveden, but his aging voice was quickly joined by many of those present because "Praise the Savior" was an anthem very familiar to the Brethren:

> Jesus is the name that charms us;
> He for conflict fits and arms us;
> Nothing moves and nothing harms us
> While we trust in Him.

A police car escorted the procession of hearses and sixty-five other vehicles to the cemetery. Other police, less conspicuous, took photographs of the cars and vans, recording their license plates.

The cortege moved through the wrought-iron gates at Evergreen Cemetery, past the Stevenson grave to a rather desolate area on the east edge of the graveyard.

The mournful silence seemed prolonged as the six pallbearers carried, in turn, each of the caskets to the grave site. Hendricks and his remaining family sat in a single row of chairs near the graves. One of the funeral-home employees tried to shield the family from the prying telephoto lenses of some news photographers.

Just as the graveside service was about to begin, David gripped the hands of his mother, who sat next to him.

"Mom, get me out of here. Take me back to the van," he pleaded.

"Dave, you can't," his mother said. It was at that moment, Laverne Hendricks believes, that her son first truly understood that his family was gone.

In his brief remarks, Lawrence Macy talked of hope beyond the grave. But virtually everyone was in tears when he ended by admitting that they all would greatly miss "gentle, gracious Susie, bright and joyful Becky and Grace, and Benjy's happy smile."

McLean County State's Attorney Ron Dozier had grown up on a farm in southern Illinois, graduated from the University of Illinois Law School, and in March of 1973 became one of three assistant state's attorneys in McLean County. Within five months, partly because of rapid turnover in the office, he was the first assistant prosecutor. Three years later he was elected state's attorney at the age of twenty-nine. Now, on November 14, 1983, he called the first of what would be almost daily conferences with representatives of the various agencies involved in the Hendricks murder investigation.

What good physical evidence did they have in the case?

None, Dozier was told. A crime-scene technician described it as "the cleanest bloody crime" he had ever seen.

The victims' blood was confined to the two bedrooms, with one exception. Police did discover a single smudge of blood at the edge of the sink in the upstairs hallway bathroom. The tests of the stained carpet fibers found that the carpeting had not been stained by blood.

"To give you an idea how clean it was," Dennis Dodwell, a crime-scene technician, volunteered, "the ax handle is red, about thirty-five inches long. There is no blood spatter, even up the handle." Dodwell said it revealed no fingerprint smudges, even from previous use. "This is unusual. Normally when we process something, you'll get something. Smudges, at least some ridges. Or even if the killer wears Playtex gloves with a design ingrained and he grabs something a couple of times, you get a little film on them. I can pick that up. We didn't even get that."

No bloodied towels or clothing was found. Every sink, bathtub, and shower in the house was dry. Yet an analysis of blood spatters on the walls, floor, and ceiling of the girls' room indicated that the killer stood between two beds when he wielded the ax and would himself have been splattered with blood.

There was no sign that any doors or windows had been pried or picked.

Dozier asked about fingerprints.

Virtually nothing unusual. No fingerprints on the ax and knife. Susan Hendricks obviously was a meticulous housekeeper. Virtually all prints that were there checked to family members. There were a couple of invisible but detectable fingerprints from the kitchen telephone receiver, several from a guest book kept in the living room, one from the purse found in the family room, and several from a wine bottle which hadn't been identified yet. And there was a single footwear impression removed from the kitchen floor near the sliding patio door.

Was there any chance the ax and knife weren't really the weapons used but were planted there to confuse police?

Unlikely, Dozier was told. The toolmark examination of the wounds showed that they could have been caused by the ax and knife. Hair fragments found on the ax and knife were consistent with Benjy's and Becky's.

What about Hendricks's car?

Nothing linking Hendricks to the crime. Some red paint chips discovered on a floor mat didn't match the ax handle. Hendricks's habit of keeping even the smallest business expense receipt yielded two pieces of paper that lent credence to his account of his Wisconsin trip. One was a handwritten receipt for fifty-eight cents for the coffee he purchased at a Bloomington restaurant on his way out of town that night. The other was a receipt from a Hardee's restaurant in Stevens Point, Wisconsin. The slip from the Hardee's computerized cash register showed a $1.56 purchase at the central Wisconsin restaurant at 7:17 the next morning.

Dozier was told the landfill search had yielded nothing useful.

Hendricks's airplane hangar? Nothing.

Hendricks's office? The same. A search warrant had also been obtained to check out Hendricks's former place of business, Illinois Orthopedic Appliance. Nothing unusual there either.

Toxicology? Again, nothing uncommon in the victims' bodies.

The same for the cup and teabag found in the kitchen.

And what about the funeral home? Anybody unusual show up there?

Not really. The one stranger who had sat smoking was a crime buff familiar to police. "I told him he should stay away from there," the man's wife told police when they showed up at her door.

The investigation was coming up with blanks.

That afternoon police officer Tom Sanders, on guard duty at the Hendricks home, answered the telephone. There was a woman on the other end.

"Killer! Killer!" the voice said. Then a click.

Sanders used his police radio to order a trace. Still holding the phone to his ear, Sanders heard a dialing sound. Then what sounded like the same voice returned.

"Who's there?" it said.

Sanders identified himself and asked the caller's name. There was a hesitation.

"I'm calling about a house."

"Did you call earlier?"

"No."

"Well, this line is being traced."

"That's okay. I'm Martha Lewis."

The woman gave her address and phone number and then volunteered that she was the sister of Susan Hendricks.

Police were interested in Susan's youngest sister. Family members had said that if there was any black sheep in the Palmer family, it was Martha. Police were told that Martha had left the Brethren several years earlier and was given to emotional outbursts.

Under police questioning, Martha denied making the "killer" call, suggesting instead that police were tapping her phone and the tap somehow became entangled with the trace.

"Will you swear on the Bible that you didn't make that call?" Detective Sergeant Irvin asked. He had one at hand. Martha examined it and then swore on it that she did not make the call.

Martha agreed to take a lie-detector test the next day. In that test she again denied making the call. The polygraph examiner believed she was lying.

Martha's husband, Jon, said he was with his wife when the call occurred and she didn't make it. Prosecutors say their phone was never tapped.

Police were also interested in Jon Lewis, who sometimes baby-sat for the Hendricks family (recently he had taken Benjy for a walk through Evergreen Cemetery) and frequently referred to Hendricks as his "millionaire brother-in-law."

Lewis said he hadn't worked in his orderly job at Brokaw Hospital the previous Monday or Tuesday; in fact, he had gone to bed at about eight o'clock the night the bodies were found and didn't learn of the murders until the next morning at work.

"You know what I think?" Lewis said. "I think somebody got an ax and knife and killed them in their sleep and then ransacked the upstairs. Somebody probably saw a movie like *Friday the 13th* and wanted to slice people up."

On November 15 police, armed with a warrant, searched the Lewis home and found nothing. The next day Lewis submitted himself for a lie-detector test, was asked about the murders, and passed the test.

And police were curious about a young couple who had spent what amounted to a five-day honeymoon in the Lewis home a month earlier.

The couple was married on October 11 and had no place to live. The minister arranged for them to stay with Jon and Martha. Their departure was unpleasant when Lewis demanded that they pay sixty dollars as their share of expenses.

In the days before his wedding, the groom had been questioned about a drug-related murder that had occurred that fall. He was released without charges. And his alibi in the Hendricks case was verified.

Hendricks, apparently convinced it would be some time before he would be able to reclaim his home, visited a realty office to inquire about renting a furnished apartment on a month-to-month basis. Pressed for his identity, he said, "I'm David Hendricks, sole survivor of the terrible tragedy. But don't tell the apartment owner until after we get an agreement. There are a lot of rumors going around."

State's Attorney Dozier had brought his first assistant, Brad

Murphy, into the case. With police detectives they put together a list of questions to submit in writing to Hendricks. There were twenty questions in all, but most were only camouflage for what police really wanted to know more about: Hendricks's activities just before and after he left for Wisconsin on the night of the killings. They would anxiously await his answers.

In the meantime police continued to search out other possible suspects. They had assembled a list of nearly one hundred persons in the central Illinois area who had been convicted of violent crimes. One by one they were crossed off the list. Some were still in prison. The rest had valid alibis.

Hendricks's attorney furnished police with the names of eleven prisoners at the nearby Pontiac Correctional Center that Hendricks had fitted for back braces. Seven of them were still in prison. Three of the four now free had been convicted of robbery, the fourth of murder. All had good alibis.

Dozier became more and more convinced that any murder case might hinge on expert opinions of when exactly the deaths occurred.

Samples of the four victims' stomach contents were given to Dr. John Dwyer, a forensic botanist from St. Louis University, for examination. Four days later Deputy Coroner Brady flew to St. Louis to pick up the specimens from Dwyer and flew on to Richmond, Virginia, where the National Medical Examiners Convention was underway. There Brady consulted with the chief medical examiners from St. Louis and Miami about what steps the McLean County Coroner's Office could take to get an accurate idea of the time of death.

But a related problem weighed on Dozier's mind. Police had verified that the Hendricks children had eaten at the Chuck E. Cheese pizza restaurant between about 6:45 and 7 P.M. But what if they had taken some of the pizza home and consumed it later? Or what if Hendricks just claimed they did? It could make time-of-death estimates based on the stomach contents much less useful.

No one at the pizza restaurant could say whether Hendricks had taken some remaining pizza home. The pass-through where leftover pizza was boxed to take home was a blind slot. Workers didn't see customers and customers didn't see workers.

Neighbors had told police they thought Hendricks took the family's garbage to the curb earlier that Monday evening for the Tuesday morning pickup. No pizza box was found in the house, and none had been found in the neighborhood garbage at the landfill. Still, if Hendricks claimed they had taken pizza home and eaten some at 8 or 9 P.M., could Dozier disprove that? It seemed unlikely.

Did Hendricks take the garbage to the curb before he and his children made their trip to the shopping mall and pizza restaurant? It was one of the twenty questions Dozier was about to submit to Hendricks in writing. And it was the question Dozier most wanted Hendricks to answer. If the garbage had been taken out before the trip to the mall and restaurant, any pizza box would likely have been found in the house. If the garbage was delivered to the curb after they got home, then it could be argued that the take-home box had been taken to and lost in the landfill.

Convinced that Hendricks and his attorney were unaware that what time the children ate could be a major factor in a case against them, Dozier wanted Hendricks's answer on the record now. But he also would rather see and hear Hendricks's answer face to face. So he called Hendricks.

"You know we'd really like to talk to you," Dozier said. "I'm really pretty confused about what the problem is here. You say you want to help police, but you won't talk with us. And we can't rule you out as a suspect until we have a chance to talk with you some more."

"Well, my attorney has advised me not to talk. I'd love to. After all, they were my children who were killed, but I can't talk without my attorney's consent."

"If you don't have anything to hide, why not talk with us? Just tell me, are you going to talk to us or not? I need to know."

"I'll ask Hal Jennings. I want to. But you know, I really don't like that Detective Crowe. He accused me, face to face, of killing my family."

"You don't have to talk to Crowe. Were there any detectives you did like?"

"That Irvin, Sergeant Irvin seemed polite. He was okay."

"All right. We'll have him talk to you."

"But I'm not sure I want to go down to the police station again."

"You don't have to. We can meet in my office."

"Can my attorney be there?"

"No problem. We'll meet anywhere you want. You set the conditions. When will you talk to us?"

"I need to talk to Jennings."

Dozier hung up in frustration, convinced that the only way he'd get the pizza and garbage question answered was in writing. The list of twenty questions was sent to Jennings.

In the meantime police were digging deeper in an effort to come up with any shred of physical evidence at 313 Carl Drive.

The city's public works department was summoned to vacuum out nearly six hundred feet of sewers connected to the Hendricks home. A test of the sewer water samples turned up no evidence of blood.

A special television camera was fed through nearly 1,500 feet of nearby sewers in the hope of turning up something used to clean the weapons and murderer after the killings. It revealed nothing.

The worker who had installed the home's plumbing was hired to remove a total of seven P-traps connected to sinks, tubs, and a washing machine. Their contents were collected and analyzed. There was no sign of blood.

Cold-air duct returns were checked. Light-switch covers were removed. There was nothing unusual. No sign of tampering.

Dozier was deeply disappointed when Hendricks responded to the list of twenty questions with only two answers. Neither had anything to do with pizza or garbage.

Through Hendricks's attorney, Dozier pressed Hendricks to take a polygraph examination. Jennings asked whether Dozier would commit himself to eliminating Hendricks as a suspect in the case if Hendricks passed the test.

Dozier thought about it for only a short time. His office policy said that the results of lie-detector tests should be considered in the light of all other available evidence. Dozier was beginning to wonder whether Hendricks really had a conscience. A lack of one could make it easier to pass a test and still be guilty. Dozier's answer was no. Then, said Jennings, Hendricks's answer was no. And the answer was also no to any additional questioning.

Dozier decided to go public in an effort to appeal to what he suspected to be an intellectual vanity on Hendricks's part. If indeed Hendricks believed himself to be smarter than police and prosecuters, maybe he would take up a public challenge.

"Mr. Hendricks is not helping in the investigation of the murders of his wife and three children," Dozier told the press. "He has refused to be interviewed by police. He's been on TV professing to be a practicing Christian and professing to be innocent. He has said publicly that he's concerned and upset and wants to cooperate. But he's not. I'd like to see the real David Hendricks stand up."

"Is Hendricks a suspect?" a reporter asked.

"I can't say he's a suspect, but there are some things about the case that point in his direction. I'd like to see him take a polygraph examination. I'm wondering why a person who really has nothing to hide, who has done nothing wrong, would object to simply going through in detail with police what his activities were the night before he left."

Hendricks told reporters he was consulting with his attorney.

By now Hendricks had been tailed by police for about two weeks. His schedule was fairly routine. He was still staying with the Lawrence Macy family, and he would be seen taking outdoor walks with Macy most evenings. Other times he would walk alone and stand for extended periods at a nearby lake. The daylight hours were filled with a short daily visit to his family's graves in Evergreen Cemetery, attendance at Brethren meetings, lengthy stays at his office, and frequent visits to attorney Hal Jennings's office.

One weekend he flew his plane to his parents' home in Allendale. The police tail continued in the air even though Hendricks had informed police where he was going.

The surveillance became almost comical at times. Hendricks once went into the building containing his friend John Cramer's faculty office at Illinois Wesleyan University. He remained inside so long that the policeman tailing Hendricks was afraid he had lost his target. As the policeman walked into the building, Hendricks walked out the same door. Hendricks greeted him.

Another time Hendricks flagged down two policemen who had followed him to the Bloomington airport. Hendricks wanted to report that his airplane hangar had been burglarized.

"You guys are doing a good job following me," he told them. "But I'm about to move into a mobile home, and I was wondering if you could be a little more discreet at the mobile home court. I'd like to keep that area as quiet as possible and not make the people there think they have a mass murderer living among them."

Two detectives visited Hendricks's parents at their southern Illinois home.

"These murders were the work of Satan to break up a good Christian family," Charles Hendricks told the investigators. He quoted some Bible verses to them and said the Hendricks family was free of worldly temptations—no TV, no radio, no smoking, no drinking.

"What would you say," Detective Greg Tulle asked Mr. Hendricks, "if I told you that a bottle of wine was found in your son's home?"

"I'd say if you find the person who brought that wine into the house, you have found the killer."

Laverne Hendricks said that Susan was her son's only girl-friend.

As the detectives were about to leave, Tulle turned to address the distressed couple.

"You know, even if your son is arrested, it doesn't mean he'll be convicted," he said. "And if he is convicted, it doesn't mean it's the end. There would still be the appellate court and the state supreme court. And although I don't practice religion like I should all the time, I believe like you do that in the end there is only one judge."

Ron Dozier returned Gene Irvin's urgent phone call.

"We might have something," Irvin said. "Hendricks may not be as clean as everyone thinks he is."

"Oh?" Dozier sat tall in his chair.

"Yeah, we're checking out a couple of tips. One is that ol' Dave might have dated some local model. The other was that Hendricks approached some young girl on the street about modeling for him."

The two men agreed that a complete check with area modeling agencies and photography studios would get top priority. If they could come up with some names, and the stories checked out, Dozier said, they might just have found Hendricks's Achilles' heel.

Dozier had received official opinions from the crime-scene technicians that the apparent burglary in the home was probably staged to mislead police. Dozier and Murphy believed what little evidence there was pointed more and more to Hendricks, and they were even more convinced that expert time-of-death estimates could be pivotal.

At a prosecutor's conference Dozier had learned that analysis of stomach contents remained the most valid method of fixing time of death. It was there that he had been introduced to Dr. Michael Baden, a New York City medical examiner.

The investigation team had the Chuck E. Cheese pizza restaurant prepare a pizza identical to the one computerized records showed David Hendricks had ordered for his children the night of the murders. Within a few hours, Deputy Coroner Dan Brady carried that pizza and the four containers of the murder victims' stomach contents into Dr. Baden's Manhattan apartment. There Baden and a colleague analyzed and compared the materials. Baden consulted by telephone with Dr. Romyn, the autopsy pathologist, and within a couple of days gave a written opinion: the children died two to four hours after they ate the pizza. In other words, between 9 P.M. and 11 P.M. if they had eaten nothing after seven o'clock that night.

The leftover pizza question continued to haunt Dozier.

Detective legwork at the modeling agencies and photography studios yielded some names and circumstances that Hendricks would have a hard time explaining to his fellow Brethren. But there was nothing as hot, as incriminating, as police had daydreamed. Something might still show up, police thought. They would keep digging.

It was just before 1 P.M. that Hendricks called the Bloomington detective division, asking for Sergeant Irvin. Charlie Crowe answered the phone.

"Yeah. Oh, hi. How're you doing, Charlie?"

"Okay."

"When will Sergeant Irvin be in?"

"Well, he usually goes to lunch somewhere about this time and is usually back about one-thirty."

"Well, that's all right. I can talk. All I need to do is give you three pieces of information." Crowe grabbed a pencil. "I just want to cooperate and help you as much as I can. One is that I've changed cars, and if you've got people that want to follow my actions, I'm in a different car now. It's a Pontiac 6000 STE. It's a new car. Doesn't even have plates on it, just the yellow window sticker, and it's brown over brown. Very distinctive-looking car and it won't be any problem to follow."

"All right."

"And then my address. I'm going to be changing in the next day or two to a mobile home that I've rented. I'm going to go and, you know, start living in a place of my own, and that will be Lot 215 Willow Creek Court. And then I intend once again to go down to

my parents' house to visit this weekend and expect to leave sometime Friday afternoon, possibly evening. Probably will drive down
there this time in that Pontiac."

"Okay."

"And this is Charlie Crowe that I'm talking to?"

"Yeah."

"Okay." Hendricks was about to hang up. Crowe didn't want
him to.

"All right now. That's the only cooperation along that line? You
still don't want to talk to us. Is that correct?"

"Well, the purpose of my call was to inform you of . . ."

"Well, I understand that. Yeah. I understand that . . ."

"Yeah. Of course, that's why I called."

"But you still don't want to talk to us right now. Is that correct?"

"Well, actually my desires really don't have anything to do with
it. I'm, as you know, following advice, and . . ."

"Well, I know that. But David, everybody has a mind of their
own is what I'm saying to you, and I think you realize that. You
have a mind of your own, I'm sure. Your attorney told you probably
not to talk to us, but you still have a mind of your own. Sometimes
you ought to use that."

Mind of your own. A phrase that Crowe thought would appeal
to Hendricks's intellectual vanity.

"You think so?" Hendricks asked.

"Well, I think so. But it's up to you. I can't tell you to or not to.
But you know you have a mind of your own, and I think you should
use it sometimes. So if you ever feel like talking to us, we're here all
the time. Come in and see us."

"Well, thank you, Charlie. Well, thank you very much."

"All right."

"Have a nice afternoon."

"Same to you. Bye."

Each night since the Hendricks murders, Detective Sergeant
Irvin, a policeman for twenty years, would strip to his undershorts
and sit on his bed to review new reports and plot the next day's
detective work. And now he had a new concern. Confidential matters that should have remained inside the detective division were
being talked about by patrol officers. And Irvin had learned from
experience that patrol officers talked to their wives and girl-

friends. And then it was all over town. He wanted to know how details of the investigations were getting out.

Irvin was particularly upset that patrol officers knew that detectives were talking to some models who had been employed by Hendricks and that the invisible but detectable footprint found in the kitchen at 313 Carl Drive hadn't been identified. Irvin had talked with individual detectives about specific aspects of the case in an effort to detect the leak. He had been unsuccessful.

The next day Irvin discovered the hole. He personally stood on a chair and ripped out the wires to a long-forgotten intercom leading from the interrogation room to the radio dispatcher's room.

Hal Jennings had told Hendricks as early as November 12 that Hendricks shouldn't be surprised if he was accused of the killings. It was now early December, and there had been no arrest.

State's Attorney Dozier, meanwhile, had received phone calls from three prosecutors in different parts of Illinois and Indiana encouraging Dozier to consider Hendricks as a likely suspect in the case. Their opinions were based only on the television interview Hendricks had done the afternoon after the murders were discovered.

Dozier consulted with two body language experts to get their opinions of the Hendricks interview. He came away with twenty-four specifics in those few minutes of Hendricks's behavior which they thought were "rife with signals of deceit."

Assistant States Attorney Murphy also saw a lot in the interview tape.

Murphy had become a born-again Christian several years earlier when his young wife died of cancer, leaving behind a baby. Murphy thought there was nothing wrong with Hendricks hoping that the killer of his family be forgiven and saved. "But he was just saying it too soon," Murphy insisted. "No mortal man can accept a loss like that so soon, particularly in the way the murders occurred. Hendricks just overplayed his hand."

To Murphy the biggest giveaway in the TV interview, though, was Hendricks's statement that "they said some things looked like some things were taken." Murphy was convinced that there was no way that Hendricks could have known that at the time without having done it himself. But the fact was that word of a burglary was on the street, even speculated on in the media. Hendricks's relatives surely had picked up on it.

Police had by now talked with nine young women hired by Hendricks to model his back brace in advertising brochures. There still was no "smoking gun," no reason why David Hendricks would want to kill his wife, let alone his children.

Was there a chance Hendricks was having an affair with his secretary–office manager? They were, after all, alone together at a couple of conventions.

Bev Crutcher was incensed at the suggestion. With her two attorneys and husband present, she told police about the time that fall when a reservation mix-up at a full convention motel caused David and her to sleep in the same room. She said she had no problem with the idea because she knew Hendricks was a perfect gentleman. She told police that they had a parlor-type room, that she slept on a hideaway bed and he on a rollaway bed, that when she woke up the next morning David had gone jogging, that she showered and dressed while he was away, and that he knocked on the door when he returned. She said they stayed in separate rooms the next night.

Ralph Storrs, the Kankakee manufacturer of Hendricks's braces, was also at that convention.

"Why didn't Hendricks and Ralph Storrs share a room and let you have a room to yourself?" Detective Tulle asked.

"We just didn't think about it."

Police heard that a twelve-year-old girl had told her Sunday School class that one of the Hendricks girls said that her father wanted to kill them.

When a detective tracked down the girl, he found that she had a learning disability. She told him one of the Hendricks girls had indeed said "Daddy is going to kill me because he doesn't love me anymore." But when shown several pictures from which to choose the Hendricks girl, the twelve-year-old selected the picture of the detective's daughter.

Police seemed fairly certain that no new evidence would be found. There were very few possibilities left to be checked. It was time to decide whether charges should be filed against Hendricks even though they had no hard evidence against him, not even a motive.

State's Attorney Dozier considered his options. He could say that police had a suspect but not enough evidence to prosecute. They would wait, he could say, in the hope that more evidence would develop rather than prematurely prosecute the case and lose the single chance they would have to convict their suspect.

But Dozier was persuaded in the opposite direction. He didn't think there was more evidence to be had. There was no missing weapon, no missing witness, no hit man to be found. Who else might be responsible for the murders? Every other good suspect had a good alibi. Dozier believed that the fact that the two weapons, a knife and an ax, came from different locations in the home pointed to Hendricks. Dozier reasoned that no one else would have gone into the garage to get an ax and to the kitchen to pick up a butcher knife.

But Dozier still worried about the leftover pizza question, a question that he couldn't get Hendricks to answer without revealing its importance to the case.

More and more of the detectives had come around to thinking Hendricks was the killer. They were particularly suspect of his calm and forgiving behavior immediately after the bodies were discovered.

Dozier's decision: let's arrest him and give it our best effort.

Dozier had another idea, too. He still believed that Hendricks's conduct with the young women he had hired to model, while not exactly execrable, was clearly something that Hendricks would find embarrassing and not in keeping with his family image.

If Hendricks suddenly learned that police knew about the models, Dozier thought, it might shake him. He might even confess. Dozier told police about his plan: let's haul in Hendricks when we can have the models at the police station giving statements. None of the detectives thought the scheme would work, but it was worth a try.

What Ron Dozier and the detectives didn't know was that one of the models happened to be a client of Hal Jennings, Hendricks's attorney. On December 3 she told Jennings that police wanted her to be at the police station to give a statement the following Monday afternoon. On Sunday, December 4, Hendricks called his parents to tell them that while he had not killed his family, he had done some things he was ashamed of.

Nine

Shortly after noon on Monday, December 5, detectives were at the state's attorney's office to pick up the warrants for Hendricks's arrest.

By 1 P.M. seven young women who modeled for Hendricks had reported to the police station as requested. They were seated with individual policemen who were taking their statements.

At 1:06 P.M. Detective Charles Crowe and three other policemen entered the CASH Manufacturing office. Hendricks was in the bathroom. Crowe knocked on the bathroom door.

"David? It's time."

A moment later Hendricks came out. As another policeman read Hendricks his rights, Crowe searched and handcuffed him. When the Miranda warning had been given, Hendricks looked at the officer.

"I wish I had my attorney with me right now," he said.

As the five men walked out the front door, Hendricks told Bev Crutcher, who was sitting at the front desk, to call his attorney.

He was silent during the short drive to the police station.

Hendricks was led into the police station, through two areas where the young women sat, and into the small interrogation room where about a month earlier he had been questioned by Crowe and O'Brien. The police left him alone there for about five minutes, time for him to think about the models' presence there, they hoped, and then took him into the booking room, adjacent to the jail.

"Do you want to make a statement?" Crowe asked.

"No, but I want to make a phone call. Why are you taking my belt?" Hendricks asked Crowe.

"You might want to do yourself in," Crowe answered.

"Well, I had a month to crash my plane into my house."

"You'd have killed policemen."

"Then I really would be in trouble."

Just before he was put into a cell, Hendricks called his office as Crowe stood nearby.

"Bev, would you call Hal Jennings, my parents, and Susie's parents to let them know what's happened? Okay. Have a nice afternoon. Yes, I will, too."

Hendricks hung up and looked at Crowe.

"Do you think I will have a nice afternoon?"

"No, I don't think you will."

The state's attorney was waiting elsewhere in city hall. When the first detective appeared, Dozier anxiously asked how Hendricks had reacted to seeing the models.

"He didn't bat an eye."

Within the hour Hendricks was transferred to the McLean County Jail, just a block away from the Bloomington Police Department. There Hendricks's attorney visited the man now formally accused of murdering his wife and children.

Hal Jennings had prepared Hendricks for the arrest and what would follow. He had warned Hendricks of the probability that he would not be set free on bond and had won Hendricks's agreement to bring a second criminal lawyer into the case. The parameters of the case, Jennings had said, required two attorneys, a division of labor.

Jennings's choice was Mike Costello, a skilled defense lawyer from the state capital of Springfield, about sixty miles away. Jennings had known Costello for years and trusted him. Costello also had access to a computerized law library and a relationship with the Southern Illinois University School of Medicine in Springfield, which would be helpful in preparing for the medical issues.

Hendricks was placed in a cell in direct view of the jail command center, a cell normally used to house prisoners for a few minutes while another cell was being prepared for them or to house persons just arrested but who were expected to get out on bond almost immediately.

That was not the case with Hendricks. Jail Superintendent Gary Ploense wanted close supervision of his best-known prisoner. He had ordered guards to log Hendricks's activity every fifteen minutes and had asked members of a local crisis team to see Hendricks to assess the likelihood of his having suicidal tendencies.

After a short visit in Hendricks's cell that same afternoon, the crisis team determined that he had no thoughts of self-destruction. Even so, Ploense ordered the four-times-hourly visual checks to continue and the cell lights to remain on twenty-four hours a day.

Toward evening, Hendricks made up his bunk and asked about the availability of radios or TVs (he was told that a limited number was rotated among inmates), asked for a Bible and some novels ("I have an active mind," he said), and inquired about haircuts for long-term inmates. He slept for the first time at 10:45 P.M., but it was a restless night. He would sleep for an hour or so, read for an hour, then sleep some more.

He was sleeping soundly when, at just before 6 A.M., guards entered his cell for the first of what would be daily, randomly scheduled shakedowns of his cell ordered by extra-cautious jail officials worried that Hendricks might harm himself. They found no contraband.

After breakfast, Hendricks requested and received a bucket and brush to wash down the walls of his cell. He washed his hair in the sink in his cell. Expressing an interest in what the news media were saying about his arrest, he again asked about getting a radio or TV. He wanted to know if he could subscribe to the local newspaper and whether he had received any calls.

The state's attorney's office had given the Federal Bureau of Investigation every known detail of the Hendricks murders and asked it to develop a psychological profile of the murderer. On the day after Hendricks's arrest, the profile arrived in the mail.

"The crime was premeditated in a 'fantasy' of a religious type nature to shock society," the profile read. "The subject desired power and control over the victims. All assaults to victims were to the facial area, indicating that the subject knew the victim and the family very well. The subject had a close personal association particularly with Benjamin due to excessive facial damage to

Benjamin. The subject's placement of the ax and knife on the bed with the two children's bodies contains some ritualism or symbolic meaning to the subject. The ax and knife were weapons of choice by the subject as opposed to weapons of opportunity. These murders were well-planned in advance. . . . [T]he subject was very familiar with the layout of the residence . . . [and] resides in an upper-middle class neighborhood and lives in close proximity to the victims."

Even though he still had no clear motive in mind, no witnesses, and no physical evidence against Hendricks, Dozier was now more convinced that he had the right man. All he and his assistant Murphy had to do was prove it.

That afternoon Hendricks made his first court appearance for his arraignment. Wearing an orange jumpsuit common to all of the jail's prisoners over a soiled and ill-fitting bulletproof vest, Hendricks looked tired and disoriented. As he pleaded "not guilty" to the charges against him, crime-scene technicians were again inside 313 Carl Drive using high-intensity lights in an effort to detect any previously unnoticed traces of blood on the floors, walls and ceilings. They gave special attention to the area around the washer and dryer, which were on the home's upper floor. They found nothing new.

After his few minutes in the courtroom, Hendricks was returned to the jail, where he first visited with his parents and then his attorney. That night he was taken to the jail's recreation area for the first time. He was there alone, except for a guard who played Ping-Pong with him. The guard found he was no match for Hendricks.

"I'll be here tomorrow," Hendricks told him, "but I hope I'm not here long enough for you to beat me."

Knowing it would probably be spring before Hendricks went to trial, Jennings's first priority was to see if he could get bond set for his client—not only for the sake of Hendricks's immediate freedom, but also because 100 percent access to Hendricks would greatly aid preparation of the defense case.

Jennings subpoenaed Coroner William Anderson to appear at the December 13 bond hearing with whatever information his office had developed about the murders. Assistant State's Attorney Murphy fought the subpoena.

"We'll provide information," Murphy told the court, "but we won't allow a fishing expedition." It was far too early, Murphy was certain, to let the defense in on what little the prosecution had. Three days later a compromise was reached. The defense was given brief access to laboratory test reports but was not allowed to take notes.

At the bond hearing, Coroner Anderson testified that there was scientific evidence that the three children had died before the time Hendricks said he left for his Wisconsin business trip. The coroner said the evidence concerning Susan Hendricks's time of death was less conclusive.

Jennings and Costello introduced affidavits from fourteen people who were willing to allow Hendricks to stay with them if bond was allowed. After a five-and-a-half-hour hearing, Associate Judge Ivan Johnson denied bond. Hendricks would have to spend the months before his trial in jail.

The McLean County grand jury began considering the evidence against Hendricks on Thursday, December 15.

Beverly Crutcher described how she came to work for Hendricks and how she accompanied Hendricks to national conventions in Houston in October of 1982 and in Phoenix the past October.

"Did you ever have much contact at all with Susan?" Dozier asked.

"Not a lot, other than when she came into the office. I went to lunch with David and her one time."

"Nothing really of a personal nature where she ever confided in you?"

"Oh no. Uh-uh."

"Did you ever have any kind of personal relationship with David?"

"No."

"Did he ever make any requests of you?"

Beverly Crutcher's attorney, present in the grand jury room, spoke up. "What do you mean by requests?"

"Did he ever ask you to be intimate with him?"

"No."

"He never made a pass at you, never kissed you?"

"No."

"In any fashion."

"No."

Hendricks's secretary said that David had started making plans for his Wisconsin trip at least by the Thursday before his Monday night departure to Wisconsin.

Most of the rest of the witnesses were investigators.

Coroner Anderson recounted his routine conversation with Hendricks at the police station early on the morning after the murders were discovered.

Detective Sergeant Irvin seemed to second-guess Dozier's decision to file charges against Hendricks when he did.

"In my own mind, I wouldn't have okayed the arrest," Irvin told the grand jurors. "Mr. Dozier okayed it in the first place. But as far as I was concerned, I would have objected to it."

Assistant State's Attorney Murphy was doing the questioning. "What was interesting, I believe—correct me if I'm wrong—but at roughly 11 P.M. the evening of Tuesday the 8th, Mr. Hendricks was told about his family. The next morning, the 9th, it was business as usual, correct?"

"He was back at his business and called a press conference," replied Irvin.

Patrolman Hibbens described finding the bodies.

Grand jurors had some questions for Crowe when he appeared before them that same day.

"When you were interrogating Mr. Hendricks that evening or early in the morning, what state of mind would you say David was in?"

"He was alert, thinking," Crowe said. "That's about all I can say about that."

"It wasn't a rambling-type thing?"

"No."

"Did he show the emotions? I mean any normal person, male anyway, to come in and find out his whole family had just been wiped out, you know . . ."

"No, he showed no . . ."

"Did he show any super emotions? I mean, even in the Bible when Job's ten children were killed, you know, he even asked God to blot out the day he was born. He was just that upset about the whole thing."

"David showed no emotions."

The grand jury proceedings would continue a week later.

That afternoon a guard saw Hendricks lingering behind a concrete wall that afforded some privacy at the toilet.

"Are you okay?" the guard asked.

"Yeah, I'm okay," Hendricks responded as he emerged into clear view. "Every now and then I think about the family, and the tears start. I go back there and hibernate for a while."

If neighbors had looked out their windows at two o'clock the next morning, they would have seen three investigators from the state crime lab quietly enter 313 Carl Drive.

Convinced that there must be more evidence inside the home, they undertook an examination that requires total darkness.

They sprayed a special chemical mixture on every surface in the home's second floor and much of its ground floor, then turned off all the lights. As their eyes adjusted to the darkness, an eerie blue luminescence appeared. The chemical was doing its job, reacting with blood and illuminating even the smallest speck. In the girls' bedroom, the walls, closet, furniture, and parts of the floor glowed with the chemical reaction. But the goal was to get a reaction where no blood had been seen before.

In the hallway bathroom, they did.

Crime-scene technicians earlier had found a smudge of blood on the edge of the sink. The chemical substance glimmered there. It also almost lit up the bathtub and shower stall.

The blue radiance was evident near the faucets, it nearly covered the bathtub floor, and there was a blotch on the back wall of the shower enclosure, about five feet from the floor.

About twenty-four hours later, a shot rang out in the Carl Drive neighborhood. It came from the Hendricks home.

The patrolman on guard alone inside the home in the hours after midnight explained that he was "dry firing" his weapon, squeezing off rounds from what he thought was an unloaded weapon. The bullet tore through the downstairs bathroom door and ricocheted off a wall.

"I have learned a valuable lesson which I will never forget," the patrolman wrote in a report to the police chief.

Some of his fellow officers thought the patrolman got spooked and shot at his fears.

On the following Thursday, Dennis Dodwell of the state crime lab was the only witness before the grand jury. He described the chemical test that he had helped conduct at the home the previous week.

He also described the crime scene as he examined it in the hours after the bodies were discovered. He described the bodies' open wounds. Susan's body, he said, exhibited eight, Grace's five, Becky's two, and Benjamin's sixteen. He said Susan's wounds included a stab wound that went through her body to the spine.

He discussed the way the bedspread in the master bedroom partly covered her body.

"It gave me the impression that it was pulled up over the head and then it was pulled back down."

"Tell us why you got that impression," Murphy prodded.

"The way the blanket was. It was as though somebody covered the body up, which has happened before. When somebody is going to spend a little time in that room, they would cover up the face or cover up the body and then uncover it before they leave so they wouldn't be staring at it themselves all the time. But it was pulled down. And as soon as I got there and saw it, I confronted all the police officers on the scene as to who pulled the blanket down. That's the way they found it."

Dodwell was also asked about how he found Susan's clothing in the master bedroom.

"They were thrown on a table against the west wall, opposite the bed. They were just kind of put down, her slip, her bra, her dress which had a small vest. Her shoes were on the floor. This would not be consistent with that house, not consistent with her at all. The same way, her panty hose were taken off. They looked like they were just thrown on top of the dresser."

"That isn't the way she kept her house?" a grand juror asked.

"If you look in the kitchen cabinets, to give you an idea, each can is placed in a row. Everything is perfect."

"It's been swept, dusted, mopped?"

"Swept, dusted, and mopped. But it looks like it's been done maybe two or three times a day. It looks like she doesn't leave. I kind of got the impression when I was there—I think I mentioned it to some people there on the first day—it appeared to be a male-dominance house. And she stays there, and she takes care of the kids, and she doesn't leave and she cleans. And I mean clean. The basement is even that way. The garage has shelves with rows. Everything is where it's supposed to be."

Dodwell was asked about the footprint that was found near the patio door and never identified.

"It may not even be a footprint," he said. "Could have been caused by a plastic bucket, a toy, a lot of things."

How long would it have taken a single person to commit the murders and ransack the house, a grand juror asked.

"It would be very easy to do the whole job in ten minutes."

That afternoon, three days before Christmas, the grand jury indicted David Hendricks for murdering his wife and children.

Ten

O n December 27, after one last walk through 313 Carl Drive
to assure themselves that they had overlooked no evidence,
prosecutors and police released the Hendricks home to the
family.

Family members and the defense team immediately checked
to see if a spare house key that David and Susan kept hidden in an
electrical box on their back porch was still there. It was, and the
key yielded no fingerprints or evidence of scarring which might
have indicated that someone unfamiliar with it had tried to improperly insert it into a lock.

Family members were repulsed by the bloodied children's
room and had to resist the urge to promptly wash and paint
everything in sight. But Jennings had warned them that defense
experts would want to examine the house as it stood.

As Illinois law permits, Jennings objected to the first two
judges assigned to the Hendricks case but was satisfied with Judge
James Knecht, a forty-year-old area native who had already spent
nine years as a judge.

In a January 20 hearing, Knecht gave defense attorneys the
right to examine with their client all of the physical evidence police
had gathered.

The defense team hoped to develop evidence that the Hendricks murders may have been the work of a serial killer and that David Hendricks didn't fit the profile of most serial murderers. Jennings and his investigators, however, could turn up no evidence of recent, similar, unsolved killings. Jennings also interviewed Susan's best friend and got no indication that Susan was unhappy in her marriage.

David Hendricks was unhappy with some of the things contained in copies of police reports already provided his defense attorneys. In a February 4 letter to a couple dozen family members, friends, and correspondents, he first described his daily jail routine and how he handled his mail. And then he got to the point:

> In reading through the discovery, I have seen many of the interviews that the police have had with some of you. I must say I have been very unpleasantly surprised at the way innocent statements of yours are twisted to make them say things that you didn't really mean to say. I say surprised, because I really expected the police and prosecutors to try to find out facts and determine the truth. But it has become obvious that they are simply interested in recording only those things that they can use to convict me. They have used guile, deceit, and outright lies. Therefore I would advise you all, if you care about me, want to help me, do not talk to the police. Don't even listen to them. They even record your "no comment" comments. You cannot help me by justifying me to them. They don't want to hear that. They record only what they want to. I know what I'm talking about because I've read everything that they have turned over! I'm not overly concerned because I think at the trial, the truth will come out. Also, that's when we'll ask you to tell your story. However, for now, silence is golden. Thanks.
>
> There are many things I want to explain to you all and share with you, but I can't because of these charges hanging over my head. However, when this is over and I am free, we'll share everything.
>
> One thing I ask your continued prayers in. I still miss Susie terribly and think of my dear children often. I thought that, perhaps by now, grief would have largely been assuaged, but it persists with seemingly undiminished force. Also, of course, your prayers regarding my upcoming trial are greatly

appreciated. I also pray for many of you each day.

I have been encouraged to think that the Lord means all this for my good and that my dear ones are happy with Him in Heaven. Soon all we who know Him as our Savior will be united with Him for eternity! What a prospect.

Please continue to write. I hope I haven't offended anyone by this impersonal response. May God richly bless each of you. I love you all.

Affectionately and appreciatively, David.

Defense hopes of linking someone else to the killings were rekindled on the morning of February 28 when the body of a bartender was found in the small tavern where he worked on Bloomington's south side. Defense attorneys fought hard to gain access to police records on the killing of Gary Sheppelman, age thirty-seven. They showed Sheppelman had been savagely beaten on his head and upper body, probably with two weapons—one sharp, the other blunt. A chain lock on the tavern's rear door had been broken. Robbery apparently was not a motive because nearly four hundred dollars remained in Sheppelman's pockets and even more in the bar's cash register.

Jennings thought there were some striking similarities to the Hendricks murders: the method (including the type of weapon or weapons used and the area of the body attacked), the fact that there was an apparent nighttime break-in, and that no sexual molestation was involved.

While Jennings waited and watched that police investigation with great interest, he was also measuring local public sentiment about the Hendricks case. The question was whether he wanted to move the case out of town—request a "change of venue."

By a February 9 hearing, Jennings had his answer.

"No case can be tried in a vacuum," he told Judge Knecht. "Our position simply is that it seems that justice requires and demands in this case that it be moved to someplace where the focus of the community is not upon the case. The Hendricks family murders were all-consuming for this community. Its residents are preoccupied with them."

Jennings said his researchers posed twenty questions to 258 people, but once there were media reports about the survey being conducted, 89 others declined to be interviewed, fearing they would be helping Hendricks.

Murphy reminded Judge Knecht that McLean County had

nearly fifty-seven thousand registered voters—all of them potential jurors.

"But, Judge," Jennings responded, "ninety-eight percent of those polled in our survey indicated that they had read about the Hendricks case. Ninety-six percent indicated they had seen it covered on television. Ninety percent heard about it on the radio. Sixty-five percent thought the defendant is guilty; ninety percent said that at the very least, he is probably guilty."

Jennings said another reason the trial should be moved out of McLean County was the fact that Dozier had challenged Hendricks, through the media, to be more cooperative. "There was a request made by the state's attorney to Mr. Hendricks not to hide behind his attorney, not to take advantage of the shield of his lawyer or the Bill of Rights, and to basically come forward and provide additional information. There's a legitimate purpose for the change of venue statute, and if it doesn't apply in this situation, I don't know when it would apply. In other words, if this is not a case for change of venue, what would it be?"

Jennings gave the judge newspaper clippings and tapes of news coverage from eight television stations and three radio stations.

"Thank you, Mr. Jennings," the judge said. "Mr. Murphy?"

"I'd like to take the liberty in the outset of my remarks," Murphy said, "to announce that Mr. Dozier and I are not available for comment after these proceedings are over."

Murphy went on to say that while there was a lot of media coverage, the coverage was factual. "I suggest the court should take into account the fact that several weeks, months now, have passed since late December, and any public furor, if it existed in the first place, has died down. I also call the court's attention to the fact that the defendant himself—the day after his family was discovered murdered—created a portion of this saturation publicity. I find it nothing short of ironic that this defendant on one hand created a portion of this publicity and is now claiming there was too much publicity."

Judge Knecht reminded Hendricks that if the trial were moved at his request, the state would not be required to bring him to trial within 120 days.

When, a few days later, the judge ruled the trial would be moved, both sides were told to submit a list of cities they would find acceptable. Both sides considered selecting a small southern Illinois community. Dozier thought he might have a "native son" edge there, but he also believed jurors there might be more difficult to convince that someone as religious as Hendricks seemed to be was capable of killing his family. He ruled it out.

Jennings's first choice was Chicago, where people, he believed, were generally critical and suspicious of police. Dozier wanted no part of the hassle several weeks of Chicago hotel living would represent. Both men found Rockford, Illinois's second-largest city, acceptable. Jennings liked it because the Hendricks murders had received relatively little publicity there. Dozier liked it because Rockford juries had been known to impose the death penalty. So Rockford, just south of the Wisconsin border, was selected.

In another letter to family and friends dated March 26, Hendricks wrote that his cell was searched three times a day and speculated that he was being kept in an area that was under constant observation in an effort to break him down psychologically. But he said he was quite used to it—except for the lack of a pillow.

"The prosecutors have made a systematic effort to prejudice the community and have been very successful," Hendricks wrote. "Not surprising, since the defense is maintaining media silence; so the only things people hear are rumors and purposefully prosecutorily-biased statements."

Within a month, it became clear that a continuing illness was preventing defense cocounsel Costello from holding up his part of the case. Hendricks's business attorney, Mercer Turner, convinced John Long to take the place of his partner, Costello, in the case. Long, also a successful criminal defense attorney, had already participated in some of the pretrial hearings. And it was he who had negotiated the original contract with Hendricks. Now Long hired another attorney to take over his existing caseload so he could spend all his time on the Hendricks defense.

Eleven

The new defense team of Jennings and Long now had access to nearly two thousand pages of information police and prosecutors had compiled on the Hendricks case. It was clear that police had found no evidence directly linking Hendricks to the murders. And there was nothing to tip off the defense on what kind of a motive prosecutors had in mind. But one matter was clear. Expert estimates on when the children died were to be an important part of the prosecution case.

Long was shocked at how little had been done in preparation of the scientific part of the defense case. He constructed a huge flow chart which mapped out the defense strategy and went to work trying to find forensic experts willing to help him. One of his first contacts was Charles Petty, the Dallas County, Texas, chief medical examiner who had been part of the Congressional reinvestigation of the John F. Kennedy assassination. Long flew to Dallas for an appointment with Petty.

"Good to meet you, Mr. Long," Petty said. "I have twenty minutes. What can I do for you?"

Long quickly outlined the facts in the case.

"Your man is guilty," Petty said. "The vast majority of

murders involving an entire family are committed by a family member."

"Will you at least look at the crime-scene photos?" Long pleaded.

"Well, if I'm going to do that, I'd like to get Irving Stone involved. Do you mind?"

Long was delighted. Stone, a former FBI agent, was chief of the physical evidence section of the Institute of Forensic Sciences in Dallas and chair of the University of Texas graduate program in forensic science. He was also close by.

Stone and Petty peered through magnifying glasses at the crime-scene photos. After a few minutes, Stone stopped.

"Why, I don't think this is a staged burglary at all," he said.

"I think I see your point," Petty answered.

The two men explained to an anxious Long that it looked like a professional burglary, not the type done by amateurs.

"Amateurs vandalize," Stone said. "They ransack a room, looking for anything valuable. Professionals know what they're looking for and they go for it. They're efficient. For instance, if you or I were looking for something, we'd probably start at the top drawer in a dresser and work our way down. A professional starts at the bottom, feels his way through the drawer, and then moves up a level. Much more efficient. That's what was done here."

Long's eyes widened. Stone and Petty agreed to go to Bloomington to examine the crime scene in person.

Long's plan was not to try to exclude his client from the list of possible suspects, but to show that Hendricks wasn't the only person who could have committed the crimes. Petty, who had written extensively about the use of stomach contents to pinpoint time of death, agreed to examine that part of the case as well.

On his flight home to Illinois, Long wondered whether any of Hendricks's competitors in the brace industry might have wanted to obtain copies of Hendricks's design drawings or computer records.

Jennings, meanwhile, was involved in a legal battle to try to limit the state's use in the coming trial of statements made by Hendricks both before and after he was read his Miranda rights during his questioning at the Bloomington Police Department.

Jennings argued that Hendricks was clearly a suspect in the minds of police hours before he was read his rights and that police had improperly delayed the routine procedure. Even after Hendricks was given his rights, Jennings said, there was some question whether his client was emotionally capable, given the circumstances, of even understanding what was happening. And Jennings wanted the judge to rule out use of any statements Hendricks made to police over the telephone when they tried to convince him that he should submit himself to further police questioning, despite his attorney's advice to the contrary.

"The question this court ought to be asking," Murphy responded, "is whether the defendant was in custody when these conversations took place. There isn't any question we have interrogation, but the defendant was not in custody on November 8th or 9th or on December 1st when these conversations occurred. The only time he was given the rights is at the Bloomington Police Department at about 2:35 A.M. He clearly indicated an understanding of the rights and a willingness to talk to the officers, as he had earlier that evening, just as he had indicated to his own family members that he wanted to cooperate.

"Whose rights are we talking about here, anyway?" Murphy continued. "Does Mr. Jennings have a right to have Mr. Hendricks keep his mouth closed? Doesn't it clearly show that David Hendricks understood his rights, and that Detective Crowe understood his rights, saying, 'You've got a mind of your own. Why don't you use it?' "

Judge Knecht ruled that all of Hendricks's statements were admissible as evidence.

At the same time, a psychological examination of Hendricks found he was fit to stand trial.

"David Hendricks is psychologically stable and healthy," wrote Dr. Robert Chapman, a local psychiatrist. "He shows no mental disease or defect, and therefore does not meet the requirements of statutory insanity or incompetence to stand trial."

In a May 1 letter to friends and family, Hendricks said he had asked to remain in the twenty-four-hour observation cell because there was more direct contact with the jail staff there. He said that even though he had to take his occasional outdoor recreation alone, he enjoyed it, particularly basketball. "There is also a volleyball net, but, as with the Ping-Pong, I'm not fast enough to play it alone.

"I find that, emotionally, each week there is progress. I no longer have the sleepless, dream-filled nights. I have gotten an interest in life back, and, in fact, am starting to be anxious about getting out and picking up the pieces. For a long time, I just didn't care. Also, I seem to be getting my interest in business back, something else I had completely lost."

Long continued to develop his case, which he hoped would show that while stomach contents might be helpful in establishing when a person died, they were not absolute proof. He was certain his experts' testimony would contradict any prosecution testimony that would categorically say the children died before their father left for Wisconsin. All Long wanted to do was to open a window of opportunity for someone other than Hendricks to have committed the murders.

Long asked Hendricks whether he wanted to go to the expense of sending him to Great Britain to interview some leading international experts on the subject.

"Do it," said Hendricks. "If I'm convicted, I'll spend more money on candy bars in prison than you'll spend going to London."

Long made appointments with three experts in the field but was able to meet with only two of them. To Long's dismay, the third was in the United States, attending to Britain's team at the Los Angeles Olympics. While in England, Long also did some research into the history and practices of the Plymouth Brethren.

On July 17, Petty and Stone arrived from Dallas to examine 313 Carl Drive. Just a few days before, Long had made a discovery on his own. A close examination of a photo taken of the carpeted stairway in the Hendricks home just after the bodies were discovered revealed a small, unidentified object, something that first appeared to be a flaw in the film. A photo blowup showed the object to be what looked like a wooden matchstick. Long had determined there were no such matchsticks elsewhere in the house. He felt confident that the object would further convince jurors that it was possible some intruder had killed Susan and the children. Now he was hopeful that Petty and Stone would find even more important evidence.

They examined the pattern of blood on the walls of the children's room, hoping to get an idea of the number and height of the assailants. Together, with magnifying glasses in hand, they crawled down the hallway, looking for anything undetected by police investigators. They did discover a couple droplets of blood, but the trail was eight months old. Stone also found a child's tooth in the girls' bedroom. He examined the nightgown worn by Susan and the bedspread that covered her body. When their on-site investigation was done, they had discovered little new evidence, except that they were convinced the murders could have been committed by more than one person.

In the meantime, the defense case seemed to be falling apart. One after another, most of the experts contacted by Long were calling to say they didn't want to be part of the defense. Long had stressed that he wanted their testimony to be well-grounded in scientific principles. Now the experts were having doubts. Long got Petty to intercede and pleaded with them to sign on. Most did.

While Petty and Stone were in Bloomington, a strange-sounding, garbled message was left on the automatic telephone answering machine at CASH Manufacturing. The voice was guttural, and its message seemed to be "Keep your barn door closed." A Chicago sound specialist confirmed Long's suspicion: it was a backward recording, accomplished with very sophisticated equipment. When played as originally recorded, the message was "Hello to you who murdered all those people."

With the expert examination complete, Hendricks's mother and mother-in-law set out to clean the house. It was a wrenching experience, scrubbing their grandchildren's blood from the walls, carting out blood-stained mattresses, and packing up toys, photos, and schoolwork that had shown so much promise. It was something they at once felt could better be handled by professional cleaners and movers, yet was too deeply personal a matter to be taken care of by indifferent outsiders. Laverne Hendricks especially felt that way when she discovered, to her shock and horror, a piece of one of the children's gum tissue in a corner of their bedroom.

In the basement, she found a small box whose contents stirred an uneasy memory. The previous summer Susan had purchased a wind chime and hung it on her back porch. During a visit there, Charles Hendricks noticed the wind chime contained some astrological figures. Having just listened to a religious tape on the subject, he told Susan there was an inherent spiritual danger in such things. Susan took down the chime, carefully wrapped it in tissue paper and put it in a box on a basement shelf. Now its parts, still in the box Laverne Hendricks held, lay shattered. She wondered if some evil force was responsible.

With August came a series of pretrial hearings at which the defense hoped to convince Judge Knecht to order two things: a ban on the introduction of certain evidence at the trial, and a detailed explanation from the prosecution of its theory of motive in the killings.

Long asked that the evidence issues be discussed in the judge's chambers, outside the hearing of the public and the press.

"This trial has been moved some two hundred miles to ensure the defendant receives a fair trial," Long said. "News coverage about evidence which might subsequently be prohibited or suppressed by this court could very well reach prospective jurors."

The judge ruled that a fair trial could be assured even with a public hearing.

"It's preferable for this case, most cases, perhaps all cases to be heard on the record and subject to the scrutiny of the public eye, while at the same time making the effort to preserve the defendant's right to a fair trial," Judge Knecht said. "I think that this court has done that by sealing a great deal of discovery and by moving the case to another circuit."

One of the issues the defense hoped to keep out of the trial was any testimony from Hendricks's former employer, Heinz Brinkmann, that Hendricks's personal lifestyle was inappropriate for a member of the Brethren.

Jennings argued that any discussion of the obscure and socially unrecognized religious group "may to a great degree affect the defendant's ability to receive a fair trial from a jury. If we let a man's religious beliefs become an issue, particularly if they're misstated or mischaracterized under the guise of somehow relating to the state's motive theory," he continued, "it's like saying that an individual's life history should be presented in any criminal case because of a violation of the Ten Commandments. The fact is that this type of evidence should not be admitted at all."

Even more important to the defense was whether the young women who had modeled for Hendricks would be allowed to testify. Murphy suggested that Judge Knecht wait until the trial to rule on the matter. Knecht didn't like the idea and suggested Murphy explain why the models ought to be allowed to testify and what connection they had with the crime.

"I'm willing to do that in general terms, Your Honor," Murphy said. "The sequence of models would show a continuing sexual aggression by the defendant. They would show the defendant's continuing interest in women other than his wife. It's an important part of the motive for her death in this case."

Judge Knecht said he wasn't ready to rule on any of the evi-

dence issues yet. That caused Jennings and Long to urge the judge
to require the state to be more specific in its motive theory.

"As I understand it," Judge Knecht said, "the question is
whether the specific motive theory must be disclosed in an entirely
circumstantial evidence case."

"I'm not suggesting that evidence to support the motive theory
can be withheld," answered Murphy, who knew all too well that he
and Dozier had developed only a general motive theory, nothing as
specific as the defense was requesting. "All the evidence bearing on
motive has been disclosed. It's certainly not our problem if the
defense can't glean from that what the motive or motives would be."

That brought Long to his feet.

"It comes down to an analysis of this case stripped of innuendo,
of conclusory ideas, stripped of prejudice and bias. And what have
we found?" Long's arm was outstretched, his palm up. "Within the
nineteen-hundred-odd pages of discovery, the state tells us there
are statements of supposed adultery, although the people have got
up and stated that they had no direct evidence of adultery. Conclusions that at one time the defendant may or may not have gotten the
better of somebody in a business deal. Conclusions or prejudices
that the defendant may have all of a sudden made a great amount of
money and may be trying to live on a fast track. Innuendo and
suspicion because the defendant has lost weight. Now if the shoe
were on the other foot and the defendant were to say he committed
the crime in self-defense, he would have to disclose to the state the
exact motive for his act. If that law applies to a defendant, why
doesn't it apply to the state?"

Murphy was ready to respond. "What we have here, in my
estimation, is a deliberate attempt to cite a proposition to the court
that doesn't stand. The defense wants the court to do something
there is no authority for. Now they can see that their cases don't say
what they cited them to say, but they're now saying, 'Give it to us
anyway.' I suggest that's inappropriate, that trial tactics, strategy,
and theories that the prosecution has need not be disclosed to the
defense and no such order should be entered here."

Judge Knecht gave both sides credit for being vigorous advo-
cates for their cause.

"I don't think it's really fair at this point for us to say or pretend
that the defendant is entirely in the dark as to the motive theory,"
the judge said. "But at the same time, I understand the defendant's
wish to narrow that even further, to make it more specific. Evidence of prior misdeeds and questionable judgment and personal

habits ought not be used to show that a defendant is a bad person. We know that. We all learned that in law school. But we all also learned that sometimes that sort of evidence is admissible to prove motive. Whether the evidence which the state wishes to offer is admissible is yet to be determined. But for now, the court rules that the state need not prove motive. And it also rules that the state need not disclose its theory of motive, because its theory is a part of trial tactic and procedure and goes to the heart of why we have lawyers representing the people and why we have lawyers representing the defendant."

The defense had struck out twice—once on getting the models' testimony barred, next on getting the state to be specific about its motive theory. Now it was at bat again to see whether Hendricks's behavior could be contrasted with his religious belief.

"The issue here," Jennings said, "is not so much who the witness is but the subject matter concerning the defendant's religious beliefs, his philosophies, his attitudes as they pertain to the scripture. We think the defendant should not be placed in the position of being tried for his religious beliefs, attitudes, or philosophies."

Judge Knecht asked the state to explain how Hendricks's religion related to the state's motive theory.

"The evidence will show," Murphy said, "that David Hendricks was so disturbed by his failure to live according to his own religious beliefs—one example being his conduct with the models—that he decided to kill his children and wife. We believe we also must show what those fundamental beliefs were, and that the defendant had knowledge of those beliefs through his practice."

Judge Knecht ruled in favor of the state. "While I'll make no ruling in advance as to the admissibility of this evidence, I believe the state has advanced an arguable theory which they're entitled to attempt to prove. They ought not be limited in their attempts by a blanket pretrial ruling that would prohibit them from even trying to prove motive in that fashion."

Twelve

Five days before jury selection was to begin, Ron Dozier, just back from interviewing a pair of expert witnesses in Texas, learned that Hendricks wanted to talk with him. Dozier had long before given up any hope of such a meeting. Hendricks had refused his requests and rejected his challenges, apparently on the advice of his attorneys. But now there were signs that Hendricks had become insistent that such a meeting should take place, and Dozier was prepared to move.

Dozier, who had been reared in a fundamentalist Christian faith, thought that he had a handle on why Hendricks killed his family, and he was prepared to test his theory on Hendricks. Maybe, just maybe, Dozier thought, if Hendricks found that someone understood what caused him to do what he had done, he would be willing to plead guilty in return for Dozier's guarantee that he would not seek the death penalty. Dozier would have a conviction and the county would be spared an expensive and lengthy trial with a doubtful outcome.

Dozier told Jennings that he would agree that none of Hendricks's comments in the proposed meeting that would exclude Hendricks's attorney could be used against Hendricks and that Dozier would record the meeting on tape and immediately give the tape to Hendricks. Jennings said it would also be necessary that the meeting be kept secret. When Dozier agreed, Jennings drafted a two-page letter, which both Jennings and Dozier signed. It was addressed to Dozier and began:

This letter is to confirm that your request to meet privately with David Hendricks prior to the trial proceeding has been transmitted to Mr. Hendricks. He has expressed the desire to meet and talk informally with you. Both John Long and myself have advised Mr. Hendricks against this meeting from a professional and attorney-client standpoint. Mr. Hendricks however persists in his wish to honor your request and to meet with you.

The letter went on to state the agreement: that the conversation would be off the record, that no part of the discussion would be used directly or indirectly in the trial, and that "the purpose of the meeting is personal and theological in nature," and that it would not be eavesdropped on but that Dozier would record the conversation and immediately give the tape to Hendricks.

Under those conditions, Jennings said, Hendricks would meet with Dozier for about an hour that very night, Thursday, September 6.

The meeting took place in a vacant detective's office, one floor below the jail cell where Hendricks had spent the past ten months.

Dozier suggested they begin with a prayer. Hendricks readily agreed. "Lord, we pray that this discussion be fruitful and that the truth be known to all," Dozier said aloud. It was the same prayer he had said privately before he walked into the room where Hendricks waited.

The prosecutor switched on a mini-cassette recorder. The two men sat face to face in the tiny room.

"Now I hope you'll hear me out," Dozier began. "None of what we talk about here tonight can be used against you, so let's not back ourselves needlessly into some positions we have to defend later on, because there won't be a need to defend what we say here tonight."

His first words came out smoothly. They were well rehearsed.

"I think I know what happened to you and how you got yourself in this situation," Dozier continued. He told Hendricks about his own background in a fundamental and strict religious environment with rigid teachings about sex and how, as a developing adolescent, he found them hard to follow.

"I passed my crisis at that point in life," Dozier said. "And I think you, coming from a more conservative and austere upbringing than even I had, have passed a very similar crisis. I think you fully loved your family—you loved your children and your wife—but you were doing these things with these models. You didn't want to, but you couldn't stop yourself. It was getting worse and worse. And you were so bothered by the fact that somebody with as much religious upbringing as you couldn't stop himself from being corrupted in this horrible, corrupting world, that you thought the best possible thing you could do for them was to kill them and send them on to heaven now before they would be similarly corrupted by this world.

"And even though you killed your family, I don't think you're an evil man. I just think you were misguided and you know that now."

Hendricks listened intently.

"If you truly believe in God and His forgiveness," Dozier said, "then you can confess your wrongdoing."

Dozier was ready to offer a deal. "I can help the public understand why you did what you did, that you weren't motivated by evil intentions but by misguided intentions. I can make the public understand why the death penalty isn't justified in this situation."

It was Hendricks's turn to speak. He looked Dozier squarely in the eye.

"Mr. Dozier, I know you think that's what happened, but it's not what happened. It isn't the case.

"You think that I was feeling very guilty about my dealings with the models, but you're wrong. I won't kid you. I wanted to have sex with those women and if it wasn't for this tragedy that happened to my family, I probably would have eventually succeeded. But I wasn't feeling guilty about it.

"Then this terrible tragedy struck and after the initial shock left me, I was certain that it was God's way of punishing me because I hadn't shown any remorse over my dealings with the models."

The color drained from Dozier's face. He wasn't expecting this.

Hendricks continued. "After a while, I realized I was wrong. But it took me some time to realize that's not the way God works. He wouldn't take a man's wife and three children as revenge."

At that moment, Ron Dozier was convinced that Hendricks was wrongly accused. The prosecutor's mind was racing. He understood everything that Hendricks had said. Dozier's own background told him it made sense. What Hendricks said was indeed plausible. It could very well be the truth.

Hendricks continued. "Now, about your theory. I had a wife that was a year older than I am. She was thirty at the time and as pure as pure can be—totally uncorrupted by this world. And I killed her, too? Why?"

"Well, basically for the same reason," Dozier said. "To keep her from being corrupted at some point in the future."

"That's absolute nonsense. My religion would never guide me to do such a thing," Hendricks responded. "The way I understand your motive, you don't think it's like I went nuts and don't know that I did anything, but that I'm fully aware that I did it and I'm just lying about it."

"That's right."

"My religion is against murder and it's also against lying. Even if I did kill my family for religious reasons, that same religion wouldn't let me lie about it. We can commit all types of sin and be forgiven, but consistently lying about an act of murder like this could not be accepted."

Nothing was said for a moment, and then Hendricks continued.

"As I understand your theory, I planned the murders several days in advance, and I lived with my family through those days, that I hugged and kissed and slept with my wife, hugged my children—all of whom I loved dearly—knowing that I was going to kill them. Is that correct?"

"Yeah," said Dozier. There was little enthusiasm in his voice. "That's what we're thinking. That's our theory."

"That's preposterous!" Hendricks answered. Dozier nodded ever so slightly but said nothing. "Do you think," Hendricks continued, "that I could have picked up an ax and crashed it down on the heads of my wife, my children?"

"Well, the only way I can justify that is that you just figured they would die painlessly, if you did it fast and efficiently, that the method didn't matter and it was a good way to conceal the crime.

"Whoever did this," Dozier continued, "carefully planned it out and concealed it. You fit that, too, because you think about things, you plan them out, you're methodical and very intelligent."

"Wouldn't I have used a more humane method?" Hendricks asked.

"Well, actually, even though it looked so bad, it's pretty humane. I do have problems thinking that you did what was done to Benjy, but I can justify that only in that you must have thought, 'Well, what difference did it make? No pain. No problem. Once he's dead, what does it matter what I do to the body?' "

Dozier began asking Hendricks questions about the case, not in a challenging way, but in an effort to get explanations.

"Why haven't you ever been willing to take a polygraph test?"

"That's one area my attorneys told me not to talk with you about tonight."

Dozier was frustrated. Now, instead of trying to work toward a plea bargain, he found himself grasping for reasons to justify dropping the charges just days before the murder trial was to start. A lie-detector test showing Hendricks innocent might help. But Hendricks wouldn't even talk about it. He would try another approach.

"If you didn't kill your family, who did?"

"That's the other area I'm not supposed to talk about tonight. We have some ideas about that, but we're saving that for the trial."

"You, better than anyone else, should know if anyone has a grudge against you or your family, and you won't talk to me about it? If you want us to let you off the hook, give us somebody else."

"I can't. Not now. I don't know for sure of anybody that I can point to and say, 'That's who did it.'

"Look, Mr. Dozier," Hendricks continued, "Hal Jennings and some other people have told me that you're a fair man and that you try to do right. That's why I wanted to talk with you tonight. That's why I've always wanted to talk with you because I've always believed that if we could talk man to man, you'd understand why your whole case against me is off base.

"I realize you're in a political job, and I know the police were under a lot of pressure to charge someone with this awful crime and that I was a convenient suspect, a scapegoat. And I honestly don't think you'll let these charges stand against me if you don't think I killed my family. I just think that's the kind of person you are. You're not like Murphy. I've never thought much of him, not after the one statement he made about me and Jim Jones."

Dozier's mind flashed back to a pretrial hearing months before when Murphy equated Hendricks with the religious zealot who had led hundreds into suicide in what became known in 1978 as the Jonestown Massacre.

"Religion isn't a motive for murder," Jennings had told the judge.

Dozier didn't tell Hendricks that he had leaned over to Murphy at that point and whispered, "Oh yeah? What about Jimmy Jones?" Murphy had used the idea in his rebuttal. Hendricks and family members present in the courtroom that day were livid.

But now, in this detective's office in the same building, Dozier did defend Murphy to Hendricks, telling him how Murphy had become a born-again Christian after his wife died of cancer, leaving behind a premature baby. "Intense" was a word frequently used to describe Murphy.

"Brad's the type of guy," Dozier continued, "who's just gung-ho. Like at a Sunday School picnic and softball game, when everybody is supposed to be out there having fun, Brad's the guy out there to win, yelling at people for not trying hard enough."

The Hendricks-Dozier conversation dwindled to nothing. The hour-long tape ran out. Neither man seemed to have any more to say, but neither seemed anxious to end the conversation. Dozier tried to make one more effort to find good reason to drop the charges.

"What do you think happened at your house the night you went to Wisconsin?"

"What do you mean?"

"Do you think it was just sheer coincidence that somebody randomly tried to get into your house the night you happened to be gone and forgot to lock the door?" Dozier wasn't being accusatory. He was searching for answers. "Why do you think they tried to make it look like a burglary was committed? Why did they use those weapons from your house? How can we explain these things?"

Dozier put a new cassette in the machine and turned it on as Hendricks responded.

"I just don't know who killed my family, and because I don't know who did it, I really don't have a theory on why they did it or how they did it. But I will tell you this. For me to work up a scenario on why someone would have wanted to do this, it would have to be almost as bizarre or screwy as the motive you've come up with."

A smile crossed Dozier's lips. "I know what you mean. Yes, it is kind of absurd. Maybe you'd have to come up with one even more absurd. That's my problem." The state's attorney suggested that Hendricks take a lie-detector test under his attorney's supervision and provide the results to prosecutors only if the results were favorable to Hendricks.

"Would you drop the charges then?"

"Well, at this stage of the game, it's kind of late to, uh . . ."

Dozier paused. "Well, I'll tell you. To dismiss charges at this point, I'd probably need two out of three polygraph tests indicating you're innocent."

"Can you commit yourself to that at this point?"

"I'm not sure. I'll have to think about it. Back in February if you had presented me with a polygraph and a suspect, I would have dropped the charges."

Now it was Hendricks's turn to propose a deal.

"I'm sure my attorneys have told you that we're going to file a lawsuit against the police department and your office once this case is over."

"Yes," Dozier lied. It was the first he had heard of it.

"Well, you don't have to worry about that if you drop the charges against me."

Dozier didn't respond.

"If you can see your way clear to drop the charges against me because you think I'm innocent and your conscience simply won't allow you to continue, there are two things I can do. I'll guarantee you no lawsuit of any kind, and I will publicly exonerate you and I'll do it effectively."

For the first time in an hour, Dozier's attitude toward Hendricks turned negative. He didn't like the carrot-and-stick approach. Dozier made movements to leave. His head was spinning.

"What are you going to do?" Hendricks wanted to know. "What do you think?"

Dozier was standing. "I don't understand this. I was afraid this would happen. You are either a hell of a good salesman or you're innocent. And I don't know which. You've obviously given me lots of things to think about. And to tell you the truth, I'm kind of a sucker for a good story. So I'm not going to make a decision now. I'll need a couple of days to think about it."

Hendricks pressed him. "What else do you need? If you have serious doubts about this case, it's your duty to drop the charges, right? My whole purpose in talking with you is to lay a guilt trip on you, to make you realize that if you succeed in this, you'll be convicting an innocent man. And if you do that, how are you going to live with yourself the rest of your life? That would be worse for you than any political problems that would come from losing the case. I think you're a loser if you lose, and you're a loser if you win."

"You're overestimating the politics of the situation," Dozier said, rather wearily. "If I lose this case, I'm going to be elected in November. It's an uncontested election."

The prosecutor's head was bowed. He turned off the recorder and handed Hendricks the cassettes.

"You started this with a prayer," Hendricks said, "so I'd like to end this with a prayer."

"Okay."

"We pray, God, that You will give us the love and courage to see that justice is done. Amen."

Dozier offered Hendricks his hand, something he hadn't done at the start of the meeting.

"Do you pray?" Hendricks asked.

"Not as much as I should."

"Well, pray about this."

"I will."

The prosecutor left the room and motioned to a jail guard who was standing several doors away.

Dozier was confused and overwhelmed. Here he was, some eighty hours away from what promised to be an exhausting, complex, and expensive trial with dozens of witnesses coming from thousands of miles away to testify, and he was now worried that the charges against Hendricks were a big mistake. He reminded himself of his own standard: if *I* couldn't vote for guilt beyond a reasonable doubt, knowing everything I know about a case, then I should never ask a jury to do the same.

Ron Dozier didn't sleep that night.

The next day Dozier met with Murphy and Crowe to tell them about his conversation and serious doubts.

"What did you expect?" was Murphy's response. "Hendricks is a slick salesman."

Dozier knew that, but he still had strong reservations about the case. He talked out loud about seeking a delay for the trial, at least long enough to schedule a lie-detector test for Hendricks. Or to wait for new research being done by a Colorado scientist into time-of-death estimates based on stomach contents. Why go ahead with the trial, Dozier wondered, if there's any doubt we have the right man?

Murphy and Crowe took Dozier through the evidence step by step in an attempt to reconvince the state's attorney that Hendricks was guilty.

Dozier prayed for a sign that he was doing the right thing. He prayed more than at any other time in his life, except just before he went to Vietnam.

That day the Bloomington *Daily Pantagraph* had printed a letter to the editor from Hendricks.

"Recently, while reading a book by an attorney who has been both a prosecutor and defense lawyer and is now a writer (Louis Nizer, *The Implosion Conspiracy*) I came across the following quote in the introduction:

I am constantly astounded by the definite opinion people have about cases based on newspaper reports of a trial still in progress. At dinner tables, intelligent men and women, who would stoutly defend the presumption of innocence of any accused person, will condemn the defendant as guilty, substituting vehemence for their lack of knowledge, and holding forth authoritatively on testimony they have never heard, and of which newspaper accounts give the most fragmentary version.

Barest inferences and suspicions are elevated to incontestable truth. After the debate has raged for a while, someone, out of consideration for my supposed expertise, will turn to me and ask my opinion.

I reply that I do not understand how they could have judgments when the defense has not even been heard yet, and when the evidence which has been adduced might fill five hundred pages of the record and of which they have read a diluted, selected version of ten or twelve paragraphs in a newspaper.

"This is so clearly put," Hendricks continued, "that nothing I could add would improve it. I do, however, wish to add a request that praying Christians please pray for me! If they don't know exactly how to pray or what to pray for, I understand; they should simply request that justice be done. That will suit me fine."

The next morning Dozier and Murphy loaded up a car with suitcases and cartons of files and made the trip to the trial site, Rockford, a three-hour drive up Route 51, the same road Hendricks traveled to Wisconsin the night of the murders. The two prosecutors talked more about the case during that drive. Dozier's faith was being slowly restored.

When they checked into the Clock Tower Inn, a message awaited them. It said Judge Knecht had been hospitalized with a recurring back problem and that the trial would be postponed.

Dozier thought it was a joke. It wasn't. In fact, a new judge would be assigned to the case in a few days.

On Monday, September 10, 126 prospective jurors showed up at the Winnebago County Courthouse. No one had thought to tell them the trial was postponed.

The new judge chosen by the circuit's chief judge after consulting with attorneys for both sides was Judge Richard Baner. He was a former prosecutor and now the only judge in Woodford County, where the county seat contained a population of 4,306 and Eureka College, then-President Ronald Reagan's alma mater. Judge Baner's regular court reporter was Hal Jennings's wife. She would not be involved in this case.

Jury selection would begin two weeks later than originally scheduled.

Thirteen

T he largest courtroom in the Winnebago County Courthouse was filled with prospective jurors.

At the defense table, wearing a blue business suit, sat David Hendricks, indistinguishable from the defense attorneys.

Judge Baner told the potential jurors that the trial was expected to last six to eight weeks and that jurors might be asked to consider the death penalty. "The court will at this time consider those who wish to be excused for various reasons," he said.

A total of forty-five asked to be excused for reasons ranging from business matters and wedding plans to having a son in juvenile court. One said he couldn't serve as a juror because he had to urinate frequently. He, along with forty-one others, was excused.

The actual *voir dire*, the jury selection, took place in a much smaller courtroom. It got off to a fast start with the prosecution and defense each accepting two of the first three persons to be interviewed. Each had been asked about three hundred questions during an hour-long interview with the judge and attorneys for both sides. Then the pace slowed. Greatly.

Judge Baner quizzed each person about what he or she knew about the Hendricks murders. Prosecutors focused mostly on each prospective juror's religious background and familiarity with the

Plymouth Brethren. Defense attorneys, who consulted each time with a psychologist and their client, spent a lot of time probing each person's feelings about the death penalty and asking about reading habits.

Finally, at 5:40 P.M. on Friday, October 5, after nine laborious days of questioning seventy-six persons, the twelve jurors and four alternates were selected. The principal twelve included two secretaries, a factory worker, an aviation engineer, a real estate agent, a drugstore manager, a hospital pharmacy technician, a buyer, a grocery store employee, a heating plant operator, a bank teller, and a financial analyst. Six men and six women, all white, average age of thirty-three.

Attorneys and Judge Baner headed home for a three-day weekend. The actual trial would begin on Tuesday, the day after a Columbus Day holiday.

Dozier was in bed at eleven o'clock Saturday night when the phone rang. The shift commander at the Bloomington Police Department was calling.

"Ron, I'm sorry to bother you, but you'd better come down here," the officer said. "We've had a report that someone has dug up the bodies of the Hendricks children, and it's apparently true."

As Dozier pulled on his clothes, his stomach began churning. What kind of pervert would do a thing like that, Dozier said to himself as he hurriedly drove downtown. What are they going to do? Dump the bodies on my doorstep? This will be in the morning headlines for sure, the tense prosecutor thought. Then there will be a mistrial after just getting the jury chosen.

Only a sliver of a moon was shining as Dozier and a policeman drove into Evergreen Cemetery, past the graves of Civil War soldiers, by the Stevenson grave, to the east edge of the graveyard where the Hendricks family was buried. Several other policemen were there. Flashlights illuminated a deep, rectangular hole. Nothing but dirt was visible at its bottom. A cemetery custodian had been summoned.

When the cemetery employee arrived, there were relieved chuckles all around. The hole, he said, was dug for concrete footings to be poured as the base for a large monument to be erected over the Hendricks graves.

That same night, Dozier woke up with severe chest pains. He later attributed them to indigestion.

"Are we ready to bring in the jury?"

Judge Baner looked small and thin now that he sat behind a large, high bench in the big courtroom. Now that actual testimony was to begin, the trial had been moved to the largest courtroom, which could accommodate 150 spectators. On this day, October 9, 1984, perhaps half the seats were filled.

It was 10:15 A.M., nineteen days since the first of the jurors had been selected to decide the Hendricks case. And even though attorneys for both sides had studied those citizens' faces and body language for a hint of predisposition for or against the defendant, their names were largely forgotten. Now, there they sat. Together for the first time.

There were now two court stenographers, one taking the official transcript, the other hired by the defense to provide overnight transcripts of prosecution testimony. The armed jail guard, who had been stationed close to Hendricks throughout the jury selection process, was now posted outside the courtroom door.

Hendricks looked uneasy as he leaned forward at the defense table. Brad Murphy was about to begin the prosecution's opening statement. He and Dozier had struck a bargain. Murphy got to make the opening statement, but Dozier would cross-examine Hendricks. They would share the closing argument.

Murphy was almost casual, but businesslike, in his approach, certainly soft-spoken. And there was a hint of sorrow in his voice. Sorrow that a mother and three young children were dead, sorrow that this trial even had to occur.

He briefly discussed the trial format and the propositions of law "that are going to govern us not only right now, but completely during the course of this trial." Murphy's hand rested on the front ledge of the jury box. He looked at each juror in turn as he spoke.

"One of those propositions—and I think you have already heard reference to this in *voir dire* examination—is the presumption of innocence of the defendant. The defendant is by law presumed to be innocent of these charges. The State has the burden of proof in this case. That's not a burden of proof that we shy away from or shrink from. It is the same burden of proof that's been around in criminal cases for over two hundred years in this great country of ours."

Murphy asked the jurors to pay close attention to the witnesses for both sides, and then he cited the charges against Hendricks.

"The defendant has been indicted by a McLean County grand jury for the murder of four persons on or about Monday, November

7th, 1983. He is first charged with the murder of his thirty-year-old wife, Susan Hendricks; secondly, the murder of his nine-year-old daughter, Rebekah Hendricks; thirdly, the murder of his seven-year-old daughter, Grace Hendricks; and lastly, the murder of his five-year-old son, Benjamin Hendricks. He is charged with killing these individuals by striking them on or about the head or neck area with an object that caused fatal injuries; and that in performing those acts, he either intended to kill each of those individuals or he knew that his acts created a strong probability of death or great bodily harm to those individuals."

He moved on to the evidence, saying it would show that the murders may have occurred as early as 9 P.M., some three hours before Hendricks said he left home on a Wisconsin business trip.

A series of telephone calls from Hendricks, Murphy said, led to the discovery of the bodies of his wife and children in their beds. Murphy's voice rose in pitch but not volume as he spoke of the crime and investigation in the future tense.

"The scene will give the appearance of being ransacked; yet, upon closer inspection, it will be obvious to the investigators that there are inconsistencies present and that this is indeed a set-up burglary. More importantly, the evidence will show that the scene was set up to look as a burglary occurring after the death of the victims, after the murders occurred."

Four of the jurors took notes on the small yellow notepads they had been given.

"The crime scene is organized, showing the preplanning of the murders. And although drawers have been opened, it appears again to be orderly, as opposed to having been opened during the course of a ransacking of the household. It will be apparent from the evidence that the ax was used because it was a powerful and efficient weapon, that it effectively eliminated multiple victims in a short period of time without the murderer losing control of the situation."

Murphy focused the jurors' attention on "the struggle that was going on inside of David Hendricks.

"The evidence is going to show that David Hendricks was living a dual life. The evidence will disclose David Hendricks to be an example of an individual who appears to live a life as a model husband, father, as well as a Christian with a high degree of self-discipline, but who in actuality is materialistic and indulges in luxuries that he will not allow other members of his family.

"The evidence will show that he's had a recent change in his personal appearance to the extent of losing approximately forty to fifty pounds, changing his hair style, shaving off his mustache, as well as developing a newer and a freer lifestyle where he traveled extensively. The evidence will show that the improved self-appearance and freer lifestyle were the result of desired sexual experiences."

Now the volume of Murphy's voice increased. "It was those experiences that created a problem for the defendant, David Hendricks. The defendant's religion and his religious affiliations would not allow him to be involved with other women without resulting in guilt and shame.

"The evidence will show that David Hendricks had seen enough of the corruption of this world that he became concerned about himself and his own interests in other women. This facade that surrounds David Hendricks will be further illustrated by the dishonest, deviate sexual approach that he used with his sexual targets.

"The evidence will also show that the defendant's inability to control these sexual experiences was a blatant weakness on his part which left him feeling embarrassed, humiliated, and guilty for his acts. The evidence will also show that it has been through his religious rationalizations that he has been able to control his own feelings of guilt and remorse, as the evidence will show, the defendant expressing in his own words that the victims in this case, the four of them, are better off now, as they are in heaven. And also that these deaths would be worth it if one person found their way to heaven.

"Such statements by the defendant serve as confirmation of the unacceptable religious rationalization for these killings by the one person who, despite all other outward appearances, was capable of killing his entire immediate family.

"The evidence will show David Hendricks to be struggling with the moral crisis that his dual lifestyle caused him, and it would be his own feelings about himself and for his family that bring each one of us to this courtroom today.

"I give you one last caution in listening to and reviewing the evidence in this case. I ask that you please pay close attention to what is real and what is perceived to be real. Look closely at the perception of the Wisconsin sales trip. You will see that in reality, it is a prearranged alibi which again shows the preplanning on the part of the defendant. The reality of the business trip is that the defendant needed time to gain control and composure of himself.

"Look closely at this set-up burglary. You will see the perception here is that a burglary occurred, and yet on closer examination, the reality is that the killer did this to cast suspicion away from himself.

"Look closely at the defendant's lifestyle. Which is his real nature and what is it that appears to be real to most people? Now I point this out to you for a reason, so that you might be able to consider the evidence over the next few weeks in the context of seeking a true and just verdict based on the evidence, because that's what the state is going to seek in this case. We view a trial as a search for the truth.

"I remind you at this time of that oath that each one of you has taken as a juror, because you have an obligation to return in this case verdicts which are both true and just. The people of the State of Illinois are confident after hearing all of the evidence in this case that you will be able to return those verdicts which are both true and just."

Murphy had spoken for thirty-eight minutes.

Jennings would give the first part of the defense team's opening statement. He, too, was soft-spoken and joined Murphy in asking the jury to pay attention to the evidence.

"Do not decide the issues in this case based on a feeling, a hunch, a guess, a snap judgment. Be patient, as you told us you would." In a sweeping gesture, Jennings motioned to the defense table where Hendricks sat, his eyes fixed on the jury, an uneasy look on his face as he was surveyed now by twelve peers who would decide his future.

"The evidence will show that this young man is the only surviving member of what on November 7th, 1983, was a happy, functioning, middle-class Christian family in the community of Bloomington, Illinois."

Jennings described the Hendrickses' family life and told how the murder victims' bodies were found by police. "A knife and an ax were found near the children. The house showed that closets and filing and vanity and dresser drawers had been opened and gone through. The house was ransacked. Money, it is believed, was missing."

As Jennings spoke, Hendricks closed his eyes tightly, as if to squeeze back tears.

Jennings said Hendricks's neighbors and relatives witnessed

his shock and that police immediately assigned a detective to question him.

"The assignment of that detective, the evidence will show, was a regrettable choice. The detective lived in the same neighborhood as the Hendrickses. His home, his neighborhood was the same as David's. You can almost throw a rock from David's house to the front doorstep of the interrogator's home. That detective, the evidence will show, was moved by the crimes virtually done at his own front door. He came to interrogate David, the evidence will show, with emotion, bias, and with prejudice. He did not know David Hendricks, but the evidence will show that he decided David Hendricks was the murderer based on a few minutes of questioning in the Cramer house."

Jennings said the detective came to an early conclusion that Hendricks was the killer despite the fact he was cooperative and truthful.

"We'll see in this case that what the officer did not believe was the complete truth. David answered questions. The officer chose to disbelieve. The evidence will show that the officer was wrong. The evidence will show that he was terribly wrong in this case. The information given to the detective turned out to be true. This can and will be shown by the evidence."

Jennings described how Hendricks told police he had stayed with his children while his wife attended a baby shower. "He told them that she had returned home after ten-thirty, that he had been resting that evening after the kids were in bed. He told them that he had a business sales trip planned to Wisconsin. When his wife came home, they discussed some personal matters. In particular, the adoption of a little boy, the subject being brought up to David and Susan by a letter that they had recently received from friends. He talked to his wife about that subject. His wife went to bed. The kids were in bed.

"A short time thereafter, he got up. kissed his family, and left home before midnight to drive on his trip."

Now Hendricks had a folded handkerchief out, blotting tears from his eyes. Defense cocounsel Long, sitting next to Hendricks, put his arm around Hendricks's shoulder, patting him gently on the back. Long made an obvious visual sweep of the jury box, perhaps to call the jurors' attention to the fact that Hendricks was weeping. If they noticed, there was no sign of any sympathy.

Jennings again stressed to the jury that the first detective to interrogate Hendricks simply chose not to believe Hendricks.

"There was clear evidence of an entry into the Hendricks home, to steal and to murder. This was evidence of entry by night stalkers, thieves who were or became killers. That, the evidence will be, was the first option: to seek, to find, to identify those nameless killers.

"The other choice was the choice made—David Hendricks. That choice was made first by a police interrogator because he did not believe what he heard from the defendant, then another detective who heard the first detective say that he thought Hendricks was a killer, and who also decided to agree."

Jennings said the police focused on Hendricks because he was the sole surviving member of his family.

"David was sitting in front of a police investigator. He was present. The evidence will show he was alive. He was visible. He had a name. He had a face. He had an identity. He was tangible. He could be touched. He could be described. He could be identified. He could be interrogated, and he was. He could be scrutinized, and he was. And he could be held accountable."

Jennings told the jurors one of the reasons the police targeted Hendricks so soon was his response to the news of the murders.

"When police heard or thought they heard David deal with the death of his loved ones in terms of his religion, they immediately felt that he was not acting right. The evidence will be that police did not understand David's religion or his beliefs then, and they do not understand his religion and his beliefs now.

"Keep in mind as the evidence unfolds that the evidence will show that the police decided this man was guilty only minutes after he was first seen by them. The facts will show, the proof will be, the evidence will be that when this decision was made, there was no admission or confession by David. There was no witness who had seen or observed anything. There was no motive known, no reason found to believe that David had reason to harm his family.

"The conclusion was made. The evidence will be that a then so-called police science went to work. Thousands of man-hours focused upon Hendricks in the hours, days, weeks, and months that followed. Untold man-hours focused on that crime scene. The evidence will show that the scene was sealed off and pored over by police and technicians for two months. The results of hundreds, if not thousands, of hours and the application of science to find whatever science could find was no fingerprints to link the defendant to the crime, no blood stains to link the defendant to the crime, no fiber analyses to link David to the crime. No footprints, no impressions, no imprints, no stains, no tracks of any kind to link David to the crime. No clothes, no fabric, no items of wearing apparel found microscopically to link David to the crime. No hairs found microscopically to link David to the crime."

Jennings said they found nothing because there was nothing to find.

"The evidence will be that police then became immersed in the process of trying to locate a motive for David Hendricks to kill his family. The evidence will show that they went further. They tore into the man's history, his wife's history, his family's history, his business history. They dug, scratched, and picked at every corner of his life.

"The evidence will show that they looked anywhere and everywhere for anything suggestive. What did they find? The evidence will be that they found David Hendricks was and is a good man. Not a perfect man, but a good man.

"The evidence will show that the police discovered that most people who knew David held him in high regard. He was a man from a religious background. He belonged to a Christian fellowship group who studies the Bible together with his family. Susan and the children were of the same religious persuasion. David and Susan had met and become husband and wife as the result of a common and shared religious background. The evidence will show that David loved his children. The evidence will show that he was a good father. He was and is a gentle, nonviolent, compassionate man.

"The evidence will be that he loved his wife. He shared with her. He gave to her. She loved him, and she gave to him and shared with him."

Jennings shifted again to the night of the murders, when Hendricks stayed with the children while his wife attended the baby shower. Jennings said Hendricks "spent time with his kids by choice, not by obligation. One daughter, on the evening in question, had an art project, a poster on display from her grade school at the local shopping mall. After his evening jog, David took all his kids out to the mall to see the daughter's art exhibit. They admired it."

Again Hendricks, at the defense table, quietly cried.

Jennings continued that Hendricks was a successful businessman who was generous with a fellowship fund he had established.

"The evidence will be that the police also moved heaven and earth to find a girlfriend as a motive. A paramour, a lover. The evidence will be that police found no paramour, no lover, no girlfriend." What police did find, Jennings continued, was that Hendricks had contact with some young women who modeled his invention, the back brace, in advertising pictures.

"Several of these women claim now, after the killings in question, that in their opinion, David Hendricks engaged in conduct or said things to them that they now disapprove of. The evidence is not that he asked them to go to bed or that he solicited sexual intercourse or sex. In fact, the evidence is that there was no intercourse, but rather several of these girls now suggest that a touch when fitting the brace or a statement made to one of the models or several of the models was considered by them in retrospect in some ways suggestive."

Jennings raised his voice in a climactic end to his part of the defense opening statement.

"We will have predicated for you by the state that when they discovered that a good and generous Christian man who loved his family and whose family loved him was found to have contact with some women in his business, that we now know the reason he would kill his wife and children with an ax. The evidence will show that all it shows is that David Hendricks was not perfect. But the evidence will be that he is not a murderer.

"The state says 'Find David guilty!' The state says they will not accept this as a case of burglary, robbery, and murders done thereby. We believe that the evidence in this case is that a wrong choice has been made. We believe that when this case is done, that you as jurors sworn to uphold the law, sworn to seek the truth and search it out however painful, will concur in the belief that the choice made by the police and prosecutors is not the path of truth."

Jennings, who had spoken for exactly a half hour, introduced his cocounsel, Long. It was Long's job to attack the idea that the time a person died can be accurately determined by examining stomach contents.

Long, in a style more dramatic than either of the other two attorneys who had spoken, told the jurors that there simply were too many variables possible to establish a time of death based on "a two-milliliter eyeball of something."

Long was more entertaining to listen to. And he drove his point home forcefully. "An analysis of gastric contents to determine time of death is totally improper, is totally unscientific, and is totally unreliable."

He flashed an unbelieving Cheshire grin at the jurors.

"So what is the evidence in this case going to show? The

evidence in this case is going to show that these children met their deaths sometime after they ate supper. And that's all the evidence is going to show."

Long moved to crime-scene evidence. He reminded the jurors of his cocounsel's statement that there was no physical evidence linking Hendricks to the crime, and he said that the defense's own crime-scene experts disputed some of the state investigators' findings.

The defense investigators would testify, he said, that two or perhaps even three weapons were used in the murders, that the burglary was indeed a burglary, not an attempt to cover up something else, and that at least two—and perhaps three—persons were responsible for the killings.

"So." Long looked at his watch. "You must do one thing at this stage: you must do what you swore on an oath to all of us you would do, and that is to withhold your decision until you view all of that evidence and all of those exhibits and all of the weight to be given to both, and then see if you can convict beyond a reasonable doubt. Because, once all of the evidence is heard—not what you may have read, not what some news director may have told you by conjecture, but solely from the cold, hard evidence—I do believe that you are going to agree with us that you cannot find guilt beyond a reasonable doubt in this case. Thank you."

The opening arguments had taken the entire morning. For the first time jurors were escorted in a group two blocks to a restaurant which would become all too familiar. A wider variety of convenient restaurants by now had been located by other trial participants, except for Hendricks. His noontime meals were whatever was served in the Winnebago County Jail. The half-dozen reporters who were now covering the trial full-time converged on a nearby café where they could all sit around one large table, discuss the trial, be served lunch quickly, and still have time to file their afternoon stories.

When Judge Baner entered the courtroom that afternoon, everyone was well settled, eager for the state to present its first witnesses.

Prosecutors considered McLean County Coroner William Anderson a routine, fact-establishing witness. Defense attorney Long saw him as an opportunity to strike hard and early at the state's scientific evidence.

After establishing that Anderson farmed part-time in addition to being the county's full-time elected coroner, Long focused on the coroner's statement to the grand jury that the Hendricks children died between one and three hours after they last ate.

"And upon what do you feel confident in making that statement?" Long asked.

"From the testing done by the doctors that have looked at the stomach contents."

"So if they have made a mistake, then you have made a mistake. Would that be a fair statement?"

"Yes."

"Did you determine before you made this statement under oath to the grand jury whether or not any of the decedents had suffered from a condition of pyloric stenosis?"

"No, sir."

"Do you know what pyloric stenosis is?"

"No, I do not."

"Do you know or did you investigate whether or not exercise has anything to do with the condition of the gastric contents?"

"I personally have not looked into that. No."

"Did you make any determination of whether or not any of these victims were engaged in any kind of activity prior to meeting their deaths which would have an effect on gastric content?"

"Yes. From the police my understanding was that they were playing at Chuck E. Cheese."

"And what, if anything, did that tell you?"

Coroner Anderson, who did not enjoy being portrayed as a country bumpkin coroner, slouched in the witness box, staring straight ahead.

"That they were at Chuck E. Cheese at a particular time."

"Did it tell you anything beyond that?"

"No, sir."

"Were you aware of the long-standing rule that there are certain activities or certain conditions which cause gastric retention? In other words, slows down or retards the gastric process?"

"I am not personally aware of that. No."

Under further questioning, Anderson told the jury that only about an ounce of each murder victim's stomach contents was delivered to the experts for their examination and that only two or three milliliters were actually studied.

"And what were your personal observations," Long wanted to know, "which led you to the conclusion that these children died one to three hours after they ate?"

"The actual stomach contents that I saw with my naked eye."

"Okay. What training, would you tell us, have you had in determining the degree of digestion from the examination of stomach contents?"

Anderson continued to stare straight ahead.

"I have no training."

"What courses, if any, have you taken with respect to the analyzation and determination of time of death based on an examination of gastric contents?"

"None."

"Do you have an opinion as to the degree of or the effect osmolarity may have on stomach contents in a deceased?"

"No, I do not."

"Do you know what the term means?"

"No, I do not."

"Can you describe for us what gastric contents look like in a decedent when the known time of death occurs five hours after the last meal?"

"No, I cannot."

"Can you tell us what it looks like four hours after the last meal?"

"No, I cannot."

Long, who had been pacing a short path between the defense table and the witness box, now stopped, facing Anderson, and spread his arms, palms upward.

"Then, pray tell, how can you from your personal observation conclude that these gastric contents represent food digested one to three hours after a last meal?"

"Because I could see mushrooms and tomatoes and so forth."

"Are you saying that you can't see mushrooms and tomatoes after four hours?"

"I don't know, sir."

The state's second witness was Janet Featherly, who would perform a dual role. As the coroner's photographer, she would describe photo slides of the murder victims' stomach contents. The second role would become evident later in her testimony.

With the courtroom darkened, the slides, projected on a large screen, revealed quantities of what appeared to be mostly vegetable matter sprinkled onto a paper towel. When it became clear what they were viewing, some people in the courtroom wished their own lunches hadn't been so recent.

In the upper portion of each picture was a white card. Brad Murphy asked his witness to read the card.

"Rebekah Hendricks, November 29, 1983, gastric contents, McLean County Coroner. Photographs by Janet S. Featherly."

In the lower portion of the photo lay a state law enforcement department ruler. It showed that while the food particles appeared quite large on the screen, they were only millimeters in length or width.

Pictures were shown of the stomach contents of the other two children. All appeared similar.

Another series of photographs showed the preparation of a vegetarian pizza at Chuck E. Cheese. The last of twenty-one pictures flashed onto the screen.

"That's the actual pizza you photographed being built after it came out of the oven?" Murphy asked.

"Yes. That's after they sliced the pizza."

"Thank you. Can we have the lights again?"

As the banks of fluorescent lights flickered on, Murphy continued. "Ms. Featherly, did you ever have any personal contact with the defendant, David Hendricks?"

"Yes."

"When was that, please?"

"The first time was in April of 1982. I—we bought a house from him. April in 1982 is the first time that I looked at the house. I first talked to him on the telephone and then went to Stanford to see the house. His wife showed me the house the first time. Then, a couple of days later, my husband and I both went and looked at the house together, and Mr. Hendricks was there, also."

The defense, while knowing the Featherly-Hendricks connection, had not expected the witness to be questioned about it.

"Would you describe for us the physical appearance of Mr. Hendricks when you first met him in April of 1982?"

"He was overweight. He had darker hair than he has now, a greasy hairstyle. And a scraggly mustache."

"When you used the term 'overweight,' can you be any more descriptive of Mr. Hendricks's condition at that time?"

"Fat."

As jurors looked across the room at the defendant, studiously taking notes, they saw a David Hendricks who was not overweight, whose hair was smooth and dry, whose upper lip was cleanly shaved.

John Long used his cross-examination to make sure jurors understood just how tiny the solid particles of food that loomed so large on the projection screen really were. He handed the witness a tiny bottle like the one used to store the stomach contents.

"If you'll take the cap off of that, take a look at the mouth of that bottle," Long said as the courtroom lights flicked off and an image of food particles again showed on the screen. "Now." Long used a pointer to indicate a single particle. "You see this piece right here?"

"Yes." The witness's voice could barely be heard over the hum of the slide projector.

"Do you have an opinion, since you were there photographing it, whether this piece," Long moved his pointer, "this piece, or this piece would fit through the mouth of that bottle? Just dropped in, I mean. Not squished through."

"Do I have an opinion?"

"Uh-huh."

"Yes, they would."

It was a new day when Ron Dozier called the state's next witness. And Dozier knew his case could very well rest on how convincing this witness's testimony was.

Dr. Michael Baden was an expert among experts. As a twenty-year-plus employee in the New York City Medical Examiner's Office, he had performed fifteen thousand autopsies, personally supervised twice that many, and testified in hundreds of murder trials. Through the years he had risen through the ranks, and in 1978, based on competitive exams, he became New York City's chief medical examiner. One year later and a day before the position would become legally his as long as he wanted it, New York City Mayor Edward Koch demoted Baden because of allegations of "sloppy record keeping, poor judgment, and lack of cooperation."

Senior medical examiners and pathologists from across the country came to Baden's defense. But Koch stuck with his decision amid rumors that the real reason Baden was fired was that he had enlivened a professional meeting with the scurrilous details of Nelson Rockefeller's death. So Baden returned to a position he had held earlier as New York City's deputy chief medical examiner. He received national attention as a special consultant to the Congressional reinvestigations of the assassinations of John F. Kennedy and Martin Luther King and chaired the committee of nine forensic pathologists that handled the scientific inquiry. He was past president of the Society of Jurisprudence and former vice president of the American Academy of Forensic Sciences.

And now he sat in the witness box in the Winnebago County Courthouse, prepared to help Dozier lay the groundwork for his all-important time-of-death testimony.

The state's attorney wanted to know what factors a pathologist considers when he tries to determine a time of death. Dr. Baden was prepared with a light lecture on the subject.

"Certain matters such as when was the person last seen alive; newspapers at the door; when was the mail last taken; dates of milk containers or grocery receipts in the house all will be taken into consideration. Then, the actual condition of the body is a factor; the stiffening of the body which takes a certain time period called 'rigor mortis'; the discoloration of the body as blood settles after death, called 'livor mortis'; and the changing in temperature of the body once the heart and brain stopped functioning. The body becomes like an inanimate object such as a piece of furniture as far as loss of heat goes. And the body temperature falls usually, or some might rise to the ambient temperature.

"All of these processes take a certain amount of time and are taken into consideration in determining time of death. Also, any evidence of decomposition. That will also depend on weather conditions, how hot the environment is. With passage of time, various kinds of fly and animal infestations are helpful."

Several members of the jury squirmed noticeably in their seats.

"At the time of autopsy, other factors are looked at that may be helpful in associating the death with an act—such as the person found in a nightgown or in the same street clothes that the person was last seen in. Certain chemical tests can be done. Certain changes of chemicals in the eye fluid, potassium, is helpful in determining postmortem interval.

"The most important factor of associative evidence in linking the death to an act is the stomach content identification and evaluation of foodstuffs in the stomach to identify what the last meal was and the time interval since the last meal. That's a piece of evidence that stops at the time of death, whereas many of the other factors start. The clock starts ticking for rigor and lividity after that occurs, and all these factors are used in trying to arrive at the best determination of time of death."

Dozier was pleased with Baden's explanation, but he needed to reinforce part of it.

"What are you saying stops at the time of death?"

"The digestion of foodstuff in the stomach essentially stops after death. There is some digestion that does occur in some of the carbohydrates, but the stomach doesn't empty its food out after death, so the amount of food in the stomach and the state of the food in the stomach becomes an indicator of what was eaten in the last meal and how long before death the last meal occurred."

Next Dozier placed four covered Styrofoam cups on the front ledge of the witness box, immediately in front of his witness.

"Would you examine those, please, and see if you recognize them."

Dr. Baden popped the lid off the first container, looked inside and then held it to his nose. He repeated the act with each of the other three containers and identified them as the four murder victims' stomach contents given him for examination when Deputy Coroner Brady visited Baden at his home a month after the murders.

"I opened the containers and removed the solid material and examined them on a blotter-type material with the naked eye, using a hand lens with appropriate lighting. I was able to see intact fragments of mushrooms, black olives, onions, and tomato in exhibits 2, 3, and 4, not in 1, which, to the best of my recollection, had no solid material."

That sample had come from Susan Hendricks's stomach.

Dozier asked what other information was given to Baden.

"I was given the autopsy reports, x-rays taken at the time of autopsy, various police reports, photographs of the decedents at the scene of death and also at the autopsy, some newspaper articles."

And now Dozier's big question.

"On the basis of your education, training, and experience, your personal observations of the stomach contents as you have described in viewing them on the date of December 1st, 1983, and the information provided to you by Assistant Coroner Brady, do you have an opinion as to a reasonable degree of medical certainty on the time of death of the children with regard to when they ate their last meal?"

"Yes."

"And what is that opinion?"

"My opinion is that the last meal was consumed approximately two hours prior to death of the three children."

There was a stir in the courtroom. Based on what both sides had said in their opening statements, that would put the time of the killings at about 9 P.M.—some three hours before Hendricks supposedly left for his trip to Wisconsin.

Dozier had the courtroom lights turned off and the slide projector turned on. There again on the screen was one of the young victim's stomach contents. Dozier asked Dr. Baden to explain to the jury what it was about the vegetable material that led him to conclude that the material had been under digestion for only about two hours.

"The vegetable material is still quite recognizable. Some other slides show fresher material. But some of the different vegetable fragments appear to be quite undisturbed by digestion, while others show some considerable digestion—but not sufficient to permit exit from the stomach in this chyme-like material."

The lights came back on.

"Let me ask you another question," Dozier said. "On December 1st, 1983, after you talked to Mr. Brady, you gave him an opinion that the time of death was from two to four hours, is that correct?"

"I believe so. I was asked to give the outermost limit of length of time, and I thought—and still do—that the gastric contents as I viewed them and as described at autopsy could not have been in the stomach more than four hours. I still believe that. But I think it's more likely to be closer to the two-hour figure, and that goes on the basis of just thinking further about the stomach contents, examining the material more, and examining some of the additional expert reports.

"So the information persuaded me closer to the two-hour figure, and I would still put four hours as the outside. But I think it's more likely two hours."

"Is there any way that these stomach contents could have been under digestion for as long as five, six, or even eight hours?"

"No. Not in my opinion."

Baden was turned over to John Long for cross-examination. Dr. Baden used the momentary break to ask the bailiff for a glass of water.

Long's first move would be to question Baden's expertise in determining time of death through examination of stomach contents.

The bailiff returned with the witness's water, contained in a Styrofoam cup markedly similar to the four specimen cups that still sat in front of Baden. He drank the water down and asked for a refill.

"We have just discussed, Doctor, that from the time you became a pathologist, you have served continuously as an active member in twelve different organizations where you have either been on the board or on a task force or on a committee or an editor or an author on problems dealing with drug abuse and alcohol abuse."

"Yes," Baden said, setting his refilled cup of water on the same ledge where the four similar cups sat. "But that goes largely to the '60s and early '70s when there was a great program in New York City to upgrade awareness about drug abuse."

"To bring it closer up to date." Long paused to look at his notes. "You are Distinguished Lecturer in the New York City Police Department on the parameters of responsible alcohol-taking and the codirector of the American College of Physicians course on the medical aspect of drug abuse in New York City. Is that correct?"

"Yes."

"How about acting as a consultant for the conference under development for a uniform system of reporting and recording drug-related and drug-induced deaths in Newport, California?"

"Yes."

"How about the American Academy of Family Physicians Symposium on Drug Abuse Treatment in Portland, Oregon?"

"The Portland, Oregon, one was 1973."

"I note that in addition to this, you are also and have been a consultant with the Firestone Rubber Company in dealing with occupational exposure to vinyl chloride. Would that have to do in part with your interest in toxicology?"

Baden reached up for a drink of water and momentarily had his hand on the wrong cup.

"Yeah. In toxicology and occupational medicine. That was an issue as to cancers of the lung caused by exposure to vinyl chloride."

"As late as 1979 and 1980, did you also apply for research grants to do study in sudden infant death syndrome?"

"I think around that time, '78, '79. I was coinvestigator of a sudden infant death syndrome project in New York City, yes. That was based in the Medical Examiner's office."

"In all of the years from the time you received certification as a forensic pathologist, Doctor, to the present time, have you ever sought or obtained any research grant dealing with the analysis of gastric contents either to determine time of death or cause of death?"

"No."

Long cited a list of seventy-four articles Baden authored. "Isn't it a fact that all but nine of them dealt with narcotics addiction, narcotics abuse, alcohol addiction, and alcohol abuse?"

Baden was drinking more water, causing the courtroom observers to wonder if this pathologist knew something about water that no one else knew.

"My main field of interest was in those areas, but there were some other papers on child abuse."

"Well, I tell you the reason I'm asking," Long said as he circled behind his seat at the defense table. "Because of what we've just gone through here—all of the articles which you had to research and author, all the committees that you have served on since 1966, all of the research grants that you have done since 1966; and you have also told us that you have done approximately an even 20,000 hours' worth of autopsy work, and you have squeezed all of that into 36,400 hours. And I guess my question is during all of that time, did you ever author one thing on the analysis of gastric content as a means for determining time of death?"

"During all that time, I haven't authored anything on gastric contents, but during that time, I have studied gastric contents in every autopsy that I have looked at."

Long thought he had made his point. As the bailiff refilled Baden's water cup a fourth time, Long attacked Baden's time-of-death opinion on a second front. "When Mr. Brady visited you in your home, one of the items that he brought upon which you could make a studied medical evaluation were newspaper articles concerning this case. Is that correct?"

Baden knew this was going to be a rhetorical tug-of-war. He took another drink.

"I think some of the items that he had with him were newspaper articles, which I reviewed. That isn't necessarily for medical information, but I do find newspaper articles in this kind of matter helpful in the sense of putting what's being presented in better perspective. I am always concerned about biases of somebody presenting a case."

"Sure." Long flashed his Cheshire grin. Baden took a drink.

"I mean, whether it is a defense attorney or prosecutor, there tends to be biases in presentation of a case to an expert, and I think I read those articles that he brought with him just to see if there were other things involved that might not be so helpful or whatever to his theory of the case."

"So." An air of incredulity materialized in Long's voice. "In a case when you are being asked to consult, where a man is being accused of the ax murder of his wife and three children, you thought you might get an unbiased point of view to help make a medical determination by reading a newspaper article?" The last three words echoed in the courtroom.

"No, I didn't say that. I didn't say that. I read and reviewed all the material that Mr. Brady had. Some things I gave more weight than others. Obviously, I didn't give much weight to newspaper articles as far as any medical evaluation."

As Dr. Baden drank, Long moved to a third front by citing three forensic science textbooks that downgraded the use of stomach contents to determine the time of death. Baden said the books were old and outdated.

"As a forensic pathologist," Long continued, "can you tell me whether there has been any individual who has collated the various factors that can retard gastric emptying?"

"Surely. A lot of people have. I think you may be referring to a paper by Dr. Earl Rose, a forensic pathologist who collated a lot of material."

"Dr. Rose has collated a lot of material?"

"Yeah, I believe."

"Would you consider—"

Baden preempted Long, knowing what he was after. "Yes, I think Dr. Rose is an excellent and superior forensic pathologist, one of the few pathologists who has taken the time on this small area of forensic pathology."

"Well, fate has given me Dr. Rose's latest article."

"I thought so." Another gulp of water for Baden.

"And let me read to you, Doctor, Dr. Rose's latest article: 'The following rules should be kept in mind when one attempts to estimate the time interval between the last meal and death, basing this estimate on the presence of food in the stomach. One, emptying of a solid meal would never exceed six hours. Two, the emptying of a solid meal may be as little as three hours.'

"Now, according to Dr. Rose, whose experience you have just informed us of, that's a three- to six-hour time frame. And you are sitting here telling us that it is one to possibly two hours in this case. How do you explain your disagreement?"

"In this paper entitled 'Factors Influencing Gastric Emptying,' I agree with much of what he writes—not necessarily everything."

"Would this digestive time make any difference to you if you found out that the decedents bolted their food?"

"I think we're talking about a small meal of pizza."

"How do you know that, Doctor? Do you know how much pizza they ate?"

"There were three children, an adult, and one medium-size pie. And comparing it to my children—they eat a lot of pizza—"

"But your children aren't dead, Doctor. Do you know how much pizza the decedents ate on the night in question? Yes or no."

"I know it was less than a full pie. But I don't know specifically how much. You are correct."

"Okay. You don't know how much, and you don't know that they bolted their food."

"When you say bolted the food, I don't see much in the way of chewing marks on the vegetable matter."

"Would that indicate to you that they may have, as children sometimes do, eaten their food in a very hurried fashion?"

"That's possible. Yes."

Long showed Baden a medical article listing one hundred reasons why food might remain in a stomach longer than the usual period. He asked Baden to read the list aloud. It contained such factors as migraine, fainting, and brain tumors.

"Then, under that, deformities. The person has various abnormalities of the spine; radiation in animals; drugs such as morphine, atropine; muscle disease like polio. Then we get down to miscellaneous."

"Ah," said Long. "Now we're getting interesting."

The judge interrupted. "We're going to have to stop at this time today, gentlemen. We are past recess for the jury." He turned to the jury. "You'll receive information in a few moments as to what time you are to return tomorrow."

"Morning, Doctor."

"Morning, Mr. Long."

Both Baden and Long appeared revived after the previous day's long day of testimony. When Judge Baner rather abruptly had ended the day's session, Long had been upset. Not only had he been about to make an important point, but he had been within minutes of ending his cross-examination. Today, however, he was armed with new questions, new research, and new points of attack on the idea that stomach contents are reliable in determining time of death.

Dr. Baden was also ready. He had his cup of water.

"One of the things that you read to the ladies and gentlemen of the jury was from a work that you testified that you thought was an authoritative work entitled 'Gastric Retention Without Medical Obstruction.' One of the items that the authors of that authoritative work indicate can retard or delay gastric emptying was exercise."

"Yes, I noticed that." Baden flashed a knowing smile.

"Now, not from what you know today—but I want to go back with you to December of 1983. I want to go back to your living room, your dining room table where you testified yesterday you and Deputy Coroner Brady sat and examined all this material which consisted of gastric contents, of pizza pie and some newspaper articles and the autopsy protocol. At that time, did you take into consideration any factors which might have resulted in gastric retention or a delaying of gastric emptying?"

Long was zeroing in on the fact that the Hendricks children had done considerable jumping and running in the pizza parlor's play area shortly after they ate, which could have slowed down the digestion process.

"From the police reports and from Mr. Brady, I did have some indication of some activity, that is, going to the pizza parlor and then coming home, without much detail."

"Do you have an opinion based upon a reasonable degree of medical certainty of whether or not, as stated in this authoritative article, exercise can retard or delay gastric emptying?"

"My opinion is that exercise has little, very little if any, effect on gastric emptying. I have not in my experience noted it to be a factor in autopsies, nor in literature."

"Okay. And if in fact there are articles that say that it does, you would discount those articles?"

"No, no, no." Baden was getting impatient. "I would take it into consideration certainly, and my opinions, as you see from December 1st, are not written in granite. I make the best opinions I can on the basis of the information available. I did so on December 1st. I also did so when I testified yesterday when I had additional information available from both your experts and from Mr. Dozier's experts, which I included. And if you would have shown me something contrary to my information, or if somebody saw these children fine at one o'clock in the morning, I would have to severely reconsider my opinion. It is not written in granite. But it is based on a reasonable medical certainty at this moment to all the information I now have at hand."

The wrangling over whether or not stomach contents are useful in determining a time of death went on for several hours more. Both

Long and Dozier had Baden read articles about scientific research on the subject and then debated their significance. Sometimes the discussion got testy. But there were lighter moments.

At one point, Long tried to reintroduce the Styrofoam cups containing the samples of stomach contents, but he couldn't get the lid off the larger canister that held them.

"Did you do this, Ron?" Long asked the state's attorney.

"I had trouble, too," Dozier said as he took the canister and tried to remove its screw-on top.

"What a guy, what a guy," Long said. "You can tell the inordinate strength of the prosecution in this case, Doctor. Ron's a runner, Doctor, so he can do this."

But Dozier couldn't do it. Instead, the defense investigator, Brian Briggs, took the canister from the courtroom and returned a few moments later, its lid removed. Long took the individual containers from the canister and in the process some of the fluid leaked from them. Hendricks offered Long his handkerchief to wipe his hands.

Later there was an intense discussion over the size of pieces of chicken liver fed to volunteers in an experiment to time the digestive process. Long handed Dr. Baden a ruler and asked him to show the jury the size of one cubic centimeter.

The ruler bore the inscription "Ron Dozier for State's Attorney." Dozier was in no position to dispute the ruler's accuracy.

As the second afternoon of Baden testimony wore on, Dozier tried to bring all of the discussion about the value of stomach content analysis into focus.

"Dr. Baden, you have run through a lot of literature in the last couple of days. Would it be fair in your opinion to say that there's a divergence of opinion among the experts on this subject of gastric emptying?"

"There is a divergence in certain areas. One question that has arisen is whether gastric emptying time has any value at all, and one could find statements perhaps in literature that it isn't of value. I disagree with that totally. It is of value and the extent of its value depends on how much is known about circumstances—eating time—and the findings in the stomach. It is of more value if you find a lot of food in the stomach than if you find a little food in the stomach. I think the interpretation of the emptying time does permit a difference of opinion, how to interpret it. But I do think that without question it is of value."

Long had tried time and again to discredit the reliability of Baden's time-of-death estimate. He would try one last time. But Baden was almost on the offense.

"The best I can do," Baden said, "is take in and make a judgment, not just on these articles which Mr. Dozier chose to show me, but on all my experience. And that's what I'm trying to do. And I'm not trying to say with precision that the children died exactly 120 minutes after they ate. I am saying what I think the outer limits are and what is most likely, based on all my experience and not necessarily just on these articles."

"So," Long countered, "it is now your position that you cannot say with any degree of medical and scientific certainty that these children died 120 minutes after ingestion of the pizza. Is that what you have just told us?"

"No. No. No. No." Baden was emphatic. "What I am saying is that to the best of my judgment and beyond a reasonable medical certainty—which in my mind is 99.9 percent, not 100 percent—that these children died approximately two hours after eating the last meal and definitely less than four hours after eating the last meal."

"And all of that conclusion is based on everything that you have told us over the last two days?"

"Yes."

"I have nothing further, Doctor."

After a total of nine hours in the witness box, New York City's deputy chief medical examiner stepped down.

The state's next expert witness was John Dwyer, a senior botanist and professor at St. Louis University. He was among those who had examined the victims' stomach contents early in the investigation. Now he was being called as a witness to establish the degree of digestion.

Dozier asked Dr. Dwyer's opinion about how much the vegetable matter in the children's stomachs had been broken down by the digestive process.

"If I were to score it on a one to a hundred percentage, I would say the rate was about a 10 percent breakdown. In other words, very incomplete. Fresh."

In his cross-examination, Long was almost fierce.

"Do you consider yourself an expert on digestion?" Long asked Dwyer at one point.

"No."

"So any opinion you would have as to the degree of digestion would be, with respect to any of these food particles, the opinion of a nonexpert. Is that not true?"

"I prefer to think that I can make a good calculated judgment with experience. If I see something, if I see a few raindrops on a hot summer sidewalk in Rockford with the sun blazing, I know those raindrops were there a short time."

Dwyer was almost antagonistic in some of his answers to Long. Perhaps Dwyer knew what was coming.

"Would you agree with me that in the accomplishment and furtherance of science and of doing research in order to ascertain truth that extreme and inordinate care must be taken in the methodology used in getting results?"

"The answer is yes."

"You were asked on the 12th of November, 1983, by Mr. Dan Brady to examine four vials containing gastric contents and to give your opinion with respect to those vials."

"That's correct."

"Isn't it a fact that in those four vials, you could identify vegetable content or pizza contents in two of the four vials, according to this report?"

"I believe that is true."

"Okay. And that report was dictated by you on the 29th of November?"

"That's not true. It was hand-typed by me."

"All right. I beg your pardon. Hand-typed by you on the 29th of November. I want to call your attention to on or about February 6th, 1984. Did you receive further communication from anybody from McLean County with respect to your findings on those four vials?"

"It was indicated to me that there was something in the initial report that needed to be rechecked."

"And where did they indicate to you that the problem might lie?"

"That presumably I had written down a report twice, and what happened was that Mr. Brad Murphy brought down a vial of Grace's, so that I could recheck, and I rechecked and submitted the report."

What Long was after, and eventually succeeded in getting, was an admission from Dwyer that his original analysis of Grace's stomach contents showed only highly digested material. "Ringlike masses that possessed cell walls so there was no doubt that the material was vegetable. From the condition of the cellular mass," the report continued, "it was impossible to determine their vegetable source." The February analysis of the material labeled as Grace's stomach contents found only slightly digested black olive, tomato, onion, and large pieces of mushroom.

Dwyer explained the first report as an error. He had mistakenly examined the vial of Susan's stomach contents twice and failed to look at Grace's.

To Hendricks's parents and in-laws, the discrepancy was significant. Seven-year-old Grace, they insisted, hated mushrooms and would meticulously remove them from any pizza before she would take a bite.

The chief medical examiner of Dade County, Florida, Dr. Joseph Davis, was the next expert in the prosecution's attempt to use the victims' stomach contents to establish that they died before Hendricks said he departed for Wisconsin.

Dr. Davis told the jury that if the children had eaten at about 7 P.M., they were dead before 11:30 P.M.

"And what factors do you think are significant in your mind in establishing the opinion?" Dozier asked.

"I think the time that they ate the pizza. The factor of being normal children is important. The degree of digestion that had taken place and, more importantly, the degree of digestion that had not taken place."

Davis said the children's stomachs contained vegetable matter that was easily identified by the naked eye.

"In fact I may be hard pressed from looking at those pictures to say that they had ever even been inside a stomach, just from the appearance, although I know they were because they came from the stomach. But they are surprisingly well preserved."

Dozier wanted to preempt the defense on the exercise issue.

"In your experience, training, and education," Dozier said, "what effect, if any, does exercise have on the rate of digestion?"

"I don't believe that exercise *per se* has any particular effect. Exercise that is accompanied by, say, very severe emotional stress or highly competitive exercise might have an adverse effect on digestive processes. But I don't believe there is any grounds to believe that just normal exercise would have an adverse effect. If it did, my seven children and my eleven grandchildren would be suffering from indigestion all the time."

"In the information that has been given you regarding the

Hendricks case," Dozier continued, "were you made aware that the Hendricks children, after consuming this vegetarian pizza, may have played in the playroom at Chuck E. Cheese and engaged in such activity as bouncing in an air pillow apparatus, hanging from a rope that slides down, sliding down a rope and dropping off, climbing into a playhouse of some sort and sliding down a circular slide, running back and forth between these activities, and so on. Were you made aware of that fact?"

"Yes."

"In your opinion, would that type of exercise have had any effect on the rate of digestion or on your estimates of the time of death in this case?"

"In my opinion, it should not have affected it."

"Doctor, what would you have expected to see in the stomach contents if you were to assume that these children had lived longer than four and a half hours after they had eaten this food? What condition would you expect the stomach contents to be?"

"I would expect to see, if anything, just some indeterminate chyme, a sort of thick, milky material. I would certainly not expect to see identifiable fragments of vegetable like we see here."

Dozier returned to his seat, confident that any credibility his scientific case had lost with Dwyer had now been restored with Davis.

Long was prepared to attack Davis's opinion that the deaths occurred before 11:30 P.M.

"What would have been the difference in what you saw in the photographs of the stomach contents if death would have come at twelve midnight on the dot instead of 11:30? What would have been the difference in appearance?"

"I think that if we had added another half hour to that time," Davis said, "what would have been there would be less—if anything. I am not inferring that what I see in these photographs and what is described in that autopsy report is what was there when the 11:30 hour rolled around. This does not appear to me to be material that was there at 11:30. This appears to be material that was there earlier than 11:30."

"How much earlier?"

"Again we get into the lack of precision because we are in ranges. But we know it cannot be earlier than, say, close to the nine o'clock period because that's the time the children were getting ready for bed. Let's see, 8:15 they would have to leave, get ready, and so forth, 8:30 to 9:00, somewhere along in there."

"They were seen alive by somebody other than the defendant at 8:15. What is your opinion now?"

"At 8:15?"

"Uh-huh."

"I would have to know where that person saw them, what they were dressed in, what they were doing."

"Let's say they were seen alive at the bookmobile, leaving the bookmobile at 8:15."

"Dressed in pajamas?"

"No. Street clothes."

"Well, then. Obviously there's a time lag. They would have had to go home, they would have had to change and get into bedclothes. So that adds on. And so what other factors are there? The distance, the time it takes to get from the bookmobile would have to be added in there."

"Five minutes."

"Changing, getting ready for bed. That's not extremely fast with small children. Perhaps fifteen minutes, another twenty. It's hard to say. It would seem to me that it would be getting closer to the 8:30 or nine o'clock time—along in that range that they finally go to bed. So obviously if they are alive during that period, they cannot already be dead."

"That's correct." Long liked the way this was going. "So let's say that we are up to the nine o'clock time. What did the stomach contents look like at nine o'clock?"

"At nine o'clock I can't be certain."

"What did they look like at ten o'clock?"

"I would say they probably looked pretty close to what we see here. But again, it's a range. I can't be absolutely sure because there is no precision to this."

"Since there isn't any precision and since it is a range, would it be a fair statement to say that instead of 11:30, it could just as easily have been twelve o'clock?"

"I don't think so, based on what I saw."

"Well, the point I'm trying to make is that when you get right down to the bottom line, Doctor, isn't what you're doing here today nothing more than a guess? Aren't you in fact guessing from an examination of these contents, guessing and setting an arbitrary time of 11:30—something that you have told us is unreliable and covers a wide range?"

"Well, I'm not guessing in that respect. I am estimating based on all the facts available to me."

"Do you know Dr. Michael Baden?"

"Yes."

"He has been here and has given evidence that in his opinion, death took place two hours postprandial with about a one-hour variation. Did you agree or disagree with that opinion?"

"I would tend to make it a little longer than two hours, plus or minus one hour. In other words, one hour after they ate is one of those parameters which means that they are killed at eight o'clock. If they are at the bookmobile reading, it's impossible. That's why I don't believe in trying to be too precise in these things."

"Do you know Dr. Bernard Knight?"

"I don't know him personally. He is my counterpart in Wales."

"Do you know him to be an expert in forensic pathology?"

"I really don't know. I'm sorry, but I don't know the man personally."

"You know nothing about his background?"

"Very little. I know that he helped write a book once, and that's about all I know."

"Are you familiar with an article he wrote entitled 'Forensic Mythology'?"

"No, I'm not. I would like to read it."

"Would you?"

"Certainly."

"Well, as luck would have it." Long produced the article. "He has written about gastric contents and examination of same. And I would like you to read the part marked in red."

As Dr. Davis read, Long made eye contact with members of the jury. Davis looked up from the article.

"I wouldn't be as strong as he is in this. He says there was only one thing to say about stomach contents as an aid in estimating the time of death, and here I am quoting exactly: 'They are utterly useless' with an exclamation mark. I wouldn't be quite that strong."

"I have nothing further." Long sat down.

The prosecution's final witness in the stomach-contents issue was John Spikes, the chief toxicologist for the Illinois Department of Public Health. He had been in the headlines nationwide two years earlier as a lead investigator in Chicago's Tylenol killings. Dozier had two objectives in Dr. Spikes's testimony: remove any doubts raised during Dr. Dwyer's testimony about the authenticity of the stomach samples, and get Spikes's opinion about how much digestion those samples reflected.

The first goal seemed to be accomplished easily. Dozier had Spikes explain in detail how he had examined all four samples on November 10—two days before Dwyer had access to them—and found pizza ingredients in the samples from all three young victims' stomachs.

And Spikes's opinion of the degree of digestion?

"That there had been very little active digestion take place upon the gastric contents."

In his cross-examination, Long was anxious to try to discredit Spikes's opinion.

"Can you tell us what you mean be 'very little'?" Long asked.

"The material that was there appeared almost intact, almost as if it had not been touched by digestion. There was a slight slurring of the edges and a slight eroding of the smooth surfaces. However, the slurring and erosion was minimal."

"Is your opinion based in part on your training?"

"Partially upon training, partially upon experience."

"Okay. With respect to your training, can you tell us what textbooks you have studied that would give rise to having formed this opinion?"

"One of the major texts that we used in the study of the digestive process was a treatise on digestion by Captain William Beaumont, United States Army."

"When was the Beaumont research done?"

"I can't give you the exact date on it. It was in the 1800s, I believe."

"Would 1822 be an approximate date?"

"I can't argue against that."

Long felt he had won that round. On to round 2.

"In the case of the three children, did you indicate in your report how much of a sample you took for analysis?"

"Approximately three cc's."

Long brought forward a vial containing coffee, an eyedropper, and a measuring cup.

"Would you please show us, if you would, approximately how much three cc's is by removing coffee from that vial and putting it in that other container that I provided for you there?"

Spikes squeezed the bulb on the eyedropper until the dropper was about half full and put its contents into the milk-colored cup.

"Okay. Now, just so we understand the quantities that we are working with, Doctor, would it be a fair statement that the liquid in this cup doesn't even cover the bottom?"

"No, it does not."

"And it is from this"—Long put the emphasis on "this"—"that you made a determination of the degree to which this food had been subjected to the digestive process?"

"Objection, your honor." It was Ron Dozier.

"Objection to that?" Judge Baner asked.

"Not if we have in the record some mention of the size of the bottom of the cup," Dozier responded.

"I'll be glad to do that," Long said. "For purposes of the record, I am not concerned with the bottom of the cup. I can pour it into a glass. But this is approximately three cc's, is it not?"

"That's correct," the witness said.

Long poured the tiny quantity of coffee from the white measuring cup into a clear drinking glass.

"Now with respect to the three cc's which you examined, did you make any inquiry as to any information regarding how you came to obtain this sample?"

"Not prior to my examination, no."

Long held the clear glass, in which the coffee was barely discernible, high in the air.

"Your Honor." It was Dozier again. "I'm going to object to counsel. Now he has poured it into another glass. Obviously he didn't get it all out of the first one. He's holding it up. I don't know for what purpose. Is there some reason you didn't leave it in the first one?"

"Yeah, it was unwieldy and you couldn't see it. It was just too small."

The judge sustained Dozier's objection. Long felt he had made his point and moved on to the next round.

"How many times in the past have you ever been called upon to give an opinion, Dr. Spikes, based upon the degree to which food had been subjected to the digestive process?"

"Requested by whom, sir?"

"Requested by anybody, Doctor."

"Approximately sixty times."

"How many times have you been called upon to give evidence on the subject in a court of law?"

"I have not been requested in a court of law."

"This is the first time?"

"That's correct."

Long felt he had won the match.

Jurors received their first indication of just how gruesome the murders were from testimony by Dr. Antonie Romyn, the Bloomington pathologist who autopsied the four murder victims' bodies a day after they were discovered.

He described in explicit detail how each of the autopsies was performed. And each time Dr. Romyn itemized a gash, a laceration, or a skull-hacking injury Susan or one of the three children had suffered, David Hendricks lowered his head and closed his eyes.

Susan, Romyn said, probably lost consciousness and died within twenty minutes—either from extensive loss of blood from the worst of her nine injuries (a gaping three-and-a-half-inch cut that exposed her skull and first vertebra of her neck) or from a brain hemorrhage.

Becky, he testified, had three wounds, the fewest of any of the victims, and probably died within seconds because of a skull fracture and injury to the brain.

Brad Murphy asked Dr. Romyn if he had an opinion about the type of weapon used on Becky.

"The wound had an impression with a small angle on it, like a blunt weapon that's used," he said. "It had at least one ninety-degree corner—like a hammer-type object, the back of an ax, or something like that."

Dr. Romyn believed Grace and Benjy had died instantly. Grace, he said, had a total of six injuries and died from head injuries and a loss of blood where several major blood vessels in the neck were severed. And Benjamin suffered some sixteen injuries, including a broken jaw, and died as a result of major blood loss, a skull fracture, and brain injury.

Edward Books, Jr., had been a deputy coroner in McLean County for five years when the Hendricks killings occurred. He had not been present for the autopsy on Susan Hendricks's body but was present for the other three.

Brad Murphy thought he had better focus on Books's handling of Grace's stomach contents. If he didn't, Murphy figured that Long would.

"Doctor Romyn opened up the stomach and took out the stomach contents that he could get in a ladle—a stainless steel ladle," Books said. "We transferred them into a plastic-type cup that I could form into a funnel to direct the contents into the container with a shallow neck, so I could send them to the lab."

"What was the purpose of collecting the gastric contents at that point?" Murphy asked.

"Toxicology reasons."

"Do you know what quantity was held by the bottle?"

"Thirty cc's, three milliliters—the same."

"After placing some of the stomach contents of Grace Hendricks in the bottle, was there other of her stomach contents that were not in the bottle?"

"Yes, there was."

"And what did you do with that?"

"After I got the full bottle, I sealed it, washed it, and at that time, I washed off the rest of the pieces of food that were left in the plastic cup—I noticed I could identify some of them as food particles—and then they were washed down the drain."

At the defense table, color rushed from Long's face. He hadn't heard this before. He made notes to be sure to come back to this topic during cross-examination.

Books also testified that during the autopsy on Benjamin's body, he noticed something unusual on the back of the boy's hand. "Benjamin's right hand had a greenish-blue stamp of a cartoon-type character, Jasper Jowls—a character of Chuck E. Cheese pizza world."

This day's testimony had held precious little to smile about. Several jurors seized the chance to smile now.

"How were you familiar with that character?"

"I have a five-year-old and a four-year-old daughter and a young son, and we go to Chuck E. Cheese. The stamp is placed on the back of a child's hand to allow them to go into a playground area inside. Kids can go in and out to play before and after their pizza is ready."

Books said he had found the same stamp impression on Grace's hand but not on Becky's.

In cross-examination, Long launched into the stomach contents issue. "Let me get this straight," he said in almost mock seriousness. "After you filled that bottle with what you thought, or what you personally felt, was a random sampling of those gastric contents, you washed off the remainder, described it to the people in the room, and flushed the rest of it down the drain?"

"Yes, sir."

"Deputy Coroner, how long have you been a deputy coroner?"

"It will be six years in November."

"And what training have you had in pathology, histology, or toxicology?"

"None."

"Did you have any conception that you might be washing valuable evidence down the drain?"

"At that time, no."

"Do you now?"

"Yes, sir."

"When you're not acting as deputy coroner, what do you do for a living?"

"I'm an industrial sales engineer."

"Do you think as an industrial sales engineer, you have the training to determine what is an adequate random sampling to take a toxicology analysis?"

"Not toxicology. No."

"But you made the determination in there as to what was going to the toxicologist?"

"Yes, sir."

"And washed the rest down the drain."

"Yes, sir."

"Was Coroner Anderson present during all four autopsies to watch the ladling of that gastric material into any vials?"

"No, sir."

"He, in fact, was only there for Susan. Isn't that correct?"

"I don't know. I wasn't there then. I believe he was. He was in the room when I got there."

"And he certainly wasn't there for Grace, Rebekah, or Benjamin, was he?"

"No, sir."

"Now by the time you got to the other vials that are there, tell us what you did with those vials. How you filled them."

"After I decided I made a mistake on the first one, I kept everything from the second two and put them in a larger container, cottage cheese-type—everything that the doctor gave me went into those containers, tagged and marked with the people's names."

It was a refreshing break when the next series of prosecution witnesses had nothing to do with autopsies, head injuries, or stomach contents. They were there to trace David Hendricks's activities on November 8, 1983.

James Peck was director of physical therapy at the Wausau, Wisconsin, Hospital Center—as far north into Wisconsin as Hen-

dricks's trip had taken him. Peck testified that he had a three- or
four-minute conversation with Hendricks in the reception area of
the physical therapy department shortly after 8 A.M.

"Mr. Hendricks made a presentation to me and handed me a
flier on a particular type of garment called a CASH orthosis," Peck
said. "I think I was quite impressed that it was much more econom-
ical to buy them directly from the company this way than it would
be going through another orthotist-prosthetist, and we talked a
couple of minutes about that. And I think he stressed that there
were two different types, one with a hinge on it and one without a
hinge. I didn't realize that we had the option on that. And that's
about the extent of it."

"Do you recall," Brad Murphy asked, "if Mr. Hendricks had a
sample of his brace along with him at that point?"

"He didn't have a sample. He did have the brochure, and I said I
have received this brochure through the mail. I told him we had
also been using them on patients. I was familiar with them. So I
didn't need a sample at that point. I didn't ask for one automatically."

Under cross-examination, Peck said it was "quite ordinary" for
salespeople to just drop in to make a sales call without an appointment, as Hendricks had that morning.

Charlene Dineen had known Hendricks years earlier when he
worked for Heinz Brinkmann's company and she was a physical
therapy assistant at St. Michael's Hospital in Stevens Point. She
was still employed there when Hendricks appeared shortly after 9
A.M. on November 8.

"David walked into the department and I knew him immediately," Dineen testified. "And it was 'Hello, David' and 'Hello,
Char,' He was bringing in the brochures of his new adaptation that
he had on his CASH orthosis, and we went through the material.
We were familiar with the garment to begin with, so it didn't take a
whole lot of words to describe what he had done. And he inquired
about my old boss, and we just chatted maybe ten minutes."

When cross-examined, Dineen said it was not at all unusual for
salespeople to show up unannounced and that her hospital ordered
some of the new braces immediately.

"And was that as a result of the information in the brochure
and David's explanation and his appearance there?" Hal Jennings
asked.

"Yes, it was."

"With respect to his appearance, how did David appear to you when he talked to you?"

"Just fine."

With the final four rows of seats in the courtroom area filled with schoolchildren on a field trip, eight more witnesses came to the stand as the state tried to show that Hendricks covered a lot of ground in a short amount of time on November 8. One was Tamiko Yamate, who with her husband operated Madison Prosthetics and Orthotics. She testified that it was not unusual for salespeople to drop by.

"He came in and asked if we sold CASH orthoses, and we said yes, we did sell them. He asked if we were buying directly from Bloomington, and we said yes. Oh, then he said he was out on an extended vacation and was making the rounds."

"Do you have any recollection of how long this salesman talk went on?" asked Murphy.

"Probably five minutes or so."

"What happened at the end of the five minutes?"

"Well, he says, 'I got to go on,' so he left."

After another witness testified that it was unusual that Hendricks had a new product to sell but didn't have it with him to show, Carol Brausen took the stand. She was an employee of Badger Medical Supply Company in Madison.

"Did you notice anything unusual about either his attitude or his demeanor while he was there?" Murphy asked.

"He wasn't nervous to the point that he was shaking," she said. "I guess I would have to say he was like he had to be someplace in a hurry. If you're waiting for your wife and she wasn't ready and you knew you had to be someplace at a time—that's the type of nervousness he was showing."

"Was there anything out of the ordinary about the sales call?"

"First of all, the majority of the salespeople that see me stop at the front desk to see our salesmen. They, in turn, come in to see if I have time to see that person.

"Number two, I can't say all of them, but a majority of them call and set up appointments. When they come in to see me, they have a product and a business card, and normally they've got a pen out, wanting to know if I'm going to place an order."

Hendricks, she said, did none of those things.

The Hendricks trial was a major ongoing news story in the

northern two-thirds of Illinois. Jim Browne was at work as the overnight deejay on radio station WJBC, back in Bloomington, when he answered the phone. It was the same man who had called earlier to request a record. He had sounded drunk then, more sober now.

"What do you think about that murder case?" the middle-aged, male voice asked. "The Hendricks case."

"I really can't comment on that," Browne responded.

"I can. I done it."

Browne paused, asking himself if he heard the man correctly.

"Uh-huh," Browne said. "And what's your name and address?"

The caller hung up but called again a few minutes later.

"You going to play Don Williams?" he asked.

"I'm afraid I'm not going to be able to," Browne answered. "Why don't you give me your phone number and I'll get back to you?"

"I'm at the phone booth."

"Well, where is it? I can get the numbers for a phone booth."

"You're not going to trace my call."

The phone slammed down.

Defense attorneys Jennings and Long were preparing their last-ditch efforts to get Judge Baner to bar the testimony of the models, something they had been unable to convince Judge Knecht to do.

Their argument would be that the models' testimony would be little more than negative character evidence which would be more prejudicial than relevant. Now, with the jury still out of the courtroom, Jennings was making his point.

"The state is espousing in this case a really bizarre theory of motivation hinging on the inference of a psychological conflict allegedly resulting from the defendant's having lust in his heart and religious beliefs," Jennings told the judge.

The motive theory was so speculative, Jennings said, that the models' testimony should not be allowed, at least not without some expert testimony that the theory even made sense.

"The testimony of some of these models," Jennings continued, "would undoubtedly have the prejudicial effect of portraying the defendant as an immoral or perhaps a perverse individual, in spite of the fact that his idiosyncrasies have nothing whatsoever to do with the crimes involved in this case."

Dozier responded that any evidence that tended to show guilt of any kind could be characterized as "negative character evidence," but in this case he thought it was particularly relevant to the state's theory on why Hendricks murdered his family. Some of the things the models would testify that Hendricks had said to them, Dozier said, "can imply unhappiness with the sexual relationship at home with his wife. And we don't believe it takes any experts to testify that that can offer a motive for the killing of one's wife."

After more than an hour of reviewing case law presented by each side, Judge Baner made his decision. The models would be allowed to testify, but their testimony was to be considered only as it might relate to the state's motive theory.

"It must not be considered by you," the judge told the jurors, "as evidence of the defendant's character or that he is a bad person."

Fourteen

B ecause of all the legal argument and publicity about whether the models should be allowed to testify in the case, the courtroom became crowded with spectators when word spread that the first of the women was about to take the stand.

Dozier was nervous. He knew that even in the limited way the jury was to consider the models' testimony, this part of the case was pivotal—at least in terms of the thin string of a motive the prosecution was suggesting for the killings. The strategy was simple. Present the young women in a rough chronological order. A pattern of accelerating sexual aggressiveness, Dozier hoped, would be obvious.

Hendricks appeared ill at ease as the first of the women was called to the stand.

Echo Wulf Atwell, a very attractive woman with long, flowing auburn hair, had been eighteen years old when Hendricks had hired her in the summer of 1981 to model his new back brace in an advertising brochure. Hendricks had been at the typesetting firm owned by Echo's father, getting prices. When Hendricks mentioned that he was looking for a model for the brochure, Larry Wulf suggested his daughter, who had done some part-time modeling.

Atwell had made an afternoon appointment to be fitted for the brace at Hendricks's office. She used a dressing room to change into the dark-colored leotard and bodysuit she would wear for the photo session at a commercial photographer's studio.

Dozier asked the witness whether there were any adjustments that had to be made on the brace as Hendricks fit it to her.

"He adjusted it for my torso. You know, the length. And then he buckled it on."

"Okay. Can you tell me approximately how long it took for him to fit the brace to your size?"

"I would say probably five minutes. Not very long. Just long enough to put it up against me and to buckle it, however long it took to adjust it."

"What happened then, after the brace was fitted?"

"I believe that I changed my clothes and I left."

Echo described the photo session that occurred the following day and identified the CASH Brace brochure that contained her picture.

"At any time in the course of being fitted for this brace, did you remove any of your clothing?"

"No."

"At any time during the fitting of the brace, did Mr. Hendricks make any marks on your body?" Courtroom spectators suddenly wondered whether a dirty hint of sadism was about to be introduced.

"No."

Jennings followed a similar course in cross-examination, asking whether Hendricks had ever physically hurt her.

"No."

"Did David, while in your presence, ever cause you any physical pain in any way?"

"No."

"Did Dave, while in your presence, threaten you with injury?"

"No."

"Did David Hendricks, while in your presence, threaten you with any form of bodily harm?"

"No."

"Did Dave Hendricks leave any marks or bruises or scratches or physical signs of damage or trauma to your person?"

"No."

"Did Dave Hendricks physically restrain you in any way?"

"No."

"Did Dave Hendricks restrict your physical movements in any way?"

"The back brace was a little restricting, and I couldn't bend over."

"Okay. Other than that, did he physically restrict your motion in any way?"

"No."

Jennings continued the line of questioning for several minutes, asking the young woman if Hendricks made any effort to keep her from leaving, whether she made any effort to get away from him, whether she was offended by his conduct in any way. The answer, each time, was no.

"Was there at any time, either in connection with these fitting contacts or modeling photography sessions, any sexual relations of any kind between you and Dave Hendricks?"

"No."

"Did Dave Hendricks ever ask you to have sexual relations with him in any way?"

"No."

"Did Dave Hendricks ever ask you to meet him for a drink?"

"No."

Perhaps without knowing it, the defense had helped the prosecution make its point: that in the summer of 1981, with a good-looking young woman, David Hendricks had been very business-like. A perfect gentleman. A demeanor prosecutors would try to show gradually changed.

A few months before that, a modeling agency had given Diana Payne, then nineteen years old, a fitting and photography job for Hendricks. She testified that Hendricks wanted to arrange a fitting session at his office for either early some morning or some evening.

"We arrived at seven in the morning. My mother and I walked in. I introduced her to Mr. Hendricks. Then he took us to his fitting room and instructed me to disrobe, and—"

"How were you dressed at the time?" Dozier interrupted.

"I was wearing a blouse and skirt."

"Okay. Go ahead. What happened next?"

"He instructed me to disrobe down to my bra and panties, which I did, and he left the room while I disrobed. My mother stayed."

"Did you understand when you arrived for the session that you were going to be fitted in bra and panties?"

"Yes."

"What happened next?"

"I disrobed, then Mr. Hendricks came back in the room and was assembling materials together to make a brace. Then he started to get the mixture together to make a plasterlike substance that he said you would use as a cast material for perhaps a broken limb—that's the example he used—and told me that it would be necessary to remove my bra. We asked why, and he said the plasterlike substance would stick to the bra material."

"Prior to him telling you it would be necessary for you to remove your bra, had you had any indication from him that would be necessary?"

"No."

"What happened next?"

"He informed my mother that he would like her to leave the room. And she asked why, and he said, 'Because you'll be embarrassed.' She said she would not be embarrassed and then he looked at me and said, 'Well, your daughter will be embarrassed.' And I said, 'I will not be embarrassed.' And then he said he would be embarrassed, so then she left the room and told me she would be right outside."

"Okay."

"And then I proceeded to take off my bra."

"Okay. After you did take off your bra, what were you wearing at that time?"

"I was wearing panties."

"What happened next?"

"He took a Vaseline-like substance and rubbed it from just below my panty line and right below my breasts on my stomach area, and then he applied a plaster-like material that hardened very quickly, and he took that off."

She testified that one evening about five weeks later, pictures were taken of her and another young woman, modeling the brace, at the modeling agency office.

Jennings thought it was time to push the defense contention that all of the models' testimony had been shaped, somehow tailored together when they were summoned, unsuspecting, to the Bloomington Police Department some eleven months earlier when Hendricks was to be arrested.

Jennings handed Diana Payne a copy of a statement she gave police that day at the police station.

"Do you recall what time you gave the statement, or what time you started making the statement?"

"After lunch, around one o'clock."

"Do you recall how you happened to be at the station on December 5th?"

"Yes. A policeman called up and said that he would like me to come in and answer some questions."

"Were you told what time to come in?"

"Yes."

"When you went into the police station on December 5th, did you know that David Hendricks was a suspect in the murder case?"

Dozier stood up. "Your Honor, I'm going to object. I think that calls for a conclusion. It's also irrelevant."

"You're overruled," Judge Baner said. "It's a yes or no question, ma'am. Did you know Mr. Hendricks was a suspect when you made your written statement?"

"Yes."

Jennings pressed on. "Did you know, when you went into the police station, whether or not David Hendricks would be present there?"

"Same objection," said Dozier.

"What's the objection this time, Mr. Dozier?" asked the judge.

"Relevance."

"Sustained."

Jennings asked to argue the issue. Judge Baner sent the jury and witness from the courtroom.

Jennings said Payne and the other young women had been asked to be at the police station so Hendricks could be "exhibited" to them. He said Payne's testimony "would lead a reasonable person to the conclusion that there was, in fact, attempts to sabotage or manipulate her attitude with respect to description and characterizations of the subject."

Judge Baner said he was unaware of any case law that addressed the issue.

Jennings responded that this was the first time in twenty years that he had seen a case where many of the witnesses were asked to give statements at the same time and place where the defendant was arrested and taken into custody. He said twenty-nine days elapsed between the murders and the day the women gave their statements, that they were there for no legitimate purpose, and that the jury was entitled to know it was no coincidence.

Judge Baner ruled that the information could not be presented to the jury, but he would allow the defense to present the information outside the presence of the jury. As part of the transcript of the case, it could be the basis of an appeal to a higher court. With the jury still out of the courtroom, Jennings proceeded.

Diana Payne told the court that there were about eight young women giving statements to several different policemen when she saw Hendricks shortly after his arrest. "He came in in handcuffs, looked at us very briefly and was put in a room by himself for a few minutes, and then they opened the door and took him out of the room."

"And was there any explanation made as to why he was brought into the room where you and the other girls were?"

"I believe a policeman just said that he was being arrested."

"Okay. For what?"

"He didn't say. He just said he was being arrested."

"Did you know for what at that time?"

"I assumed it was in relation to his wife and children."

It was Dozier's turn to ask the questions. He had only one.

"Miss Payne, to the best of your knowledge, has anyone from the McLean County State's Attorney's Office or the Bloomington Police Department ever tried to influence you in giving any testimony or making any statement about Mr. Hendricks or the Hendricks case that was untruthful?"

"No, not at all."

"No further questions."

With jurors again present, Cindy Baird Segobiano testified that she was employed as a model and instructor at a Bloomington modeling agency in 1982 when Hendricks visited the agency office to arrange for some young women to model braces and artificial limbs for a catalog he was planning. She and Diana Payne were assigned the job. They were directed to wear dark leotards and tights for the fitting and photo sessions. Segobiano said her fitting session occurred one afternoon at Hendricks's office.

"I was directed into a private room, and I took off my slacks and sweater and had my leotard and tights underneath, and Mr. Hendricks took measurements."

"Can you be more specific as to how he went about taking these measurements?" Dozier asked.

"He used a tape measure, and he took measurements of my leg, length of my arm, circumference of my waist, my hips, my thighs, and diagonally across my chest. And then he could not get a close enough fitting for what he needed, what he needed to make that brace, so he asked me to remove everything except my bra and panties. He gave me a gown from his office to put on, and he left the room while I changed. He came back and remeasured."

"You say he could not get a close enough measurement. How did you know that?"

"Because he told me. He told me he could not get a close enough measurement in the leotard and tights."

"And so you took off the leotard and tights."

"Yes. He left the room, and I took off my leotard and tights and put on a gown that he had given me, comparable to a doctor's office gown."

"And at that time you were wearing what?"

"Bra, panties, and gown and socks."

"What happened next?"

"Mr. Hendricks measured the same points, and clearly in my mind I remember being nervous because it wasn't exactly what I expected, and I was holding myself."

Defense counsel Jennings objected, and Judge Baner sustained the objection.

Segobiano went on to testify that after the measurements were taken for a second time, Hendricks had her lie facedown on an examination table. He examined her back and told her she had a straight spine. And then he had her sit in a chair and made a cast of her left leg.

"I just sat in the chair, and he put on a gauzelike material and then a substance on my leg that hardened."

"How long did that take?" Dozier asked.

"Perhaps between twenty minutes and a half hour. After that, I dressed and left."

"At any time while you were there, did you actually see any brace, or were any braces fitted to you or tried on or anything like that?"

"No."

The witness went on to say that at a later photo session at the modeling agency, she did wear a brace over leotards and tights and a sweater-dress.

"Do you know whether or not any of those photographs made at the photography session were made into a brochure?"

"I never saw a brochure of my own pictures or a tear sheet or anything."

"At any time at the photography session did you ever wear a brace that would go on your leg at any time?"

"No, I did not."

"At any time during either the fitting session or the photography session did Mr. Hendricks explain the purpose of the leg cast?"

"No."

Under cross-examination, the young woman said that Hendricks had briefly explained that he made artificial limbs and braces. But Jennings didn't inquire whether Hendricks had indicated he was conducting research for a new product.

Also in the early spring of 1981, Kathy Harper, a young mother, grocery store cashier, and part-time model, was hired by Hendricks for a modeling session. A friend had told the attractive blond that Hendricks had seen her photo composite and was interested in having her pose for some pictures for his brochure. She had called Hendricks and arranged for a fitting session at his office late the next afternoon.

"Who was present when you arrived?" Dozier asked the new witness.

"His receptionist was in the lobby, and he was in one of the back rooms." Harper said she was wearing a blouse and slacks and that he asked her to strip down to her panties.

"I asked him if the shoot would be done with clothes on, and he said yes, and I said, well, I didn't see any point in taking the blouse off if it was going to be done with clothes on. He said he wanted the brace to be fitted tight enough that it would look right, you know, through the session. So I went ahead and disrobed my blouse."

"Did you take off your bra or your slacks?"

"No, I didn't. No, later on through the session, he stated that he thought the pants—"

"Let's go in order down the line. What happened next after you took off your blouse?"

"He took the brace out of a box and he began to fit it to me. He put the brace on me, held it up to my chest, held it up to the front of me, and began marking with a pen where the ends of the brace met. And then he strapped it around me."

"All right. Was it necessary for you to adjust or remove any other items of clothing in order for these measurements to be made?"

"Mr. Hendricks felt like it was necessary that I unzip my pants. He felt like they came too high. So I did."

"Okay. Any other items of your clothing have to be adjusted?"

"No."

After the brace fitting, she said, they discussed what Hendricks wanted her to wear and how she should fix her hair and makeup for the photo session.

"He was impressed with the way that I was so thin after having two children and inquired about if I had any type of relationship going with anybody at this time."

"Was that the word he used, relationship, or do you recall?"

"No, he just referred to it as 'Do you have a boyfriend?' He wanted to know if I had a boyfriend."

Under cross-examination by Jennings, the witness said that as far as she knew, Hendricks's receptionist was in the building the entire time she was being fitted for the brace.

"When Mr. Hendricks was making the marks on your person that you have described for the jury and for Mr. Dozier, do you recall whether or not he was taking any notes or writing anything down?"

"It seems like he was writing something."

Jennings then went through a list of questions about whether Harper had been physically harmed or threatened by Hendricks. The answer each time was no.

The jury was then excused, and Jennings questioned the witness about her presence at the police station the afternoon Hendricks was arrested.

"You indicated when you saw him, he was brought into the room where you were, is that correct?"

"Yes."

"Did that have an effect or an impact on you, Miss Harper?"

The woman didn't answer right away. She fought to keep her composure. And then, through a flood of tears, she said, "It was unexpected."

"Okay. How did you react to that?"

The woman was still crying.

"If you need some time—you want to stop for a few minutes and compose yourself, Miss Harper? You're welcome to do that."

"Do you want to take a brief break, ma'am?" Judge Baner asked.

There was a brief recess.

When she returned to the stand, Dozier asked her whether

anyone from the police department or state's attorney's office had tried to influence her to tell anything but the truth that day at the police department. She, like the other women before her, answered no.

Dawn Rueger was sixteen years old when she modeled for Hendricks in February of 1982. Her father had fabricated the CASH Brace for Hendricks before Hendricks moved the manufacturing to Ralph Storrs's plant in Kankakee. Hendricks had asked Dawn's father, Terry, whether his daughter would be interested in modeling the brace. A brace fitting session took place in the Rueger home. Dawn's mother was present.

"My brother was upstairs in his room."

"Okay," Dozier continued. "How were you dressed for the fitting session?"

"I had on underwear and a bra and a robe over that."

"Please describe in as much detail, as you can recall now, what took place at the fitting session."

"He just had the back braces with him, and he put them on and measured them, made sure they fit right, and that was basically about it. He wrote down the measurements." She said he fitted four or five braces to her. "From what I can remember, he just put them on, made marks, and adjusted the braces."

"What kind of marks? What did he use to mark them with? Where did he mark you?"

"On the front area and in the back. I can't really remember, but I guess he used a marker or something."

"Okay. At any time during the fitting process, did you remove any of the three items of clothing that you've told us about?"

"No."

"At any time, did you have to adjust any of the items of clothing in order for him to make marks or fit?"

"Yes."

"In what way?"

"I had to lift up my bra a bit so he could adjust one of the braces."

"Okay. How long, if you recall, did the fitting session take?"

"Approximately a half hour to forty-five minutes."

She, too, identified an advertising piece that contained two pictures of her wearing the brace. The pictures, she said, were taken by Hendricks in the basement of his home about a week after the fitting session. She said Hendricks's wife, son, and a daughter watched the photo session. It was her first job as a model. She wore her mother's light blue leotard and tights.

The next witness was Penny Peavler. She testified that she had met Hendricks in July of 1983. She said she was walking alone to a city swimming pool, wearing a swimsuit and short shorts when she saw Hendricks's car circle the block and then stop.

"He asked me my name, and I told him my name was Penny Peavler. He told me that he worked for CASH, his business, and then he asked me if, well, he told me he was looking for models to model for his business, and he asked me if I'd like to be one, and then he asked me how old I was, and I said I was sixteen. And then he gave me his business card, and he said that I'd have to make sure it was all right with my parents and talk to them about it."

Jennings cross-examined.

"You did, in fact, call Mr. Hendricks's place of business about the modeling?"

"No, sir, I didn't. My mother did."

Dozier brought Peavler's mother to the stand. But before she could testify, Jennings asked to address the court without the jury present. After the jurors left the courtroom, Jennings asked the judge to bar the mother's testimony because it would be more prejudicial than relevant.

Dozier argued that the mother would testify that she was upset that her daughter was approached on the street and that she called him at his home to tell him so. She would testify, Dozier said, that Hendricks wouldn't discuss his conduct with her and said that it didn't matter anyway because he had hired another model.

Judge Baner allowed the defense motion and barred the mother's testimony. Dozier moved on to the next model.

Nancy Jarrett testified that Hendricks appeared at her apartment door early one weekday evening in the summer of 1983 to say that he was looking for a model. She had been doing some part-time modeling on a free-lance basis.

"Prior to that time," Dozier asked, "had you had any contact with him in any way, by telephone or through intermediaries or anything else?"

"No."

"Did you have any kind of appointment with him when he came to your door that evening?"

"No."

Jarrett said that she was just headed out the door for a long-distance bike ride when Hendricks showed up. "He said he wanted to do the fitting that night and asked if I would be back later. I said between seven-thirty and eight. He asked if he could come back to the house then and I said yes. He said he needed to fit the back brace before he could do the photography work."

"Were there any further explanations of what was involved in the fitting?"

"No, he didn't explain the fitting. I just asked him about the business then, like do you sell the brace here in town? He said no, a lot of the business was done overseas. He then showed me a picture of the last brochure that had Kathy Harper in it and Echo. I knew those two. He said he would come back later."

The young woman said Hendricks was waiting for her when she returned from her bike ride at 8 P.M.

"He asked me if I wanted to take a shower because I had been biking. And I said no."

"How were you dressed at that time?"

"I had a legatard and shorts on."

"After you said no to taking a shower, what happened next?"

"He said that he could go ahead and do the fitting but that he would need me without a bra and panties. I said, I prefer to do it in the legatard."

"Prior to that moment, had there been any conversation between you and him about how you would have to be dressed for the fitting?"

"No. He just said that in order to do the measuring, he couldn't get the markings and stuff with the legatard. I said, 'Let's go ahead and try it with the legatards. I feel more comfortable with a legatard on.' That's the way he started out with the measuring. He said, 'We need to move the legatard down because I need to make marks underneath your breasts where the brace would be.'"

"Okay. And what did you do then?"

"I went ahead and lowered them because he came off, you know, professional. Like this was the way it had to be done. I never had done a brace before. So we had a conversation, and I felt like he knew what he was doing. So I went ahead and lowered it to just below the stomach and so I was there with no bra."

"Okay. What happened next?"

"He began to mark with the brace. He had it up against me and he touched my breast and marked underneath the breast with a felt-tip marker."

Jarrett said the measuring and marking took ten or fifteen minutes.

"During the time when he made the marks around your breast area, did he touch any part of your breast?"

"Yes, he did. The lower part. The brace is kind of flat. And he just kind of scooted up and touched the boobs from underneath."

There was a slight rustle. One wondered when the last time the word "boobs" had been used in a courtroom. But State's Attorney Dozier had either missed it or was unaffected. He charged on.

"Did he touch you with his hands or just the brace then?"

"Both his hands and the brace."

"What part of his hand did he touch your breast with?"

"Probably with the inside palm."

The witness said Hendricks had her pull the legatard back up and then took an instant photo of her holding the brace against herself.

"He said he needed me to go out and purchase a tight-fitting blue leotard that crossed over in the front. He did specifically say, 'I do not want you to wear a bra or legatards through the photography work.' At that time I had a very dark tan. And he said he really liked the dark tan as opposed to having a pair of hose on."

"Did anything else occur at that fitting session?"

"No."

"During the fitting, the actual marking session, he did walk over and close the drapes in your apartment?"

"Yes."

"Did you request him to do that?"

"No, I did not."

"After that was over, did you happen to see Mr. Hendricks again?"

"No. He called me the next day. He wanted me to go out and purchase the legatard that day, and he wanted to come over and pick it up. He planned to take it over to the photographer and pin it up on a board to see what the color would look like."

The woman said that a photo session occurred one evening about a week later at a photo studio. About a dozen pictures were taken with the brace on.

Jarrett testified that she called CASH Manufacturing the day after the photo session and talked with Hendricks's secretary.

"Why did you call?" Dozier asked.

"To find out—" Jennings cut her off.

"I'm going to object, Judge. Why should she be allowed to

testify about this if she never talked to the defendant?"

Judge Baner shifted his gaze. "Mr. Dozier?"

"Well, I believe it's relevant to show the witness's state of mind at that time. I think there's a real question about what was occurring at the fitting and photography sessions. And it's an issue in this trial. And I think that her testimony about why she called the next day is relevant to that issue."

Judge Baner sent the jury from the courtroom. Dozier continued.

"Miss Jarrett, would you tell us why you tried to contact Mr. Hendricks the day after the fitting session?"

"To find out more about the company, how stable it was. I had not heard of it. And since I lived in Bloomington, I wanted to find out a little bit more about it."

"Was there a reason why you were curious about the company?"

"I was kind of up in the air on why the fitting was not done at the office as opposed to my apartment."

"And why were you up in the air about that?"

"I guess I was having second thoughts about the fitting, how it was done."

"And what kind of concerns did you have about how it was done?"

"I was wondering if, you know, I needed to be exposed like I was, if the brace just could have been fitted on me."

Dozier turned to the judge. "That's the nature of the statement, Your Honor, that I wanted her to testify to."

Judge Baner ruled the jury could not hear the testimony.

With the jury back in the box, Dozier resumed.

"Miss Jarrett, were you paid for the modeling session?"

"Yes. I was paid the same night the photography work was done. I left the photography work, and he said he would send me the check in the mail. I went home. I was beginning to take my makeup off and get ready to go to bed. And there was a knock at the door. It was Mr. Hendricks. He decided to bring the check to my house and pay me."

"What time was that?"

"Approximately nine-thirty."

In cross-examination, Jennings asked Jarrett whether anyone came to her apartment during the fitting session with Hendricks.

"Yes, my two sisters."

"And do you recall why they were there?"

"To visit."

"Were you expecting them?"

"No, they just dropped in."

"Do you recall how long they were there?"

"Maybe ten minutes. Not very long."

"Did you ask them to leave, or did they have to leave on their own?"

"They had to leave on their own."

"Did you ask them, either one of them, to stay while the fitting session and measuring was going on?"

"No."

"Ms. Jarrett, do you recall at the photography session what your wearing apparel was?"

"Yes, a blue legatard."

"And were you asked as far as the photography session is concerned to do that shoot without an undergarment, braless?"

"Yes."

"Okay. And did you in fact do that shoot without an undergarment and in a braless manner?"

"Yes."

"Okay. And you indicated that Mr. Hendricks brought your pay by that same evening after the photography session. How long were you in his company at that time?"

"Maybe two or three minutes. He just handed it over to me at the door."

"Then left?"

"Then left."

Jarrett said that she got angry with Hendricks at one point. Jennings asked her to explain.

"When I got the prints back and I was over at his office looking at them, Mr. Hendricks, at that time, had looked at the prints and said that I had too much makeup on and my hair wasn't right, that he decided not to use me. And I was angry because he had looked down the camera and saw how the pictures were going to come out."

"I need to ask you several questions for the record. And I do not ask these questions to offend you," Jennings said. "My apologies if they appear offensive. But did David Hendricks ever on the four occasions that you had contact with him or at any other time and place ever have sexual relations with you?"

"No."

"Did he ever ask you to have sexual relations with him?"

"No."

"Did David ever ask you to meet him some place intimate or at some location alone to have a drink or something of that nature?"

"No."

"I need to ask you in connection with a possible later witness, not to offend you, have you ever as a professional model done any nude photography work?"

"No, I have not."

With the jury out of the courtroom, Jennings had Jarrett explain the circumstances of her being at the Bloomington Police Department the afternoon Hendricks was arrested.

She said she reported to the police department on the afternoon of December 5 as requested and found about ten other young women present. She said that a policeman informed them as a group that Hendricks would be coming in and that officers would be taking their statements.

"And do you recall him saying, if anything, the reason for Mr. Hendricks being there?" Jennings asked.

"He was being arrested for murder."

She said she and Kathy Harper were in a room with an officer when Hendricks was brought through. "We were sitting in a chair giving our statements. And they brought Mr. Hendricks through with an officer on each side of him. They just brought him through the room and out the door."

"Do you recall whether or not he was handcuffed?"

"I don't remember."

"Was there any comment or any statements made either by Mr. Hendricks or by the officers accompanying him or by the officer who was taking your and Kathy's statement?"

"The officer just wanted to see if Mr. Hendricks had made any kind of facial expression to us when we looked at him. We just said no."

"Were you and Kathy interviewed by the same officer?"

"Yes."

"Did you hear her statement?"

"No. She heard mine."

"Did you sit through any portion of hers?"

"Only the very first part."

When it was his turn to cross-examine, Dozier asked what had now become a standard question. "At any time that you were at the

Bloomington Police Department on that day, December 5th, 1983, did anyone from the Bloomington Police Department or the state's attorney's office or anyone connected with law enforcement at any time attempt to influence you to say something about Mr. Hendricks or put anything in a statement that wasn't the absolute truth?"

"No, they did not."

"At any time, did Kathy Harper attempt to influence you to say anything about Mr. Hendricks that was not the truth?"

"No, she did not."

Lee Ann Wilmoth, an insurance company secretary and part-time model with long blond hair, was the next prosecution witness. She said that about eight-thirty one night in early August Hendricks unexpectedly had shown up at her apartment. She said she had heard of him from another model.

"He introduced himself and showed me his business card. He told me who gave him my name and showed me a pamphlet of a girl that had done some modeling. I knew the girl, so I let him in. We sat down and he showed me all the information that he had about his business and talked about what he wanted me to do. The job."

"Could you describe what he specifically said about the job?" Dozier asked.

"Well, he wanted to take pictures of me wearing the brace. And he said he would have to measure me for the brace and that all I could wear is underpants. He asked if that made me uncomfortable. I said yes. I told him I was going to wear my bathing suit bottoms instead. He said that would be okay. And he asked me if I wanted to do it then or the next day. I said I wanted to do it then and just get it over with."

She said Hendricks left for about ten minutes and returned with the brace. In the meantime she put on her swimsuit bottoms and a long bathrobe. The measurement session would take place in the living room.

"He had a piece of paper that he was going to write the measurements on. He got the brace out and showed me what it was and then he went ahead and started measuring me. I had the bathrobe on backwards. He opened it and made marks on my back."

"Why did you have the bathrobe on backwards?"

"So my front was covered."

"But had you and he discussed how you should wear the bathrobe?"

"Yeah. He told me I could put it on that way."

Wilmoth testified that he measured her back, and then, at Hendricks's request, she went into a bedroom, reversed the bathrobe so it would open in the front, and returned to the living room.

"He pulled it aside on the shoulder and made marks on my ribs and on my hip bones. We were talking about what I was going to wear. He was telling me I could go out and buy a leotard. We were making all kinds of general conversation. And I told him that I had a leotard and he wanted to see it. So I went back into my bedroom and put my leotard on."

"Can you describe the leotard?"

"It was a one-piece purple color and just had straps, V neck, like a bathing suit. Top of the legs clear up to here." The attractive blond rose slightly in her seat in the witness box to indicate the top of her legs.

"All right. What happened after you came back out?"

"Well, he was looking over the measurements and he started telling me that I had a tilted pelvis or asymmetric frame or something just talking about bone structure. I told him that a doctor had told me that I had a tilted pelvis. And we just made conversation about that. And I told him that I thought I had a rib out of place. And I kind of pointed at it."

"Would you exhibit how you did that?"

The young woman arched her back and placed her thumb and two fingers against a rib just under her left breast.

"I just went like that."

"Okay. Did that involve exposing your breasts?"

"No, I had my bodysuit on."

"Okay. What happened then?"

"Then he said he had to come over and see, so he came over and touched my ribs."

"Would you explain the manner and place that he touched you?"

"He started at the bottom and just was kind of counting ribs and went from the bottom of my rib cage clear up to my shoulder bone."

"And what parts of the body then did that involve him touching?"

"All the way up my left side."

"Can you be more specific?"

"My breast."

"You still had your bodysuit on?"

"Yes."

"Could you explain in detail how this touching occurred, what part of his hand touched what part of you?"

"Just his fingers going across my ribs, up the ribs as if to count them."

"Did he go around your breast or over it?"

"No, just straight up. His hand went straight up my rib cage."

"What did you do?"

"It was so fast, I just stood there."

"And then what happened?"

"And then he stepped back and we just, you know, continued to make conversation. And I don't remember how we got on to it, but then he said he had to check something else out. So he said that I had to lay down to do that. I trusted him, so I said okay and went and laid down on my stomach."

"Where did you lay down?"

"On my bed."

"And then what happened?"

"Then he started going up my back, the rib cage in my back, on both sides. And then he kind of started massaging my back and up my shoulders."

"How long did that go on?"

"Thirty seconds to a minute. Not very long."

"What happened next?"

"Well, then he asked me to turn over, and he started to do the same thing on the front."

"And could you describe specifically what he did on the front?"

"Taking his fingers up the rib cage towards my breasts."

"Can you explain what parts of your body he touched when he was doing that?"

"Just my ribs and started up towards my breasts."

"How close did he get? Did he actually touch them?"

"Yes."

"What parts of your breast did he touch?"

"All of them. Just took his hand and touched me."

"Were you still wearing the bodysuit you talked about?"

"Yes."

"Were you wearing any bra underneath that?"

"I don't think so. I don't remember. I don't think I was because I didn't have one on to start with."

"What happened next?"

"Then he . . . " The young woman paused and looked at Hendricks. "Then he got close to my face and bent down. I thought he was going to kiss me, so I pushed him away and told him he had to leave."

Jennings was on his feet. "Judge, I'm going to object to what she thought and ask it be stricken."

"Overruled."

"How close to your face did he get?" Dozier continued.

"I don't know. Maybe about that far," she said as she held her two index fingers about six inches apart.

"With what part of his body?"

"With his face."

"And how did you push him away?"

"My hands on his shoulders."

"And what did you say to him at that time?"

"I said, 'I think you ought to leave.' "

"What did he do or say next?"

"He stepped back and he looked at me and said, 'I thought that's what you wanted. I'm sorry.' And I said, 'No. No, it's not.' "

"Did he say anything then or do anything else?"

"Yeah. He backed away and said he was sorry and that was about it."

"Do you remember anything else that he said at that time?"

The witness silently shook her head.

"What happened immediately after that?"

"Then I got up and put my bathrobe back on, and he went in and started gathering up all his stuff and kept apologizing. I got everything that he'd brought over and packed it all up. He was telling me what time he wanted me to show up for the photography session and talking more about that, trying to change the subject. I said okay, okay. And he said he would call me, and I said okay. And he went out the door."

"Did you agree to do the photography session?"

"Yes."

"Why did you do that?"

"Because it was at a studio and I didn't think I'd have to be alone."

Jennings spoke up. "I object to her reasons and move to strike."

"Sustained," said the judge. "Mr. Dozier."

"How long did this session take? How long was he at your apartment that evening from the time he arrived with the brace until the time he left?"

"I think about an hour and a half."

"When did you next see or hear from Mr. Hendricks?"

"As soon as he left. A few minutes later he came back and said he thought he left his watch. I looked around and told him I didn't see it. He said he must have left it in his office. And he left again. Then a few minutes after that, he called me and asked me if I would still do the job and apologized again. I said that was okay and yes, I would still do it. I just wanted to forget it, and I would still do the job."

Wilmoth said Hendricks called about a week later to schedule a photo session. She said the session occurred about a week after that at a photo studio. The entire session, including the brace fitting, she testified, lasted only fifteen minutes.

In cross-examination, Jennings asked how the young woman was paid for the modeling.

"After the photography session, he said he forgot his checkbook. He left it in his office. He asked me to come back to his office. So I went back to the office and then he wrote me out a check."

"Was that during business hours?"

"No."

"Do you recall if anything occurred other than him giving you the check?"

"He made conversation about my car, and that was all I can remember."

Of all the young women who would testify, Susan Ryburn came closest to resembling a high-fashion model. Hendricks looked away to the courtroom clock on the wall as the striking brunette walked to the witness stand.

In a soft voice, Ryburn testified that she was now employed as a hostess in a Chicago restaurant and as a part-time model. She said she lived in Bloomington in October of 1983 when the owner of a photo studio called to ask her to model Hendricks's back brace for a photo session. She agreed. It would be her first modeling job. She was told to report to Hendricks's office at seven o'clock that night for a fitting session.

"We got out of the car and walked up. We weren't sure which building it was because it was all dark. And my husband went around the side of the building and looked for the door. And then he came back around front and the door was opened then, so we knew which way to go."

Murphy was asking the questions now.

"When you indicate that the door was open at that time, did you have occasion then to see Mr. Hendricks?"

"Yes. He was opening the door."

"Could you describe Mr. Hendricks as you saw him that particular evening?"

"I'm going to object, Judge," Jennings said.

"Physical appearance?" the judge asked. "Is that what you're asking for, Mr. Murphy?"

"Yes."

"Overruled."

"Please." Murphy motioned Ryburn to continue.

"He had on a dark green Polo-type shirt and tan pants. His hair was freshly combed."

Jennings spoke up again. "I'm going to object to characterization, Judge."

"Overruled."

"Please proceed," said Murphy.

"And he had a very strong amount of cologne on."

This time Jennings's voice was louder. "I'm going to object, Judge. Characterizations. Move to strike."

"Overruled."

"Was there anything else?" Murphy asked.

"When I said, 'This is my husband,' his mouth dropped open."

"I am going to object and move to strike, Judge," Jennings said in a still louder and more insistent voice.

Once again, after some argument outside the jury's presence and after a short recess to check some case law, Judge Baner overruled the defense objections.

When the jury had returned to the courtroom, Ryburn said that she and her husband accompanied Hendricks to a small room in his office.

"Mr. Hendricks asked me if I had brought my modeling portfolio with me."

"What did you say?"

"I said no, I did not. He said I should always bring my portfolio with me when I was auditioning or applying for a modeling job. Then Mr. Hendricks explained what it was that I was coming to audition for, to model the back brace. And he said how it worked and what it was."

"Did he actually show you one?"

"Not at that time, no."

"After he explained to you about the brace itself, what was next done or said? What happened?"

"He told me that he thought I would be too tall to model his brace. He left the room and came back with one of the braces."

She said he held up the back to her body and said her height of five feet and eleven inches was too much for the brace to accommodate. "He wasn't going to use me as a model because he thought I was too tall. And then we had a little further conversation. He told us about the other braces and artificial limbs and things that he developed for about another ten, fifteen minutes. And then we said we had to go and we left."

"Did you have any further contact with Mr. Hendricks at all after that?"

"No, I did not."

In cross-examination, Jennings zeroed in on Ryburn's description of Hendricks—the smell of cologne, his freshly combed hair.

"Do you recall whether Mr. Hendricks said anything to you about his having been jogging that day or that evening?"

"No."

"Did he say anything to your husband about his having been jogging or running that evening?"

"Not that I know of."

"Do you recall whether or not he told you or said anything to you concerning the fact that he had turned down or rejected another model as being too tall within the last few months?"

"No, I don't believe he said anything like that."

The prosecution's next witness was Susan Ryburn's husband. Like his wife, Stanley Ryburn appeared to be fashion-conscious. He wore a stylish sports coat and narrow tie, loosely knotted, against a dark shirt. Murphy asked Ryburn to describe the Ryburns' visit to Hendricks's office.

"When we got there, the place was dim. There were no front lights on, so we checked around the side of the building to see if any other lights were lit. Then I stepped around to the front door, and Mr. Hendricks answered the door. He asked me what I was doing there."

"What did you say, if anything?" Murphy asked.

"At that time, Susan approached and she said, 'This is my husband. I'm here for a seven o'clock appointment,' at which time his mouth dropped completely open."

That brought Jennings to his feet.

"I'm going to again object, Judge. The man is volunteering information and characterizing and drawing conclusions as to conduct. Move to strike."

"Overruled."

If Susan Ryburn was the image of a sophisticated and educated young woman, Tammy Ledbetter was nearly the opposite.

She was attractive enough, curly brown hair framing her twenty-year-old face. But she appeared to be only moments past her bubble-gum–chewing days. And as she described her encounter with Hendricks in October of 1983, she gave the impression of a young woman who grew up too fast and now amazingly, implausibly, found herself far from her Phoenix, Arizona, home, a witness in the trial of an accused ax murderer.

Ledbetter said she was employed as a cocktail waitress and had been doing part-time modeling since she was fourteen. She testified that her agent had called her with instructions to meet Hendricks at his room in the Phoenix Hyatt Hotel at 9 P.M. to be fitted for a back brace she would model in a trade show the following two days. Her grandmother accompanied Ledbetter that night, but Hendricks couldn't be found. She returned alone to the Hyatt the next morning and met Hendricks in his room.

She removed a long-sleeved red blouse to show Hendricks the bodysuit she was wearing.

"And he didn't like that, so I showed him my other one. And then I went into the bathroom to try it on."

"You changed into your second one?"

"Right. And no skirt on after that. Just my bodysuit and leotard."

"Did you have any underclothing on?"

"I had on a bra."

"What happened then after you came out in this second outfit?"

"He said that one would be all right. And then he tried on the brace I was going to wear. He said that it didn't quite fit right. And he fiddled around with it and tried to work with it. And then he told me he needed to make markings to fit me for the brace. Then he said I needed to remove my bodysuit to make the markings."

"What did you say or do?"

"Then I did that."

"Where did you do that?"

"In the bathroom."

"You came back out and what were you wearing?"

The witness's answers came slowly.

"A bra and my leotards."

"The bottoms?"

Another pause.

"Right."

"Okay. What happened next?"

"Then he put the brace on again and told me that I needed to remove my bra because he couldn't make the right markings with it on."

"What did you do next?"

"I asked him why I needed to remove my bra. That's when he told me that he needed to fit it, and don't be embarrassed or anything because he was a doctor, and he had seen many other people before so it wouldn't make a big difference."

"What happened then?"

"Then I removed my bra, and I had my shirt and my blouse and my bra in front of me. And then he told me to raise my arms out like this in front of me."

"And did you do that?"

"Yes."

"So then you had nothing on from the waist up?"

"No."

"And you had your arms out to your sides?"

"Yes."

"What happened next?"

"Then he held the brace up in front of me and made markings with his pen. Little dots, I think, and crosses."

"On where? Where on your body?"

The young women gestured as she said, "It was right here, one here, and one here." Defense attorney Long spoke up.

"Would you stand up and point, ma'am? I can't see from where I'm seated here."

Ledbetter stood. "Right here," she said, as she pointed below her breast, "and right below right where my hip bones are."

"What happened after he made those marks?" Dozier asked.

"He put the brace up against me where the markings were. Then he told me it still wouldn't fit me and he would like to crack my back."

"What did you say to that?"

"I told him no, I didn't want him to crack my back because I have scoliosis and that really hurts. I remember going to the doctor and having that done and it hurt me. He said that it wouldn't hurt me. But I still refused. And he said he would give me a massage and that would make me fit the back brace. He said that it would

relax my muscles and that he could see my curvature and it would make the back brace fit."

"Okay. So what happened after he said that?"

"He told me to lie on the couch."

"And did you do so?"

"Yeah. Facedown, you know. Straight leg all the way, lying down. That's when he massaged my back."

"And could you explain in detail how he went about massaging your back?"

"He massaged my shoulders and the higher part of my back. And it was with all palms, all hands, and pressing my back to one side."

"About how long did he massage your back?"

"A couple of minutes. Two, three." Her voice trailed off.

"Was there any conversation going on while he was engaging in this?"

Even the jurors had to strain to hear her response when it came a few moments later.

"He asked me if it felt good."

"I'm sorry," Long's voice boomed. "I'm having trouble understanding you."

"He asked me if the massage felt good."

"Thank you."

Dozier continued.

"Do you remember what you replied or if you replied?"

"I think I said yes."

"Then what happened?"

"He told me to lay on my back."

"Did you do that?"

"Yes."

"What happened next?"

"Then he told me to put my arms outward like I had done before, and he massaged my front, my ribs."

"Could you go into detail? What part of his body touched what part of your body during this massage?"

"Both of his hands were massaging my left side, the opposite way he had been doing my back."

"Where did he touch your body?" Dozier asked almost apologetically.

"My whole front. My whole breast, not including my nipple."

"About how long did this go on?"

"I'd say the same length of time. Two or three minutes."

"What occurred next?"

"Then I had mentioned that I thought we were in a hurry, that we needed to hurry because I didn't get to be fitted the night before, that he was in a big rush, and we had to hurry up and get downstairs because the whole convention had already started."

"So you reminded him of that?"

"Yes."

"And then what did he do?"

"Said okay. And then I got dressed, and he had put the brace on one more time."

"What were you wearing when he put the brace on?"

"My bra, my bodysuit, my tights, and my skirt."

"And where did the brace fit in relation to your clothing?"

"On top."

"What did you do down at the convention center that day?"

"I modeled the back brace in his exhibits. And the clients came by and looked at me standing there with the brace on top of all my clothes."

"Had you been hired to model the back brace for a specific length of time?"

"Yes. I was supposed to do part of the morning when I could get there and the whole rest of the afternoon until whenever the exhibit was over, about five o'clock."

"Okay. Did you fulfill that length of time?"

"No, I didn't. I had a break around one-thirty, and I went and made a phone call to my agent. I told him that I wasn't going to be able to finish the job, and I needed a replacement and could they send one. I had told them also that I wasn't going to model two days. I said I was not going to be there the next day either, just not finish the job."

"Why did you not finish the job?"

"Because—well, the whole time in the room when I was being fitted for the brace, I was very uncomfortable about the situation."

"Ob-jeck-shun!" Long bellowed.

"Sustained," the judge quickly responded.

"Did Mr. Hendricks," Dozier continued, "do anything to you up in the room during the fitting that was unpleasant for you?"

"Objection," Long countered.

"Sustained."

"Why did you allow Mr. Hendricks to touch your breast during this fitting procedure when you described the massage?"

"Objection," Long said.

"Overruled."

"Because," Ledbetter answered, "he had told me that he was a doctor and he had studied for years about this. And I felt it was just like I was at a doctor's office, I was with a doctor."

"So what time did you quit the job that day approximately?"

"I'd say after the replacement got there at two o'clock."

"Did you tell Mr. Hendricks why you were leaving?"

"I told him that I had another appointment that I was supposed to be at."

"Was that the truth?"

"No."

"What was the real reason you were leaving?"

Long objected again, and Judge Baner sustained the objection. Dozier ended his examination by having the young woman identify Hendricks in the courtroom.

Now it was Long's turn.

"Miss Ledbetter, if you don't mind, I'll examine you from a standing position because I can't see you sitting here."

The witness looked at the judge. "Me?"

"No," said the judge. "He's going to stand up."

"I'll stand," Long said as he walked toward the witness. "And then when I get tired, you can."

Long moved quickly to the issue of her scoliosis.

"Isn't it a fact, Miss Ledbetter, that when you were trying this back brace on, the reason it wouldn't fit was because of your scoliosis?"

"Could you say that again?"

"Yeah. Isn't it a fact that the reason that Mr. Hendricks had a problem fitting the back brace on you and the reason it wouldn't fit is because of your scoliosis?"

"Your Honor," Dozier interrupted. "That calls for a conclusion, I would think, of a medical nature."

"Sustained."

"Did Mr. Hendricks say to you," Long continued, "that he was having trouble getting the back brace to fit you?"

"Yes, after I had told him."

"Pardon me?"

"After I had told him I had scoliosis, he told me."

"And he had already, by that time, tried to put the brace on you and to fit it. Is that not correct?"

"Yes."

"And, as a matter of fact, he tried to bend the brace even to get it to fit to your body. Isn't that correct?"

"Yes."

"And it still would not fit right, would it?"

"No. He said he had to make the markings."

"In order to get it to fit?"

"Yes."

"And at the time," Long loudly questioned, "that he had to make the markings, you didn't have to undress in front of him, did you?"

"Wait," Ms. Ledbetter said. She paused. "At the time—"

"You undressed to make the markings." Long continued. "You did not have to undress in front of him."

"Yes, I did."

"Didn't you just tell us a moment ago you went into the bathroom to undress?"

"Yes, but then he told me to take off my top and my bra in order to make the markings to fit me."

"Yes, but you had already changed clothes in the bathroom, had you not?"

"Yes, but I had to change again, take them off."

"After you finally got the massage done, isn't it a fact that the massage was always on one side of your body, and that's the side that you have the scoliosis problem?"

"I'm not sure what side has the problem." She paused. "No, as a matter of fact, it wasn't. My lower back is where I have my problem. That's not where he was massaging me."

Long was pacing now.

"When he was massaging you, did you ever ask him to stop massaging you?"

"No, because he told me why he was doing it."

"No," Long said in a complaining voice. "Just did you ever—"

"No."

"—ask him to stop massaging you. You didn't, did you?"

"Uh-uh."

"When he asked you to turn over, you indicated that he massaged you on one side on the front as well. Is that correct?"

"Uh-huh."

"Isn't it a fact that the massage was always confined to one side of your body?"

"I can't remember."

"Do you remember giving a sworn statement in this case to a Ms. Nancy Wilson, a statement that was sworn and subscribed to by you on the 20th day of August, 1984, at 3:40 P.M?"

"Uh-huh."

"Do you remember at that time this question being asked you: 'Did he massage both your left side of your back and your right side of your back?' And you answered no."

"I said my left side of my front."

"I'm sorry. Excuse us for just a minute."

Long walked to the defense table and retrieved a document. He handed it to the clerk, who affixed an identification sticker. Long then gave it to the witness.

"Miss Ledbetter, I'd like to hand you what has been marked as defendant's exhibit V, group exhibit V for identification, and ask you to please take a minute and peruse that exhibit."

Long paused a moment. He looked at members of the jury, giving them a look that seemed to simultaneously say, Aren't I polite—isn't this amazing—we must be patient.

"Is that a sworn statement," Long continued, "made by you and signed under oath on August 20th, 1984?"

"I don't understand. What are you saying that I said?"

"No, no. No, no." Long gave the jurors another glance. "I'll ask—I'll try asking the question and you try answering it. We'll work on that basis for a moment. Is that a signed statement signed by you on August 20th, 1984?"

"Uh-huh. Yes."

"Calling your attention to page 11 of your statement, were you asked this question, and was this answer given by you? 'Question: did he massage both your left side of your back and your right side of your back? Answer: no. Question: what side did he massage? Answer: I think my right. Question: he massaged the right side of your back? Answer: uh-huh. Question: he never touched the left side? Answer: no.' "

Long removed his reading glasses and looked at the witness.

"Were those questions asked you, and were those answers given by you in that sworn statement?"

"Yes. That's what I thought—" Long cut her off.

"No, no. I don't want to know what you thought then. I want to know if those answers were made by you at that time under oath."

"Uh-huh."

"My question to you, is it not a fact, Miss Ledbetter, when he massaged you, he only massaged you on one side of your body?"

"I can't really remember now. I can't remember."

"Okay. And when he finished with your back, you turned over, did you not?"

"Yes."

"And he asked you to turn over, did he not?"

"Uh-huh."

"And did you ever object to turning over?"

"No."

"That is when he massaged the left side of your front. Is that not correct?"

"Right. Uh-huh."

"And only the left side of your front."

"Of my front. Right."

"And he touched your breast."

"Yes."

"During the course of the massage, he touched your breast."

Now the young woman was taking a long time before responding.

"Yes."

"Now." Long walked up to the witness stand and placed his hand on the front edge. "You made a point of telling us on direct examination, Miss Ledbetter, 'exclusive of the nipple.' "

"Uh-huh."

"Why did you say that?"

" 'Cause he had asked me where exactly did he touch you. He touched me everywhere but my nipple."

"Isn't it a fact, Ms. Ledbetter, that when he massaged you, he massaged you under the arm at the axillary region, and the part of the breast he touched was the left side of your breast?"

"No." The answer came quicker this time.

"Have you ever had your breasts checked by any physician to determine whether or not you had a lump?"

"Yes."

"When that happens, isn't it true that a physician massages the entirety of the breast all the way around?"

"Yes, the entire thing. The entire—all of it."

"Yeah. Did Mr. Hendricks massage the entire breast?"

"What part are you including?"

"Whatever you consider entire, Miss Ledbetter. Did he or did he not?"

"Yeah."

"In the same sworn statement that you've just identified for us, on page 12, Miss Ledbetter, do you recall this question being asked to you and this sworn answer being given by you? 'Question: would it be as if a doctor would check for lumps on a breast, how they touch around the breast area? Answer: no, it wasn't like that.' "

"How he massaged me wasn't like that."

" 'Question: was it more explicit? Answer: it was something like that, but not really.' "

That brought Dozier to his feet to object, saying Ledbetter's earlier statement didn't contradict what she was saying now. Judge Baner sustained the objection.

The state's attorney decided he had a few more questions for the young woman. Dozier's approach was decidedly more friendly than Long's.

"Miss Ledbetter, at the time that you took this job with Mr. Hendricks, did you do nude or partially nude modeling?"

"No. Never."

"Why did you wait three months to tell the modeling agency why you left the job?"

"Because I was too embarrassed to tell my agency what had happened because I felt—"

Judge Baner cut her off. "I think that's a sufficient answer for your question, Mr. Dozier."

Long sat in his chair for his re-cross-examination.

"Now, in answer to a question that was just asked you by Mr. Dozier about why you didn't tell the agency, the fact of the matter is, you didn't have contact with the agency for three full months after this job. Isn't that right?"

"No. They had to pay me."

"So you had plenty of opportunities to state what had happened on this job."

"Yes."

With that, Tammy Ledbetter was excused as a witness. She quickly made her way to the women's restroom just outside the courtroom door and promptly vomited.

Prosecutors expected the final two of the twelve models to testify to be the most convincing and the most damaging to Hendricks's case.

Libby Tomlinson, a personnel assistant at a Phoenix-area junior college and a part-time model, had been sent by the modeling agency to Hendricks's hotel room to replace Tammy Ledbetter the afternoon she decided she didn't want the work. As she took her place in the witness box, she appeared attractive but prim, Victorian compared to some of the other young women who had testified.

She wore frameless glasses and a frilly blouse that buttoned at her neck.

Under Dozier's questioning, she testified that at the suggestion of the modeling agency, she wore a leotard, tights, and a wrap-around dance skirt to the modeling job. She said Hendricks explained that she would model a back brace at his booth in the exhibit hall and that he would need to fit the brace on her. Then he asked her to please remove her clothing.

"I said, 'Pardon me?' I said the agency had not said anything about having to remove any clothing for any type of a fitting."

"What did he say?" Dozier asked.

"He said, 'Oh, well. If it makes you feel any better, I am a doctor, and I do this sort of thing all the time.' "

"Okay. Then what happened?"

"I hesitated a little bit longer, but—"

John Long was out of his seat. "I'm going to object to the characterization of her actions. She can testify what she did."

Judge Baner looked at Dozier. "Perhaps you should phrase your question in such a way that elicits what she did, Mr. Dozier."

"What did you do next?"

"I went into the bathroom and removed my leotards and tights and dance skirt."

"What did that leave you wearing?"

"Nothing."

"You had no undergarments on at that time?"

"No, sir."

"Okay. What did you do next?"

"I took one of the towels and wrapped it around me, took a deep breath and went back—"

Long was out of his chair again. "Objection to this characterization for taking a deep breath, and ask that it be stricken unless the testimony be that the towel wouldn't stay up around her without a lung full of air."

"Overruled."

"Okay. And then you went out?" Dozier continued.

"Yes, sir."

"How did you have this towel wrapped around you?"

"I had it—I was holding both ends of it such that my arms were across my chest."

"Just holding it in front of you, up against you?"

"Wrapped completely around me. When I came out of the bathroom, he was standing in front of one of the couches in the room. And he asked me to open the towel so that he could place the brace up against my chest to start making measurements."

"Okay. What, if anything, did you say or do then?"

"I did as he asked. He placed the brace up against me. As I recall, he removed some of the pieces to a higher position or lower position. And then he took it away from me in order to make some adjustments at which time I put the towel back across my front covering myself again."

"And then what happened?"

"After he made those adjustments, I opened my towel again. At this time he took a pen and made a couple of Xs, one on each hip bone, one underneath each breast. And he asked me to turn around, at which time I lowered the towel and draped the towel then fully in front of me, leaving the back open. He felt along my spine with his fingers down towards the buttocks."

"Now, at this point, did you have anything on at all other than the towel?"

"No. No, sir. Nothing other than the towel. He felt along the base of my spine and out to the outer edges of my buttocks. He made a couple of more marks with a pen. He said that I could drop the towel if I wanted to. And I said I did not want to."

"Okay. What happened after that, after he made marks on your back?"

"He went into the bathroom to run some hot water over the polyurethane or foam pieces in order to be able to form them closer to my body. He said that I had a fairly straight spine but that I did have some scoliosis or something along those lines, some word I'm not absolutely sure what it was."

"Had you ever been told that before?"

"No, sir."

"What happened next?"

"He said that he would need to try to correct that temporarily by pushing it—pushing my spine into place. And at that time he asked me to lay down on one of the couches, first on my stomach, which I did, keeping the towel in front of me but exposing my back. And he pressed mainly on my left side—the left side of my spine pushing over to my right."

"About how long were you there laying facedown while this was going on?"

"I would say at most five minutes."

"What happened after that?"

"He asked me to turn over. And then he was going to do some

adjustments from the front at which time I again switched the towel and turned over on my back. And he took his hands and on my rib cage pushed from the right side to the left."

"At any time while he was doing that, did he touch your breasts?"

"No, sir."

"How was the towel arranged around you at that time while you were lying on your back?"

"I believe I just had it . . . it was . . . although it was on my back and I was holding the edges of it, I had it open."

"How much of your body was exposed at that time?"

"All of it."

The witness said that after a few minutes she dressed and modeled the brace over her leotards and tights in the exhibit hall.

"At any time," Dozier asked, "while you were actually modeling the brace for the exhibitors, were you ever required to wear the brace next to your skin?"

"No, sir."

"Were you ever required to expose your breast or any other private parts of your body while you were modeling the brace?"

"No, sir."

"How long did you model the brace that day?"

"I believe it was three hours, from 2 P.M. until 5 P.M."

"What happened after that?"

"Mr. Hendricks wanted me to model his new product, which had swivels at the top and at the bottom. He told me that I would have to be fitted for that brace."

Tomlinson testified that she and Hendricks returned to the hotel room, where she again disrobed, and he fitted her for the swivel brace.

"However, this time he said he didn't have to make too many measurements since he already had his marks on me."

"How long did this second measuring session take?"

"Between twenty and thirty minutes."

The young woman said that she returned to model the swivel brace the next day from 10 A.M. until 5 P.M.

"He said that there was some type of a president's council or reception that was going to be held that evening there in the exhibit hall. He asked if I could come back that evening and again model the brace for approximately two hours for the individuals that would be attending this reception."

"What did you say?"

"I said yes, I was available."

"Okay. What occurred after that?"

"He had asked several questions throughout the day about Phoenix and what it had to offer in the way of sights, landmarks, nice places to see. And I told him some of the nicer places to see, some of the things that were of interest to be seen. And as the afternoon progressed, he asked if I could show him around town."

"Do you remember if anyone else was present other than you and Mr. Hendricks when he asked that?"

"I believe his office manager, Beverly, was there at that time."

"Okay. Would you go ahead and complete the conversation then?"

"I said that I would be more than happy to show them around the town, as is tradition in our family when visitors come to Phoenix and are interested in what's available in the city for sightseeing. And I said yes, I would take them, meaning Mr. Hendricks and Beverly, as I understood it, around the town and show them the sights.

"At five o'clock I did return to my home to get a change of clothing, as Mr. Hendricks suggested, so that when the sightseeing was done, we might stop and get a bite to eat."

"Okay."

"I returned to the exhibit hall shortly before 7 P.M., at which time I met Mr. Hendricks, and we went into the exhibit hall. He placed the back brace on me. We stood around for a little bit and came to the realization that the people who were attending this reception were attending it as a casual, social affair—not as something where individuals would be going through the exhibit hall itself and looking at products. In other words, everyone was in the lounge area, in the refreshment area having hors d'oeuvres and drinks."

"And you and Mr. Hendricks were there with a brace and no customers?"

"Yes, sir. He suggested that since nobody was going to be really looking at products at that time that I go ahead and change and just attend the reception, and then later on we would go out and see the sights of Phoenix."

"All right. What happened next?"

"We went back over to the hotel, and I changed into my dress that I had brought with me. And we went back over to the exhibit hall. We got into a discussion of religion. He said that he had been raised in a very religious home, that he was not part of any particular denomination. We did not really get into a doctrine discussion, but he did say that he was—he had some doubts about his faith. He had done a lot of reading in the scriptures, and that he was not sure that his God was the right God or that his religion was the right religion, the only religion. I said, 'At that point, that is where your faith has to come in.' He said that since he could not come to any conclusions as to whether his faith was right or not, that he really was not practicing his faith, had kind of dropped out of his faith because of his doubts in that area."

"During this time, after you arrived at the exhibit hall and decided not to exhibit and when you went back and changed, was Mrs. Crutcher around?"

"She was there briefly when we first got there. Mr. Hendricks and I had been talking about what was available in Phoenix to be seen. At one point, Mr. Hendricks left the booth space, and I asked Mrs. Crutcher if there would be any problem with me going out showing the sights, having a bite to eat with Mr. Hendricks, that he wasn't going to make any advances on me."

"Did you subsequently then go out to show the sights of the city to Mr. Hendricks?"

"Yes, sir, I did."

"And did Mrs. Crutcher accompany you?"

"No, sir."

Tomlinson told the court that she and Hendricks took his rented car first to the Arizona State University campus at Tempe.

"The conversation had turned toward relationships, and he began speaking about his wife. He said to me, 'Well, I've had—I've had several affairs, and I don't think there's anything wrong with them.' And he said, 'If I told my wife and hurt her, that would be wrong.' And he said, 'I guess you think that's a pretty bad attitude.'"

"Did you reply?"

"Yes, sir. I said, 'I think that's lousy, because in other words what your wife doesn't know doesn't hurt her.' He says, 'Yes.'"

The witness said she and Hendricks continued their drive north into Scottsdale, where they stopped at Jed Nolan's Music Hall, and then drove up Camelback Mountain.

"I took Mr. Hendricks up there—or told him how to get up the mountain—to show him the lights of the city, which is a usual stop in our family's traditional sightseeing tour of Phoenix. We went across the highest road looking at the lights. When we got to a hairpin turn which would have led us back down the mountain, he turned around and went back up to the highest road and stopped on the right side of the road."

"Is there an overlook or a place for cars to park up at that area?"

"No, sir. There is no parking in that area."

"What happened then?"

"He said he wanted to hear the night sounds, so he reached across me and rolled down my window."

"Let me ask you at that time, had you suggested that he make the turn at the hairpin and go back up to the top again?"

"No, sir, I did not."

"Had you suggested that he stop at that location at the top of the mountain again?"

"No, sir."

"Was the engine still running in the car when he pulled over there?"

"No, sir."

"So he reached across and rolled down the window, he said, to hear the night sounds?"

"Yes, sir."

"What happened next?"

"He asked a few questions about some long bright strings of lights, asking what they were, one of which was Camelback Road, one was Indian School Road, the major thoroughfares in Phoenix."

"Then what happened?"

"He put his arm on the back—he put his right arm on the back of the seat."

"Whose seat?"

"It was a bench seat, so it was the seat we were both sitting on."

"Okay. Then what happened?"

"And scooted a little closer to look out the window a little better."

"Which window, the driver's side?"

"My window."

"Then what?"

"He said, 'I probably shouldn't do this but I'm going to anyway,' and he leaned over and tried to give me a kiss on the left cheek, at which point I said, 'Don't try it. Don't even think about—don't even try it.' "

"Then what did he say or do?"

"He backed off for a minute and said, 'But you're so pretty,' and I said, 'I did not bring you up here for this. I brought you up here to see the city lights and that's it.'

"At this point he moved back over to his seat, sat there quietly for a moment, started up the car, and we started back down the mountain. He said—he said, 'I'm calmer now.' I said, 'I did not bring you up here for that kind of activity.' He said, 'I thought you had wanted something like that because you got so quiet.' I said, 'No, sir. I'm sorry if I led you to believe that but that is not the reason why I brought you up here.' "

The witness continued that she and Hendricks drove down the mountain, and by the time they got to the restaurant where they had planned to eat at ten-fifteen, the restaurant no longer had food service. She said that at her suggestion they decided to call it a night.

"We went back to the hotel. The conversation at that time dropped to basically nothing. I had to go back up to his room to pick up my modeling clothes, my leotards, and tights and skirt. As we got into his room, he—and I was going to pick up my clothes, he said, 'Well, I'd like to pay you for showing me the city.' And I said, 'No, no, I don't want any money.' And he was insistent that I take money. And I said, 'No, the agency will pay me.' He said, 'Thank you very much for all the hard work that you've put in and for showing me the city. Since you won't take any payment, just let me give you a hug and say I'm sorry if I offended you.' "

"What did you say or do?"

"I said, 'It's okay. It's all right. It's not necessary.' But he did give me a brief hug. And as I was going out the door, he had stuck his head between the door and the post, where it closed, and he looked at me and he said, 'Well, since you wouldn't—since you wouldn't let me up on the mountain, can I at least fantasize?' And I turned to him and said, 'When I'm gone, you can do whatever you want to.' And I left."

"I have no further questions."

Long began his cross-examination by focusing on what Tomlinson said was her family's tradition of taking people sightseeing in Phoenix.

"And approximately how many times had you shown total strangers around the Phoenix-Scottsdale area?"

"Total strangers? None."

"And how many times—if this was the first time you showed a

stranger around—how many times with people you knew did you show them around the Phoenix-Scottsdale area at ten o'clock at night?"

"None."

"So what we have here is for the first time you showed a total stranger around the Phoenix-Scottsdale area and it was at ten o'clock at night."

"Yes, sir."

"Would you agree with me, Miss Tomlinson, that viewing the sights in Scottsdale and Phoenix at ten o'clock at night is somewhat difficult to do?"

"No, sir."

"Would you agree with me that it's easier to see a building or easier to see sights in the daytime as opposed to ten o'clock at night?"

"No, sir."

Her voice remained calm.

"When you were going out with a total stranger at ten o'clock at night, Mrs. Tomlinson—Miss Tomlinson—to show them the sights, you were prepared for a social evening at that time, were you not?"

"Yes, sir."

"You brought along a change of clothes, in point of fact."

"As requested by Mr. Hendricks, yes, sir."

"And," Long's voice gained in pitch and volume, "you brought a change of clothes to go out sightseeing with a total stranger at ten o'clock at night after you had been measured for braces in this case. Is that not correct?"

"That's true."

"So notwithstanding that you went through this whole procedure that you've told us about, you were not in any type of fear or intimidation or apprehension about going out at ten o'clock at night with a total stranger, socially, to show him the sights, were you?"

"Yes, sir. I had some apprehension."

"But you went."

"Yes, sir."

"Were you forced to go?"

"No, sir."

Long drove home the point that many of the more interesting rock formations on Camelback Mountain are not visible at night.

"With your earlier testimony in mind, is it your testimony that you took a stranger at night, who was not familiar with the location, who was driving a rented car, up a series of sharp hairpin curves, up the side of a mountain where there is no place to stop, no place to park, and no place to pull over, where there are sheer drop-offs, in order to look at a vista of the city?"

"Yes, sir."

"And you felt that while he was trying to control the car, he would be able to look at all the sights that you had laid out before him. Is that correct?"

"Yes, sir."

"Isn't it a fact that you suggested he stop the car in order to get a view of the city?"

"I don't recall that."

"My question is, is it possible then that you in fact requested that he stop the car so that he could get a view of the city from the top of Camelback Mountain?"

"It is possible."

"And when you requested, if it is possible that you requested that he stop the car, at that time, is that when he leaned over and tried to roll the window down?"

"Yes, sir."

"And at that time there was silence between you."

"Yes, sir."

"There was nothing but the city out in front of you, and it was dark, and you could see the twinkling lights of the city off to the southwest."

"That's correct."

"That is when he tried to kiss you on the cheek?"

"Yes, sir."

"And when you told him to back off, he backed off, didn't he?"

"Yes, sir."

"At any time did he use any force?"

"No, sir."

"At any time did he use any coercion?"

"No, sir."

"At any time did he make any threats of any nature whatsoever?"

"No, sir."

"Isn't it a fact, ma'am, that he was responding to the situation into which you had brought him?"

"It's possible."

"When you confronted him with this, did you confront him indignantly?"

" 'Firmly' would be my word."

"And you still planned to go to dinner with him after he had made this advance towards you. Isn't that a fact?"

"Yes, sir."

"And you told the ladies and gentlemen of the jury that he had indicated that he had affairs but didn't want to tell his wife about it because he thought it might hurt her."

"He said it would be wrong to hurt his wife."

"Isn't it a fact that you took him out of your way to show him Phoenix's gay community and a gay bar?"

"That is not true. The route that we were taking passed by a place known as Hot Bods, The Desert Dance Palace, which happens to be a gay bar-discotheque. It was not an out-of-the-way trip."

"Did you take time to point that out to him as one of the sights that you as a family tradition show out-of-town visitors?"

"No, sir. I just mentioned that we do have a gay community in Phoenix, and that was one of their major hangouts."

Long switched gears.

"I would like to go back with you to your testimony that you gave with respect to the manner in which the brace was fitted. Did I understand you to give testimony to the effect that no improper sexual advances were made to you at that time?"

"That is correct."

"Now, I think you indicated something about Mr. Hendricks saying that he was a doctor. Did I understand you to say that?"

"He told me that he was a doctor."

"Did you, in fact, have a conversation with his office manager and ask his office manager whether or not he was a doctor?"

"Yes, I did."

"And were you in fact told that he was not a doctor?"

"No, sir, I was not."

"You were not told that?"

"No, sir, I was not."

Long's cross-examination was over. Dozier rose from his chair.

"Miss Tomlinson, would you tell us what conversation you did have with David's secretary, Mrs. Crutcher, concerning David?"

"At one point, I believe, I said, 'Is he really a doctor?' And her response was, 'If that's what he said.'"

"You had another conversation with her about Mr. Hendricks, did you not, before you left with him that evening?"

"Yes, sir."

"And did you ask her specific questions about what type of person he was?"

"Yes, sir, I did."

"What did she tell you then?"

"She told me that he was an easygoing guy, happily married, and that I would be all right."

"And is that something you relied on then in agreeing to go out and show him the sights of the city that evening?"

"Yes, sir."

"Did you at any time either prior to or during that evening desire to have a sexual relationship with Mr. Hendricks?"

"Absolutely not."

"As far as any intention on your part, did you do anything purposely or intentionally to lead him to believe that you wanted any type of relationship like that?"

"Absolutely not."

"How would you describe the view of the lights of Phoenix at night from the drive up Camelback Mountain?"

"Very nice. Very easy to see. Very expansive."

"Very beautiful?"

"Yes, sir. Very beautiful."

"Can you see the lights of Phoenix from Camelback Mountain in the daytime?"

"You see mainly smog but not necessarily lights."

"That's all I have." Dozier sat down. Long remained in his seat.

"In addition to being very expansive, very bright, very beautiful, these lights of Phoenix," Long asked, "isn't it a fact that they're also very romantic at that point?"

"When you take it in the romantic sense, yes."

"You have now told us that you did all of this upon Mrs. Crutcher's representations and your feelings, having been measured by him already in the motel room in the manner in which you've already told us, that he was a good and honest man, and that you felt safe with him."

"That's correct."

"And all of this took place after you had been measured while holding your towel around yourself, and been marked upon your body, and been massaged as you've testified, and everything else that took place up in that motel room. Isn't that also correct?"

"I do not consider that I was massaged."

"I beg your pardon. I am only—I don't mean to imply anything by that. But you were touched by Mr. Hendricks. Is that not correct?"

"That is correct."

Long had ended his re-cross-examination. Dozier was on his feet again.

"Did you believe him when he said he was a doctor?"

"Yes, sir, I did. Otherwise I would not have taken off my clothing."

"When did you change your mind about Mr. Hendricks in terms of your feelings about him?"

"As he put the moves on me, if I may use that expression, up on Camelback Mountain."

"Nothing further."

"Any additional re-cross?" Judge Baner asked.

"Oh, yes," Long said, still seated at the defense counsel table. "Ms. Tomlinson"—a hint of sarcasm entered Long's voice—"other than him, meaning Mr. Hendricks, putting the moves on you, which I understand consisted of putting his hand over the back of a bench seat, leaning over, and attempting to kiss you on the cheek, were there any other moves he tried to put on you on Camelback Mountain?"

"No, sir."

"And is that what so offended you, Miss Tomlinson?"

"Yes, sir, from a married man."

"Thank you, Miss Tomlinson," said Long.

"Nothing further," said Dozier.

For two and a half days now, jurors had been listening to young women recount their dealings with David Hendricks. Now, Tuesday, October 23, they were about to hear from the final model.

Outside the courtroom, as usual, stood Laverne Hendricks, today with her husband Charles. Like all future witnesses, they were excluded from the courtroom. Charles told a reporter that he supported his son 100 percent.

"I'm convinced, like so many others, that the authorities have wrongly accused David," he said. "But I know that most people would expect that from a father. I just know if my son were guilty, I would want him to be punished."

"What about this testimony showing David had made advances on some of the models he employed?" the reporter asked.

"He's not perfect," Charles Hendricks replied. "Neither am I. We're all sinners. That's why we need a savior."

Inside the courtroom, Carla Webb—twenty-six years old, a buxom blond who worked as an aerobics instructor and part-time actress, dancer, and model—sat in the witness box.

In August of 1983, a photographer had mentioned to her that Hendricks might like to use her as a model for his back brace. Then in mid-October the photographer, Bill Ortleb, called to say that Hendricks wanted to drop by her home that afternoon to talk about the modeling job.

Carla's girlfriend was there when Hendricks had Carla try on the variety of colored leotards she owned, selected two of them, and arranged for her to meet him at his office at eight o'clock that night for a brace fitting.

"Had Mr. Hendricks made any mention of any necessity of disrobing your clothing during the fitting process?" Dozier asked his witness.

"No, he did not," Carla Webb answered in a clear voice. "As a matter of fact, when I tried on a particular type of dancewear, he said he was concerned because I was a bit more endowed than the other models that had used the brace, because the brace apparently would be a cross-type brace, and he explained that. I think he used the word 'cruciform.' Said I was a bit more endowed than he had been used to using. And I blushed. I reacted to that. And he said, 'Don't get me wrong. I enjoy your figure.' "

Webb testified that she wore the white leotard he had selected along with a pink skirt, panty hose, and shoes to Hendricks's office that night. She said Hendricks made small talk about her acting and modeling work and then began fitting the brace.

"He asked me if I could stand up very straight, and I did. And he asked me if I could lift myself, meaning my breasts, to fit the brace."

"Okay," said Dozier. "You were a little too well-endowed for the crossbeam to fit underneath? You had to stand up straighter?"

"Well, when I stood up, it would work."

The witness said Hendricks then explained that he would have to make some measurements.

"I asked at the time, 'Is this what you would like me to wear, or should I try on the ones that you have?' So then he pulled out a navy blue bodysuit. I went back in the bathroom, came back out with it on and with my skirt and everything else. And he looked at it and said he wanted to proceed with the measurements.

"And I said fine, and I stood there for a moment. He pulled out a paper-type gown and he asked me if I would put it on. I had assumed I would be measured in the bodysuit. I said, 'This fits very snugly. Maybe we can do it in this.' He said he needed to do it just like a regular patient. And I guess I gave a reaction at the time because he said, 'All this is standard procedure. All the models go through it. I'm a doctor.' Because I seemed very nervous, I guess, for a moment."

"Just tell us what he said and what you said. Did he say he was a doctor?"

"He said—I believe he said, 'I'm a doctor.' I can't use the exact term. I know he did not say he was a chiropractor. But I was led to believe he was a doctor."

"I'm going to object, Judge, to her characterization and move to strike it," Jennings said in a louder than usual voice. "I do not object to what he said."

"Objection will be sustained," Judge Baner said. "Characterization will be stricken."

"You're only allowed to testify to what he said," Dozier told his witness. "Not what you believe."

"He said it was standard procedure—I would be treated just as a normal patient. And, well, I can't say that he said he was a doctor."

"What happened next?"

"At that time I went into the restroom and put on the plastic gown. It was baggy. It was slit, and I put the slit on in the back so that it was completely covering the front. No sleeves in it."

"Had you ever seen a gown like that type before?"

"In doctors' offices, yes. My gynecologist."

"Now, at the time you put on the gown, what were you wearing underneath it?"

"I had my skirt, panty hose, and shoes. I had taken off my Danskin."

"And the slit was in the back?"

"Yes, sir. He sat down at his desk and asked me to come over, you know, stand next to him to do the measurements. I went over there. And at that time I saw the form. It just had a body on it, a figure—figures and lines. He told me he was going to make some marks on my back with a felt-tip pen, wouldn't hurt or anything. He turned me around and began marking on my back. He opened up the gown a bit and began marking. He made marks on my midback, up and down my spine, and then he went to my upper back, my shoulders, and made several marks. And then down to my lower back and then he asked me if I would lower my skirt a little bit because he needed to make marks a little bit lower on the lower part of my spine."

The witness estimated that Hendricks made a total of at least twenty-five marks on her back over a fifteen-minute period—all the time talking with her about her acting.

"We were discussing my shows, where I'm from. I mentioned I was from Kentucky and I liked the Bloomington area a lot, but I didn't like the weather here as well as I do in Kentucky. He said he would need to make some marks on my front, and I needed to turn the gown around. I went back to the bathroom to turn the gown around and came back out with the gown closed and walked back out there.

"He then began making marks on my midriff, lower midriff, the tummy area. He pulled the gown back, but I wasn't exposed. The gown was moved back slightly. And he made marks on this area." The witness pointed to her rib area.

"And as he made the marks, then I could see that he was writing down little measurements, and then occasionally would take a tape measure and measure from one spot to another spot and record that. And he moved up to the top of the part around my shoulders and this area." Now she motioned to the area above her large breasts.

"And still the gown is not actually open. He's making marks here and writing them down. He told me he would need to open the gown to make a few more marks."

"So what happened then?"

"At this point I guess I began to look a little bit more nervous, because he said it was okay once again, this was standard procedure, and we began talking more about me and where I went to school and all of this. Then he told me he would have to pull the gown back. And he pulled it back off to the side."

"So that exposed your breasts for the first time?"

"Yes, it did. Right after he opened the gown, he began making marks directly above my breasts. And then he asked me—he turned me a little bit, grabbed me. I moved to the side so he could make marks there. He measured a couple marks on the side."

"On the side of what?"

"On the side of my breasts, level with my breasts on the side."

"Still making marks with a marking pen?"

"And he was still writing them down. The marks on the side level with the breasts were not corresponding. He wrote them at the bottom of the paper. That's the first time I noticed marks had not corresponded with the little figure."

Dozier, who had been standing near the witness box, now

backed away, looked at Hendricks, and leaned against the defense table.

"Did his hand come in contact with your breasts when he was making marks on the side of your breasts?"

"With the side of my breast, it did, where he was making the mark. He then proceeded to make a mark underneath my breasts. And by this time, he made maybe twenty marks in and around. For those, he changed the way he held the pen because he was trying to get underneath. He had one hand resting on my midriff and the other held the pen. And the hand that marked, you know, brushed up against me.

"And when he made that one, I noticed it didn't correspond. Then he started to make one in the center. And that's when I suggested to him that I had a nine-thirty rehearsal, but I really needed to get there early, and it was getting kind of late. And so that I—you know—I felt like I needed to go. Also I suggested that it was cold in the room. I was beginning to get a little cold."

"Did you notice anything unusual about him at that time?"

"Yes, I did. He didn't go back and mark anything on the paper at that time. And he had not made eye contact with me or talked with me for a while about weather and things like this. He was also sweating, you know. I just noticed he was shining a little bit. He was sweating. At this time I said I needed to go to rehearsal. He said, 'Wait a minute.' He got up and walked over and grabbed the cruciform. He said, 'Come here and let's see this.' He wanted to try the cruciform on me like this."

"Had he done any bending on it that you knew of at that time?"

"No, not at that time."

Webb said he first held the brace up to her.

"And then he started to hook it on the back. And he said, 'Bend over. I want to show you something.' So he took the back portion with one hand and he held the movable part with the swivel part with the other and bent me over to show how it swiveled. And he said that's what was different about his type of brace, that it moved up here, would give when people bent so it was more comfortable. And I suggested then, 'Well that's, you know, that's really neat. But I really need to go now.' He said, 'Wait a minute,' and pulled out another cruciform, another brace, and said, 'Here. Try this.' And he put it on me. Once again just set it on. I remarked that that one felt a lot better. It fit me better. It was a lot more comfortable. He said, 'It's not mine.' So I kind of laughed about that. And then he said,

'Did you know that you have scoliosis?' It was just out of the blue because he told me earlier that I had good posture. By this time, I was just a little bit upset because I wanted to go. I was a little bit irritated about the time."

"Judge," Jennings said matter-of-factly. "I'm going to apologize for interrupting the narrative, but I object to the characterizations."

"Objection will be sustained."

"He went over and sat back down at the desk when he said, 'Do you know that you have scoliosis?' I just didn't react. I gave a nonverbal reaction because then he said, 'Do you know what scoliosis is?' I said, 'Yes, a curvature of the spine.' Then I made a joke or remarked I had switched to medical school after law school or something like this so I was aware of what it was."

"Had you ever been told before that you had scoliosis?" Dozier asked.

"No. And I was joking with him about the fact that, you know, I had switched from law school to medical school and all this, you know. He showed me a little difference between—"

"Showed you on what?"

"On the chart. He had a piece of paper. He said, 'See, this is eight and three-quarters. This is this and this and this. And that's your curve.' As he was explaining the curvature of my spine to me, I was looking at the paper. And he grabbed the lower portion of my back with his hand, with his right hand, and then the lower portion of my abdomen with his other hand."

"And you still are wearing the gown-type thing?"

"Yes, I am."

"His hands are on the outside of the gown?"

"Yes, they are."

"What did you do then?"

"He's moving up. It's actually the lower part of the gown because the gown didn't come down that far. He's moving up, feeling my spine, making rubbing motions on my spine, explaining, 'This is where it's located.'"

"His hand is touching your skin underneath the gown at that point or on the outside?"

"It's underneath in the back. It's lower than the gown, so it's on the skin. And he's moving up my spine to show me where the curve is. And he moved up, he moved up with his hand in the front corresponding, and he was touching me in the center portion of my breast."

"Did that require his left hand touching both your breasts as he went in the area between them?"

"Yes, it was touching the area in between. And then he made me stand straighter. He pushed me from the side, which resulted in touching my right breast. At that moment in time, I said I really needed to go."

"How close are you to him at that time?"

"He had a hand on my back and he moved it up. As he did that, I made eye contact with him. As I looked to make eye contact with him, he pulled me in. He put his hands around my back completely and he pulled me in."

"Towards him?"

"Yes."

"Both hands on your back?"

"On my back."

"Now is he sitting or standing at that time?"

"He's sitting. I'm standing."

"What is he sitting on?"

"He's sitting at the desk in a chair. And I'm standing."

"Where would his eyes be in relation to your body as you're standing there?"

"His eyes would probably be chest level."

"And then he switched from one hand on your back and one in the front to both hands on your back? How close does he pull you towards him?"

"All within an inch of his face. As he pulled me in, I had my hands on his shoulders. And I patted his shoulders and then I pushed him back after I patted his shoulders. We never really completely made contact but felt very close. I felt his breath. I patted his shoulders and pushed him back and said, 'I really need to go.' "

"What happened next?"

"He then set down the pen, looked at the floor, backed up, stood up, and then he looked at me, and his eyes were very red. And that's when I noticed he was teary-eyed. He said, 'I'm a good Christian.' And there was a pause because I didn't know exactly how to react to that. And then he said, 'I'm married.' I said, 'That's okay. Nothing happened. I'm just going to go now.' And I turned to walk out of the room to go back to the bathroom. As I did that, he said, 'My wife can't find out.' I said, 'Nothing happened. There's no problem. I'm just going to go change.' I went to the bathroom and changed and came back out to get my purse, which was in the office. When I came back out, he was looking through some shelves and got some brochures of other girls who had modeled and what they looked like to show me. I said I was very interested in doing the modeling, you know, just to give Chelsea Studio a call when he was ready. He said that he wanted to work around the fact that I was endowed because he liked my look and wanted to go ahead and use me. He mentioned to me he wanted me to be in *The Journal of Orthopedics and Prosthetics*, I believe. I don't know what it was. He pulled the medical journal out and showed me. He said I would be good material for that. And I said, 'Well, that's good. I'm very interested in doing it.' And I'm walking out the door.

"He said, 'If you ever need anybody to talk to, just give me a call.' I said, 'Okay.' When I got to the door, he said, 'I have a plane. If you want to go to Kentucky some afternoon, I can take you there.' I said, 'Well, that would be great.' And that was it. I left."

Carla Webb went on to tell the jury that Hendricks called her a few days later to say that he was going out of town for a few days but remained very much interested in using her for some photo work. A few days after that, she said, Hendricks showed up at her home.

"He said he tried to phone me, couldn't reach me by phone," she said. "He had just gotten back in town, so he just thought he'd drop by and let me know he wanted to use me for the modeling. He kept reassuring me of that and told me I should go to Bergner's and pick out a flesh-toned or pink color leotard because he decided he wanted to do color photos."

"Instead of black and white?"

"Yes. And go to Bergner's to pick one out, and to save the receipt and he'd take care of it."

Webb said a friend was present when Hendricks stopped by, both that afternoon and again a few afternoons after that.

"He asked me if I had been to Bergner's yet. I said no, I hadn't. He reassured me I should go to Bergner's and pick something out and he'd take care of it. He had been talking to Chelsea and narrowing it down to probably sometime in early November for the shooting at this point."

"Did Mr. Hendricks come into your apartment on that occasion?"

"Generally he came to the front door and would come into the living room."

She said there was a third visit a few days later. Again a friend was there when Hendricks arrived.

"At this point he told me he had set a date with Chelsea and that we would do the shooting November 12th. He wanted to know if it was okay. I said sure. Had I gone to Bergner's? No, because I had been very busy. I promised I was going to go on the weekend and pick it out. He told me to let him know, drop by and show it, or give him a call. He wanted to see the Danskin I had chosen."

A few days later, Webb said, Hendricks telephoned to say that the photo session was still set for November 12.

"He also said that he had an abdominal brace that he would be interested in me modeling. And we needed to do another fitting for this particular brace. I told him I would be extremely busy all the next week, and I didn't think I would be able to see him before the shooting of the photos. He said he really wanted to get a fitting for this, and we could do the fitting on the 12th for the abdominal brace as well. I said, 'Well, why don't I try dropping by your office sometime.' And then he stated, 'Well, the office—I just got back in town. The office is in shambles. We're meeting on the east side.' I thought he meant an east-side location. He told me at that time then that he would like to get together Monday, Tuesday, or early in the week. And I said, 'I will be really tied up at the beginning of the week.' He said he'd give me a call around Monday to confirm where the location was where we would meet."

"Do you recall the events of the following week?"

"I recall Monday only because I was deliberately gone. I had a lot to do as far as the show went, and I didn't want to do another fitting. I wanted to model."

"I'm going to object, Judge," Jennings said. "And please ask it to be stricken."

"Objection will be sustained," Judge Baner ordered. "The testimony will be stricken. Ma'am, please listen to the questions and just try to answer the question you're asked. You are allowed to say what happened and what did not, not what you assume, felt, or thought, or things of that nature. Mr. Dozier."

"Specifically, do you recall hearing about the tragedy that occurred the following week?"

"Yes, I do."

"Do you recall what day you heard about that?"

"Wednesday."

"Did you ever then go for the modeling photography session on Saturday, November 12th?"

"No. I received a letter through the mail, a memo from his office, stating that the shooting would be postponed indefinitely due to the recent tragedy, and they would be back in contact with me."

In his cross-examination, Jennings questioned Carla Webb about the incident in which she said Hendricks pulled her toward him, putting her breasts only inches from his face.

"You said something to him or did something at that point. Is that correct?"

"Yes. I was patting him on the shoulders. And when my breasts got close to his face, I just broke away. I just pushed him back."

"Was this done with any force or violence or in a gentle manner by you?"

"By me?"

"Yes."

"I broke. I wasn't very forceful, no."

"Would it be fair simply to indicate that what you were doing was suggesting to him or telling him by your movements that you did not wish him to do what he was doing? Is that correct?"

"Yes."

"Did you say anything to him at that time, anything verbal like, 'Don't do that?'"

"No. I said that I needed to go."

Jennings quizzed the witness about her statement that Hendricks got "teary-eyed."

"Did you have the feeling at the time that this incident happened with Mr. Hendricks on South Evans that he was quite emotional or very emotional, considering the circumstances?"

"Uh-huh. At one moment he appeared emotional about the fact that he was a good Christian. That's when I thought he was emotional."

"And did you have occasion to tell the police about your observations of his emotional reaction?"

"I told Detective O'Brien about it."

"Did you tell O'Brien that you thought he was very emotional about apologizing for simply copping a feel? Is that the way you described it?"

"Copping a feel is not my term, you know. I suggested that I thought Mr. Hendricks was very emotional and apologetic after it happened because that's why I felt very awkward about it. And that's why I went on to say, 'It's no big deal.'"

"If I understand the sequence of events, immediately after he touched you and he held you as you described, you made it clear to him by your conduct that you didn't want him to do that. Is that correct?"

"Yes."

"And he immediately stopped what he was doing, as I understand your testimony?"

"I pushed him back. Yes."

"And he did not attempt in any manner to force himself upon you or to persist in his conduct. Is that correct?"

"Yes."

"Shortly after that, you had a discussion about your desire and your willingness to do the modeling for him. Is that correct?"

"Uh-huh."

"He asked you if you would do it, and you indicated that you were perfectly willing to do the modeling that you and he had discussed earlier. Is that correct?"

"Yes."

Jennings seemed to have made the point that despite Hendricks's alleged indiscretions, she was still very willing to model for him. The point was not lost on Dozier.

"What was your understanding on how the photo session was to be conducted?" Dozier asked.

"It was to be conducted at Chelsea Studio with my photographer."

"Were you agreeable to do any more fitting sessions with Mr. Hendricks?"

"No. No, sir."

"Nothing further."

Fifteen

J urors closest to the witness box strained to get a glimpse of the photograph being handed Kathleen Starkey, the young assistant manager of Chuck E. Cheese and one of several restaurant employees called by the prosecution.

It was a picture of Becky, Grace, and Benjy. The jurors were still having a difficult time seeing it.

Brad Murphy was doing the questioning.

"Were you able to identify for the police any of those individuals in the photograph?"

"Yes, I was. The two girls. I saw them at Chuck E. Cheese."

"And that was on November 7th, 1983?"

"Yes."

The picture was returned to an evidence envelope, the jury still having no image to attach to the children's identities.

With his wife and young son, Jeffrey Monahan had visited the Hendrickses' next-door neighbors, the Bob Phillips family, the night of the killings, November 7. And now Monahan was in the witness chair.

The Monahans had gone to the Phillips home at about 8 P.M. to pick up Rodney Blair, a teenaged boy who had been staying with the Phillipses. Rodney was to spend the night at the Monahan home in LeRoy, a town about fifteen minutes outside Bloomington, and help Monahan with some odd jobs the next day.

Shortly after 9 P.M., Monahan testified, he was sitting in his pickup truck in the Phillipses' driveway, waiting for his wife, son, and Rodney to follow him out of the house, when he saw a man walk down the Hendricks driveway and get into a car.

Murphy asked the witness to describe the person he had seen.

"As far as seeing, no, I can't. But I know he was a, you know, a fairly good-sized man. I don't know. I would say probably my height, which is six-two, in that area, six-foot. Something like that."

"Can you estimate anything in terms of weight?" Murphy asked.

"Didn't seem that he was as, you know, as heavy or as big as I am. That's about 225, 230."

"Where was this individual when you first recall seeing the individual?"

"Walking down the driveway."

"What did that individual do as he walked down the driveway?"

"Just walked to the car and opened the car door. I can remember the dome light coming on, and he got in and drove away."

Murphy asked whether he had seen the man come out of the Hendricks home.

"I didn't see anybody come out of the house. All I saw was somebody walking away from the house, down the drive."

"Could you recollect whether you heard any doors open or shut?"

"No, I don't."

"Do you have any specific recollection as to whether the garage door was open in that driveway adjacent to you?"

"I don't know that either."

Murphy showed Monahan two pictures of Hendricks's blue 1977 Buick Electra with a conventional engine. Could it be the same car that Monahan saw pull away that night?

"The vehicle that I saw leave was a light blue four-door. And it did have square headlights. I thought it was an Oldsmobile. The two cars are both full-sized cars. This car is very similar to what I saw. That's all. I can't say that I know for a fact that it was his car."

"Okay." Murphy had been hoping for a positive identification on the car but hadn't expected it. "Mr. Monahan, I neglected to ask you how you were employed."

"I'm a body man, a painter."

"Are you generally familiar with the body styles and the models of motor vehicles for some number of years?"

"Yes."

Under cross-examination, Monahan told Jennings that he did not see the face of that man who drove away. And he conceded that in his written statement given to police two days after the murders were discovered, Monahan described the car not only as an Oldsmobile, but as an Oldsmobile with a diesel engine.

If Murphy was disappointed in Monahan's testimony, he was to be pleased with the testimony of the next witness, Rodney Blair. The nineteen-year-old, in previous interviews, had been reluctant to positively identify Hendricks as the driver of the car in question. But now Blair was testifying that he saw the car back down the Hendrickses' driveway and pull away just as he came out of the Phillips home.

"Did you recognize the vehicle?" Murphy asked.

"Yes, I did. It was Mr. Hendricks's car."

"Had you seen it on prior occasions?"

"Yes, I had."

"Did you have occasion to observe any of the occupants of that vehicle?"

"Yes, I did. One person."

"Where were you at the time that you could observe that there was one person?"

"I was already at the truck."

"And where was Mr. Hendricks's vehicle at that time?"

"It was just passing behind the truck."

"Did you recognize the occupant of the vehicle at that time?"

"Yes, I did."

"And who was it?"

"Mr. David Hendricks."

Jennings, in his cross-examination, took Blair back to minutes after midnight on the night the murders were discovered. Blair said he answered the door to find a detective there, explained that the house belonged to Bob and Debbie Phillips, and that they had children but that he was "kind of like a foster child to the Phillipses."

"Did the officer explain why he was there?"

"He said the family next door had expired and he was there to ask some questions. I went upstairs to wake the Phillipses up."

"Okay. And did the Phillipses come downstairs?"

"Yes, they did."

"And did you stay away from the remaining conversation?"

"Yes, I went back downstairs to the basement. I was watching the TV."

Jennings handed Blair a copy of the statement he gave to police two days after the bodies were found.

"Was your recollection of the events of November 7th, 1983, better on November 10th, 1983, than today?"

"It was better then."

"At any place in the written statement, defendant's exhibit H, does it say you saw David Hendricks on the evening of November 7th?"

"No, it does not."

Murphy was asking the questions again.

"During the course of your statement to police, were you ever asked specifically by the officer taking that statement if you could identify the driver of the vehicle as Mr. Hendricks?"

"No, I was not."

"You did clearly indicate to him that you saw Mr. Hendricks's car in the street with the lights on and it went north on Carl Drive?"

"Yes, I did."

"And later you were asked what kind of car does Mr. Hendricks have and you said a blue Buick, four-door?"

"Correct."

Jennings again.

"Mr. Blair, the question you were asked that you responded to concerning what you had seen was, 'Tell me about any activity the evening of the 7th at the Hendricks home.' Correct?"

"Correct."

"Either at the time of the written statement or prior to that time, did any police officer ask you if you had seen anyone at the house?"

"No, he did not."

A hint of incredulity entered Jennings's voice.

"The police got you down to the police station concerning November 7th at the Hendricks house and no one asked you if you'd seen anybody at the Hendricks house on November 7th?"

"No, they did not."

Dozier needed to show that even under the most innocent of conditions, all of the nudity, body markings, and time spent with the models was unnecessary. And to do that he called Ed Roman as a witness. Hendricks gave Roman a small wave and a half-smile when Roman, who had purchased Hendricks's patient-care business in 1981, took the stand.

Using the teenaged daughter of one of Dozier's employees as a "patient," Roman stood before the jury box to demonstrate how he fitted the CASH Brace to a patient. It was immediately clear that the fitting process was not a prolonged one.

Under questioning, Roman said he normally spent twenty or thirty minutes with a patient when the CASH Brace was fitted.

"What do you do during that twenty minutes or half hour?" Dozier asked.

"In addition to the fitting of the orthosis, I try to explain to the patient what I'm doing, why I'm doing it, what benefits they would receive from wearing the orthosis, asking them what the doctor's instructions were as far as the patient to wear it, whether it's twenty-four hours a day or just while they're awake. Explain how to care for it, how to clean it, what they can do, what they can't do."

"When you indicated twenty or thirty minutes, was that including the time for all this general conversation, or was that just the time to do the actual fitting of the brace?"

"No," Roman answered. "That's the patient coming in the front door and walking out the front door. That's all the paperwork necessary for it and insurance forms, Medicare forms, whatever."

"Assuming a patient of ordinary height and weight, how long does it normally take just for the portion of fitting the brace?"

"If I said nothing and just did the fitting, it probably could be accomplished in three, four minutes—possibly even less."

Dozier felt he had scored the point about time. Now, about nudity.

"When you fit a patient, what do you have them wear? Do you have them wear anything special?"

"No, I do not. As I indicated, I do some in the hospital and some in my office. I could fit the orthosis over whatever—usually over whatever they're wearing, unless it's an extremely bulky sweater."

"Now, you fit other brands of back braces as well. Is that correct?"

"Correct."

"How does the CASH Brace compare in terms of its ease of fitting?"

"This is probably one of the easiest back braces to fit."

Hendricks looked up from the legal pad where he was taking notes. A flash of pride seemed to flow over his face.

"How is it designed to be worn with regard to the person's clothing?"

"I recommend that the patient wear it over T-shirt–type material," Roman said. "There is plastic in the pads, and plastic up against the skin can be uncomfortable."

"In your fitting of patients," Dozier continued, "do you ever have occasion to require any patient to disrobe either fully or from the waist up?"

"Not on the fitting. No."

"At any time in your dealing with the CASH orthosis and the patient?"

"No. No."

"Let me ask you again to make sure." Dozier wanted to make certain the jurors didn't miss this point. "If you are fitting patients with a CASH orthosis, do you ever find it necessary for a patient to either be completely nude or nude from the waist up?"

"No, I do not."

"In your fitting of the CASH orthosis to your patients, do you ever find it necessary to make marks such as with a pen or pencil on the body of your patient?"

"No, I have not."

His point made, Dozier moved on to another issue which he found particularly intriguing. "Did you have a conversation with Mr. Hendricks shortly after the deaths of his family in which there was an exchange of something?"

"I believe it was maybe two weeks after that date. He had stopped by the office and he returned the keys."

Jennings stood up.

"Judge, I'm going to object to this unless there's going to be some relevancy as to something he did two weeks later. I don't know where it's going, but I want to object to it before it goes to left field."

Judge Baner cleared his throat.

"Well, I have no idea where we're headed here, Mr. Dozier. Do you want to do it outside the jury's presence?"

"I think it would be best," Dozier said.

The judge sent the jury from the courtroom and then spoke to Dozier. "Want to indicate the relevancy of this line of questioning?"

"Your Honor, the question is going to disclose a conversation and event in which Mr. Hendricks a couple of weeks after the deaths dropped by Mr. Roman's place of business, gave Mr. Roman a key to the business, and made a statement to Mr. Roman that he was giving it to Mr. Roman so that the police would not discover that he, Mr. Hendricks, had this key to Mr. Roman's business and would not, therefore, be searching Mr. Roman's business place for evidence. The state also intends to bring out the relatively short distance between Mr. Roman's place of business and the Hendricks home where the murders occurred. Given the closeness and the fact that Mr. Hendricks had a key, coupled with the testimony of the previous witness who saw Mr. Hendricks leave the Hendricks home around nine o'clock the night of the murders—it's all an indication of where he might have gone on that occasion."

"Is where he might have gone relevant?" the judge asked.

"We'd certainly like to know where he might have gone."

"That's not my question. You have to prove something with this."

"Is there," Jennings asked, "any evidence that he was there?"

"Your Honor," Dozier responded, "I can only tell you that we have no other evidence to show whether or not Mr. Hendricks went to Mr. Roman's place that night or that any activity of any nature occurred there. We still have a desire to have this conversation about his returning the key, so that the police would not find it and then search Mr. Roman's place, admitted."

"What is that going to prove?" the judge asked.

"I think it could indicate that Mr. Hendricks was expecting to be searched on his person. And I think it may imply he was expecting to be arrested, which again I realize there is more than one interpretation. But I think the jury can infer on that some degree of perhaps guilty knowledge."

"Expectation of arrest," Judge Baner countered, "creates a guilty knowledge or even an inference of it? Is that what you're suggesting?"

"I think that's one inference that could be drawn."

"Has any case that would indicate that proposition ever been accepted by anybody, Mr. Dozier? Anybody in the country?"

"A case, Your Honor?" Dozier shifted his weight from one foot to the other and back again. "I've not done research on the area."

"I'd be amazed if there were such a case," the judge said. "The objection will be sustained."

In cross-examination, Jennings was anxious to show that the

The Hendricks family on the front porch of their home in May 1983.

The Hendricks home, where the murders occurred. (Photo by Lori Ann Cook)

Becky, Grace, and Benjy Hendricks in a department store photo taken three weeks before they were murdered.

Susan and David in Great Britain on a tenth-wedding-anniversary trip in the fall of 1983.

Susan and David Hendricks
on their wedding day, July 28, 1973.

David and Benjy three months before the killings.

Hendricks as he appeared in a television interview the afternoon after the murders were discovered.

Ron Dozier,
McLean County state's attorney.

Brad Murphy,
McLean County assistant state's attorney.

Hal Jennings,
defense attorney.

John Long,
defense attorney.

Echo Wulf Atwell, the first of the models, demonstrating Hendricks's patented brace for an advertising brochure. (Photo by Robert E. Handley)

Carla Webb, the last of Hendricks's models, in a photo used as evidence in Hendricks's murder trial. Webb is now a police officer in Tennessee.

Hendricks, his new wife, Pat, and her children, Rachel and Ryan, shortly after David and Pat were married in a prison ceremony, December 20, 1988. The next day the Illinois Supreme Court issued a ruling in Hendricks's case.

The Hendricks grave. The space for an epitaph below the names has been left blank. (Photo by Lori Ann Cook)

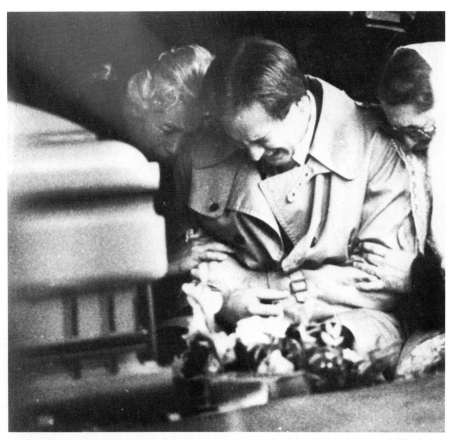

Hendricks breaks down at the graveside service for his wife and three children. His mother, Laverne Hendricks, is on the left. His mother-in-law, Nadine Palmer, is on the right. Hendricks was charged with the killings a month later. (AP/Wide World Photos)

time and methods used with the models could have been legitimate. Coincidentally, he would also help Dozier make at least part of his point about Hendricks's having a key to Roman's office.

"Mr. Roman," Jennings asked, "did you have conversations with David Hendricks concerning research projects he was working on?"

"Yes."

"And did he, in fact, from time to time use your facilities in any way in connection with any of these projects?"

"Dave came to me and said that he didn't want to spend a lot of money on tools and equipment and asked me if I'd be willing to let him use my lab when I wasn't there. We signed an agreement. I believe it was for fifty dollars a month and whatever materials were used by him that I had in stock. And he was given a set of keys to the place. And I usually could tell when he was in because something was just a little bit off center from where I left it the last time. I know just before the convention he was working on the CASH orthosis, the pubic pad. I know one of the models was formed around our garbage can because it had a nice radius."

Roman looked at Hendricks. They exchanged smiles.

"Are you aware of whether or not he was working on any spinal brace system?" Jennings asked.

"I know he had discussed it in that he was attempting to come up with ways to provide other types of back braces. I believe he was trying for a universally accepted size."

"Do you know, if in connection with the spinal brace system or process he was working on, whether or not he used or obtained measurements from time to time?"

"I'm sure he did, because that's the basis you make a chairback brace on."

"Mr. Roman, in the practice of orthotics, are there, from time to time, occasions when you are mistaken for a doctor?"

"Yes."

"And is that, from time to time, by patients or clients in the ordinary course of your business?"

"Yes."

Jennings next would try to show that Hendricks's Wisconsin trip was not unusual.

"Tell me if you get calls from people involving products— orthotic, prosthetic equipment?"

"Yes, I do."

"Are they scheduled appointments or cold calls?"

"Cold calls."

"Is that almost universal?"

"Yes."

"What's the average length on a cold call from a salesman who comes in to sell you an orthotic or prosthetic appliance?"

"It could be anywhere from a couple of minutes to four or five hours. I'd say the average is ten to fifteen minutes."

"When these sales folks come in from time to time, do they usually bring their product line with them?"

"Into the office?"

"Yeah."

"Not always."

"Do they generally leave anything with you when they drop in?"

"Usually their business card and promotional brochure describing whatever products. Sometimes catalogs and price lists."

Dozier wasn't going to let that pass.

"When salesmen have a new product or product line, Mr. Roman, do they normally bring any of their product information about it?"

"Yes. Well, they'll bring information on it and if I desire them to go further, they usually would go back out to the car and bring it in for me."

"That's all," Dozier concluded.

The witness was dismissed.

When the next morning marked the seventh week of the trial and the defense had not yet presented its first witness, there were revised predictions about how long the trial might last. And the defense was deeply troubled by an article about the trial in that morning's *Rockford Register-Star*.

The article contained several paragraphs about Dozier's efforts to have testimony that Hendricks had returned the key to Roman's office allowed. It quoted Dozier as saying the testimony would not only prove that Hendricks expected to be searched and arrested, but that he "might have disposed of other evidence."

Before the day of testimony began, Hal Jennings asked Judge Baner to sequester the jury.

"While there has been, in previous reporting, some degree of misstatements and mischaracterization of evidence, I believe this morning is the first occasion in which the problem of evidence or nonevidence specifically and expressly excluded from the purview of the jury has been reported."

Judge Baner took a brief recess to read the article and the previous day's court record and ask Dozier whether he had made this statement privately to the reporter. He returned to the bench with a stern look on his face.

"The court finds there to be absolutely no basis in fact for what is reported in this article. The article is inaccurate in an important area of the case and if read by a juror could produce prejudice as far as the verdict in this case in concerned."

The judge, prepared to excuse any juror who read the newspaper story, went into the jury room.

"A problem, or at least a possible problem, has developed this morning," he told them. "Before I proceed, I want you all to understand that your earlier oath still applies, and that any questions you are asked about your services here are still under oath."

Several jurors looked at each other, wondering what this could be about.

"In this morning's *Register-Star*, there was an article reportedly discussing what transpired in court here yesterday—including things that were presented to you and things that were not. There is nothing legally improper about the press reporting things outside the jury's presence, although that does not assist the process. My concern," the judge continued, "is that there was something reported to have happened yesterday that did not, in fact, at all occur. Now, my question to each of you today is has any of you read today's paper concerning this case?"

The judge pointed in turn to each of the twelve regular jurors and four alternates, getting either an audible "no" or a shake of the head from each of them.

Baner was relieved. He could deny the request to sequester the jury.

The next prosecution witness was Bev Crutcher, who had been Hendricks's only full-time employee. Following his arrest, she had taken over the day-to-day operation of CASH Manufacturing.

A slim brunette with a wedge hairstyle made popular a couple of years earlier by skater Dorothy Hamill, Crutcher never once looked directly at Hendricks during her eight hours of testimony spread over two days. At one point, when the attorneys and Judge Baner went to his chambers for a brief conference, Hendricks, left alone at the defense table, looked uneasy when repeated attempts to make eye contact with Crutcher, still seated in the witness box, failed. Some jurors noticed.

Much of Bev Crutcher's testimony focused on CASH Manufacturing's financial success. But another major part concerned her contact with Hendricks before and during his Wisconsin trip.

She told prosecutor Murphy that at about 8:30 on the morning before the bodies were discovered, Hendricks called her from Wausau. "He told me that he was ready to start making his calls, and that he was going to stop at a couple of places and talk about the brace and make his way down to Madison. And I told him about a hospital that was up in the area that I wasn't sure I had put on the list for him."

"Did you later on that day have any further contact with the defendant, David Hendricks?"

"Yes. He called later in the afternoon. A little before four o'clock, though I'm not sure of the exact time period. He gave me the name of the motel where he was staying and the room number. I believe also the phone number. And I asked him if I should call Susan for him and tell her where he was. And he expressed that he would like me to try because he had already tried and couldn't reach her. And he was ready to go to sleep because he'd been up quite some time and was pretty tired. He also said he knew she had a dinner engagement that night and he didn't want her to worry if he didn't reach her before she left for dinner. So I agreed to try to reach her for him."

"Okay. Now, was it you who volunteered to call Susie for him?"

"Yes, I always did. And he said that I should just keep trying to reach Susie."

"Prior to Mr. Hendricks making a trip to Wisconsin on November 7th, 1983, were you aware that there were plans for such a trip?"

"Yes."

"Do you have a recollection as to how long in advance you were aware of the plans for the trip?"

"It was the week before he was to leave. I don't recall the exact day. It was as early as Thursday."

"Were you requested by Mr. Hendricks to make any arrangements for purposes of that trip?"

"Yes. I was to get customer names in the area that he was going to call on."

"Do you recall how that was communicated to you by Mr. Hendricks?"

"He would have just asked me. Verbal."

"On Monday, November 7th, 1983, or some time prior to that, did you have a conversation with David Hendricks concerning this trip to Wisconsin that he was planning?"

"Yes."

"During the course of that conversation, did you discuss the time he was to depart on his trip?"

"Yes. I believe he said he was going to leave late in the evening and drive through the night so he could start calling on customers first thing in the morning."

"Did he provide any more specific time to you?"

"I believe that he said he was going to leave about midnight."

Murphy was ready to ask the clincher question.

"On any prior occasion on such sales trips, did he ever tell you what time he was departing or going to be leaving on a sales trip?" Murphy thought back ten months earlier to Crutcher's testimony before the grand jury. When he had asked her if it was unusual for Hendricks to leave on sales trips at midnight or late in the evening, she'd answered, "I didn't always know when he left." "Were you ever aware of him doing that before?" Murphy had asked. "I don't recall," she had told the grand jury. "I don't think that I knew of another time."

Now Murphy waited for a similar answer to his question about whether Hendricks had ever before told her of his departure plans.

"I believe he did."

Murphy looked stunned. Defense attorney Long spoke up.

"Excuse me. Excuse me, counsel. Your Honor, I beg your pardon. May I ask that the court have that question and answer read back to me. I was looking up something and . . ."

The judge ordered the court reporter to read the question and answer. Murphy approached the bench, and the judge sent the jury from the room.

Murphy told the judge that based on the conflict between what Bev Crutcher had testified before the grand jury, had told him in a pretrial interview, and had just testified to, he was prepared to impeach the witness. Judge Baner reminded Murphy that Murphy himself might have to testify in such a situation.

"We also," Long interjected, "have the right to cross-examine Mr. Murphy."

"Absolutely," said the judge, "if he becomes a witness like any other witness in the case."

It was time for a recess. When it was over, Murphy had changed his mind.

"During the recess I have been requested, if not directed, not to interject my credibility into this trial. So I'm going to abandon the questioning. I'm not going to attempt to impeach the witness."

So it was Long's turn to cross-examine Crutcher, and he wasn't about to let loose of what Murphy had started.

"I believe your testimony was that in the week prior to the November 7th trip, he had asked you to begin making arrangements for that trip. Is that correct?"

"Yes."

"And part of those arrangements was to begin to collate and assemble various prospects for sales calls."

"Yes."

"Had he done this in this same fashion on previous occasions?"

"Many times."

"And had he made plans in order to drive and make sales contacts on previous occasions as he was going to do on November 7th?"

"Yes."

"And he in fact on those days indicated to you that he was going to leave at night and drive somewhere in order to make calls in the morning."

"I believe that he did."

"Did you find anything unusual in his request to you in that week preceding November 7th relating to the trip to Wisconsin?"

"Nothing out of the ordinary."

"And as a result of your responsibilities with CASH Manufacturing, you were familiar, were you not, with David's working habits?"

"Yes."

"With respect to those working habits, was it normal for him to make cold calls on customers?"

Bev's intonation reflected unconditional certainty. "Oh, yes."

"And was this done in the ordinary course of business times prior to November 7th?"

"Yes."

Long liked the way this was going.

"Can you state whether or not his calling you at eight-thirty in the morning from his location would have been a usual thing for him to do when he was on business trips such as the one to Wisconsin?"

"Very much so."

"Did he have a habit of doing that as a normal course of business?"

"Calling in? Yes."

"And did he always call you either first thing in the morning when you arrived or last thing at night?"

"It always seemed that way."

A hint of humor entered Long's voice. "Had nothing to do with checking to make sure you were in the office?"

"I was never sure of that."

"But either the very first thing in the morning or very last thing at night you got a phone call from David Hendricks."

"Yes."

"When he called you at 8:30 in the morning on November 8th, 1983, what, if anything, did he say to you during the conversation?"

"That was the conversation we had where he told me he was in Wausau and ready to start his calls."

"And can you state whether he made that statement to you in a normal tone of voice?"

"Yes."

"Did you notice anything unusual about his voice at all?"

"No."

"You next heard from him later that afternoon?"

"Yes."

"Would you say, without putting you on the spot, Mrs. Crutcher, that David Hendricks could sometimes be snug with a buck?"

Hendricks smiled. Beverly grimaced. "Yes."

"If David Hendricks didn't have to spend a nickel, he wouldn't spend it, would he?"

"Yes."

"You had a WATS line, did you not?"

"Yes."

"And can you state whether or not he used to call you on other business trips prior to November 7th, 1983, and ask you to call his wife because he could call you on a toll-free line?"

"Many times."

"And did he ever specifically state to you during these times to call her so he could save the cost of the phone call?"

"Yes, he did."

The next morning there was another problem with an article in the Rockford newspaper. It inaccurately reported that there had been a request for a mistrial.

Jennings renewed his request that the jury be sequestered and now did move for a mistrial.

"Your complaint," asked Judge Baner, "has to do with what is reported today, not yesterday?"

"What was reported today that didn't happen yesterday."

Judge Baner went into the jury room again to address the sixteen men and women he had talked with twenty-four hours earlier.

"I hope this doesn't become a daily occurrence," he began. "We've had an additional problem again this morning with a press release in the local paper, which I guess is this time not chargeable to the local paper, but to the Associated Press because it's a wire article. What I've decided to do—and I don't do it in any way meaning to offend any of you—but rather than have to go through this process every morning when I pick up a paper and see something reported there that we all know didn't happen in court, even with you present, what I'm going to do is prepare a form which I'm going to have the bailiff provide new each day to you that simply indicates in the heading paragraph that each of you, by signing that form, has not seen or read or heard anything and that this is being signed under your oath so you won't have to be sworn each day. Does anybody have any questions at all about that?"

Nobody moved.

"Okay. We'll get you one for today that will cover the article we're concerned about. We're ready to start here in a few minutes."

The murmuring of three dozen courtroom spectators stopped as they discerned the shape of the brown paper container being handled by the witness. It contained the ax used to murder Susan and her three children.

Rodney Wamsley was the first of the five state crime laboratory technicians brought to the stand. Both the prosecution and the defense used Wamsley's testimony to introduce a total of twenty-eight pieces of evidence that he had collected. Each item was sealed and labeled in its own cardboard or paper evidence container. Nineteen of the items belonged to the prosecution. There were the ax and the butcher knife, three swatches of downstairs carpeting, the bloodied bedspread and sheets from the master bedroom, some doorknobs, a palm print, some blood swabbed from the marble vanity top in the upstairs hallway bathroom, and Susan's black purse, whose contents were found spilled on the family-room floor. Among the nine defense exhibits were three impressions of foot-wear taken from the kitchen floor.

When jurors entered the courtroom for the fourteenth day of testimony, they found a pair of slide screens standing side by side, directly across the room from the jury box and near the defense table.

Missing from the defense table was David Hendricks. John Long told reporters that Hendricks had never viewed the crime-scene photos and that he recommended that Hendricks not see them.

Baner explained Hendricks's absence to the jury: "Ladies and gentlemen, the defendant has been granted permission by the court to be absent during the testimony of certain witnesses. His absence should not be considered by you in any way at arriving at your verdict in this case. For the benefit of you who are here observing, all the lights are going to be shut off. If that makes you nervous, I'm telling you that in advance. The state may proceed."

The courtroom darkened, and the sudden drone of a pair of slide projectors announced the appearance of two images on the twin screens. On the right appeared a floor plan of the Hendricks home's first floor. On the left screen was a view of the front of 313 Carl Drive, its dark brown siding with a partial brick facade denying the horrible events that had happened inside. Only the wide, yellow crime-scene tape in the picture's foreground betrayed that there was anything unusual about this house.

In the witness box was Dennis Dodwell, another crime-scene technician, who testified that he spent parts of nine days in the home, searching for evidence. He had taken most of the photo-graphs.

Brad Murphy's voice strained to be heard well over the sound of the two projectors.

"I show you a slide that's marked ninety-one-dash-one. What is that, sir?"

"That's a photograph of 313 Carl Drive northeasterly from the home looking into the front."

The slide on the left suddenly disappeared, and another re-placed it.

"This is ninety-one-dash-two. What is this, please?"

"This is almost the same angle. Only thing is that it's back farther from the northeast to take in part of the driveway next door at 311 Carl Drive."

That slide was replaced by another.

"Ninety-one-dash-three?"

"This shows the north end of the home, crime-scene tape going across. The evening we arrived, we went along the tape and went up to the rear patio door."

Slide by slide, Murphy and his witness took the jurors and other courtroom observers on a tour of the home's interior, starting just as the police had, on the screened-in porch, into the family room where some drawers stood open and a purse lay on the floor, its contents spilled. In the kitchen, a single cabinet door was open. And a close-up of a wood block containing several sharp knives revealed that one slot, the top one, was vacant. It was labeled *butcher*.

More photos through the dining room and living room, into a front hallway, and past a bathroom. Jurors were seeing a modern home, well kept and organized, except that in virtually every room drawers and cabinets had been opened. Rarely, however, had their contents been disturbed.

Some jurors, only an outline in the courtroom darkness, seemed to brace themselves as the floor plan of the second story flashed onto the screen at the right and the photos made a turn up the stairs into the master bedroom. They showed a very large room, big enough to accommodate a large bed, pair of dressers, sewing table and chair, bookcase, hope chest, two stereo speakers, and couch, and still look somewhat underfurnished.

A small wooden box on one dresser had been overturned. The coins and combs it had contained were on the floor.

One photo showed a corner of the bed. And there was Susan Hendricks's body on its right side, mostly under a blue bedspread, head on a pillow. The picture was taken at a distance and angle that showed none of the wounds.

The large master dressing room was ransacked. A drawer from a file cabinet inside a closet had been removed. Inside a linen closet, numerous shoe boxes had been disturbed. A quilt had been pulled from its shelf partly onto the floor. An umbrellalike sweater dryer balanced on the edge of a partly opened drawer.

Next the photo tour moved into Benjy's room. A bed that looked like it had hardly been slept in, some toys on the floor, closet doors open, a box with rolls of wallpaper spilled out, and a chest of drawers tilted forward by the weight of its pulled-out drawers.

And now into the girls' room. First a picture of a light switch cover depicting a sleeping elf, and just above it a splatter of blood about the size of a half dollar. Then a view of much of the room, showing only the foot of the beds, a dresser and desk with their drawers open, and a pair of end tables. Some close-ups of some of the room's contents, including a white lampshade spattered with blood.

Dodwell continued to describe the slides.

"This is on the same side of the dresser. The bottom third drawer has also been removed, now depicting the two shoes." A pair of black patent-leather girl's shoes glistened.

"The shoe is up underneath the dresser just a little bit, and inside—as you can see—is a red substance that appeared to be blood."

"What was the position of that lower drawer with reference to those shoes when you first saw it?" Murphy asked.

"You couldn't see the shoes. The drawer itself was out, covering the shoes."

Then, a picture of two beds and three young bodies.

In the foreground, Becky, face down, her hair in pigtails. In the background on the second bed, Grace, partially on her side, her head lightly touching her brother's. Benjy was on his back, his arms outstretched, one leg hanging over the edge of the bed.

The camera angle spared the courtroom much of the gore that had confronted the two Bloomington policemen a year earlier. But the shock of seeing the apparent murder weapons was still there. The ax and long butcher knife, their blades bloody but their handles clean, lay parallel across the foot of the bed that held two of the bodies.

Crash! A startling, almost explosive sound pierced the courtroom darkness, causing more than a few people to jump in their seats. Dodwell had inadvertently struck the microphone in the witness box with his hand.

After lunch, Murphy turned Dodwell's attention to his analysis of the spatterings of blood on the girls' bedroom walls. Dodwell said it was clear that the blood had come from the victims' heads.

Murphy asked where he found the blood.

"Across the bed, on the end table, the wall, the end of the closet door, inside the closet, on some items and clothing on the floor, by the light switch, on top of the dresser, and on the face of the drawers of the dresser."

Some of it, he said, was a result of what he called "castoff"— blood leaving the ax with centrifugal force as the killer stood between the two beds and made repeated strikes with the weapon.

Long later questioned Dodwell about the crime technicians' late-night visit to the Hendricks home about a month after the killings. "You indicated that when you spray Luminol, you want it as dark as possible, so you went to 313 Carl Drive at two o'clock in the morning."

"Approximately, yes, sir."

"And you sprayed this, looking for luminescence because there's a blue luminescence that occurs when Luminol hits something that it will react with?"

"Yes, sir."

"And blood is one of the things."

"Yes, sir."

"But it will also react with other organic compounds, will it not?"

"Yes, sir."

"That will also create a blue luminescence, will it not?"

"Yes."

"If you get a reaction, a blue luminescence from Luminol, that in and of itself just tells you to check this area that's glowing blue, right?"

"Yes, sir."

"Yeah." Long was pressing the point especially hard because it was Friday afternoon and the jury had had a hard week. "That doesn't say we've got blood here. All it says is we've got something, you better test further because there's a possibility that there's blood here."

"Yes. To identify it as blood, there would be a secondary test."

"Sure. Now, you testified under direct examination that you sprayed this tub and shower in the upstairs and that the entire bottom of it glowed."

"Yes, sir."

"And was that entire shower bottom subject to any other tests to determine whether it was blood?"

"No, sir."

"Were the P-traps and drains in that shower checked?"

"Yes, sir."

"Was blood found in the P-traps or drains?"

"No, sir."

"Would it be a fair statement to say that every single P-trap and drain in this house was pulled by a plumber under the direction of your department?"

"I believe two P-traps were not pulled—the ones in the kitchen sink and in the downstairs bathroom vanity."

"With the exception of those two, were they all pulled?"

"Yes."

"And were they all subjected to laboratory analysis at the Morton crime lab?"

"Yes, sir."

"And was blood identified in any of them?"

"No, sir."

"As a matter of fact, you as crime-scene technician do not believe that the luminescence in that bathtub was caused by blood, do you?"

"I don't know whether I could positively say either way."

"You never wrote a report or mentioned that you had an opinion that there was blood in the shower, did you?"

"No, sir."

"If a substance has an organic base, such as shampoo or conditioner or body lotions or some type of bubble bath that would be used for children and left a soap scum in a bath tub, it's conceivable Luminol would pick that up, won't it?"

"I don't believe it would all brands."

"I don't mean all brands either. But it would in some cases, would it not?"

"It could possibly."

Dodwell said his own tests found that Luminol reacted with bleach, Cascade, and Sno-Bol.

"These are items that are used to clean bathroom fixtures and are normally found in a bathroom. Is that correct?"

"At times. Yes, sir."

"Now if a cleanser—common bathroom cleanser, kitchen cleanser has bleach in it, and something is washed with that bleach and it isn't all rinsed out, would that show positive with Luminol?"

"Yes, it could."

"Could that be the reason that the entire floor of the bathtub glowed blue?"

"It could be."

Under further questioning by Long, Dodwell testified that an analysis of the hair found on the ax blade was consistent with hair samples from Benjamin and Becky.

"And the butcher knife?"

Dodwell read from a report: "A few Caucasian head hair fragments present consistent with head hair samples from Benjamin Hendricks. A few Caucasian head hair fragments present consistent with head hair samples from Becky Hendricks. Several Caucasian hair fragments present insufficient characteristics for comparison."

"Is there anything in the reports or in your personal observations of any evidence of any of the blood of Susan Hendricks on either the ax or the knife?"

"I see nothing here, and I don't know anything other than that."

"Do you have an opinion about the absence of blood spatters and castoffs in the bedroom occupied by Susan Hendricks?"

"Yes. That because there was no spatter or castoff, because there were cuts in the bedspread, and because the bedspread was positioned as though a thumb was used to pull it back toward the foot from the head, I believe Susan Hendricks had the blanket up over her head."

"Now correct me if I'm wrong, because I want to state the facts as accurately as possible." Long was about to summarize. "You've testified that there was an absence of blood spatter and castoff in the master bedroom. You've testified further that the ax and the knife were found in the southwest bedroom and that they were heavily stained with blood. You've testified further that there were hairs on the ax and knife that were identified as belonging to the two children who were laying in the bed upon which the ax and the knife were found. You testified further that there were blood spatters and castoffs at least on three walls of that room. Based upon all of that, do you have an opinion as to whether or not Susan Hendricks was murdered first and then the weapons used on the children or not?"

"I object for several reasons," Murphy said.

"Sustained."

Long shifted focus and moved to the issue of whether any incriminating blood was found on David Hendricks's clothing and other items. He started with item 20, a white T-shirt taken from the master bath.

"You just want the results?" Dodwell asked.

"Yep."

"No blood identified. A few hairs present."

A few minutes later Long was up to item 79. "Trap from south washbasin in master bedroom."

The answer was the same as the jury had already heard every time before. "No blood identified."

A few minutes later, Long had reached item 88. Judge Baner interrupted him.

"Mr. Long, it's about twenty-five after four. Just wanted to bring that to your attention."

"Yeah. I'm just about done with this section. Let me move down for a moment to number 99. Right shoe from David Hendricks."

"No blood identified."

"Number 100. Pair of blue slacks from David Hendricks."

"No blood identified. A few hairs present."

"Number 101. Plaid shirt from David Hendricks."

"No blood identified."

The litany continued through number 111.

"Now," Long said, "just to end up for this evening and make sure that I understand your testimony, based upon the reports that we've read and your personal analysis, there wasn't any blood identified in any of the traps, wash basins, contents from same, or any of the clothing identified as belonging to David Hendricks. Is that correct?"

"To the best of my knowledge, yes, sir."

Hendricks remained in his Winnebago County jail cell Monday morning when Long put Dodwell back in the witness box to return to the issue of blood evidence.

He had Dodwell reiterate that no blood was positively identified anywhere outside the bedrooms, except for a tiny amount on the vanity in the upstairs hallway bath, an amount too small to link to any of the victims. No blood, Dodwell testified, was found in Hendricks's car or on any of his clothing or personal items.

With a floor plan of the girls' room now on the slide screen, Long had Dodwell point out an area between the two beds where he believed the killer had stood when Grace and Benjy were struck. And he had Dodwell describe again where the blood spatters and castoffs had occurred.

"And did you not also tell us, Mr. Dodwell, that one of the bases for your opinion was that the absence of blood any place else would indicate that the assailant, in part, was shielding parts of the other surfaces from the blood splatter?"

"Yes, sir."

"And we may infer from that that it would be your opinion given the crime scene and your personal investigation and your experience and expertise in blood splatter analysis that the assailant got blood on him?"

"Yes, sir."

"Enough blood to shield the westernmost and northwesternmost end of the north wall of that room. Is that correct?"

"Yes, sir. Through there."

"Because he would have been standing there, his body would have caught the blood, and it would not have traveled to these other locations because he, in fact, shielded that direction of flow. Is that correct?"

"Yes, sir."

"And you found it highly unusual that there was no blood on towels, on bathmats, in the bathroom, and what have you?"

"I didn't find any towels—"

"That had any blood on them," Long finished.

"That's correct."

"And you find, in addition to that, none on the clothing belonging to—and including the shoes, wristwatch, and belt—belonging to David Hendricks that has any trace of blood on it. Isn't that a fact?"

"That is correct, sir."

"Okay. Did you not tell us that on the upper floor there was a closetlike area wherein was located a washer and dryer?"

"Yes, sir."

"And the traps or filters from that washer and dryer were also part of the serology report. Were they not?"

"The P-traps. Yes, sir."

"And was there any blood found in them or any trace of blood?"

"No blood identified."

Long had the slide projector turned on again. A photo of the stairway leading to the upstairs of the Hendricks home appeared. It had been taken shortly after the crime-scene technicians entered the home.

"Okay. Now I want to call your attention to the elongated white marking that is on the second riser, or second tread, up from the bottom. What is that?"

"I don't recall exactly what it was."

"Well, if you were to get up and take a close look at it, would you be able to identify that as a wooden matchstick?"

"I don't know whether I would or not, sir."

"Why don't you try?" Long emphasized each word. Dodwell left the witness box and walked to within inches of the screen. A blowup of the light wood-colored object replaced the stairway picture. Long drummed his pen on the defense table. "Have you had a chance to take a look at it?"

"Yes, sir." Dodwell made his way back to the witness box.

"What does it appear to be?"

"It appears to be a match."

"Were you, during the course of your investigation, ever able to determine whether or not either David Hendricks or Susan Hendricks smoked?"

"I have no personal knowledge."

"In your walk-through and investigation of the house did you find any evidence of ashtrays, filled ashtrays, or of anybody of the residence using cigarettes or tobacco products?"

"No, sir."

"Was that matchstick collected as evidence?"

"No, sir."

"Did any member of your group supervised by you or working with you smoke?"

"Yes, sir."

"Who was that?"

"I do."

"Did you leave that matchstick on the stairs?"

"No, sir."

"Did you inquire of anybody who had been in there before you about who might have left a matchstick on the stairs in the Hendricks house?"

"Could I clarify one thing?"

"Sure," said Long.

"By looking at the photograph, it appears to be a matchstick. I don't recall it as a matchstick. I recall just a sliver of wood. I don't recall exactly what that was."

"Even if you recall it as a sliver of wood and assuming that it might be, Mr. Dodwell, was a sliver of wood in that location ever examined to determine whether it had evidential value?"

"I remember examining something on the stairs. I don't recall what it was. It was not collected."

"Okay. So my last question to you is, if in the event that it is a matchstick, there is nothing that you did in the course of your duties to determine the source from which that matchstick might have come. Is that correct?"

"Yes, sir."

"I have nothing further."

Murphy had a follow-up question.

"Did you also find a stack of wood out in the garage?"

"Yes, sir."

"Did you find a fireplace in the family room?"

"Yes, sir."

Alexander Mankevich, a Connecticut native employed as a fingerprint examiner by the Illinois Department of Law Enforcement, told jurors that he conducted five different types of tests on the ax and butcher knife but could come up with no fingerprints. He said tests on numerous other items revealed not only fingerprints and palm prints belonging to the five members of the Hendricks family but several other prints which couldn't be linked to anybody but definitely did not belong to any Hendricks family members.

"Was anything done," Long asked, "by the Department of Law Enforcement to try to determine who owned those fingerprints?"

"I did my part as far as I can," said Mankevich in a high, choppy voice. "I have reported, you know, that they were unidentified latent prints. I am unaware . . . I had not received any further inked fingerprints cards after February."

When questioned by Murphy, Mankevich testified that there was no way to determine the age of any of the prints.

Next on the stand was Mankevich's colleague, James Roberts, whose specialty was given as identification of tool marks, firearms, and footprints.

Murphy asked the bearded witness to explain what a tool mark is and how he goes about connecting a mark with an individual tool.

"There are basically two types of tool marks—either impression-type tool marks or striated," Roberts said. "An impression-type tool mark is caused by a harder object impressing its shape onto a softer object. A shoe print would be an example of an impression-type tool mark, or the mark left behind by the face of a hammer when it strikes a softer object. A striated tool mark is caused by a harder object sliding across and leaving striations on a softer object. Striations are basically a pattern of scratches to simply identify it."

"How do you go about making identification?"

"One would go examine a tool mark for its class characteristics, those predictable characteristics that define the group of tools that could have caused that kind of mark. And then one examines the individual characteristics. Normally this is done on comparison microscopes by making a test with the tool and comparing it directly to the tool mark. Every object has its unique characteristics."

Roberts went on to say that he attended the autopsies to make sure that evidence was collected to help in the tool-mark-identification process.

"I examined various items that the doctor removed for me. I made some casts from sections of Grace's trachea."

"Were there also sections of the trachea or vertebrae of Benjamin Hendricks that were cast by you?"

"Those casts were made later in the laboratory and used in addition to the casts that were attempted at autopsy."

"Can you describe the area or location of the vertebrae that was cast?"

"No, I cannot. The doctor removed it and gave it to me. I recall it being from the neck area."

Roberts said he tried to match up the ax and knife with not only some bone injuries but also to some damage done on some barrettes from Grace's hair.

"And how did you go about doing that, please?" Murphy asked.

"An examination under the stereomicroscope. And when it was determined there was sufficient individual characteristics present for additional comparisons, tests were made using the tools submitted, and comparisons were made between the casts and casts of those tests under this comparison microscope."

"So you actually used the ax and the knife to make known tool marks on another object and compared them to these marks?"

"Yes."

"Did you form any opinion or conclusion with regard to the tool that made the marks?"

"The tool involved was an edged instrument. I could not determine what instrument."

"Were you able to exclude the knife or the ax as being a weapon that could have caused such marks?"

"No, I was not able to exclude them."

Roberts also told Murphy that his examination of doorknobs and locks from the Hendricks home showed no sign of having been tampered with. And he said that he determined that none of Hendricks's footwear caused any of the three partial shoe prints found on the kitchen floor. Murphy brought up the subject because he knew Long would if he didn't."

That done, it was Long's turn.

"Let me ask you a question. When a lock is picked, are there always traces of tool marks?"

"Not always. It's possible, I suppose, to use a type of tool that would buffer the metal surfaces so they did not come in contact."

"And there are types of tools that can do that?"

"I'm not particularly familiar with any brand name that has that feature, but I'm sure that one could be created easily enough."

The state's final crime-scene expert was Tommy Martin. The supervisor of other crime-scene technicians in the middle third of Illinois told the jury that he had been involved in at least four thousand criminal investigations—roughly half of them involving burglaries, another eight hundred involving death. He also had spent parts of several days at 313 Carl Drive taking measurements and searching for evidence.

"I was looking for anything unusual," Martin said. "It had previously been processed by crime-scene technician Wamsley, and I was merely checking to make sure everything had been processed. Then I examined the air ducts, the crawl space, and the attic."

"Did you find anything unusual or of evidential value?"

"No, nothing."

"Based upon your experience and your training, Mr. Martin, and your examination of the scene, what is your opinion as to whether or not a burglary in fact occurred at 313 Carl Drive in Bloomington?"

"It is my opinion that a burglary did not occur at 313 Carl Drive."

Murphy had the courtroom lights dimmed and a slide projector turned on. Murphy asked Martin to use photos of the crime scene to illustrate why he thought a burglary had been faked. Hendricks remained in the courtroom.

A slide of the family room with its fireplace framed by bookcases and cabinets was on the screen. Martin was on his feet, near the screen. "The picture and a mirror on the wall did not appear to have been disturbed, nor did any of the books on the bookshelf appear to be disturbed."

"What in particular," Murphy asked, "did you notice about the books on the bookshelf?"

"It's not unusual for people to hide wall safes behind books or behind photographs. Oftentimes a burglar will take the pictures down, take the books out or at least lift up the corner of the picture. When they let the picture go, it's not hanging straight any more. Generally speaking it will be off-level. The books were in a very neat and orderly fashion. In fact, they all faced exactly to the front of the shelf on a level line."

Another photo showed a desk, some of its drawers pulled out. "The black object here, I believe, was a camera. Neither the paper bag nor the pink cloth sack had been gone through."

More pictures and similar observations with some valuables in clear view and undisturbed; drawers or cabinets open but nothing inside apparently disturbed. There was a photo of a china cabinet in the dining room. "Contained in the china cabinet were small figurines, china objects, decorative knickknack type things. By taking a hand-held flashlight and shining oblique lighting on the bottom of the shelving, you could see a very, very fine layer of dust on the shelf. After the outside was processed, I then opened that and carefully picked up one item, and you could clearly see the circle where the shelf had been protected from the dust around it. None of those items had been moved."

When pictures of the master bedroom appeared on the screen, Hendricks lowered his head and appeared not to watch. Martin went on. "Here we have an electric typewriter and case here. And you can see the drawers have been opened on both the dresser and the chest. This is a cedar chest at the foot of the bed, and the cedar chest does not appear to have been gone through, although the dresser and chest were."

"Was there any type of lock on that cedar chest?" asked Murphy.

"If I remember correctly, there was a push button to release the mechanism, and there was a key lock inside that. But it was not engaged. It was unlocked."

"Was the interior of the cedar chest examined?"

"Yes, I examined it. It contained bed clothing, sheets, blankets."

"Did they appear to have been disturbed?"

"No, they did not."

Another slide filled the screen. Long nudged his client, directing him to look at the picture.

"Was there any jewelry on or about this chest of drawers?" Murphy asked.

"Yes, on top of this chest I believe there was a silver-colored plain band like a wedding band, and I believe there were two silver dollars and one Kennedy half-dollar laying on top of the chest."

Another slide. "This depicts the dresser again in the master bedroom. It apparently has been disturbed more so than the others. This particular drawer at the lower right-hand corner was empty, and there was a pile of clothing on the floor here." Martin continued to point and Hendricks continued to look. "The top drawer at first glance appears to have been rifled or ransacked, gone through extensively. If you will notice along the front of the drawer, these are socks. They are folded and lined up very neatly, obviously they are still very neatly lined up. It indicates to me that these articles have been removed from the back corner and just drug forward, rather than actually looked through."

Another slide. "This is apparently a jewelry box, which appears to have been dumped onto the center of the dresser. Chains, brooches, pins, and that is a lady's watch, a ring box—all these items are still there." In other slides, Martin noted a container that still held a few dollars in coins, then a cassette tape player, turntable, and tape deck. "The electronic gear is something that's in rather high demand by burglars, something easily removed and has a relatively good value."

Another slide. "This is a photograph shooting from the master bedroom toward the master bath. There is a vanity area with sinks. The thing I noted about this particular area, the drawers are open. However, in this drawer and this drawer the contents did not appear to have been disturbed. The item up here is like a nylon mesh sweater dryer. As you can see, it has a sweater lying on it. The only thing holding it at this particular point is the edge of the drawer. If the drawer were moved a fraction in or out, the dryer and sweater would fall to the floor."

There were more slides and more comments from Martin pointing out details he considered to be inconsistent with a burglary. When the scenes moved into Benjy's room and Martin called attention to a green turtle bank on the floor with money in it, Hendricks began to cry into a handkerchief. Even though the courtroom was darkened, some of the jurors seemed to notice.

As Hendricks used his hand to shield his eyes from the pictures, slides were shown of the dresser drawers in the girls' room and of the shoe with the drop of blood inside.

"The drawers had been opened, in my opinion, after the attack, due to the splattering on the front of the drawers and nothing on the inside of them," Martin said. He added that a pulled-out drawer protected the shoe, that the drawer had to have been closed and the shoe unprotected in order for a spurt of blood to reach inside the shoe.

"Do you have specific experience or training in what are referred to as 'subterfuge crimes'?" Murphy asked.

"If you are referring to crimes which are set up or used to cover other acts, yes, I have."

"What type of subterfuge crimes have you had specific experience with?"

"Burglaries, arsons, auto theft."

And what about 313 Carl Drive? Murphy wanted to know.

"It is my opinion that a burglary was staged at this location in order to throw investigators onto perhaps a false lead, a false trail."

John Long was on his feet. The slide projector had been turned off, and the lights were on.

"Mr. Martin." Long moved close to the witness box, his hand resting on its front. "Can you tell me whether or not, based upon your experience and the number of courses that you have taken in this subject, are there parts of this crime scene that were consistent with a burglary?"

"Yes. That is true."

"Does everything in a burglary scene have to be disturbed?"

"No. It's very rare that everything is disturbed."

"Now with respect to some of the items that you say were not taken, in your investigation did you ever learn personally or through any other police agency that there was a report of currency not found in the home that might have been taken?"

"I first learned that last week when I came here."

"And what you learned was that there were several hundred dollars to have been considered missing. Is that correct?"

"Yes, that's correct."

"You indicate that the drawers were opened in some respect after the attack on the victims in their home. If one were attempting not to be caught or to be identified, one wouldn't ransack a place before getting rid of the people who could identify one, would one?"

"Correct."

"Isn't therefore this crime scene also consistent with the fact that the murders interrupted what you would consider a normal burglary?"

"No, sir. I can't agree with that."

"Tell us why you can't."

"There were no defensive wounds. There was nothing to indicate that the victims had been alerted to the fact that an intruder was in the house. The final resting places of each of the victims did not indicate to me that they had awoke, that they suspected anything to be wrong."

Murphy had only one area of questions in his re-direct examination.

"Assume, as Mr. Long suggests in one of his questions, that

there may have been some money in the home that is gone, and assume that as part of the other facts that you know about this case. How, if at all, does that change your opinion in this case?"

"It does not change my opinion."

"Why is that?"

"It's not unusual for someone to stage a burglary and either physically take something or report something is missing to help verify that a burglary did in fact occur."

"You have had specific experience in the past with that situation?"

"Yes, I have."

The next part of the prosecution strategy was to show that Hendricks was acutely aware of what might happen to a member of the Brethren who sought and obtained a divorce. The witness was Sandy Bumpus, a Bloomington teacher who had known David and Susan since the three of them were children and had attended Brethren meetings and other gatherings with their parents.

Murphy questioned her about her attendance as a Brethren member at meetings of the Bloomington group. "Were you aware, Miss Bumpus, whether the defendant, David Hendricks, held any position of leadership among the believers there at the Bloomington meeting?"

"Yes. He would give meetings and led prayers and such. He would outline the gospel."

"Miss Bumpus, when were you divorced?"

"In August of 1980."

"Were you at that time regularly attending the meetings?"

"Yes."

"And how often did they meet?"

"Three times a week. Sunday morning, Sunday evening, and Wednesday evening."

The witness testified that shortly after her divorce, she received a letter signed by Hendricks and three other of the Bloomington meeting's leaders who were her relatives. The letter informed her that she was being barred from taking communion and from socializing with members of the Brethren except at church events. The letter was delivered to her by Hendricks and one of her relatives.

"The letter just stated that I would not be able to remember the Lord with them on Sundays. I could be at the meetings, but I could not socialize with them outside of the meeting."

"Was there any conversation about why this was occurring?"

"David explained to me that as far as the Bible states, there is no basis for divorce except . . . ummm . . . I forget what the word is. Can you give me a clue?"

Jennings was up. "I'm going to object to this, Judge."

"Object to what?"

"To the request of the witness for information and interrogation of counsel by the witness."

"Can you restate your question, Mr. Murphy?" Judge Baner asked.

"Yes. As best you can recall, would you relate at the time you received the letter what the conversation was and please indicate who was saying what."

"If I can figure out what that word is, I can tell you."

There was a pause.

"Adultery. Okay. There is no basis in the Bible, there is no reason, no excuse for divorce in the Bible unless the other person has committed adultery, and therefore if I was initiating the divorce, it was going against the vow that I took when I married."

"After receiving the letter, did you attend the meetings?"

"No."

"Going back to one specific aspect of the letter that you received, who is it that you were not allowed to socialize with?"

"Anyone in the meeting."

"At that time, were there any close relatives of yours in the meeting?"

"Yes. Father and mother, aunts, uncles, cousins."

Bill Ortleb, a photographer who had done photo work for Hendricks's brace brochures, was next on the stand. He said Hendricks had stopped by his office about three weeks before the killings.

"He wanted to get some new photos made up because he was coming out with a new back brace, and he had shown an interest in Carla Webb doing some photos for him in the past, and he wanted me to try and arrange a meeting between her and him. I called her up to try to arrange something. He said that if she was ready, he would like to see her that afternoon, and she said that was fine."

"What occurred next?" Dozier asked.

"Well, I was on the phone, and after I was talking to Carla—all of a sudden I was getting this funny feeling in the corner of my eye—"

Jennings objected to the characterization.

"You can only testify as to what you saw and did," Dozier reminded the witness.

"Well, out of the corner of my eye, I saw Mr. Hendricks staring intently at the photo of Carla Webb."

"Do you have an estimate of the period of time he stared at the photo?"

"It was for quite a few seconds."

"Then what happened?"

"I looked at him, and he saw me looking at him. And he finally stopped looking at it and kind of blushed. And kind of gave a nervous smile."

"Could you tell us what the photo of Carla Webb looked like, what did it depict?"

"Blond woman wearing a striped knit top that was cut pretty low and just a nice smile. And she was kind of holding glasses in her hand up to her face."

"What portion of Carla Webb was showing in the photo?"

"I would say about the waist up."

"On any of these occasions when Mr. Hendricks talked to you about using Carla Webb as a model, was there any conversation with him about why he desired to use her particularly?"

"Yes. He said that he thought that Carla was an attractive woman, and that she photographed well, and that most of the models that he had been using were, oh, tall and kind of, you know, thin. And he was looking for someone who was a little bit more, and he kind of used his hands. I can't remember the exact adjective that was used, but—"

"Could you describe for the record," Dozier said as he motioned to the court reporter's machine, "because that little machine cannot see what you're doing. Can you state how he used his hands?"

"Emphasizing breasts."

"Mr. Ortleb." Hal Jennings was sounding casual but firm. "With respect to your recollection concerning your contact with Mr. Hendricks and your observations concerning him, you were interviewed by the police within a week after the murders in Bloomington, were you not?"

"Yes, sir."

"Did you tell them anything about this conversation involving Mr. Hendricks and Carla Webb and the description that you have given us today concerning his comments about her buxom nature?"

"No, I didn't."

"With respect to another interview concerning this case, you talked to Mr. Dozier sometime in 1984 in his office concerning this same set of circumstances. Is that correct?"

"Yes."

"Did you say to Mr. Dozier at the time you talked to him in 1984 anything about this conversation with David Hendricks concerning Carla Webb and her buxomness?"

"At that time I didn't."

"When did you first talk to anybody in connection with this case about this conversation concerning Carla Webb and Mr. Hendricks, discussing or describing in some physical manner her buxomness? Was it in fact right before you went on the stand today?"

"That was the first time that I recalled it. Yes, sir."

Carolyn Johnston, a college student who had done a little modeling, lived in an apartment house next door to CASH Manufacturing's Evans Street office. Now on the witness stand for the prosecution, she said she was trying to start her car on a cold day in March of 1983 when Hendricks approached her and asked to talk to her in his office when she had a moment.

"He asked me if I would be interested in modeling the back brace for him. He had some brochures lying on the table in a folder, and he showed me pictures of the back brace. There was, you know, a picture of a model wearing the back brace, and he told me that he would pay me fifty dollars an hour in the studio, and I don't remember if it was fifty dollars an hour to be measured also or if it was twenty-five dollars an hour to be measured. I'm not really sure of the prices quoted. He said I would have to be measured in the nude, but when I went to the studio, I would wear a bodysuit which I think he said he would provide."

"What happened next?"

"He then stated that he was a professional and that there was no need for me to worry about anything, that he had a business that he had sold before he went into the manufacturing of back braces. Then I asked him could I at least wear my underclothing to be measured, and he said that I could wear the bottoms but not the tops. And I asked why, and he said that he had to measure the bones and mark the measurements on the body in order to properly fit the back brace."

"Did you at that time agree to model for him?"

"No. I think I said I would think about it and left."

"Did you subsequently contact him or he contact you?"

"I contacted his secretary the next day to tell her that I was too busy."

"Did you have any more contact with Mr. Hendricks?"

"Yes. It was probably the day after I had called his secretary."

"Okay. What happened then? When and where did it occur?"

"At my apartment. He came to my apartment one morning and—"

"Were you expecting him at that time?"

"No. He asked me if he could measure me for the back brace. And I said that I didn't have time to do the modeling."

"Was there anyone else present during that conversation?"

"My boyfriend was there."

"And then what occurred?"

"And then that was the end. He was like okay. That was the end of the whole thing."

"And so you never did model for him."

"No."

It was already another Friday morning when Ernie Mountjoy, a twenty-year veteran of the Bloomington Police Department, took the stand for the prosecution, explaining how a close examination of the Hendricks house found about twenty-one dollars in currency and change in various drawers and children's banks. Now Long was cross-examining him about the possible latent footprints which Mountjoy had been asked to analyze.

"Can you state whether or not you obtained the shoes worn by Dan Brady, Detective Scott, Officer Hibbens, Detective O'Brien, and Detective Bagnell, as well as shoes worn by David Hendricks, to determine whether they matched any of the impressions of the footwear found at the crime scene?"

"I did."

"And isn't it also a fact that was done in order to exclude those people who were physically in the crime scene as people who might have made those shoe prints?"

"That is true."

"Isn't it also fact that those shoe prints found in the crime scene don't compare with any of the officers' who investigated the crime scene or anybody first in the crime scene or David Hendricks?"

"They did not compare."

Next there was a written statement presented as evidence

from Sharon Zwanzig, one of two women who had driven with Susan Hendricks to the baby shower near Delavan just hours before the murders occurred. One part of the statement covered what Susan had talked about during the drive. "Generally we talked about children. Susan talked about how the kids were doing in school and how they were really enjoying school, and she talked to Paula about the upcoming teacher's conference and things like that. Then we asked Susan if Dave had any trips planned lately, and she said he was leaving as soon as she got home, but she didn't say where he was going. We asked her if she liked that, and she said that she didn't like the ones that took a week or so but when he was only gone for a couple of nights that wasn't so bad because he was real good about calling her."

When court resumed after lunch, a large-screen television sat in front of the jury box. The prosecution planned to show jurors the unedited television interview Hendricks did with two TV reporters the afternoon after the murders were discovered. Jennings, calling the tape irrelevant and inflammatory, asked Judge Baner to bar its use.

"When all is said and done, it will simply be an argument to the jury that a statement of religious belief by the defendant is somehow inappropriate and that a person who utters such a statement is guilty. It seems to me that would create a violation of the defendant's First Amendment rights as far as his freedom of religion is concerned." Jennings also objected because the tape showed Hendricks's response to a reporter's question about capital punishment for whoever killed his wife and children.

Dozier said he couldn't understand the defense objection to showing the videotape. "There is no assertion being made that it was not a free and voluntary statement by the defendant concerning the offense. This videotape is the best evidence of the questions asked and answers given and everything that goes with that. It is far more accurate and truthful than perhaps a witness testifying from memory. In addition, I think it goes to motive. Shown in its best light of the state's evidence, there are answers that could relate, again depending on how the jury views the evidence."

Jennings was now standing in front of the bench. "The real purpose for this, Judge, are the religious statements made by the defendant in an attempt to have the jury make a judgment as to whether or not they are appropriate."

Judge Baner ruled in favor of the prosecution but accepted a defense objection that the large-screen TV was unnecessary. When the jury came into the courtroom, a standard-sized television sat in front of the jury box. WEEK-TV reporter Christine Zak explained how the interview came about. Then color bars appeared on the TV set and a man's voice was heard as a close-up picture of David Hendricks came into focus.

"Yes, they are all three in school."

Hendricks looked toward the camera and gave what looked like a nervous half-smile.

"Are you rolling?" It was Zak's voice. "Are you guys ready to go? Okay. Now the last time you talked to your wife was late Monday?"

"Yes. Monday night." Hendricks's voice sounded tired. His hair was messy. His eyes appeared watery, tired.

"And then you called around noon, but you weren't alarmed at all. And then what happened?"

"Then I called again about three o'clock when the kids got home from school and knew she would be home. But there was no response then either." Hendricks's voice was flat and somewhat nasal. "I still wasn't alarmed because she could easily have been out, so I called later about five-thirty when she was supposed to be at her brother's for dinner. I knew she had an appointment there. And she wasn't there, and that is why I began to get alarmed, because Susie was always timely. And then when they called, I gave them my number up there in my motel, and they called me back about a half hour later, and she still wasn't there. I called a neighbor, who knocked on the door for me and came back and said she's not at home either. So—"

Zak interrupted. "But her car was back?"

"It was in the garage, so nobody could tell whether it was there or not, so I suspected there had been an accident on the road and called the police, and they reported no accident. And after waiting for a while longer, I kept trying to call home, thought I better check out of my motel and come right down and cut the second day of my sales trip short. And so I did and drove right down and got here about eleven-ten at night. And what had happened was a lot worse than just the accident I thought."

Another man's voice was heard. It was another TV reporter, Gary Lane. "What did the neighbors say? Did they see anything?"

"I haven't talked to any neighbors. The police advised me to stay away from my home because of all the news people out there."

"Who do you think might have done something like this?" Lane asked.

"I have no idea." Hendricks's gaze dropped to his feet. "The people asked me when they interviewed me last night, interrogated me last night. I have no idea."

"Do they know what was the motive for this?" Zak asked. "Was there anything missing in the house itself? Were you at the house itself?"

"No, I was not at the house. I was never in the house, but they said that some things looked like some things were taken. I suppose I will be the one to find that out when I get there, but I haven't been there yet."

"What will you do now?" Zak asked. "This is probably the worst thing that will ever happen to you in your life. You are young. Where do you go from here?"

"Well, I guess that is a question that I haven't really allowed myself to answer. I have been—" Hendricks paused and swallowed hard. "Been dwelling on more short-term things the last couple of days, but I know that Susie and my three children are much better off, and I wish them back for me as a selfish thing. But I know that they are with the Lord Jesus in heaven, and I am satisfied now in knowing that."

"Dave," Lane jumped in, "you are a fairly religious person. If they find the person who did this, do you believe in the death penalty? What would you like to see happen?"

"I would like to see him get saved. It would be worth it if one person found their way to heaven, don't you think so?"

"Well—" Lane's voice was the last thing heard on the tape.

It was now late Friday afternoon on the sixth week of the trial. And there was only one more matter to be addressed. At the defense's urging, Judge Baner instructed the jury not to watch NBC's announcements promoting its upcoming miniseries "Fatal Vision," based on the Jeffrey MacDonald family murders at Fort Bragg, North Carolina—a crime that had some similarities with the Hendricks killings.

Back in Bloomington that night, a man attended a Halloween costume party dressed as David Hendricks. He wore a three-piece suit and a Chuck E. Cheese hat and carried a Bible and an ax. On his back was a bumper sticker distributed by Wisconsin's state tourism office. It read, "Escape to Wisconsin."

On Monday, the prosecution's next-to-last witness, David Hendricks's longtime friend Lawrence Macy, took the stand. The Bloomington man, about twenty years Hendricks's senior, had known David since he was a boy. Over the past five years, they had been brothers in the Bloomington assembly of the Plymouth Brethren. Macy's testimony about the Brethren's marriage tenets, Dozier believed, would be pivotal in trying to establish a motive for the murders.

With a stern and serious bearing, Macy told Dozier that God instituted marriage when Eve was presented to Adam as a help-mate.

"Are you familiar with the basic beliefs of the Brethren on the subject of divorce?" Dozier asked.

"Divorce was permitted in the early days of the law by Moses. The Lord told his disciples that Moses permitted it because of the hardness of their hearts. But then the Lord went on to say that in God's eyes, divorce was not permitted except for the case where the spouse perhaps had committed adultery, been unfaithful, and had left his wife."

"And is that the teaching that is followed by the Brethren to this day?"

"Yes."

"When you speak of adultery in that context, could you tell us what is the understanding of that term within the context of the Brethren's beliefs?"

"Well, adultery is the instance where one or both members are unfaithful to the other in the marriage connection. They go outside the marriage and seek illicit affairs."

"Can you tell me, if a member of the Brethren were to commit adultery as you have defined it, what are the consequences within the fellowship of the Brethren?"

"Well, it has to be known. It has to be revealed. Then we have to examine it by a committee, and then it's brought before the assembly as a whole, and the decision to either allow them to remain in fellowship with us or to be set aside is done by majority decision."

"Can you explain what is the procedure by which this decision is made and who makes such a decision? You used the term 'we.' Who were you referring to that starts the process?"

"It's generally some of the perhaps older brothers in the assembly or those more learned."

"Would you explain what it means to be a brother in the assembly?"

"Well, to be a brother in the assembly could be one who is the Lord's, who has been saved, who knows the Lord Jesus Christ as their savior."

"And you used the term 'setting aside' a while ago. What does it mean?"

"Setting aside, of course, is just telling them they cannot remember the Lord in his death, cannot partake of the emblems. They can still come to the meetings. They can remember the Lord in their heart, but they're set aside in that way."

"Are there any other sanctions or discipline or consequences specifically for the matter of adultery?"

"They're not allowed to have specific fellowship with those who are gathered. If you want to call it social functions. This does not mean necessarily their parents or family—but with others."

"Can it also apply to their parents or close relatives?"

"The very extreme case."

"How long is a person who has committed adultery put aside or set aside for that transgression?"

"Every case is different. It depends on the severity of the case, on the spirit of the person who's been set aside, whether they're really repentant, really sorry. Depends on whether they continue to come out to the meetings."

"Do you know, Mr. Macy, whether the defendant, David Hendricks, is familiar with the basic beliefs of the Brethren on marriage, divorce, and adultery that you have outlined for us today?"

"Yes."

"How are you aware?"

"Just from having talked with him, having him in our assembly."

Dozier reached into a file and pulled out three pages of typewritten text. It was his next question.

"Mr. Macy, I have a rather long question to ask you, but based upon your experience and knowledge of the Brethren as you have testified here today, I want to ask you this question. Assume a brother of the fellowship is married, and he and his family are regular and active members of the fellowship. Assume that he has engaged in the following behaviors: that in the course of conducting fitting sessions for the stated purpose of preparing female models for photographic sessions wherein they would be modeling back braces for an advertising brochure, the subject requested at least three such models to disrobe entirely to the nude and directed and caused at least five such models to disrobe from the waist up, thereby exposing their breasts to him in the course of the fitting sessions."

The question went on and on, Dozier having his witness assume that a member of the Brethren had done everything the models had testified to—the touching, massaging, the efforts to kiss. "And further assume that each of the aforesaid models is young, physically mature, and physically attractive. And further assume that the subject engaged in the aforesaid behaviors described as occurring during the fitting sessions were not for the stated purpose of obtaining a proper fit for the brace for photographic advertising purposes but for the purpose of his own sexual gratification. Assuming all of these facts to be true, can you tell me what, if any, penalties, sanctions, or discipline could be imposed by the assembly of the Bloomington Brethren on such a subject for such behavior or conduct?"

The question had taken six minutes to read. Now it was time for Macy's answer. "Are you asking me to speak for the Brethren?"

"No. I'm asking you in your opinion what, if any, penalty or range of penalties could be imposed if those circumstances were taken as correct?"

"Well, this is a hard question to answer, because you don't enter into these things lightly. You don't make decisions in a few minutes. I believe it's something that would have to be deliberated by an individual and by a group before anything—any kind of corrective measures could be taken."

Annoyed, Dozier turned to the judge. "Your Honor, I'm having trouble getting the witness to understand. I'm not asking Mr. Macy for the procedures to be followed." He turned back to the witness. "I'm simply asking you, given those facts and assuming those facts for the purpose of this question that I have stated, what, in your opinion, could be imposed as a discipline or penalty for those behaviors?"

Macy's stonelike features didn't budge. "And, I repeat, I couldn't go on record of making any opinions right away. I would have to deliberate about it."

"Mr. Macy." Dozier's voice took on a firmness that hadn't been heard before. "Do you understand we're not asking you to make a decision on an actual case? We're asking you to assume certain facts as correct and then indicate what, if any, range of penalties could be imposed, in your opinion."

Jennings spoke up. "Judge, I object, because the witness has simply said that neither he nor others would make such a decision based on a hypothetical set of facts read to him, whether true or untrue. And the fact is that counsel may not like the answer, but he has answered."

"Objection is overruled," Judge Baner said.

Dozier turned to Macy. "You may answer the last question."

"Well, I can give the range of what might be decided. One would be a public rebuke before the assembly, depending on the severity. And in this case it might amount to that. Or it could be a silencing of the individual where he couldn't take part in any of the group giving out the Word or himself in prayer. Or he could be set aside where he would not be allowed to partake of the emblems."

Dozier's sigh was almost audible. "I believe that's all the questions we have."

In his cross-examination, Jennings attempted to downplay the religious and social significance of a reprimand of a member of the Brethren. "As far as your religious service is concerned, is there any sermon or preaching by any minister, equivalent of a minister, or any deacon or elder? Is there a presentation or a sermon in connection with your religious service?"

"No. There's no formal program. There's no minister. We're just led by the spirit. Whoever feels led to give out a hymn, it's all done according to scripture."

"Is it true that in your service, brothers simply state a request for a particular hymn or state a prayer in terms of a particular reading of scripture?"

"Yes."

"And by 'silencing,' do you mean anything other than a brother would not be called upon to refer to a scriptural passage or prayer or to call for a particular hymn?"

"Yes. That's what we mean."

"Now you mentioned that it's possible that given some act of conduct that a brother could be set aside. Tell me when you use the term 'set aside,' what do you mean?"

"To be set aside, of course, would be to be restricted from partaking of the emblems, to be restricted from certain fellowship with others of the assembly. Not family necessarily, but other members of the group."

"By 'emblems,' are you referring to anything more than the loaf and the cup?"

"No."

"With respect to being restricted as far as activities are concerned, are you referring to activities of the assembly whether they are characterized as gospel meeting or prayer meeting or social meeting? Is that what you're referring to?"

"Yes. I shouldn't use the term 'social meeting,' but a social function such as a group getting together for a potluck or a picnic or something like that. We always invite them to continue coming out to the meetings, the gospel meetings, Wednesday morning meetings."

"You're not suggesting by noting a restriction on religious, prayer, or social functions that a person would be removed from contact with their relatives or with their friends or former acquaintances, are you, Mr. Macy?"

"No."

"When somebody is set aside, as far as your faith is concerned, does that have to do with the act of the person or the attitude of the person?"

"Well, I think there's some of both."

"Tell me what you mean by that."

"There is the overt act that has to be dealt with. It's as if our children did something naughty and we had to spank them. It's done in love. It's not done with malice in our hearts. We want to bring that person back. For one thing, the very first thing that we have to remember is that the person is responsible to God for his actions. We have to bring that before him very forcibly, and then in love seek to restore him back into fellowship."

"When someone is set aside, are they removed, are they excommunicated, are they kicked out of the fellowship?"

"They're not removed, not kicked out. They're told by letter that they are no longer in fellowship. They're encouraged to continue to come out to meetings. They're told of our love for them and our desire to have them restored."

"Is that status something that's permanent or is it temporary?"

"It's temporary, except for the cases where the one set aside leaves and no longer has a desire to come back."

In his second round of questioning with Macy, Dozier asked whether the Brethren consider it adultery when someone seeks but is refused sex with someone other than his or her spouse.

"We never really have been faced with that kind of situation," Macy responded. "I would say that it's not if it's not an act. A person is on dangerous grounds as far as that goes. He may be going on the wrong course and sooner or later things would generate into the actual act."

Jennings wanted to know whether there are divorced people in the Bloomington assembly.

"Yes."

"Are there people in the Bloomington assembly who have been restored after being set aside?"

"Yes."

"Are there people who have been restored after having committed a sexual transgression?"

"Yes."

"Such as bearing a child out of wedlock?"

"Yes."

"I have nothing further."

The state's last witness was Detective Charles Crowe. When questioned by Murphy, Crowe painstakingly recounted his interviewing, interrogating, and finally accusing Hendricks in the hours after the bodies were found. Now Jennings was cross-examining Crowe, whom he had cross-examined in countless other criminal cases. They were friends. And they were adversaries; Crowe trying to put defendants behind bars; Jennings working to keep them out. Now Crowe sat straight, almost starched, in the witness box, eyes straight ahead, concentrating.

"Detective Crowe," Jennings began, "during the interrogation process, did you say to David Hendricks that you knew he had committed the murders of his wife and children?"

"Yes." Crowe's voice was flat.

"Did you also say that you were going to get him for that murder sooner or later?"

"Yes."

"How many murder cases do you believe, Detective Crowe, that you have worked on while you have been a detective for the city of Bloomington?"

"Twenty-five or thirty."

"And that twenty-five or thirty, would that be half the cases of a homicidal nature that have occurred in Bloomington since you became a detective, a third of them, all of them? What would you judge?"

"All of them."

"Are you familiar specifically with the neighborhood around Carl Drive?"

"Yes."

"Is it fair to characterize that area as a white-collar neighborhood?"

"Yes."

"Is the neighborhood around Carl Drive also your home neighborhood?"

"I live eight to ten blocks from there."

"Do you visit back and forth in that neighborhood around Carl Drive from time to time?"

"Yes."

"And are there other police officers that live close by?"

"Yes."

"Detective Crowe, have you ever worked a murder case in Bloomington where four people were killed?"

"No."

"Have you ever worked one where three people were killed?"

"No."

"Have you ever worked a double homicide in the city of Bloomington since 1972?"

"I can't think of any."

"Have you ever worked on a case where children have been murdered since you became a detective in '72?"

"One that I can recall."

"Have you ever worked a murder in your neighborhood before, Detective Crowe, within a half mile, quarter mile, six blocks, anything that close?"

"Three-quarters of a mile."

Jennings took Crowe back to the detective's questioning of Hendricks in the Cramer home shortly after the murders were discovered. Had Crowe known, when he questioned Hendricks, that the Hendricks home may have been burglarized, that relatives were at the house when police first arrived, what information they may have given police, or even that Hendricks had arrived at his home after police had found the bodies? The answer each time was a curt "no."

"When you first saw Hendricks at the Cramers', where was he and what was he doing? Do you recall?"

"He was sitting in the living room in a chair." Crowe's eyes remained straight ahead, his voice flatter than before. "Had something draped around his shoulders. I don't recall what it was."

"Do you recall what you first said or did with respect to your initial contact with Hendricks?"

"Told him I wanted to talk to him."

"Did you shake his hand or did you offer any statement of condolence or sympathy or saying anything like that?"

"I just indicated I wanted to talk to him."

"Did you note any reluctance or hesitation on his part when you asked permission to search the airplane, the motorcycle, the hangar?"

"No."

"Did he state any reluctance when you asked to search the house and the car?"

"No."

"Detective Crowe, when you asked Hendricks to go down to the police station for additional questioning, did you have any knowledge at that particular time, from any other officers or any other source, that any of the information that David Hendricks had given you in that interview up there in the bedroom was a lie or factually inaccurate?"

"No."

"Did you, at the conclusion of that interview in the Cramer bedroom, say to other officers that you believed that David Hendricks was dirty or guilty of the murder?"

"Yes."

"Before you made that statement, had you asked David who lived in the house at 313 Carl Drive? Did you ever ask him that question?"

"No."

"Did you ever ask him whether any persons other than himself or Susan or the three slain children had lived at 313 Carl Drive in the past?"

"No."

"Did you ask him if there were any visitors, family members, or non-family members expected at the Carl Drive home on November 7th or 8th?"

"No."

"Did you ask him if he knew of any other persons other than himself or Susan or the three kids who might have physically been inside the house on November 7th?"

"No."

"Did you ask him if he saw anyone when he left the house on November 7th, '83?"

"No."

"Did you ask him if there was anything suspicious when he left the house on November 7th inside, outside, anywhere?"

"No."

Jennings's questions continued eight minutes more as he tried to show that Crowe had left a lot of questions unasked yet had come to a conclusion of guilt. Had Crowe asked who knew Hendricks was going to Wisconsin, whether his home had been broken into before, whether he had been threatened or feared anybody, whether he had any crank or suspicious phone calls, whether he had financial problems, whether money was kept in the house, or whether Hendricks knew of any possible suspects or motives? Had Crowe asked Hendricks any of those questions before concluding to his fellow policemen that Hendricks was dirty? Each time the answer was a single word: no.

"Detective Crowe, when you told David Hendricks on November 9th that sooner or later you intended to 'get him' for this offense, were you telling him the truth?"

"Yes, I truthfully and honestly thought that we would be getting him sooner or later."

Murphy had some more questions.

"In the course of the initial interview at the Cramer home," Murphy asked, "did the defendant give answers to questions that were not in direct response to your questions?"

"Yes."

"During the course of the interrogation down at the police department, did you feel that the defendant was trying to present himself in his most favorable light to you?"

"Yes."

"Can you give us a couple of examples of answers he gave in which you concluded that?"

"When I asked him if his wife was awake when he left, he said yes, and he hugged her and kissed her good-bye."

"He added that?"

"Yes."

"Any others?"

"When we went through the part about the age of the kids and where they were, he added that he kissed them good-bye."

"You didn't specifically ask him then what his actions were when he left?"

"No."

"Detective Crowe, in the manner in which you go about your

duties trying to solve crimes for the Bloomington Police Department, does it make any difference to you what the location of the crime is or what neighborhood it occurred in?"

"No."

"Concerning the conclusion that you reached after your interview of the defendant at the Cramer home, was that based in part upon your seventeen years' experience as a police officer?"

"Yes."

"Specifically in part upon the hundreds of interrogations that you've been involved in as a police officer and detective?"

"Yes."

Now, Jennings's last questions for Crowe.

"Again, Detective Crowe, was your conclusion that you reached at the end of the interview with the defendant that the defendant was dirty in this case based on any facts that you had at hand concerning the crime scene or any misrepresentation or untruths spoken to you by the defendant concerning where he had been, when he'd called, what he'd done, who he'd seen, anything at all having to do with what the man had just told you by way of factual information?"

"Yes. Some of those things he had told me."

"Some of those things he had told you you knew to be false?"

"I didn't say that."

"Did you have any information from any collateral source concerning anything the man said to you up there in that room that you knew to be false?"

"No."

"And in fact, the investigation in the case that followed in whole or in part had to do with determining the accuracy of what he told you up there in the bedroom, correct?"

"Yes."

"You indicated that, in your opinion, David Hendricks tried to present himself in a favorable picture when he told you that before he left for Wisconsin he had kissed his wife and given her a hug. Is that correct?"

"Yes."

"And that he was trying to present himself in a favorable fashion when he said that he kissed his children before he left for the trip to Wisconsin?"

"Yes."

"When you leave on a business trip, Detective Crowe, do you kiss your wife good-bye?"

"Yes."

"Detective Crowe, when you leave on a business trip, do you kiss your children?"

"They're in Boulder, Colorado. But if they were at home, I probably would."

As the prosecution's seventy-sixth and last witness left the stand, David Hendricks blotted some tears from his eyes.

Sixteen

The defense of David Hendricks began on Election Day, November 6, 1984.

But first, John Long sought a directed verdict of not guilty. With the jury out of the courtroom, Long tried to convince Judge Baner that the directed verdict was in order. He stood at a podium before the judge.

"When the evidence that has been elicited at this trial is viewed even in a most favorable light to the state," Long told the judge, "a conviction could not stand. And this court, with all due respect, has an obligation to enter a directed verdict of acquittal—notwithstanding the sensational nature of this case."

Long said the state's case was entirely circumstantial, and no motive had been established.

"The state has not offered evidence—not one iota of evidence—that there is such a thing as progressive sexual aggression. There has not been a single witness testify with respect to the behavioral sciences or anything else that there is in fact such a thing as a progressive sexual aggression. Yet this is the basis that the state would urge upon us as their motive for the defendant to take an ax and/or knife and slay his wife and his three children as they lay sleeping.

"Even if we admitted that there was such a thing as progressive sexual aggression, what evidence has been shown that progressive sexual aggression will lead one to commit the act of murder? Not murder, Your Honor, of a lover. Not murder of somebody in a heat of passion but, by implication, a cold deliberate act of ax murder of one's wife and children."

Long moved on to the related issue of Hendricks's religion. There was no evidence, Long said, that Hendricks had done anything that would cause the Brethren to set him aside, or silence him, or even take the least severe step, a reprimand. Even so, Long asked, would the mere possibility of a reprimand cause a man to take the action Hendricks was accused of taking?

"The possibility of a reprimand would be sufficient for a man to take an ax, a long-handled ax, and hit his wife in the head at least three times with it? To take the same ax and hit his children in the face with it? To take a butcher knife and to slit their throats with it because he might be reprimanded?

"Motive means motivation. Is there a scintilla of evidence in the trial to this point which would show by word, by deed, by demonstrative evidence that the defendant feared a possibility of rebuke to such an extent that his only recourse was to kill his wife and children?

"Can the court see or find anything that's been presented to show the relationship or the actions of this defendant any different from the actions of many individuals who may be indiscreet or may stray or may do a wrong thing? Instead, what the evidence here has shown is that the defendant is not perfect. The bottom line of this, Your Honor, is that there's no showing—no showing whatsoever—that the only recourse that the defendant had was to get rid of his wife and children. And how in heaven's name does getting rid of his wife and children obviate the fact that he still might be discovered in an adultery and still might be set aside?"

Dozier's response was brief. He felt there was literally no chance Judge Baner would enter a directed verdict.

"Your Honor, I believe that Mr. Long has made a good speech that certainly would sound good in final argument, but the purpose for this hearing is to determine whether the state's evidence viewed in its light most favorable to the state is sufficient to support as a matter of law a verdict of guilty in the case. And we believe it is.

"Experts called by the state established that the three children were violently slain at a time period when, by the defendant's own statement to police, he was the only one in the home alone with them."

It was time for lunch. Judge Baner promised a ruling on the request for a directed verdict immediately afterward. As Long left the courtroom, a reporter asked him the chances that he would win an immediate acquittal. "I'm an optimist by nature," he responded. "But I'm not a fool."

After lunch the motion was denied. The defense case would begin immediately. Its first witness would be familiar to the jurors.

Bev Crutcher seemed a bit more self-assured as she stepped into the witness box a second time. Knowing more of what to expect as a defense witness, she even gave her boss an uneasy smile.

Long asked her to explain what duties she had in connection with Hendricks's business trips.

"It would start with his announcement of taking a sales trip," she said. "He would tell me the area he was going to and ask me to pull customers that we had so that he could call on them. Sometimes I would pack his briefcase for him, lay out his business cards, paper, pens, the names and addresses of the customers. When he got to the area, he would call back and read more names from the phone book to see if they were either on the list or if I had heard from them in the past. And on his return, he would hand over all of his notes, and we would do several letters to these people as follow-up. I would also take care of the receipts from the trips, the expense receipts."

"In the year leading up to and including November 7th of 1983, how many business trips do your records indicate Mr. Hendricks took?"

"About thirteen."

"And can you state whether when he announced in the week prior to the 7th of November that he was to take a business trip to Wisconsin, whether it was done in the same manner that he had made these announcements in the past?"

"Yes."

"And you found nothing unusual about it?"

"Nothing whatsoever."

Crutcher testified that several times a month Susan Hendricks and the children would stop by the CASH Manufacturing office.

"At any time other than an office setting did you ever have occasion to see David Hendricks in the company of his wife and children?"

"One that I can think of offhand. I think it was May 21st of 1983 in the hospital. I had just given birth to my second son. The family came up to see me."

"Did you ever see or hear an argument between David Hendricks and his wife or his children?"

Crutcher's voice took on the tone of someone who was shocked by the question. "No. Never."

"At any time did you ever observe any discord or any anger or any shouting between the two?"

"No."

"Or between David and the children?"

"Never."

"What, if anything, did you observe the actions to be between David and his wife and children when they were in your presence in the office setting?"

"Extreme happiness. You could feel the love fill the room."

"With respect to November 7th, 1983, you indicated in your earlier testimony that Benjamin Hendricks was left in the office by his mother. What, if anything, did you observe about the relationship or actions between Benjamin and his father on that date?"

"Dave was just beaming with pride over Benjy. Benjy was excited at being at Daddy's office and sitting at his desk. And they talked. Benjy had lunch. Most of the time I was in the other room."

"Other than the business trips, are you aware of any trips taken by David with his family?"

"Yes."

"And approximately how often did David take trips with his wife or his wife and children?"

"Oh, they went many times to many different places."

"Can you state what that last trip was?"

"One that sticks out in my mind that David took with Susan was to London. I think it was in August of '83."

"What, if anything, did he say to you about that trip when they returned?"

"He said that they really enjoyed the trip—it was a combination business-vacation trip for the two of them—and that they planned, they were planning on taking the children back in the summer of 1984."

More tears from David Hendricks.

"And can you state whether you had a conversation with David Hendricks during the week of November 1st, 1983, regarding the adoption of a child?"

"Yes. It was just between David and myself. He came in and announced that they had a line on a possible adoption of a young boy. I don't remember if it was an infant or toddler. And that he had heard about it from some friends in Wyoming, and they were really excited about it, and they were in discussion."

"Now, lastly, Mrs. Crutcher, I believe you gave evidence with respect to your attendance at a convention in Phoenix, Arizona. And you were aware that certain models had been arranged to model a back brace on the convention floor."

"Yes."

"At that convention, do you recall meeting a model by the name of Elizabeth, also known as Libby, Tomlinson?"

"Yes."

"At any time during the course of your stay at Phoenix, can you state whether Libby Tomlinson ever inquired of you whether the defendant, David Hendricks, was a doctor?"

"Yes. She asked me if he was a doctor."

"And what, if anything, did you say?"

"I told her no, he wasn't a doctor, that he was an orthotist, and that they're both at least in the medical field, but that an orthotist makes braces on orders of doctors."

"I have nothing further. Thank you."

On cross-examination, Murphy would question Crutcher's account of how many business trips Hendricks had taken over the twelve months before the murders occurred. He referred to February 1983 visits to Nashville and Memphis.

"Did the defendant drive or fly?"

"He flew."

"Now in this thirteen number that you gave us, did you count that as one or two trips?"

"I believe I counted the cities he contacted as a trip."

"So you counted that as two, then, in your number of thirteen?"

"I believe so. Yes."

Murphy asked about May of 1983. "What city was visited then?"

"There were three total: Indianapolis, Indiana; Toledo, Ohio; and Ann Arbor, Michigan."

"How many sales trips did you count that as in telling us he made thirteen?"

"Three different cities. Counted it as three."

"Okay. Mrs. Crutcher, were you aware that on the sales trip that the defendant took into Wisconsin on the 7th and 8th of November of 1983 that he intended to visit the towns of Wausau, Stevens Point, Portage, and Madison?"

"Yes."

"Would that, in your view, count as four sales trips?"

"In this particular case, I suppose I would have to in the way I did the other ones."

"What I'd like you to do now is to exclude those trips which were either vacations in whole or part and tell me the number of trips that were only sales trips. Would you do that for me?"

Crutcher's dark eyes focused on the ceiling. She counted on her fingers. "Eight."

"Okay. You're still counting the trip to Nashville and Memphis as two sales trips."

"Uh-huh."

"You're counting the trips to Indianapolis, Toledo, and Ann Arbor as three."

"Uh-huh."

"Nothing further."

Judge Baner looked at John Long. "Redirect?"

"Yes, briefly," Long responded. "Let's just talk about the total number of trips, leaving Bloomington and returning to Bloomington. Not counting the trip he took to Wisconsin on November 7th, 1983, what is the total number of trips?"

"Eight."

"And of those eight, how many were taken without his wife and family or without there being any vacation or religious trip?"

"Five."

"And if you counted the trip to Wisconsin on the 7th, that would have made nine trips. Is that correct?"

"Yes."

"And that would have meant six out of the nine would have been taken without his family. Two-thirds of the total number of business trips that he took."

"Right."

"But at least one-third of the times that he left during 1983, he took his wife and family with him. Correct?"

"Yes."

Ralph Storrs, whose Kankakee company manufactured the CASH Brace for Hendricks, was next on the stand. Jennings asked about Storrs's knowledge of Hendricks's business and sleep habits.

"On many occasions he came into my office early in the morning—quite early in the morning," Storrs said, "and looked very haggard and drawn out. And upon questioning why, I would learn that he had—"

Murphy interrupted. "I would object."

"He had been—" Storrs continued, but Murphy's loud objection drowned out Storrs.

"I'm going to object. The fact that he's at an office early in the morning doesn't indicate anything about sleep habits."

"The fact is," Jennings responded, "that it has to do with the basis for his knowledge, not the truthfulness of what somebody may have told him."

"To the extent this witness has personal experience with regard to doing business at particular hours," Judge Baner ruled, "he'll be allowed to testify."

Jennings resumed. "Have you had occasion, Mr. Storrs, to have the defendant, in a business context, present himself to you during the very early morning hours?"

"Yes, sir."

"Tell me how he has presented himself on those occasions with respect to outside of usual hours."

"Looking like he needed sleep."

"When would he show up? What would be the purpose?"

"Prior to seven in the morning to discuss business."

"Would these be on occasions in which he has been in town?"

"He had come from Bloomington to Kankakee."

"Mr. Storrs, can you tell me whether or not you had any prior knowledge of a business trip as far as Mr. Hendricks was concerned during the same week his family was slain?"

"I was aware of the fact that he was going to leave Monday evening on a business trip to Wisconsin."

"During your contact with David Hendricks since 1981 or prior to that for that matter, have you had occasion from time to time to see him in the company of his family members?"

"Yes, sir. A number of times with his wife and three children in my office."

"What, if anything, did you see or observe with respect to the relationship between David and Susan as husband and wife?"

"A relationship of great love and affection."

"Tell me what, if anything, you saw and observed with respect to the relationship of David and his children?"

"The same."

"And based upon your own relationship with David Hendricks,

did you form an opinion as to his reputation with respect to truth-fulness and veracity?"

"Yes. Well-respected individual. Excellent."

Murphy pursued the same area in cross-examination.

"Mr. Storrs," he began, "with regard to that last question about your opinion as to the reputation of the defendant, were you relating to us your own personal opinion or opinions you've heard discussed by others?"

"Both."

"Tell me when, please, was the last time anybody told you of their opinion of the defendant for truthfulness and veracity?"

"I don't think I can answer that question. All I can say is I never heard anything negative."

"In terms of your overall operation, Mr. Storrs, what percent-age of your total manufacturing operation does the manufacture of Mr. Hendricks's brace occupy?"

"Probably 20 percent."

"Were you referring to 20 percent of your time or 20 percent of your sales or revenue?"

"Probably 20 percent of everything—just off the top of my head."

"Had you ever had discussions with the defendant about any other type of business relationship other than just manufacturing the brace for him, sir?"

"Yes, sir."

"Is it correct that you specifically talked to him in the past about joining your firm?"

"Yes."

"In Kankakee?"

"Yes, sir."

"When were those discussions, Mr. Storrs?"

"Probably starting in the middle of 1982."

"And how long did they continue, sir?"

"They're ongoing."

James Russ, director of orthotic education at Northwestern University and Hendricks's former professor as well as an orthotics businessman, was on the stand for the defense.

"Tell me," Jennings asked, "with respect to the teaching at Northwestern that you do and have done in the past, describe the process for me by which your students at Northwestern are taught to determine landmarks on the body of a patient, customer, or client and the manner in which measurements are taken. Tell me your teaching philosophy or approach, how students are taught."

"Okay," Russ began, "classes are very small because it's a private university. So what we do is that I measure you and you measure me, or I do the landmarks on you and you do them on me. The student marks the landmarks with a dull pencil. And we have a grade sheet, so the instructor evaluates whether the marking is correct or incorrect. We do it on each other to start, so we really learn to develop those skills on each other before we try them out on patients."

"Is the marking on the skin surface or over some sort of a garment?"

"We do it on skin surface, and we do it on shorts and on T-shirts and just whatever."

"Tell me what reason, if any, that you teach students of orthotics at Northwestern to make marks on individuals with an indelible marking pen."

"We have three instructors with eighteen or twenty students, twenty-two students, and each instructor takes a third of the class. So I would be responsible for six or seven students, and they would work independently. They palpate the bony prominence, then they mark it. And when they're ready, they have all the landmarks marked, then they call an instructor. He goes in and grades—yes, it's right, or, no, it's wrong—by looking at where he's marked."

"With respect to your professional practice in orthotics, do you continue to measure and mark with an indelible pencil of some sort?"

"Sure. That's why we do it in school for grading purposes. But carrying that over into private practice as an orthotist or prosthetist, I feel that when you mark on people, it's like going to the doctor, and he marks on my arm where he's going to do surgery. Then I go home and show my wife, you know, where he's going to do surgery. And she understands what was going on as if she were in the room with the doctor and me. I can also go home and get some sympathy from her and so on." There were several chuckles in the courtroom.

"I think it's great marking on people," Russ continued. "On little kids, funny faces and all that stuff. That's how you calm little children down, by drawing pictures all over them. They go home and say 'Look. He drew all over my leg. It hurts so much.'"

"Do you continue to mark in order to track your measurements?"

"You really don't have to, but I think that's part of it. A person comes in and they're going to get a one-hundred-dollar orthosis or a thousand-dollar orthosis. You have to give them something to take away. You put a lot of marks on them, so this is what I got for my hundred dollars initially, anyway."

"Can you tell me with respect to your business as far as the manufacture and fabrication of custom products, do you also have occasion to measure and mark?"

"Has to happen. In other words, if I see the patient and I take the impressions, then I'm going to send it to you to manufacture. I've got to mark the landmarks. If someone takes an impression of my torso, especially my torso, they wouldn't know the top from the bottom or front from back because I look like a tube. Someone with a very defined waist wouldn't be any problem."

"Have you had occasion in your business to be involved in the development of orthotic devices and appliances, braces—the general line products in that area?"

"Yes. We're in the process of developing a knee orthosis."

"Do you use patients to measure and mark in connection with that development, or do you use some other source?"

"We've used both. We've used patients, but usually a patient is there to receive a product and receive orthotic treatment. They're not going to be interested if you're developing a product. Usually what we do is use the people in our business. We have thirteen people—big people, small people, fat people, thin people—so we can fit it around all the people within our business and get a pretty good range of sizing by doing it internally without using patients."

"Do you also use other individuals for sizing and for measuring?"

"Yes, I've used my children. I've used my employees' children, wives, or husbands."

"Do you also use students from time to time?"

"Students. Right."

"Do you use males and females?"

"Males and females. Right."

"And with respect to the measuring and marking, is it done in the same manner that you teach?"

"Yes. You have to have the same consistency. In other words, if we teach someone how to measure and don't follow it up in our laboratory services, there's no cohesiveness in the end product."

"And is there a difference in the way that you approach the students and the people that work in your lab for you as far as research is concerned and in the way you approach patients?"

"Oh, two entirely different things. A patient is a person that's paying for services and/or a product related to that service. So you certainly wouldn't treat them like you'd treat Harry's wife."

Dozier would do the cross-examination.

"From your knowledge of the CASH orthosis, do you know of any reason why it would be necessary to make markings on the back of a patient with a pen or indelible pencil?"

"Well, the only reason I can think of is if the person had a compression fracture at a certain level. You'd palpate to find that level and you'd mark that level."

"Do you teach ethics with regard to the practice of orthotics?"

"Yes."

"And where do those ethics or ethical standards come from?"

"They come from the background that I've had practicing as an orthotist."

"Are the ethical principles you teach your own personal ethical principles, or are they a body of principles that occur in the field of orthotics? Are they generally accepted in the field?"

"I think so."

"Were those ethical principles taught at the time that the defendant, David Hendricks, was a student at Northwestern?"

"Yes."

"When you use your employees or their families and so on for the purpose of doing research, do you inform them of what you're doing?"

"Of course."

"And do you consider it proper to do so?"

"Of course."

"Would you consider it proper to use anyone for research and not tell them what you're doing?"

"No, I don't think it's proper. I think you should tell them what you're doing."

Harold Donald, a prosthetist in Madison, Wisconsin, and a classmate of Hendricks's at Northwestern, testified that he saw Hendricks on November 8, 1983. "I was attending a patient and had left the room when David stepped out from behind the door as a prearranged kind of practical joke and gave me quite a surprise," he testified. "And we had a rather friendly exchange at that time. He stayed for about a half hour."

"Tell me what you talked about."

"General amenities, of course. Then we talked just slightly about his product. Being a prosthetist, I leave that to the other professionals. We did talk about where he's now living. Somehow we got on different subjects. One of the things that really comes to mind is the fact that he had driven all night the night before, which I was amazed at. He told me that he doesn't necessarily have to have as much sleep as most folks. And we talked quite a bit about that."

"Did he say what he was doing there, or did you know?"

"Well, I figured it was a sales call. And I'm certain that must have come out, because he had told me that he had originated his trip to what I thought was a backward situation. He had gone all the way to Wausau first and then began his circuit to come back down through Madison, was seeing me on his way back down to Rockford and a couple more facilities on the way, and finally on home."

"Did you talk to him about how frequently he made sales trips?"

"I don't know whether they were necessarily sales trips. Well, I'd have to say they were because he said at least once a month he stayed up all night because if he slept too much, it worked against him. So he would utilize that time to drive to distant places."

"Can you tell me whether he talked to your brace man at your place of business?"

"Yes, he did. He talked to both of them. And they discussed different dissatisfactions Mr. Burk had with the brace. And Dave said those had been corrected, and they, you know, interchanged a little bit of information there. I didn't just stand there and hover. I was in and out."

"Did you, from time to time, find yourself approached by people who are selling, marketing products?"

"Every day."

"With respect to David's appearance there at your place of business in Madison on November 8th, did you notice anything unusual at all about the manner in which he called upon the place of business? Can you tell me whether he was there with an appointment or did not have an appointment?"

"He did not have an appointment. Very few people offering a product will have an appointment because we won't fool with them. We don't have time. They come in with a potluck attitude and take what they can get and take who they can get. If you can't see them, you state so. They're the ones selling the product. You don't have to be amenable to them when your patient comes first."

"Was there anything unusual with respect to the length of time that David was there?"

"No, he wasn't in the way. He said what he had to say. He and I were glad to see each other. I had to get back to my patient and he took off."

"Did you find anything unusual about the manner and form in which he discussed or promoted his product?"

"Nothing."

The first phase of the defense case was now complete. Next the defense was ready with a strong attack on the idea that time of death can be accurately determined by an examination of stomach contents. Hendricks's own testimony and that of his family and friends would be last. Jennings and Long had long before abandoned the idea of presenting evidence about the Sheppelman murder case which had occurred in Bloomington some three months after Hendricks was jailed. They decided it had at least as many dissimilarities as similarities and would only muddy the defense focus, which would be to convince the jury that Hendricks wasn't the only person who could have committed the crime.

The first salvo on the subject of stomach contents would come from Dr. Ross Zumwalt, an associate professor of pathology at the University of Cincinnati and deputy coroner in Hamilton County, Ohio. He had written at least twenty books or articles about forensic pathology and taught law enforcement classes about how autopsy findings can help determine a time of death.

He shifted in the witness box to face the jurors almost directly when he answered Long's bottom-line question. "My opinion is that gastric contents are not useful in determining exactly the time of death of an individual."

"Can you please state for the ladies and gentlemen of the jury the basis for that opinion?"

"There are many variable factors in the appearance of gastric contents. This is based on not only my experience in doing autopsies, but also based on my reading of the literature and my understanding of the physiology and the changes in the stomach. The only way to determine exactly when a person died is to witness the death."

Dr. Zumwalt told the jury of one of his cases, in which an eleven-year-old boy was known to have eaten pizza for lunch at a school cafeteria between noon and 1 P.M., was seen alive at 4 P.M., but found dead at 7:30 the next morning. Some five hundred cc's (more than double the amount in the three Hendricks children's stomachs combined) were found in the boy's stomach—all clearly identifiable as pizza. But Zumwalt testified that he had also conducted autopsies in which very little stomach content was found.

"Is there any type of constant emptying rate of the stomach, so one can determine the time of death with any close mathematical precision?" Long asked.

"No, sir. It varies so much on the type of food ingested, the amount of solids, the amount of liquids, and the individual variations."

"Will an examination of the degree of digestion indicate the length of time that the particle has been in the stomach?"

"No, because it doesn't digest very much in the stomach. It digests in the small bowel."

"So it is possible, or can you state whether or not you've ever seen, for example . . . " Long was having a difficult time making this come out right. "Well, the common, I guess, vegetable, for example, is corn, which is sometimes passed through the gastrointestinal tract in totally pristine form, undigested."

"Yes, sir. That's correct. Corn is probably one of the most difficult things to digest because it has so much cellulose and a very thick shell. It very often passes completely through the digestive tract undigested. I have seen other vegetables identifiable even down into the small bowel."

Now, another bottom-line question from Long: based on his examination of all the evidence available in the Hendricks case, what was his opinion about the time of death of the victims?

"I can give an estimation over a long period of time. Based on my analysis of this case, based on my experience, the deaths could have occurred as early as 9 P.M. or as late as 1:30 or two o'clock in the morning."

"And would the photographs of the gastric contents and the analysis found in here be consistent with these people being killed at one o'clock or 1:30 in the morning?"

"Yes."

"And it would be equally consistent with them being killed at twelve o'clock?"

"Yes."

"Or with them being killed at eleven o'clock?"

"Yes, sir."

"Or being killed at 12:45 in the morning?"

"Yes."

"Or 1:30 in the morning."

"It's possible. Yes."

"Can you state, therefore, Doctor, whether analysis of gastric contents alone can give an indication of time of death within a two- or three-hour period, or even two- to four-hour period in this case?"

"Yes. The analysis of gastric content in this case cannot narrow the opinion as to time of death that much. It cannot be narrowed down to a two- or three-hour period. The use of gastric contents is best used as an investigational tool to estimate the time of death within a broad range and to help indicate what the last meal was. But too much reliance on an individual time-of-death study can be detrimental to the investigation."

Long beamed as he turned over his witness to Dozier for cross-examination.

No, Dr. Zumwalt told Dozier, he had not been present at the autopsies, and he was basing his opinion on pictures and reports made available to him by John Long.

"Would you agree," asked Dozier, "that it's significant that we have here three victims who ate the same type of meal at approximately the same time?"

"Yes. It's important because we're not dealing with other variables. We're not looking at two individuals who ate at a different time and trying to coordinate their stomach contents with different time frames, or looking at people who ate two different things."

"Does that tend to eliminate or reduce the risk of individual variables?"

"Yes, that's correct."

"If you have just one individual, you don't know what the person's emotional state was or whether he had a twenty-four-hour flu bug or anything like that, do you?"

"Yes, that's correct."

"From as far as you were able to determine from viewing the photographs and so on, would you agree that these three individuals were all consistent with one another?"

"Yes."

"Would that tend then to rule out or help at least lessen the possibility of these broad range of individual differences?"

"Yes, sir, it would."

"Would you agree that persons who have had more experience in this field might be able to offer a narrower range of time as to when the deaths occurred?"

"I don't know of anybody who has had a great deal of personal experience in gastric contents. I personally don't know of any article or any study among forensic pathologists specifically studying gastric contents in an experimental study."

"Okay. You haven't done any such studies."

"No, sir. I haven't."

"And you're not aware of whether anybody else has or not."

"As far as I know, there have not been any."

"But would you concede there are people who have more experience as forensic pathologists?"

"Oh, yes. There are many forensic pathologists who've had more experience than I."

Next up for the defense was Dr. Earl Rose, a physician with a law degree, a professor of pathology at the University of Iowa who also lectured at its law school.

It was his opinion that it usually takes three to six hours after the digestive process has begun for a stomach to empty.

"We're talking three to six hours as a normal span. But there are many factors that may inhibit and a few that may accelerate gastric emptying," Dr. Rose testified.

"There are factors then," Long emphasized, "that would cause the stomach to empty slower than normal."

"Yes."

"And in those latter factors, food would be retained and not subject to the range which you gave. Would that be correct?"

"Yes, that's correct."

"What would be one of the factors that could delay gastric emptying?"

"I think that exercise could and most likely would delay gastric emptying."

Long was hoping jurors remembered that the Hendricks children had played hard in the pizza parlor's play area for about an hour after they ate.

"Dr. Rose, could the emotional state, the level of excitement of a person have an impact on gastric emptying, too?"

"Yes. I think it could delay gastric emptying."

"So the three- to six-hour period for usual gastric emptying wouldn't come into play until a period of delay for whatever reason has ceased?"

"Yes, that's correct."

"If, therefore, a person were to play in strenuous activity for an hour after eating, would gastric emptying be delayed for that hour's period?"

"Yes, I believe it would be."

"So that if you had a situation where an individual ate at seven o'clock and played until eight, would the range that you suggested of three to six hours have its onset not at seven o'clock but at eight o'clock?"

"Yes. But I have to qualify that because it isn't a start-stop-punch-the-button-go. It could be that at least some of the gastric material juices and what have you could have gotten through to a degree before the eight o'clock period. On the other hand, after the cessation of exercise, there could be a little delay before the emptying started. So it isn't an absolute type of situation. I don't want to mislead you by suggesting that at all."

As Dozier questioned Dr. Rose, the witness said the degree of delay in gastric emptying caused by exercise would depend on how vigorous the exercise was.

"Let me ask you particularly about children," Dozier continued. "Would you agree with the proposition that children generally tend to be more active than adults?"

"Yes."

"And it's not unusual for children to eat a meal and go out and play to varying degrees of activity."

"Yes, that's correct."

"And in your opinion, does normal child's play significantly affect digestion?"

"I think that it probably would, but I know of no studies that particularly address that specific item. So I can't say from either my own studies or from reading anyone else's studies, because I don't know of anyone that has addressed that subject."

The defense's big gun in its medical volley was Dr. Frederick Jaffe, a forensic pathologist and assistant professor of pathology at the University of Toronto who had performed more than twelve thousand autopsies. His mustache and long, pointed nose were reminiscent of Inspector Clouseau. But his chief notoriety had come nearly twenty years earlier when he appeared as a defense witness in the Steven Truscott case, a highly publicized Canadian case that ended when the conviction was upheld by Canada's Supreme Court.

"In that case," asked Long, "did you give evidence with respect to gastric contents?"

"Yes, I did."

"And have you given evidence in such cases since that time?"

"Not really, because it's no longer regarded as really a pertinent issue in modern practice."

Too many variables, Dr. Jaffe testified. "First of all, how active is the nervous system of the stomach in emptying it?" he began. "What food was eaten? Some foods stay in the stomach longer than other foods. How thoroughly was the food chewed? Large hunks remain in the stomach much longer than smaller particles. What was the person doing after eating? What was his mental, physical state? Excitement, fear, joy—any strong emotion as well as physical exercise can affect the rate of gastric emptying. The difficulty here is that in some people, strong emotions tend to stop stomach action, but in other people—and I think it applies to me—it tends to accelerate it. The same applies to physical exercise. It's very difficult to give you a precise answer."

"Is that because each person is unique with respect to this question?"

"Well, not only is each individual unique, but it may vary from one day to another in a given person."

Long presented to Dr. Jaffe photos of the stomach contents of the three children. "These are rather large fragments of food," the doctor said. "In each of these photographs, there's a scale. And some of these fragments are in excess of one inch in diameter. Most of them are a little smaller."

"Viewing those photographs together with the scale," asked Long, "do you have an opinion as to whether there was a short duration between the time the children ate and the time they died?"

"Well, you see, this is a question I cannot answer."

"And why is that?"

"Because as soon as I saw the photographs, it suggested to me that these were the stomach contents of children, because children don't chew very well, especially when they get eating something they like or when they're anxious to get away from the table. They gulp food."

"Would that affect your analysis of how long the food might have been in the stomach?"

"Yes, indeed. The bigger the particles, the longer they tend to remain in the stomach. During the first part of digestion, only very small particles pass—about two millimeters in size—about one-tenth of an inch. In the later stages of emptying, larger particles pass, but they tend to remain in the stomach for quite a while."

"And so is the fact that a particle is large demonstrative of the fact that death must have occurred shortly after ingestion?"

"No, not at all."

"It could, in fact, based on a reasonable doubt of medical and scientific certainty, be indicative of the fact that death occurred a long time after ingestion. Is that right, many hours afterwards?"

"Yes. I have some inhibition about the term 'certainty.' "

"And why is that?"

"Because there is no certainty about determining the time of death with regard to a meal."

Long turned to the absence of any identifiable food material in Susan Hendricks's stomach.

"If the mother were to have eaten raw vegetables, do you think evidence of that would remain in her stomach much longer than if she had eaten, for example, a sweet roll?"

"One would expect that, yes."

"And if she were to have ingested vegetables, let's say between nine o'clock and 9:30 in the evening of November 7th, would you expect to find evidence of that still in her stomach, let's say, by one o'clock the next morning?"

"It depends on the coarseness of the food and so on. If it's a coarse type of food, yes, one might expect that."

"In your experience and based on your training in this field and your study of determining time of death from gastric contents, do you think it's possible, simply by a gross examination of gastric contents, to determine time of death?"

"No. Are you referring to the stomach emptying time or are you referring to the degree of digestion?"

"The degree of digestion."

"That's the big problem here. There's no way of measuring it. It's a personal impression. One observer looks at the stomach contents and says it looks about one to three hours. And another equally competent observer will say no, it's more like two to four hours. Another observer may say it looks more like four to five or six hours. There's no way of measuring it. It's a purely subjective impression. And that makes it almost useless when it comes to the precise determination of death. It would be nice to have some way of measuring the degree of digestion. But that can't be done."

"Based upon your experience, Doctor, based upon your training, and based upon your study of the examination of gastric contents in order to determine time of death, and based further upon the fact that you've had an opportunity to review the pathology report, the autopsy protocol, crime-scene reports, photographs taken by crime-scene technicians of the stomach contents, the reports of Doctors Dwyer and Spikes—based upon all of that, can you state whether or not it can be determined that the victims in this case met their death at about midnight on November 7th, 1983?"

"Well, I think this obviously is a very important question. It is very difficult to give an upper limit, and I must say I have not seen the whole stomach contents. But in the context of this case, yes, it's quite possible these children met their death before midnight. Could they have died between twelve and two? The answer is yes, they could have."

"And is it equally possible they could have died between twelve and two as between eleven and twelve?"

"Yes, that's the point. There's no sharp line of division. Could they have died between two and four? Possibly. But again, four and six? Not likely. Between six and eight? Probably not. So there's no sharp line here. There's a graduation. And that makes it so difficult to determine the time of death with any degree of precision."

"Is there some generally accepted principle, rule, or proposition with regard to a normal digestive time for food in the stomach?" Dozier asked in cross-examination.

"You'll find that in modern medical practice and modern medical literature that people are very reluctant to use the word 'normal.' It's almost a word which is in disrepute."

"Is there, nevertheless, a textbook description of a period of time in which a meal empties from the stomach?"

"It depends very largely on the nature of the food eaten. And even then, discrepancies between various authors are very great."

"How much is 'very great'?"

"Fifty percent. Sixty. A hundred. I don't know."

"Well, I won't use the word 'normal,' " Dozier pressed. "Let me ask you if there is a generally accepted time within your profession as a physician in which food leaves the stomach, assuming a healthy—"

Dr. Jaffe interrupted. "Assuming all types of food, or—I'm sorry."

"Say the food that Americans and Canadians generally eat in their regular meals. A mixed meal, if you will."

"I don't want to be difficult," Jaffe resumed, "but I find that very difficult to answer because some constituents of the food leave before other constituents."

"But I'm talking about the total time for it all to—"

"Yes, I know that's what you want, and I can't really answer that question. Four hours is a sort of ballpark figure, but it's really basically a meaningless figure because it's so much subject to variation."

"Okay." Dozier was digging in. "I'm referring specifically to the book that you wrote called *Guide to Pathological Evidence,* second edition, page thirty-six. Do you agree with this statement: 'Generally, a meal has left the stomach after four hours, but emotional disturbances may cause considerable delay.' "

"I certainly wrote that."

"Is it a meaningless figure?"

"Yes. May I possibly read the next two sentences?"

"Well, I'm sure your attorney will give you an opportunity to read those next two sentences," Dozier answered.

John Long spoke up from the defense table. "I don't know if his attorney is even in the state, Mr. Dozier."

"And, in fact, I would invite him to," Dozier continued, ignoring Long. "Now, granted that there are a great many variables. To the extent that one can exclude those variables, the estimation of the time of death from examination of stomach contents and other relevant factors in the case can be of value, can it not?"

"I think you've put your finger right on it," Jaffe said. "You used the term 'if one could exclude the variables.' If one could exclude the variables, it would be a terrific method of determining the time of death. Unfortunately, one cannot exclude the variables. And this is the problem."

"All right. Are many of the variables that are involved medical conditions or illnesses, physical problems with the stomach?"

"Some of them are. Yes, indeed."

"In this case, are you aware of any physical or health problems that could affect the emptying time and therefore the estimation of time of death?"

"No."

"You have been made aware that the children may have played in a playroom at the pizza place where they ate."

"Yes."

"Do you have an opinion as to whether normal play of children significantly delays digestion?"

"I don't know, again, what normal—I'm sorry. I shy away from that word 'normal.' Physical activity can accelerate digestion. It can retard digestion."

"Doctor, would you agree that, based on all the factors that you considered in this case and your analysis of the photographs and autopsy reports and so on, that death of the children in this case could have occurred before midnight?"

"Yes."

"All right. Would you agree that death could have occurred as early as nine o'clock?"

"If these photographs were representative of the entire stomach contents, I would tend to agree with you."

Long would remind jurors that the stomach samples photographed may not have been representative.

"Do you have any information," Long began in his redirect, "whether these photographs are representative of the entire stomach contents?"

"I have descriptions of stomach contents by Dr. Spikes and others which do not correspond to these photographs. That's why I feel these are selected pieces picked out of the stomach contents."

"Would your opinion be strengthened if you were to determine that laypersons picked out parts of the stomach contents to put them in a thirty milliliter vial and disposed of the remainder of the stomach contents?"

"No. Of course not."

"So if, for example, out of the seventy milliliters purportedly removed from one victim, only thirty milliliters were taken and the rest disposed of, you wouldn't know what was disposed of and what was kept. Is that correct?"

"That's quite correct."

"And these photographs, therefore, do not appear to be representative of the stomach contents, but appear instead to be selected stomach contents."

"That is my impression."

"Now by the way, I'm not your attorney, am I?"

"No, you're not."

"Okay, because if I were, I haven't billed you lately." Long grinned at Dozier and then the jury. He handed Jaffe a book, *The Pathology of Homicide* by Lester Adelson and referred him to page 185. " Can you state whether or not Dr. Adelson writes that 'the physical and chemical facets of digestion are beset by so many imponderable and uncontrollable variables *in vivo*, that one cannot rely on the extent of mechanical dissolution and chemical breakdown of the gastric contents to help reach a reasonable estimate as to how long the food was present in the stomach?"

"Yes, in fact that was one sentence I wanted counsel to read."

It was Dozier's turn again.

"Dr. Jaffe, are you suggesting in your testimony that you believe that someone has selected those particles of vegetable matter that appear less digested and left out or did not use other particles to appear in the photographs?"

"Well, yes, indeed. I did not attribute any motive to the person, but it's quite clear, for instance, looking at these photographs, that the fluid isn't there. There are just solid hunks."

"Okay, the fluid isn't there. These particles have been washed. All fluid is gone, and all you see is the vegetable particles. But you're not suggesting, then, that somebody looked at all the vegetable particles and only picked the particles that looked least digested and decided to photograph those?"

"I don't know what the person decided. All I'm saying is that this is not, in my view, representative of the whole stomach contents."

"Because it does not contain any of the fluid."

"Because it doesn't contain smaller particles or fluid," Jaffe continued. "The photographs merely show some pretty sizable hunks from half an inch to one inch in diameter. And I merely expressed the opinion that this does not appear to be representative of the whole stomach contents."

"Why do you think that this is not representative of the size of the particles that were contained in the entire stomach contents? Or do you believe that?"

"I don't know. This is my opinion. I do not know."

"Okay. One more thing," said Dozier. "In 1966 you were of the opinion that estimation of time of death from stomach contents was full of variables. You testified to that effect for the defense in the Truscott case back then."

"Yes, I did."

"And you are testifying essentially to the same effect for the defense in this case."

"Yes. I have a lot more experience now than I did then."

"But throughout this period of time, you have been of the opinion that you yourself cannot estimate the time of death from analysis of stomach contents."

"Estimate the time of death with any degree of precision. Yes, you're correct."

The next defense witness in this area would be Dr. Robert Stein, the Cook County, Illinois, chief medical examiner who played a major role in the Tylenol tampering murder investigation.

John Long quickly got to the crucial question: after his study of all the material available in the Hendricks case, did he think analysis of stomach contents was a reliable way of determining the time of death in this case?

"No, it is not," Dr. Stein responded in a hoarse voice.

"And what is the basis for that opinion?"

"The basis, is, number one, the time of death; two, the amount of time the decedent was dead; three, the temperature; four, amount of putrefaction; five, the amount of gastric juice which has been submitted to determine time of death is completely, totally inadequate."

"Do gastric contents give forensic pathologists a reliable way of determining a time of death in any circumstance?"

"Reliable? I don't know. It's one of the parameters which is used. But time of death is entirely a nebulous type of thing. To state with certainty when the time of death is—that's an impossibility."

"Based upon your experience, education, and review of the documents and records in this case, can you even give a range as to the time of death, based solely on an examination of gastric contents?"

"No, I cannot."

"Based upon the principles of forensic pathology, do you think such a determination can be made?"

"No, it cannot."

Dozier would take up the same line of questioning with Stein as he used fairly successfully with Jaffe.

"Did your medical training include instruction on the normal or usual time it takes to digest food in the stomach of a healthy individual?"

"Yes. The teaching was that in a normal individual, it is an entirely unreliable type of estimation. However, some books will give you one range; another will give you another range; another text still another range. But they all will make one statement. They still don't know when digestion actually started."

"And my question is, in your training, what was the normal range of time it takes for food to digest in the stomach of a healthy individual?"

"The normal range of digestion was anywhere from four hours, six hours—in that particular range."

"And did that depend on the type of food that was ingested?"

"That's just one of the factors."

"Dr. Stein, do you have any training or experience in the speed with which liquids empty from the stomach?"

"Yes. If it's not too acid and contains no sugar, the liquid will leave very rapidly."

"What is 'very rapidly'?"

"All I can say is very rapidly. I don't know exactly the amount of time."

"Are you talking about something in excess of an hour, or something less than an hour?"

An edge entered Stein's coarse voice. "As I said, I don't know."

"What about the emptying time of starch from the stomach?"

"Starch, carbohydrates—they all leave the stomach rapidly."

"And are you able to give us a time that you mean by 'rapidly'?"

"All I can say is rapidly, sir. By rapidly, I mean in relation to proteins. The exact times, sir, cannot be stated with certainty. There are too many factors involved."

"I'm not asking you to state with certainty, but to indicate ranges."

"All I can state is that carbohydrates leave much more rapidly than proteins or fats, sir."

"Does the speed with which food empties from the stomach depend on the amount of food taken into the stomach?"

"Yes, it does."

"Do you have any range for, say, the difference between a light meal as opposed to a heavy meal?"

"I don't know what one means by light meal or what one means by heavy meal."

"I'll let you define those terms."

"For myself, a light meal would be a double hamburger or cheeseburger, Coke, and perhaps a little ice cream. That would be a light meal."

"Taking that as a light meal, can you estimate a range of time it would take such a meal to empty from the stomach?"

"Definitely not. No."

"No range at all?"

"No."

"No low end or high end?"

"No."

"Is there a maximum period?"

"Couldn't answer that question. I don't know."

The last defense witness in this area would be Charles Petty, the pathologist, chief medical examiner, and head of the criminal investigation lab in Dallas who had helped when Long first became fully involved in the Hendricks case. Now he had literally left a hospital bed, where he had been recovering from surgery, to testify in this trial, not only about the time-of-death evidence, but also about the crime scene.

Time-of-death evidence would come first. A table in front of the jury box held the containers of stomach contents, several lab dishes, and a pair of pizzas from the Chuck E. Cheese restaurant.

Dozier had had his lengthy, hypothetical question to pose earlier in the trial. Now it was Long's turn.

"Doctor, I want you to assume for a moment that three children, ages five, seven, and nine, ingested nine-tenths of a vegetarian pizza, about twelve inches in diameter and having a dry, tamped volume of approximately 1,500 milliliters. Assume further that these three children ingested with the pizza soft drinks, root beer. Assume further that the children, upon ingestion of the pizza, went to a play area where they played for approximately forty minutes. Assume further that the play consisted of bouncing on an air mattress, trampoline-type affair, diving into a pool of big, round, plastic balls, swinging on ropes, and running about.

"Assume further that after approximately forty to forty-five minutes of play, the children were taken home. One of them ran into the house, procured library books, ran into the car, and went off to a bookmobile. Assume further that the children were in a hurry or were hurried to get to the bookmobile for fear of its closing before they got there. Assume further that upon returning from the bookmobile after spending about fifteen minutes there, the children engaged in a game of hide-and-seek with each of the three children taking two turns. Assume that the children were read to for about half an hour and then put to bed.

"Assume further that sometime subsequent to their being put

to bed, the children were murdered in their beds as they slept. Assume that an autopsy was performed a period of time in excess of thirty hours postmortem. Assume further that at the time of autopsy, in the youngest child, who was about forty-six inches in length and had a weight of fifty pounds, some sixty milliliters of gastric content was removed. Assume further that in the second oldest child, about fifty-three inches in length, weighing sixty-five pounds, that approximately seventy milliliters of gastric content was removed. Assume further, in the oldest child, approximately fifty-four inches in length and weighing about ninety-five pounds, that one hundred milliliters of gastric content was removed.

"Do you have an opinion, Doctor, based upon all of those facts and based upon a reasonable degree of medical certainty, as to whether or not the volumes removed from the children, when compared to the amount possibly ingested in both food and drink, whether the gastric contents of the children indicated a relatively empty stomach or full stomach?"

"Yes. The total of the food recovered from the stomach at the time of the autopsy—one hundred, seventy, and sixty milliliters—is a total of 230 milliliters, or a total of 220 cc's. And as I understand your question, you said that they ate about nine-tenths of a tamped down, 1,500-cc meal, the pizza."

"Correct."

"Plus liquid."

"Correct."

"You didn't specify the amount of liquid. But if they ate nine-tenths of 1,500 cc's, that would mean they ate 1,350 cc's of food. Remaining in the stomachs was 230 cc's." Dr. Petty worked a hand-held calculator. "230 cc's is approximately 17 percent of what they originally ingested. So these stomachs were well along toward being empty. I wouldn't say they were virtually empty, but they were far along toward being empty, because there's only 230 cc's left of the pizza itself." Petty sounded as though he was thinking out loud. "Which is 1,350 plus whatever the gastric juices were— which may have been as much again as the pizza—plus whatever liquid they took in. So these stomachs were well along toward being empty. Virtually empty. Yes, I would use that term, too."

At Long's request, Dr. Petty stepped down from the witness box and joined Long at the table which held the cups, pizzas, and lab dishes. The stomach contents were emptied from the Styrofoam cups into the lab dishes. Courtroom spectators expected some odor, but there was none.

Long asked Petty whether the stomach contents now before him looked as if they were highly digested.

"Of the materials that I see here, some of which are unidentifiable to me and others are quite identifiable, I can easily make out onion, mushroom, olive, possibly some green pepper. Then there are some things I can't identify. Some is digested and some is not."

"Can you use these observations to determine the degree of digestion in terms of the length of time that this might have been in anyone's stomach?"

"No. In my opinion, I cannot."

"And what is the basis for that opinion?"

"Because not all of the stomach contents get digested at the same rate. The digestion starts from the outside and goes toward the center, and the center portion stays relatively stable until the digestive processes have worked on the outer layers."

"So if I understand what you're saying," Long tried to summarize, "based upon your earlier testimony, the fact that about 90 percent of what went in has been digested, the fact that you may have some portions of that remaining, 10 percent relatively undigested, that does not give you a basis to assume that death occurred shortly after eating."

"Not at all. And I would also have to add that not all of the things that go into the stomach are digested."

"And do you have an opinion, Doctor, about whether an examination of gastric contents in this case can be utilized to determine the time of death of these individuals?"

"Yes, sir. It cannot be utilized to accurately pinpoint the time of death because of two things: first, present and accounted for is a relatively small percentage of what obviously was taken in; second, there was intervening exercise which would cause a lag in the beginning of digestion."

"Do you have an opinion as to whether or not these gastric contents that we see here would be consistent with these children having been killed at nine o'clock or before on the night that they ingested this pizza?"

"Yes. This is beyond the nine o'clock time. There's too much of the pizza unaccounted for in the stomach as the autopsy surgeon saw them and estimated or measured them."

"Can you state whether the stomach contents could be consistent with the children meeting their deaths at one in the morning?"

"No, I think that would be asking me to say too much. I don't believe I can tell you when death occurred, except to say this is toward the tail end of the digestive process."

"So whether I say eleven, one, ten, two—anything like that—your testimony is that based on this method we're using, that type of determination cannot be made."

"That's correct."

Long would also use Petty's expertise in crime-scene analysis. As Long shuffled through a series of eight-by-ten photos of the crime scene, Hendricks moved away from the defense table to avoid viewing the photos. Long handed Petty a photo of the wounds to Becky Hendricks and asked him to describe the type of weapon used to inflict them.

"It's perfectly consistent with a blunt instrument."

"When we're speaking of a blunt instrument, are we thinking of things like hammers, or the blunt edge of an ax, a tire iron, a baseball bat?"

"We're speaking of instruments that are not edged in the first place."

Long presented a picture of Grace's wounds.

"It is consistent with the heavy and somewhat sharp, but not really sharp, instrument such as an ax, machete, cleaver—something of that nature."

"Is there any other evidence of trauma other than that to the left side of the head?"

"Yes. It doesn't show too well on this photograph—but there is an obvious, deep, long slash wound on the neck which goes from behind the left ear, clear across the left side of the head beneath the jaw, and as far around as I can follow it."

"Is that trauma consistent with a wound which would have been caused by an ax?"

"No. It's not consistent with the ax. It would be perfectly consistent with the knife found at the scene."

"So on this victim, Grace Hendricks, are the photographs, autopsy protocol, and crime-scene reports consistent with two weapons being used on this one victim?"

"That's correct."

Long handed Petty two photos of the shockingly mutilated upper part of Benjy Hendricks's body.

"Is the trauma to the face consistent with that made by a sharp-edged instrument?"

"No. There are at least two or three, possibly four, wounds on the face."

"Is the trauma to the neck consistent with an edged instrument, such as the butcher knife?"

"It's perfectly consistent with a knife, a butcher knife or any cutting instrument of that type."

"Then the trauma exhibited in those two photographs is consistent with the trauma having been inflicted by two different weapons?"

"Yes."

"And are all of those wounds consistent with either the ax or the butcher knife or some other edged instrument?"

"Yes, they are."

"I would like you now to examine the photographs that you have with respect to Susan Hendricks. Do you have an opinion about what instrument or what type of instrument that type of wound is consistent with?"

"I believe there are two different instruments involved here. One is a cutting instrument that's heavy, as an ax. The other is a cutting instrument, used in a stabbing manner."

Petty also testified that there was evidence Susan had been strangled.

Long handed Petty two more photos. One showed the light blue nightgown Susan wore. The other was of the dark blue bedspread that partially covered her body. Each contained a short cut or tear, a right-angled defect in the bedspread.

"Do these photographs show defects consistent with being made by an edged instrument?"

"Yes, they do."

"With the butcher knife in this case?"

"Well, I can't say whether the defect on the coverlet is consistent or not. But I can say that the defect in the sleeve of the nightie is not consistent with that particular knife because that knife has too broad a blade to have inflicted this injury."

"And so would that injury be consistent with either the ax or the butcher knife that are exhibits in this case?"

"No, it is not."

"It was, therefore, in your opinion, caused by another edged instrument unknown?"

"Another edged instrument unknown."

"So as I understand you, Doctor, what we have in this case so far are injuries to the oldest child consistent with being caused by one weapon?"

"That's correct. A blunt instrument."

"The injuries to the two youngest children are consistent with two weapons?"

"That's correct. A chopping sort of instrument and an edged weapon which has been used in a throat-slitting manner."

"And if the hands can be considered an instrument, we have trauma to Susan Hendricks which could be consistent with four weapons?"

"Not to her herself. The injuries to the body itself would have involved manual strangulation—hands; a heavy, semisharp ax, or the other side of it; and a stabbing with a cutting-edged instrument. The fourth instrument is the one that caused the injury to the nightie, and that does not fit with the knife previously mentioned."

"Do you have an opinion, then, whether multiple weapons were utilized in this crime?"

"Oh yes. There's no question about that. There are multiple weapons involved. At least three. Possibly four."

"And have you, in the span over the last thirty years you've been practicing and in your duties now as medical examiner, for as long as you've been a forensic pathologist, an opinion as to whether the use of multiple weapons is consistent with having two or more assailants?"

"Yes, I think it's consistent with two or more assailants."

A low rumble was heard from spectators in the courtroom.

"I have nothing further of this witness," said John Long as he sat down.

Dozier knew he had a lot of material to cover in cross-examination. He decided to start with the crime-scene testimony because it was fresher in his mind and those of the jurors.

"What you called a defect in the nightgown," Dozier began, "you believe it was made with a different instrument than what made the cuts on the body."

"Yes. It's only, well, almost three-quarters of an inch in length, and the butcher knife had a broader blade than that."

"What type of instrument do you believe made this?"

"I believe a single-edged instrument."

"Could this be a tear rather than a cut?"

"No."

"Why not?"

"Because it exists isolated in a sea of untouched material. If it were a tear, a rip, I would expect it along a seam or someplace near the edge or at the edge."

"Is there anything to preclude that if someone wanted to, for example, that one could have grabbed the material and pulled and maybe make a tear that could look like that?"

"No, it wouldn't look like that. It would be torn. This looks cut, and it's cut with a sharp angle at one end and a dull angle at the other." Petty pulled out a penknife and used it to demonstrate. "The sharp edge did the cutting and the dull knife tore a little bit as it went through."

"Were there any wounds on the body of this victim that correspond with the location of this cut or tear?"

"I don't see any."

"Do you have any way of determining how long this defect had been in the nightgown prior to the time it was observed?"

"Not at all."

"Then you have no way of knowing whether or not this defect in the nightgown has anything to do with the murder of this victim?"

"No."

"Doctor Petty, is there any way you can tell in what order the wounds were inflicted on the victims?"

"No, I can't tell you that."

"Is there any way you can tell whether these wounds were inflicted simultaneously—that is, any two at the exact same moment?"

"I can't tell you."

"Is there anything about these wounds to either the children or the mother that would preclude a single individual from inflicting them?"

"No, not absolutely preclude a single individual having done it."

"In your mind, he would have had to have switched from one weapon to the other, but one person could have done it?"

"One person could have switched from one weapon to another. It's sort of useless in a sense, but he could have done it."

Dozier was ready to move on to the stomach-contents issue.

"Doctor Petty, I'd like to ask you a little bit about exercise and stomach contents. In the course of the questions that you were asked by Mr. Long, we talked about tremendous exercise, strenuous exercise. Could you be more specific in terms of how you specifically feel that exercise affects the digestive process?"

"Well, the more severe and prolonged the exercise is, the slower the emptying of the stomach. Exercise, such as an individual boxing for fifteen rounds in the ring, would certainly be severe and prolonged exercise. An individual playing professional basketball, severe exercise and prolonged. How they do it, I don't know. When you get into children, however, children go at exercise in a gung ho fashion. They exercise to the full capabilities that they have. And so a child who is running or swimming or jumping exercises strenuously because he does it in a burst of enthusiasm. This is the usual way children exercise, so what appears to be less than total or strenuous exercise to you and me in a child is strenuous exercise. And that would include jumping around on a trampoline and diving into the little plastic balls. That, in my opinion, would constitute pretty severe exercise in a child."

"You, of course, did not observe the children exercising at Chuck E. Cheese."

"Well, of course not."

"And you don't know, then, what interval occurred between diving into the balls and diving again, or whether they laid there a while in the balls, do you?"

"No, of course not. They could have laid there laughing and tickling each other and screaming. I don't know."

"Or buried themselves under the balls and laid there for a while to see if anybody could find them."

"I suppose they could have, yes."

"When children play, they do some things strenuously and other things not," Dozier stated as fact.

"Well, based on being a father and watching a few children exercise, when they go to it, they go to it pretty strenuously."

"And you're saying that digestion then is not occurring in the stomachs of the children while they're performing very normal play?"

"I think it's very much delayed, in fact may be absent for a period until they finish whatever they're doing and for a prolonged period afterward, too."

"So if children eat a breakfast at eight o'clock and go out and engage in the normal play all morning and come in for lunch at noon, their food hasn't digested from breakfast."

"Their food may not have digested very well, that's true."

"And if they eat lunch and go out and play for two or three more hours, they may still have breakfast in their stomachs at three or four in the afternoon?"

"When they're exercising, yes. I didn't say play. I said exercise. They may play at cards or whatever. But that's not exercise."

Petty gently shifted in the chair, obviously in some pain.

"Doctor, you've indicated that you feel that the stomach contents were in these victims for a considerably long period of time after the meal was ingested primarily because of a small volume that was left, as indicated in the autopsy report."

"Well, yes. I think that's inescapable. There's only a small amount of the total there. Therefore the stomachs are pretty well emptied out."

"That, however, assumes, Doctor, the accuracy of the information you were provided that the children somehow split nine-tenths of a pizza that size?"

"That was the question that was put to me. Yes, sir. And I assumed the accuracy of that in making my opinion."

"And that information comes from the defendant himself. Is that correct?"

"I believe he asked the question. Yes, sir."

"You were assuming, then, that between the three children, they had to consume about 1,350 milliliters of pizza."

"That is correct."

"Would your opinion differ, depending on whether or not substantially less food was consumed?"

"Well, certainly. If the children only ate 230 milliliters of material, and that's what was recovered, then I would be forced to the conclusion that there hadn't been much digestion that had taken place."

"Doctor Petty, you have been of the opinion, have you not, for a good many years, that it is difficult to estimate the time of death from an analysis of stomach contents?"

"Yes, sir."

"Are you likewise aware that there are other forensic experts in your field who feel it can be done?"

"Yes. There are some that are quite dogmatic about it."

"And in essence this is an issue that has been in controversy in the forensic science field for a number of years, has it not?"

"To a lesser extent than 'controversy.' I think there's a difference of opinion on it, and I would differ with some of my conferrers on this."

The next defense witness was Petty's colleague, Irving Stone, the former FBI agent, a Ph.D. who now headed the physical evidence section at Dallas's Institute of Forensic Sciences. He had joined Dr. Petty in an inspection of the crime scene and had personally inspected some of the items taken by investigators from the home. Included were the ax and butcher knife. He had concluded, just as Petty had, that neither the ax nor the knife were responsible for the defect in the nightgown worn by Susan Hendricks. He believed that at least three sharp-bladed instruments were involved in the crime.

Long also wanted the jury to hear Stone's analysis of the ransacked house. "Can you state whether, based upon your review of all of the crime-scene reports, lab reports, autopsy protocols, the photographs of the crime scene, your analysis, and visit to the crime scene, whether you have an opinion whether this crime scene indicates that a burglary was committed?"

"Yes. My opinion is that a burglary did occur."

"Would you please tell us the basis of that opinion?"

Stone cited numerous situations police had found inside the house: drawers pulled out, material moved around on top of dressers, opened boxes, clothing disturbed—all indications, Stone said, that the burglar or burglars were looking for something. He focused particularly on the bedspread in the master bedroom.

"The thing that is important in my viewpoint is that the coverlet is pulled up on the edge of the bed, which is a characteristic thing that you'll see at many, many burglaries—virtually all burglaries—because they will look under the bed, under the mattress, and you see the coverlet pulled back on the corner. It's just a consistency."

Long had Stone look at a photo of the china cabinet in the dining room.

"Did it at the time of your personal examination of the crime-scene appear to be undisturbed?"

"It was undisturbed."

"What, if anything, does this mean to you with respect to your opinion that this scene indicates that a burglary took place?"

"That they were looking for certain types of things and not other types of things."

"How many burglaries have you investigated?"

"I didn't keep track of them. But more than a thousand."

"Can you state whether, based on your experience and your observations over these years and your knowledge and training, that every burglary scene that you've investigated has evidence that everything loose or available to be carried away was, in fact, carried away?"

"The answer is no. Certainly not."

"Now you indicated that you have had the crime scene reports that were prepared in this case by the Department of Law Enforcement of the State of Illinois made available to you. Is that correct?"

"That is correct."

"With reference to the basement, can you state whether there was anything that you observed that formed an additional basis that a burglary had been committed?"

"Yes. The freezer door in the basement was left partly ajar. Open."

"And what significance does that have for you with respect to your conclusions in this case?"

"That there really was a relatively wide search of the house."

Long had another bottom-line question: whether the crime scene was consistent with there being two or more assailants.

"My opinion is that this crime was perpetrated by two, possibly more, people."

Judge Baner spoke up. "The answer is going to be stricken. That's a nonresponsive answer."

"I understand," said Long. "Listen to my question, if you will, please. Can you state whether or not this crime is consistent with having been perpetrated by two or more assailants?"

"Yes, I have an opinion."

"And what is that opinion?"

"Yes, it is."

"Thank you. I have nothing further."

"Dr. Stone," Brad Murphy began, "it's appropriate to call you Doctor?"

"I'll answer to that. Yes, sir."

"But you're not a pathologist, I take it."

"They aren't the only real doctors."

Murphy showed Stone a picture of the master bedroom.

"You've been kind enough to tell us what aspects of that represent what you think were things consistent with a burglary. Now would you be kind enough to tell us what, if any, aspects of that photograph are inconsistent with a burglary?"

"Well, I guess I'm surprised that the cedar chest, which appears at the base of the bed, is not opened, although it may have been closed. That's all I can think of."

"Doctor Stone, in your opinion that you've given to us here that a burglary occurred, do you mean to exclude the possibility that this scene was set up to look like a burglary?"

"No."

"And in your opinion here today showing the possibility of multiple assailants, are you intending by that opinion to exclude completely and totally the possibility of there being a single assailant in this case?"

"No, sir."

In August of 1982, David Hendricks walked a few doors down Carl Drive to welcome his new neighbors to Bloomington. It wasn't until a couple of months later that John Cramer and Hendricks realized they had more than the same neighborhood in common. They were both associated with the Brethren. But Cramer had been part of an "open" group—one whose rules about active participation in the meetings were not so rigid.

Hendricks and Cramer would occasionally meet over coffee at a restaurant to discuss the differences between the two branches of the Brethren and to study the Bible. By January 1983, Hendricks was expressing some disappointment that Cramer hadn't joined the Bloomington meeting. Nevertheless Cramer had become one of Hendricks's best friends, their wives trading baby-sitting, the two families visiting each other's homes for dinners or Bible study sessions. Now John Cramer, a university chemistry professor, was on the stand for the defense, being asked to characterize the relationship between David and Susan Hendricks.

"I'd characterize it as a very warm, loving relationship—one of mutual esteem and respect, very caring, very warm and positive in all respects that I can recall."

"Do you recall," Hal Jennings asked, "any time or circumstance where you saw or heard David Hendricks speak in anger as far as his wife was concerned?"

"Absolutely never."

"Did you ever hear him say or demonstrate any negative reaction or statement as far as his wife was concerned?"

"Never."

"Did you ever hear or see any negative statements by Susan towards David?"

"Never."

Jennings asked the same questions about the children. Never, Cramer said, had he seen any problems between Hendricks and the children.

"How did they talk in terms of their attitude toward their father?"

"In terms of great love and respect and pride in their father."

"Did you ever see him in a situation where he disciplined the children?"

"Never any physical discipline. There may have been a situation where he spoke to them and rebuffed them verbally for some infraction. But I don't even recall that for sure."

"Can you tell me, Mr. Cramer, whether you've had occasion to be in the presence of others—either friends or family or neighbors—where the person of David Hendricks has been discussed or where comments have been made?"

"Yes, I've been in those situations."

"Do you have an opinion with respect to the reputation of David Hendricks in his community for truthfulness and veracity?"

"Yes. I'd say he had an excellent reputation, was highly esteemed."

"Based on those contacts and on that opinion, can you tell me whether you would believe David Hendricks if he were to testify under oath?"

"I would."

"In your characterization of the Hendricks family, Mr. Cramer," asked Brad Murphy, "would you describe the children as obedient children?"

"Yes, I would."

"Would you describe Susan Hendricks as an obedient wife to her husband, David Hendricks?"

"Yes. I would say that."

When Cramer's wife, Karen, testified, she questioned the use of the word "obedient." "I don't recall a situation where obedience came into question," she told Murphy. "Would you elaborate?"

"Is there anything in your range of experience with the family that would cause you to conclude that she either was or was not an obedient wife to her husband, David Hendricks?"

"I don't like that word. I don't think of marriage in those terms."

"So that's not a word that you would use to describe Susan."

"Yeah. I guess that's not a word I would use to describe a marriage."

Earlier, in a soft, almost timid voice, she had described the relationship between David and Susan. "I recall numerous occasions when David would take Susie out to eat. I was aware of those because we would trade baby-sitting. I recall an instance where David watched both my children and his children so that Susie and I could go to eat and shop. I've seen them in sort of pressured situations, like one time they were getting ready for a trip to Europe. And I was going to drive them to the bus they'd take to the airport, and they were hurried. And yet I never saw them say anything unkind to each other.

"The same thing with the Bible study. Sometimes there would

be a few dishes or something left, and things would be a little hurried and rushed. Yet I never saw them say unkind things to each other, or pressure each other, or treat each other in a—"

"Was there anything," Jennings interrupted, "you recall concerning the frequency that David and Susan would go out together?"

"No. It seemed quite often to me. I used to be kind of jealous."

"Based on what you saw and heard, how would you describe the relationship between David and his children, their interaction as children and parent, father and child?"

"I thought they had a very good relationship. I recall seeing Dave outside, playing with the children late afternoons. I recall one occasion where he had come home from work and his son was playing in the neighboring yard, and he stopped and waved to them. And that stuck in my mind because his son didn't see him right away so he stood there for the longest time until he got the child's attention. That impressed me and it stuck in my mind. I recall there were toys at David's office. I had seen the children play down there. I remember one time he took my children and his out for ice cream on one of the occasions they were baby-sitting. The thing that really sticks in my mind is—I think it must have been around Benjamin's fifth birthday—I went over to the house and he just grabbed my hand." A small smile and then tears crossed Karen Cramer's face. "He was all excited. He wanted to show me a little workbench his dad had made for him down in the basement." She choked back tears and looked toward the defense table where David Hendricks also sat crying.

A parade of more than a dozen of Hendricks's friends, former employees, and relatives followed Karen Cramer to the stand. Each testified they had seen nothing less than a kind, loving relationship between Hendricks and his wife and children. One witness, who had worked for Hendricks before he sold his Illinois Orthopedic Appliances, said that one of the reasons Hendricks sold the business was to let Hendricks have more time to spend with his family, but Hendricks didn't sell it until he had assurances that the new owner would keep his employees on staff with no loss in pay.

Another witness, Michael Adams, testified that the Hendricks family had visited him in Wyoming less than four months before the murders. "I remember Dave and Susie being very close, hugging a lot, and Susie sitting on Dave's lap. And I also remember being caught in a water fight between Dave and the kids, and how much fun they had."

Katherine Macy and her daughter, Kara, had attended the Bloomington Brethren meeting the Sunday before the murders and talked with Susan Hendricks about plans to attend the baby shower the following night.

"Dave and Sue had offered to have Kara to stay with David and the children Monday night," Ms. Macy testified. "Kara had a piano lesson in Bloomington, and they said David would pick Kara up from her lesson and take her out to eat with them, and he would take her to Heyworth to my father about eight-thirty or nine o'clock. And as it turned out, I had already made arrangements for her to stay with her cousin in Delavan. And I told them that if those arrangements didn't work out, I would have Kara stay with Dave. But as it turned out, she went to Delavan and stayed with her cousin."

"Was it your understanding," Jennings asked, "that the offer was for David to care for his children and your child in his home while you and Susie were at the shower?"

"Yes."

"And was that an invitation extended by Susie in David's presence?"

"Yes."

"Please describe for me the relationship between David and Susan."

"It was a very close relationship. You could see in their interactions together they were very close. During meeting, if one of the children did something amusing, you could see them share that in just a glance between them. I know on one occasion when we were at their home, David was teasing about something and the remark was made, 'How do you put up with his teasing?' and she said, 'I can never get mad at him because he always makes me laugh.' "

"And what about the relationship between David and his children?"

"They were very close. In the meeting room, there were five chairs in a row. And the prime seat was on the aisle by the father. The middle seat between the parents was second, and the wall seat was the lowest. They always tried to race to get in and sit on the aisle by their father."

"Was that something that you observed regularly at meeting?"

"Every week."

Seventeen

S usan Hendricks's will, dated about eleven months before her death, left her estate to her husband. But because Illinois law prevents a person convicted of murder from benefiting from the will of a victim, the money was to revert to her second choice, her children. Because they, too, were dead, the estate went to the couple's twelve brothers and sisters. Susan's six brothers and sisters and David's six brothers and sisters all agreed to transfer their inheritance—a total of about $130,000—to David to help pay his legal fees.

Money had become an issue for Hendricks and his parents. David had sold CASH Manufacturing and his back brace patent to Ralph Storrs on contract. And he had also sold his home on Carl Drive to a young childless couple for a bargain-basement $84,000—at least 15 percent under market value.

The couple was quite familiar with the home's history because they had lived in a smaller home only a few blocks away. The wife was hesitant about the move, but her husband convinced her it was a bargain too good to pass up. "If one of us couldn't have dealt with it, we wouldn't have bought it," the husband told friends. "I'm sorry for what happened in the house and to the people in it, but I don't dwell on it. It's sad that some people think something like this can't be overcome. My understanding is that some people wanted to burn it down."

Neighbors, however, were pleased that the house was again occupied.

Jennings had predicted the trial would last four to six weeks. Now the trial was about to begin its ninth week, and its end was just barely in sight. Hendricks's father, increasingly concerned about mounting expenses, had a rather bitter confrontation with Jennings and Long in a three-hour meeting one night. Charles Hendricks was upset that the two attorneys were staying at Rockford's best motel and charging the defense for their meals. He accused the legal team of taking advantage of its client.

Jennings answered that the defense case could have been shortened by reducing the number of expert witnesses, and that overall costs could have been reduced if the family had not insisted that every possible lead be checked out, no matter how obscure. But don't worry about it, said Jennings. He was having a hard time staying focused on the case with Charles Hendricks looking over his shoulder. Never mind, said Jennings, that the two defense lawyers should have adjoining rooms. He would move to a cheaper motel. Three hours of preparation time had already been lost, complained Jennings, and David Hendricks himself was to testify the following day.

Jennings, who would question Hendricks, had considered getting a theatrical coach to help Hendricks, but the idea was rejected in fear that it could backfire. When, at 1:29 P.M. on Tuesday, November 13, Jennings called Hendricks to the stand, the defendant seemed very eager. And unlike most members of the Brethren, who took an "affirmation" rather than an oath, Hendricks, wearing a blue suit, took an oath to tell the truth. The courtroom was nearly full.

Jennings first questioned Hendricks about the change in his appearance in the sixteen months leading up to his arrest.

In a calm and firm voice, Hendricks said he weighed 275 pounds when the family moved from Stanford to Bloomington in the summer of 1982, and that his doctor placed him on a diet because his blood pressure had increased. At about the same time, he said, his hairstyle changed as the result of a free haircut offered in a coupon package distributed to new residents. "There was a coupon from a specific stylist, and I simply took the coupon in and redeemed it for one free hairstyle," Hendricks said.

"Since that time, have you ever had your hair styled profession-ally?" Jennings asked.

"No."

"Was there any particular manner or style you requested?"

"I didn't ask for anything specific. I simply told her that I knew nothing about hairstyles and had never really paid any attention to mine, and that both my secretary and my wife thought it was high time I got a new one, and that whatever seemed best to her, I'd like to try it."

"At the time you had your hair styled in '82 with the coupon, did you have a mustache?"

"Yes."

"When and under what circumstances did you cut off the mustache? Do you recall?"

"I think it was July 28th, 1983—that's our anniversary—and I did it specifically on that day for Susie. She had expressed a dislike for it years before when I first put it on. I hadn't heard anything from her for years on it."

Jennings shifted the focus to Hendricks's business.

"What were you working on with respect to either the CASH Brace or any other products, devices, or appliances?"

"I had a number of things going. I had a wide pelvic band and a chin place attachment—both of those are attachments to the CASH orthosis. I was just finishing development of the final proto-types of a hinge version, was working on a one-size-fits-all spinal brace system, which would be three different kinds of braces. I was working on a one-size-fits-all Dennis Brown splint-type orthosis."

"With respect to the products or devices that you marketed prior to November of 1983, were you marketing other types of braces other than your own CASH orthosis?"

"Correct. They were not one-size-fits-all products, but the system for fitting them was my own."

"What are you referring to?"

"A scheme I devised that would fit these braces which come from manufacturers, some with over one thousand different possi-ble combinations of sizes, with just three standard measurements. The person who fit the brace would take three simple measure-ments, phone them to our company, and Bev Crutcher would know from a chart that we compiled what size to order from this manu-facturer. That's all we do."

"When did you start traveling in connection with the promotion of either your hyperextension back brace or any other of your product lines?"

"Even before the beginning of the business."

"Did you, in fact, plan and make a business trip to central and north central Wisconsin November 7th and 8th of 1983?"

"I made the trip then. I planned it earlier, of course."

"When was it that you decided to take this particular trip?"

"Specifically, the previous week."

"David, as far as your trip to Wisconsin November 7th and 8th is concerned, how did you get from your starting point to your destination?"

"Automobile."

"You have an airplane. Why didn't you fly?"

"Because while getting to Wausau the airplane would be much better, it would be perfectly useless stopping at all of these little towns on the way back."

"What was your starting point as far as this November 7th trip is concerned?"

"Three thirteen Carl Drive."

"What time did you leave 313 Carl Drive?"

"Shortly after, or right about, eleven o'clock."

Dozier, Murphy, and Long all looked up from their notes. They had expected Hendricks to testify to an 11:30 P.M. departure.

Jennings had Hendricks recount the evening he spent with his children before he left for Wisconsin.

"Susie left a little before six, and at that time I called the children in. Until that time, I was just cooling down from my run and playing with the children outside. I went upstairs and took a shower, changed, then took the children out to the Eastland Mall."

"And what reason, if any, did you have for going to the mall on that particular occasion?"

"Well, Becky had a . . ." Tears welled into Hendricks's eyes. "Excuse me. Becky had a . . . I'm sorry . . . Becky had a poster that she had made in school and won a prize, so it was posted in the mall. And she was proud and wanted to show me."

"What time would you have gotten to the mall to see Becky's poster?"

"Six-fifteen."

"Okay. Tell me of your activities after that. Where did you go?"

"We went north to Chuck E. Cheese pizza."

"We've heard a lot about Chuck E. Cheese, but for the record, what is it?"

"It's a pizza restaurant that caters to children. They have animated characters and a playroom and large-screen TV and a full-sized animated Elvis Presley. And they sell pizza, sandwiches, salads, whatnot."

"Was it someplace where the kids went frequently? How often would you say you've been there?"

"Pretty often. They liked it a lot. And they had their little birthday passes, and we went on Tuesdays usually, which was an extra token day."

"What time did you arrive there?"

"Around 6:30, I would think."

"David, had you intended to have another child with you when you went out to dinner that evening?"

"Yes. Kara Macy, Kathy Macy's daughter—Becky's best friend. In meeting on Sunday, Susie offered my services to Kara's mother for that night, which was the night of the baby shower that Kathy would be attending. What she offered was my baby-sitting services and then taxi service back to Heyworth at the end of the evening."

"Were you present when Susie suggested that Kara spend the evening with your children?"

"Yes."

"And what was the response to the invitation?"

" 'That's nice, thank you. We already have a place for her, but I think Kara would like that better. I'll talk to her and call you back tonight.' "

"And did you or did Susie hear from Kathy later that evening?"

"We did. I did. It was a telephone call from Kathy, and she said 'Thank you, but we're going to go through with the plan for her to be with Paula.' "

"Where is Heyworth from where you live on Carl Drive?"

"Almost due south, I would guess fifteen miles."

"You and your kids got to Chuck E. Cheese about 6:30. Tell me about your activities, the activities of the children, how long you were there."

"We ordered the pizza and I sat down and gave the children tokens. We had brought in an envelope full of tokens with us, had gotten a few with the pizza. I gave the children tokens, they went in and played in the designated play area. I watched TV in that large-screen TV room until about seven. The pizza came at that time, and the pitcher of root beer. I got the kids, and we ate the pizza, and the kids went back to play. I continued to watch TV until about, oh, half past seven or maybe a little after that."

"When you went in to get the kids when the pizza came, you got the kids from where?"

"They were in the play area. Two of them were bouncing on this air cushion pillow that they have, and one of them was diving into these plastic balls that they've got in a big vat."

"Tell me, to the best of your recollection, who ate what."

"I know generally we all ate the pizza and finished the soft drink."

"What part of the pizza did you eat?"

"I ate a piece. One piece."

"Any particular reason that you recall eating one piece or only one piece?"

"No particular reason. I really don't care for their pizza. It's not very good and I was continuing to try and watch my weight. It's difficult for me to maintain my weight."

"Other than the piece that you had, can you tell me what the other kids ate?"

"They ate the balance between them. I'm sorry, I simply didn't think it was important to record it. I don't remember it all."

"Can you tell me whether there was anything left?"

"They ate it all."

At the prosecution table, Dozier and Murphy looked at each other and had to suppress smiles. Finally, an almost giddy Dozier thought, we have him on record saying they ate all the pizza at the restaurant. If Hendricks had said they took some of the pizza home with them and ate it later that evening, the state's whole time-of-death case could have gone out the window. Dozier immediately felt more confident about his case.

"Give me your best judgment," Jennings was saying, "as to how long it took for the kids to eat before they returned to the play area?"

"I don't have the foggiest idea. Not very long. They ate fast."

"Then what did the children do?"

"I stayed where I was and watched TV for a little while. Then I went in and watched the kids for a little while and came back and watched TV."

"When you say you went in and watched the kids, how long did you remain there?"

"Five minutes or so. Just long enough to satisfy them. They enjoyed showing off for me." Hendricks's voice choked with emotion. "You know, bouncing as high as they could and things for their daddy."

"What did you do next?"

"I went back in to the kids and told them, 'It's time to go' and—"

"What time was this?"

"About half past seven."

"Go on."

"Well, I didn't take them at that time because they protested, you know, they were having all kinds of fun. I needed to fill the car up with gas, so I said, 'Stay in the play area. I'm going to be gone a few minutes,' and I filled the car up."

"Where did you go to fill the car up?"

"Across the street. Then I came back and watched them until about ten to eight, and then I said, 'We've got to go now.' "

"Describe for me, as best you can, David, the level of physical activity the kids engaged in immediately prior to your leaving."

"Vigorous, very high. They were having a lot of fun and they were very, very active. And even as we left, we were late. In fact, by the time I finally coaxed them out of there, it was actually more like seven minutes till eight, and it was very late to get to the bookmobile. I thought we needed to get to the bookmobile by eight, and I simply didn't think we were going to do it. So we ran to the car and drove home fast."

"Was it your belief that the bookmobile was in your neighborhood only until eight?"

"Yes. But they had just changed the schedule, and they were there until 8:15, fortunately, because we didn't make it there by eight. We came home and I just pushed the automatic garage door opener button, pulled into the garage, Grace ran into the house and got the books which were on the kitchen table and the library cards, ran back to the car, and we zoomed the car down—it's just one block—but we were that late that we drove the car back to the bookmobile, plowed out, and ran into the bookmobile. Then I found out that we had fifteen minutes to spare. We got done just shortly before they drove away about 8:15. The children selected their books, and I helped the lady fill out some information for some new library cards that we were getting—a first-time card for Benjy, and new cards for the girls. They checked out, I think, three books each, which is what we usually have allowed them to check out. Then we went home in the car into the garage."

"Was anyone else at home when you got there?"

"No. We went into the house and started to play hide-and-seek. Two rounds each of hide-and-seek. Then I read to them a little and put them to bed."

"Where did you put the children to bed?"

"They went into their own beds. The girls share a room, and Benjy has his own room."

"Do you recall whether any of the children had a bath or anything of that nature before going to bed?"

"I recall, yes—no, they didn't. I don't think."

"What time would you judge that the kids went down for bed?"

"It would be a guess. 9:00 to 9:30."

"What did you do then?"

"I read for a little bit and then went to bed myself. I just rested."

"Can you tell me what happened next with respect to Susie's arrival home or anything else?"

"That was next, her arrival home. She drove into the garage. Well, I didn't see that. I heard the garage door open and then her coming up the stairs. Then I saw her walk south down the hall to the end of the hall, and then a short time after that, she came back and got ready for bed and got into bed. Very quickly after she got home."

"What time did she get home?"

"Around 10:30."

"Can you tell me when it was that you first became aware of the plans that Susie had to attend the shower, that Susie requested that you care for the kids while she went to the shower? A day or two, or a week ahead? Do you recollect?"

"Sometime between those two, sometime during the previous week."

Under Jennings's questioning, Hendricks gave details of the several family trips and evenings out with Susie that occurred in the months before the murders.

"David, I want to ask you with respect to your relationship with Susie, had you in 1981 or '82 or '83 any problems in your relationship with Susie from the standpoint of marital disharmony or discord?"

"No."

"Had you ever been separated from her?"

"Oh, no. Nothing like that."

"Had you ever contemplated any divorce or had she ever discussed any notion of leaving you or separating or her getting a divorce?"

"Oh, no. Not even close."

"David, there has been much said here in this case about women who modeled for you at various times and places in connection with your business. With respect to a lady named Echo Wulf Atwell, do you remember her testifying?"

"Yes."

"Does your recall as to the facts and circumstances of your contact with her differ in any significant way from what she testified to?"

"Not significant. No."

Jennings asked the same questions and got the same responses concerning the testimony of Cindy Baird Segobiano, Diana Payne, Dawn Rueger, Kathy Harper, Nancy Jarrett, and Lee Ann Wilmoth. Hendricks had a different response when Jennings got to the testimony of Carolyn Johnston.

"Specifically, if I remember her testimony correctly," said Hendricks, "she said that I asked her to be nude, and I remember asking her to be partially nude or topless for the measurements. And I think one more point. If I remember her testimony—it's hard to separate them all—I think she said that she had never told me she was going to model and never made an appointment to do so. And I remember her making an appointment which she did not keep. Other than that, nothing that I can remember right now that's significant."

"Tell me about Carla Webb. Does your recall of your contacts with Carla Webb differ in any significant way from what she testified to?"

"A couple of minor points that I would call significant, yes. She said that I told her that my wife can't find out, subsequent to a hug that was given. I don't dispute the hug, but that statement, and I think she said that I offered her an airplane ride to Kentucky. That's not in my memory at all."

Hendricks's tone seemed to say that he didn't want to call Carla Webb a liar, but he certainly didn't remember anything like that. "Other than that," he said, "nothing significant that I can think of."

"Do you recall Tammy Ledbetter being here?" Jennings continued.

"Yes, and again just a couple of minor points. Well, I don't know that they're minor. She said that I told her I was a doctor. I'm sure I did not do that. She said that I offered to—I think she used the expression 'crack' or 'bend' her back. And I remember the expression she used was completely foreign to me. I don't think I used that."

"David, do you recall Elizabeth Tomlinson testifying here?"

"Yes."

"And does your recall differ in any significant way from what that young lady testified to under oath?"

"Very much so."

"How does it differ?"

"I would take issue with almost her whole narrative. I'm not sure I can remember everything now. You want me to go through what I can?"

"Tell me what your recollection is with respect to your contact and association with the young lady in Phoenix."

At the prosecution table, Ron Dozier was writing feverishly. Two jurors were also taking notes.

"I first met her in my hotel room in Phoenix. She came from the Bobbie Ball Modeling Agency as a replacement for Tammy Ledbetter about one o'clock in the afternoon. I was to fit her with a CASH orthosis, and then we were to go across the street, and she was to begin modeling at two o'clock. I asked her to be partially nude or topless for the measurements. She went into the bathroom and got completely nude. She was the only model that I dealt with that was completely nude. She came out with a towel on her. She dropped her towel for me and never replaced it. And that differs significantly from her account, if I remember her account correctly.

"I think she also said that I told her I was a doctor, which I am sure that I did not do. Anyway, I measured, I made marks on her, I fit the CASH orthosis for her, took it into the bathroom sink and ran hot water over the parts and bent the metal and adjusted the bars and everything. I did have her lie down on the couch, both supine and prone, and made marks and measurements. That's correct, and I did make a number of measurements. I did mark down her spine. She got dressed and we went across the street and she began to model a little before two o'clock. She modeled the brace at the booth for about three hours, I would guess, and at that time I asked her to come back to my room for a refitting of the swivel-type CASH which I had tried to put on her in the afternoon but didn't like the looks of at all. And we went back to my hotel room. I refit her with the CASH with the swivel attachments on both the sternum and pubic pads. That fitting didn't take as long as the earlier fitting, and she gave times which I don't dispute in those cases.

"Other than that, her narrative is essentially what I remember until the time when we went out for the ride through Phoenix and Tempe and Scottsdale. And again, her narrative is correct, except for some conversation she reports. I don't remember saying to her that I've had several affairs, and I'm sure I didn't say that because it's simply not true. I do not remember making a pass at her or coming on to her, putting my arm on the seat behind her, trying to kiss her. Other than that, again her narrative is relatively accurate. We did come down from that mountain and go to the restaurant, Garcia's of Scottsdale, which was closed. And she suggested that we not go out to eat but return home. Back at the hotel room she got her leotard and the clothes that she had left from her modeling that day and exited. She said that I hugged her at that time, and that's accurate. I gave her a brief hug, but I did not ask her if I could fantasize."

"Did you ever tell her, David, that you had quit your church or were having problems with your religion?"

"Oh, I'm sorry. I forgot that. I'm sure I didn't do that."

"In fact, has there ever been any point in your life in which you have disassociated or disaffiliated yourself with your fellowship group?"

"No. No."

"David, have there been occasions in connection with your contact with various of these ladies which has caused you to be physically attracted to any of them?"

"Yes. Obviously."

"Has that been on more than one occasion?"

"Two."

"Can you tell me whether that physical attraction in any way diminished or diminishes your feeling for Susie?"

"Oh, no."

"Before you left for Wisconsin, what was the last thing that you and Susie discussed?"

"It was about possibly adopting a young boy we had become aware of."

"Is that something that Susie wanted?"

"Yes."

Jennings's questions were coming rapidly now and almost matter-of-factly.

"For how long had that been her desire?"

"Since she lost her . . . the . . . the last baby and had . . . had a hysterectomy."

"Had that been something that you wanted and you desired?"

"Yes."

"David, did you kill Susan Hendricks?"

"No."

"Did you kill your children?"

"No."

His voice clear, almost loud, David Hendricks's direct testimony had ended after nearly two and a half hours.

At 9:15 the next morning, Hendricks was back in the witness box. And if there had been empty seats in the courtroom the previous day, they were filled now. A few people stood outside the courtroom, waiting for a seat to be vacated.

Ron Dozier had spent several hours the previous night preparing his line of questioning. His first questions had to do with Hendricks's development of the CASH orthosis, but he soon moved into a more sensitive line of questioning.

"Where is the CASH orthosis designed to be worn with regard to clothing that a patient wears?" Dozier asked.

"Over a cotton undergarment."

"And why is that?"

"Because if you wear it directly on the skin, the foam pads would irritate the skin if directly on the skin for long periods of time."

"Isn't it true that the purpose of the photographic sessions with the models is so that you can place an ad in a trade magazine showing how the brace fits on the model?"

"Or have them display it in person."

"And what are the primary considerations that you're looking for in how the brace is going to look when modeled for a brochure or advertisement?"

"Mainly you want it to look like it fits the person. You want all of the pads to lie flat, and you don't want any gaps."

"Yesterday you indicated you were physically attracted to two of the models. Which of the two models, David?"

"I'm glad you asked that because I thought about that last night. That was a bad answer. To say I was physically attracted to only two, I don't think would do justice to the situation. I physically did something about that attraction in the case of two models. That's what I meant."

"Which two were you talking about?"

"Carla Webb and Lee Ann Wilmoth."

"And Carla Webb is the one that you admit that you tried to hug?"

"No, I said I hugged her."

"Oh. You did hug her?"

"Yes."

"And Lee Ann Wilmoth is the one that you admit you tried to kiss?"

"No."

"Would you explain that?"

"I don't remember doing that."

"All right. What is it that you indicate that you did about the physical attraction in the case of Lee Ann Wilmoth?"

"I physically touched her breast. She was lying on the edge of her bed and I was next to it, and I physically massaged her back and front to some extent. I didn't spend much time touching her breasts. I was close to her physically, and she correctly said that she rebuffed my attentions and that I backed off and apologized. But I did, in fact, do that."

"She also testified that you tried to kiss her. Do you not recall that?"

"Oh, I recall the testimony. And the truth of the matter is, I wouldn't be honest with you if I said that I'm sure I didn't try to kiss her. But I don't remember doing it. I do remember being attracted at that time, and it would be a natural thing to do, so it's possible. I really don't remember doing that, though."

Dozier temporarily left the issue of the models. But he would come back to it. It was part of his strategy. He moved on to Hendricks's activities the day and night before he departed for Wisconsin.

The previous day Hendricks had said that the gas station where he fueled his car had been "across the street" from the pizza restaurant. He had been wrong about how close the gas station was, and Dozier made a point of correcting Hendricks.

"Oh, I think you're right," Hendricks responded. "I was thinking it was just south of College Avenue."

"So to get there from Chuck E. Cheese—is this correct—you would go west out of Landmark Mall, over to Towanda, drive south up to the intersection of Towanda and College, cross that intersection, go down that long winding path south on Towanda, all the way down to Vernon, cross the intersection of Vernon, and then left into the Freedom Oil Station?"

"Yeah. Yeah, that's correct. The way you described it, you take longer to tell it than it takes to drive it, but, you know, it's not real far. It's like one block when you go by the College Hills Mall."

"One real long block."

"Yes, and then turn left right after Vernon. Yes, I'm sorry. Thank you for the correction."

"It's not directly across the street from Chuck E. Cheese?"

"No, it sure is not."

"And what would you estimate the driving time of that to be? Five minutes?"

"Oh, no. It just takes a little over five minutes to get clear home from Chuck E. Cheese. I would say two minutes."

"That would depend on the lights at the intersection to some degree, wouldn't it? You have to go through two intersections to get from Chuck E. Cheese to Freedom Oil."

"Yeah. Most red lights last, what, about twenty-five seconds or so. So if you hit a light, you'd add less than a half minute maybe."

"How many of your children had school the next day?"

"Three."

"And after you got home, did you have the kids get ready for bed immediately?"

"No."

"Okay. What did you do first?"

"We played hide-and-seek."

"And they were still in their street clothes?"

"Uh-huh."

"How long did you play hide-and-seek?"

"We played two rounds each. I don't know how long that would last. Twenty minutes, a half hour maybe."

"And then what did you do?"

"I read to them."

"Where did you go at 9 P.M.?"

"Nowhere."

"You did not leave the house at 9 P.M. at all?"

"No."

"What time did Susan return home?"

"I would say around half past ten."

"I'm sorry. What did you say?" Dozier asked.

"I said I would say around half past ten."

"Did you tell Detective Crowe that she came home around 10:45?"

"That's possible. I don't remember."

"It's possible," Dozier echoed. "Is it possible she did come home as late as 10:45?"

"It's possible, but I doubt it now, knowing what I know now."

"How long did you talk with her after she arrived home?"

"Probably twenty minutes or so."

"Did you tell Detective Crowe you talked with her approximately an hour?"

"It's possible. I don't know."

"It is possible that you talked to her about an hour?"

"No, I don't think I did."

"What time did you leave the house?"

"About eleven o'clock, maybe slightly after. Not before eleven."

"When did you pack for the Wisconsin trip?"

"While the kids were getting ready for bed."

"Before Susan came home?"

"Yes."

Dozier had Hendricks retrace his business trip to Wisconsin, starting with a stop in Bloomington to get a cup of coffee, to his nap the following afternoon at the Red Roof Inn in Madison.

"How long had it been since you last slept?"

"Well, let's assume it was four o'clock in the afternoon when I laid down. I didn't sleep the previous night, and it would be until I had awakened the morning of Monday. I usually wake up at about 5:30, so it would be 5:30 to 4:00, which is ten and a half hours, plus twenty-four is thirty-four and a half plus twelve hours, or 12:00 till 4:00 in the afternoon is sixteen. Fifty hours, roughly."

Actually the correct total was thirty-four and a half hours, but Dozier didn't seem to notice. He asked, "And if I understand correctly, that is not particularly unusual for you?"

"You understand correctly."

"You do that once a month or once a week or—"

"Between those two. Once every ten days or two weeks, something like that. I did then. I don't anymore."

"When you checked out of the Red Roof motel, you told the people there that there was an emergency and you had to leave?"

"Likely."

"What time did you stop at the Standard station in Compton, Illinois, on the way home?"

"I have no idea. I hardly know where Compton is."

"You did stop and make a phone call to the Cramer residence that evening on the way home?"

"Yes."

"And did you drive straight home from there?"

"I made one more stop after that Compton stop. Just beside the road and took a walk down the road and back which is what I do at night when I'm driving and start to get drowsy. Five minutes. No big deal."

"Any recollection of where that was?"

"Uh-huh. Just south of El Paso."

"So you would, basically, then be within twenty, thirty minutes of home?"

"Yeah."

"Did you call Rebbec Motors on November 9th?"

Jennings stood up. "I'm going to object, Your Honor."

"The basis?" Judge Baner asked.

"Relevancy."

Judge Baner sent the jury from the courtroom and then asked Dozier to defend his question concerning the morning after the bodies were found.

"Your Honor, the defense brought out certain events that occurred on the 9th: who was with the defendant, what activities were occurring, what he was doing. This particular call, I believe, relates to the same time period and to activities he was doing that we believe would, at least, show that he was in full possession of his faculties and able to carry on routine functions, which I think would contrast perhaps with things that show him behaving in a different way."

"You're planning to demonstrate something other than he made a call to an automobile dealership?" Judge Baner asked.

"That he made a call, what he did, what he said," answered Dozier. "It would be a call to Rebbec Motors in which he canceled a new-car order that was for his wife."

Jennings responded that the defense never contended that Hendricks had lost control of his faculties, that the prosecution was trying to present the testimony only to indicate that Hendricks didn't show the proper amount of grief.

"Well, the court's convinced," Judge Baner said, "that the fact that he made a call to a dealer is relevant. But is the subject of the call necessary, as far as the jury is concerned?"

Dozier said he believed that the defense would eventually argue that some of Hendricks's comments in the hours after the bodies were discovered shouldn't be taken too seriously because of the tragedy and his lack of sleep. He wanted the car dealership conversation testimony heard as proof that Hendricks was thinking clearly the day after the murders were discovered.

"Well, may I assume correctly that this was not a car he was purchasing for himself?" asked the judge.

"There were two cars, Judge," said Jennings. "He had ordered both, one for himself, one for his wife. And in fact he called the car dealer, suggesting that there had been a tragedy in his family and to forget about the one car."

"What does that go to prove in this case?" the judge asked Dozier.

"Just what I indicated. His mind was functioning clearly. He was capable of remembering to do that, calling and carrying it out."

"Judge," Jennings responded, "it seems clear to me that the real motive behind it has nothing to do with the issue in evidence. It has solely to do with an attempt to prejudice the jury, to suggest to them that the call was an inappropriate response in some manner to the situation of his family slaying. The fact is that prejudice outweighs any probative value."

"The court concludes," Judge Baner ruled, "that the nature of the information has more prejudicial effect than probative value. The court is going to allow the state to present the fact that the call occurred, and to the extent that the content of the call can be demonstrated to the jury without demonstrating the beneficiary of this proposed purchase, the state will be allowed to go into it."

The jury returned, and Dozier asked Hendricks, "Did you make a call to Rebbec Motors, a car dealership in Bloomington-Normal on the 9th of November?"

"Not that I remember."

After a recess, Dozier returned to questions about the models.

"I'd like to ask you specifically," Dozier said, "were you physically attracted toward Echo Wulf Atwell?"

"I could say yes, but I'm not sure that the meaning would be what I want to say."

"You're indicating, however, with only Carla Webb and Lee Ann Wilmoth did you, quote, take action with regard to that attraction."

"Yeah, that's what I'm saying. Essentially that I'm a normal man with all of the hormones, or whatever, flowing through my body. And I think most women are attractive, but I don't mean that I go around making advances to women."

"All right. Understanding that, were you physically attracted toward Echo Wulf Atwell?"

"In a sexual way?"

"Yes," answered Dozier.

"No," responded Hendricks.

"Were you physically attracted toward Cindy Baird Segobiano?"

"Now in all of these questions, you mean in a sexual way?"

"Yes," responded Dozier.

"No," answered Hendricks.

"Were you physically attracted in a sexual way toward Diana Payne?"

"No."

"Toward Carolyn Johnston?"

"No."

"Toward Kathy Harper?"

"No."

"Toward Dawn Rueger?"

"No."

"Toward Nancy Jarrett?"

"No."

"Toward Susan Ryburn?"

"No."

"Toward Tammy Ledbetter?"

"No."

"Toward Libby Tomlinson?"

"No."

"You were, however, physically attracted in a sexual way toward Carla Webb and toward Lee Ann Wilmoth?"

"Yes, and to qualify all of the other no's, that's a very difficult question to answer because to some extent, every man is physically attracted in a sexual way."

"Not interested in philosophy. Were you physically attracted toward any other models that we have not asked about in a sexual way?"

"You mean like the model in California that's not been here on the stand?"

"Kim Taylor?"

"Kim Taylor. I would say no like I said no to the others."

"Was there a model named Chris?"

"No."

"Any others?"

"I don't think so."

"Is that a 'no'?"

"Pardon?"

"Is that a 'no' answer, Mr. Hendricks? Are you saying that you might have been? Are you saying no, there were no others?"

" 'I don't think so' is something less definite than a 'no.' "

"Are there some that you may have been physically attracted to?"

"I wouldn't pick out any particularly. You don't want any philosophy, so I'd say I'm attracted to all women."

Dozier momentarily left the models issue, asking about Hendricks's calls from Wisconsin. But then he asked about the models again.

"You recall questions being asked of those models by your attorney regarding research being done on a brace system or something along that line?"

"Yes."

"Are you contending to the ladies and gentlemen here that the measurements and markings and the partial nudity that you required had to do with research that you were doing in order to try to invent another brace?"

"Yes."

"Specifically when, and on which model, did you start doing this type of research for another brace?"

"It would be, let's see, not Echo, Cindy, or Diana. So the next model after Diana would be where I started. It was basically after the CASH began to become profitable and sell well, and I decided that inventing was a pretty good way to make a living and wanted to invent something else."

"For what purpose were Echo Wulf Atwell, Cindy Baird Segobiano, and Diana Payne hired to model for you?"

"Echo Wulf Atwell was hired specifically and only for the purpose of modeling the CASH orthosis for pictures for a brochure. That's all. Cindy and Diana were hired to take measurements and make a number of different braces on their bodies—arms, spine, legs, feet—and take photographs and put that in a catalog of services for Illinois Orthopedic Appliances."

"Did you explain this to either of them beforehand?"

"To both of them."

"What did you do with the cast that you took of the torso of Diana Payne?"

"I filled it and made a positive mold and stripped off the negative and started to make a custom-mold, polyethylene body jacket."

"Started to?"

"Didn't finish because the project was far more extensive and expensive than I initially had planned on. I was initially going to make a catalog which had all of the different kinds of orthopedic appliances that we made, made up for models and in pictures. And what I realized was, of course, in the prosthetics half of the catalog

I would have to have artists' drawings, because you can't find many models who are amputees. Then I realized that would be incompatible with the orthotic part. And then I realized it was far cheaper to just make drawings for the orthotics part of the catalog. So I hired an artist who drew a bunch of drawings for the catalog. The whole project was scratched when I started to sell my business. It was stupid to go into the expense for that project for a business that I was about to sell."

"What models did you use for the purpose of doing research for a new brace product?"

"Well, any models that I took any measurements of, because, frankly, you don't need to take measurements or make marks to fit a CASH Brace."

"Do you agree that you did not tell any of those models that you were taking these measurements of their bodies and requiring them to expose their private parts to you for the purpose of your doing research on a new brace design?"

"That's true."

"Did you deceive those models when you didn't tell them?"

"Yes, because I think that the impression—"

"I don't care why you think that," Dozier snapped. "Did you deceive them? Every one of them?"

"I think so. I can't think of any who knew exactly what I was doing."

"David, what type of research or information were you attempting to obtain from those models when you were taking these measurements?"

"Specific data that would help me develop a one-size-fits-all spinal brace system. Heights, widths, circumferences, relationship of one part of the body to the other."

"Did you ever develop the brace that you're talking about?"

"I've been interrupted in the process. I would still like to."

A faint smile crossed the mouths of some of the jurors.

"How many sets of measurements do you need to build or develop this brace?"

"Far more than I could ever get with models, you know. It would be nice to have hundreds and hundreds and hundreds. The more the better. I suppose you could say you don't need any. But the more you have, the more accurate you would be."

"Well, how is it that you felt having the measurements of approximately seven or eight of these models is going to be of significant help to you in developing a new back brace?"

"Because, as I say, measurements are a help."

"Could you not have asked friends, relatives, or colleagues to supply you with these measurements?"

"I think I could have."

"Could you have not hired people to be measured for you for that purpose?"

"I could have, I think."

"What were you paying these models? What was the rate for these sessions?"

"I don't remember any less than twenty-five dollars an hour. Specifically the part of their work in which I did the measurements, I paid them zero."

"So you were, in essence, getting that for free?"

"Right."

"So in addition to deceiving them as to the purpose for which they were being measured, you were also not paying them for exposing their body and allowing themselves to be measured by you?"

"No, I would disagree with that. I paid them for the modeling, which was a good hourly wage—sixty dollars an hour is a lot of money for these girls—and when I hired them they knew one hour would be for free."

Dozier shifted gears again.

"David, at this time I would like to go back now to the conversations you had with Detectives Crowe and Scott in the upstairs bedroom of the Cramer home when you arrived home that night of the 8th. Do you recall telling Detective Crowe on that occasion that you left the previous night at about midnight for Wausau, Wisconsin?"

"No, at this point I don't. But I probably did."

"Did you, in fact, tell Detective Crowe that when you left around midnight or at midnight, your wife was asleep in your bed in the master bedroom?"

"I remember saying that. The midnight came from him in the question. In other words, he said, 'When you left about midnight, where was she?' "

"And you said, 'She was in bed.' "

"Correct."

"Did you tell Detective Crowe that the two girls were sleeping in their bedroom, in separate beds, and that Benjy had crawled in bed with his sister, Grace?"

"Very likely."

"Did you tell Detective Crowe when he asked you when you first became concerned, 'It was hard to say. It was probably when I called Mary Ann and Susan wasn't there'?"

"I recall very well that whole line of questioning. He kept asking me maybe thirty times when, exactly, I became first concerned. He was just very, very concerned about that, and I remember not being able to pinpoint when I first became concerned. I remember we spent a long time on that issue."

"Were you asked if you remembered checking the doors before you left and told Detective Crowe that you don't specifically remember checking, but it's usually your habit to check the doors to make sure the vertical locks are in place and the wooden bar is in place on the patio?"

"I'm sure I didn't say that. I don't have vertical locks in my house. I don't even know what that would mean."

"Do you recall Detective Crowe asking you about the ax you had in your home?"

"Yes."

"Did you tell him that the ax was in your home, that it was red, and it was an old ax?"

"Yes, red-handled, I said."

"Do you recall the news conference that you had on the 9th of November in the afternoon hours with the TV station there at CASH Manufacturing?"

"I recall talking with two news cameras going, yes."

"Did you, in fact, say at that news conference, 'I was never in the house, but they said that some things looked like some things were taken'?"

"I don't remember specifically. Probably."

"Did someone say to you that some things at the house looked like some things were taken?"

"They must have."

"Who specifically said that to you?"

"One of the police. I wouldn't have any idea."

"When was that said to you?"

"Sometime during the time I was talking to the police."

"Which time?"

Dozier was trying to get under Hendricks's skin. Only a tiny bit of irritation was beginning to show.

"I have no idea," Hendricks responded.

"What do you recall about that conversation?"

"I'm sorry. Which conversation?"

"When someone said that some things looked like some things were taken."

"I don't even recall that happening."

"Did it happen?"

"It must have."

For a fourth time, Dozier turned to the models issue.

"Do you recall Nancy Jarrett's testimony that she was in leotards and shorts when she arrived, and that you told her she would have to take off her underpants and bra, but she said no? So she did not take off her underpants?"

"I'm sorry, I didn't recall that testimony. That's significant and that's different from what I remember. I didn't tell any model to be completely nude. Period."

"So all of these models who have said that are apparently mistaken?"

"The three. Yes."

"Do you recall while at Nancy Jarrett's house your going over and pulling the drapes closed?"

"Yes."

"Why did you do that?"

"Because cars were coming down IAA Drive and drivers could see right in."

"And you didn't ask her if you could do that or anything?"

"Well, I knew I could do it. Simple, just—" Now it was Hendricks's turn to get under Dozier's skin.

"You didn't ask her if it was okay for you to close her drapes?"

"Oh, no. No. I assumed it was. I was about to ask her to take her leotard down and expose her breasts, and I didn't think she'd want people driving by to see that."

"You weren't asked by your counsel yesterday if you agreed or disagreed with what Susan Ryburn testified to. Do you disagree or agree?"

"I agree in the main."

"You agree that your mouth dropped open when she introduced herself and her husband, Stanley?"

"No, I don't. Since she said that, I've tried to drop my mouth open. It's such an unnatural action, I can't imagine doing it."

"When did you first find yourself becoming sexually attracted to Lee Ann Wilmoth?"

"I want to be careful because I don't want to hurt Lee Ann's reputation at all, because I'm the one who's wrong—not she. But it

was when she opened her robe and asked me to take a look at her
rib after I was done measuring and examining her, and then
walked into the bedroom. I asked her to lay down on the bed, and
she lay down on the bed supine. And I said, 'I am going to check
your spine again.' And in fact at that point, what I was doing wasn't
what I said I was doing. I was deceiving her, and well, I really
didn't think I was deceiving her. I thought we both understood that
what I was doing was something of a somewhat sexual nature. I
was rubbing her."

"And you rubbed her back? What part of it?"

"Just all over lightly. I thought it was fairly obvious to her that
I wasn't doing anything."

"And what was she wearing at that time?"

"I'm not sure at this point because her testimony said she was
wearing a leotard, and I thought I remembered that she wasn't,
that she only had on the pajama bottoms. She might remember that
more accurately than I."

"She was, nevertheless, nude from the waist up?"

"Not according to her testimony. I thought I remembered that.
I'm not sure."

"All right. So you massaged her back first?"

"Correct."

"And then did you have her turn over?"

"Yes."

"And you massaged her front?"

"Correct."

"What did you massage there?"

"The entire front abdominal area, including part of the
breast."

"Did you touch her nipples?"

"Oh, no. When I got to her breasts, she broke it off. She said, 'I
think this is something other than an examination or taking measurements.' And I said, 'Yes, it is.' And she said, 'Well, I think we'd
better stop.' And I said, 'Okay, I'm really sorry. I didn't realize
that. I really wasn't thinking.' "

"In fact, you said, 'I thought that was what you wanted, and I'm
sorry,' or words to that effect."

"It's possible, because that's true."

"Did you try to kiss her?" Dozier asked.

"I don't remember trying to kiss her. I remember her testimony. I was definitely attracted, and it's very possible."

"And did you, in fact, after you left, and after you had forgotten your watch or came back and looked for your watch and then left, call her and ask her if she would still do the photo session and once again apologized for whatever had occurred?"

"Yeah. I don't remember asking her if she'd still do the photo session, but I called her specifically to apologize."

"And did you tell her at that time that you still wanted her to do the photo session and that she would not be alone with you again?"

"Yes. I tried to reassure her that I wasn't going to do anything like that again."

"When you were at Phoenix and you touched or manipulated— or whatever you want to call it—Tammy Ledbetter's back and then had her turn over and did the same to the front when she was nude from the waist up, what's the difference between what you were doing then and what you were doing with Lee Ann Wilmoth on this occasion?"

"What I was doing with Lee Ann was a more gentle caressing, rubbing, somewhat sexual type of thing. What I was doing with Tammy was simply pushing my hand on the side of her thorax at the apex of the curve. She had a definite scoliosis—there was no doubt about it—and I was seeing if it was manually or passively reducible. If I develop this one-size-fits-all spinal system, one of the big features was that two sizes can be made of different heights for an oblique torso or asymmetrical torso, so it can fit exactly both sizes. And I was wondering if I had her as a patient if I would have to accommodate the scoliosis, or if a brace could be fit which would be straight and reduce her scoliosis. If I would have to accommodate her scoliosis, it would make my one-size-fits-all brace a really neat product and more in demand."

"So you're indicating that the measurements that you were doing and that manipulation of the spine was research for the brace that you hoped to develop?"

"That's what I said. Yes."

"What did you do with the measurements that you took on that occasion?"

"They were written down on a piece of paper, and I kept them either in my research file, or in the models' file, or on my desk or somewhere."

"Do you know any reason why that particular piece of paper would not be included with the measurements on the rest of the models?"

"It probably wasn't found is my guess. I didn't know it wasn't included. I've been in jail, so I haven't had a chance to look for it."

"Whenever these models, as they have testified, indicated to you by word or action that they were reluctant to be nude from the waist up, didn't you, in fact, tell them that this was a routine or standard procedure, and that you were a professional of some kind, and that you had often seen patients or clients in this situation so there was nothing to worry about?"

"I would say yes, except that I would differ with the beginning of your statement. One of the things I noticed with the models—and one of the things that probably caused me to go in the path you've been trying to bring out—is the fact that they were amazingly unhesitant or unreluctant about taking off their clothes."

"You have indicated previously, in your testimony for Mr. Jennings, that you agreed about what the models had to say."

"I don't think that's particularly significant," Hendricks answered.

"Don't you recall most of the models testifying that they expressed reluctance to expose themselves from the waist up?"

"Yes."

"In fact, didn't Kathy Harper, when you told her that, ask you, 'Am I going to be in the photo session with clothes on?' "

"Yeah, I—"

"And then she said, 'Well, then, I don't see why I can't do the fitting session that way.' "

"I remember her saying that."

"And you didn't have her then be nude from the waist up. Is that correct?"

"If my memory serves me correctly, it's not. If my memory is accurate, I measured her just like the others—topless."

"Wouldn't you agree that would be a significant difference, considering the issues in this case?"

"Yeah, maybe. I'll tell you why I don't think that whole issue is significant."

"I'm not interested in that, sir. The jury's going to decide whether it's significant."

"Okay."

"But you do acknowledge that you did tell models that you were a professional, and this was a routine procedure, and there was nothing for them to be concerned with?"

"Uh-huh. Many times."

"What exactly did you tell Tammy Ledbetter would be necessary in order for her to be fitted?"

"I simply told her, 'I'm going to take some measurements. I

need you to be partially nude. That is, you can have your panties on but not anything else.' "

"Did she say anything to that?"

"Just 'Okay.' "

"Do you recall her testifying that she said, 'Pardon me, the agency didn't say anything about this'?"

"Very well."

"And are you saying that she was not telling the truth when she said that?"

"Yes, yes."

"And you're indicating she did go into the bathroom to change."

"Uh-huh."

"You agree that she was telling the truth when she said that?"

"Yes."

"And you're indicating she came out in what fashion?"

"With a towel in front of her."

"How was she holding the towel in front of her?"

"Loosely. It was draped, one arm, two arms, I'm not sure. I remember she had a towel covering her as she came out."

"What parts of her body was it covering?"

"The front of her. Those parts she would likely want to keep covered."

"Okay. And what happened next?"

"I said, 'I'm going to measure you,' and motioned for her to drop the towel, which she did. And I placed the brace on her, and fastened it up, and made some notations as to how I needed to adjust it, took it into the bathroom, poured hot water—"

"Let's stop a minute," Dozier said. "You motioned her that she would have to drop the towel, and she did?"

"Uh-huh."

"Were you surprised to find that she was wearing nothing?"

"Yeah."

"What did you do?"

"Nothing. No skin off my back."

"And so, just ignoring the fact that you have a totally nude model in front of you, you went right ahead with the fitting session in the normal fashion?"

"I thought it was rather unusual, because I had specifically said that she could keep her undies on."

"And you did your research in the normal fashion."

"Yeah."

"And you did have her lay down on her stomach, and you did your research or experiments on her back. Is that correct?"

"I made some measurements."

"Did you care about what Tammy Ledbetter's feelings were when you were doing that?"

"Not like I should have. I do now, but I really didn't think about it then."

"Did you ever tell her that you would rather she wore something on her bottom or not expose herself to you like that?"

"No, because it wouldn't have been true."

"You were enjoying the free look?"

"Why not? Yes."

"But you weren't sexually attracted to her?"

"I don't remember being particularly attracted. No."

Dozier moved to Hendricks's drive with Libby Tomlinson to Camelback Mountain.

"What happened when you pulled off the road and looked at the lights in the city?" Dozier asked.

"She rolled down her window. We looked at the lights. She described a number of different items in and around the city. I asked her what this was and what that was, and pointed out the airport to her, and said I can always spot those because I was a pilot. We talked for a little bit, and then I drove the car away."

"Do you recall Libby testifying that you said, 'I probably shouldn't do this,' and you leaned over and tried to give her a kiss on the left cheek, at which point she said, 'Don't try it'?"

"Absolutely."

"And are you denying that occurred?"

"Absolutely."

"And are you denying that you backed off and said, 'But you're so pretty'?"

"Yes."

"And are you denying that after you sat there for a moment, you said, 'I'm calmer now,' and said, 'I thought you had wanted something like that because you got so quiet'?"

"Yes."

"Did you then go to Garcia's and discover it was too late to get any food?"

"Yes."

"And then you went back to the room?"

"Correct."

"Did you try to pay her money after you got back to the room?"

"Yes."

"For showing you the sights of the city and so on?"

"Yes."

"And she wouldn't take it?"

"No, she wouldn't take it."

"And so instead, you said that you'd give her a hug."

"Oh, no. No, that had nothing to do with the money. She didn't take the money, and I gave her a hug."

"And why did you give her a hug?"

"It was a spontaneous thing. It was definitely nonsexual. It was a brief embrace. What I said specifically is, 'Okay, I'm not going to press any money on you. I understand and I thank you very, very much,' and I gave her a hug."

"But you didn't fantasize about what didn't happen up on Camelback Mountain?"

"I certainly didn't ask her if I could fantasize. I have no idea whether I fantasized anything."

"Did you have any conversation with Libby Tomlinson about your religious beliefs at that convention?"

"No."

"Did you discuss her religious beliefs?"

"She talked about them to me. I don't remember responding at all in that context."

"Did you talk to her at all about having had affairs?"

"No."

"That conversation didn't occur at all?"

"No. We did talk about moral issues when she took me by and showed me the gay bars, Hot Bods and some other gay bars that she particularly pointed out to me. And we got to talking about homosexuality and issues of morality. But I don't remember talking about marital infidelity."

Dozier, who had been standing near both the witness box and the jury box for most of his examination of Hendricks, now leaned against the defense table.

"Let's go back to Carla Webb now. You indicate that you have only two significant differences between what you recall happening and what Carla Webb has testified to."

"Yes."

"And those two are you do not recall saying, 'My wife can't find out,' and you don't recall offering to take her on an airplane trip to Kentucky."

"Right. I'm sure I didn't do either of those."

"You're sure you didn't do either of those?"

"I'm positive."

"Absolutely positive?"

"Yes, because I can't imagine why I would have done either. They would be senseless statements."

"But you do have an airplane, do you not?"

"Yes."

"Do you deny after you hugged Carla Webb, you got teary-eyed and said, 'I'm a good Christian'?"

"The teary-eyed is a characterization I would have no idea about. I would think probably that's not true. I don't usually get watery eyes."

"How about your saying, 'I'm a good Christian and I'm married.' "

"It's very possible I said that when I was apologizing."

"But at the same time you're saying it's not at all possible that you said, 'My wife can't find out.' "

"No. The reason I say that is that would be absolutely stupid. That's just asking for blackmail or whatever. I wouldn't do that. I wouldn't say that."

"Carla Webb told you she was married, didn't she? And it was no big deal. She's married, too."

"Yes. I might be wrong, but I got the impression that her system of values might be somewhat different than mine in that regard."

"On the other hand, she just might have been trying to make you feel more comfortable."

"Really." Hendricks's tone indicated he agreed.

"You would not have wanted your wife to find out about that incident, would you?"

"No."

"Absolutely not?"

"It wouldn't have caused insurmountable problems, but I certainly wouldn't have wanted it. It would have hurt her."

"Why did you set up all of these fitting sessions after business hours and at the homes of these models, where you would be there alone with them?"

"Because I had this ulterior motive of making those measurements, and I didn't want somebody else to be with me while I had a model unclothed or partially unclothed."

"So you were keeping that fact even from Bev Crutcher?"

"Yes."

"Is there any particular reason why you didn't want people to know that you were doing it for research purposes?"

"To tell them what I was doing would have meant that I would have had to explain why I was doing it. Much easier simply not to say anything."

"Was not Bev Crutcher a trusted or loyal employee of yours?"

"Oh, she's very trusted and loyal."

"And is there some particular reason that you would want to hide what you were really doing, even from her?"

"It's possible that, without realizing that, I was ashamed of it. I certainly am now, and I realize it."

"Do you recall how you paid Nancy Jarrett for her modeling session?"

"I brought a check to her home."

"Around bedtime in the evening?"

"Yes."

"After telling her she would be receiving the check in the mail?"

"Yes."

"Why did you do that?"

"I was going to Perkins at the time. She lives right next door to it, and I dropped the check off specifically because she had mentioned that she had a need for the money. I thought it was a nice thing to do."

"So after this situation with Carla Webb in which you admit you momentarily succumbed to your sexual temptation, you continued to contact Carla Webb."

"Of course."

"In fact, you contacted her at least four times between that time and the time of the deaths of your family, did you not?"

"Yes, and that's not my fault and that's not her fault. That's because the photographer kept messing me up on the time."

"And did you not, in fact, have a photography session set up for Carla Webb for Saturday, November 12th?"

"Yes, that's correct."

"And did you not attempt to set up a second fitting session to measure her for another brace prior to that?"

"A whole series of braces."

"What type of fitting session did you have in mind for that?"

"That would have been strictly fitting—because I was going to conduct it at Ed Roman's office. I was going to fit a series of braces to her to take color pictures."

"So you did not consider that you were exposing yourself to more temptation by continuing these contacts with Carla Webb?"

"Oh, no. No. They would have been photographic. They would have been that kind of contact. That doesn't have anything to do with temptation."

"Do you deny telling Libby Tomlinson that what Susan didn't know wouldn't hurt her?"

"Yes."

"I believe that's all," Dozier said. He had questioned Hendricks for a total of three and a half hours.

Jennings conferred briefly with John Long before beginning again with their client.

"David, you indicated that you would not have wanted Susie to know about these several instances in which you had an attraction to other women. Have you discussed the fact that you had a physical attraction to other women with anyone?"

"With Lawrence Macy, yes, shortly after I was incarcerated."

"Okay. Mr. Dozier asked you some questions concerning the trip to Wisconsin and the phone calls you made. When you called Mary Ann at Nate Palmer's house, did you know what time Susan was due for dinner?"

"Oh, no."

"Did you know that she was due for dinner?"

"Yes."

"How did you determine that she was due for dinner at five-thirty?"

"Mary Ann told me."

"Mr. Dozier asked you some questions about your activities on November 9th with particular reference to the news conference. David, can you tell me if you have any recollection, prior to talking to the media people in your office, do you have any recollection of how many police officers you talked to on November 8th and 9th?"

"Oh, a whole bunch. You know that night in the station, boy, I have no idea how many different ones I would have talked to—fifteen, maybe."

"Did you, prior to your TV tape that we saw here in court, also talk to Beverly Crutcher?"

"Yes."

"Did you talk to Nate Palmer?"

"Yes."

"Seth Palmer?"

"Yes."

"Any other members of the Palmer family?"

"Yes. Chuck, Nicki, my father-in-law and mother-in-law."

"Any other friends, relatives, acquaintances that you talked to?"

"All of the people that I said before were in my office."

"One last thing," Jennings said. "Why did you write down P J whatever as far as the license number was concerned if it, in fact, was not your license number?"

"It's kind of a dumb reason. There's really no good reason. It just always has irritated me that people have always asked for that kind of information, and a lot of times I write down bogus information just for the fun of it. But that's a number that I have used for years. That's the only license number that sticks in my mind. It might have been a Wisconsin plate. It might be an old Illinois plate. I don't know when I got it."

"You were not trying to conceal your identity or hide your person in any way as far as giving bogus license plate number information?"

"Oh, no. She had my credit card and my name and address."

Dozier didn't move from his seat.

"Are you saying now that it may be someone other than the police who told you that it looked like some things had been taken from the house, the statements you made in the press conference?"

"I would object to that," said Jennings. "He has not said that."

"Objections will be sustained to the form of the question," said Judge Baner.

"Mr. Jennings gave you a list of people," Dozier resumed. "I didn't write down all of the names that you talked to at the time before you had that press conference."

Hendricks rubbed the back of his neck. "Correct."

"Are you indicating that it may have been one of them who told you it looked like some things were taken from the house?"

Jennings spoke up again. "I'm going to object. I believe he's already testified he doesn't recall who told him that."

"Court's ruling is the same. Form of the question," said the judge.

"Do you," Dozier continued, "have any memory whatsoever of who or when anyone made such a statement to you?"

"No."

"Do you know whether or not anyone made such a statement to you?"

"No."

David Hendricks's testimony had ended. As Hal Jennings left the courtroom, he told reporters he thought Hendricks "did fine," but he was secretly disappointed in Hendricks's performance. Half the problem, he supposed, was simply Hendricks's personality. The other half he attributed to the stress of the situation.

As Ron Dozier left the courtroom, the chief prosecutor was, for the first time, 100 percent convinced that Hendricks had killed his wife and children.

Eighteen

I t was a peculiar sight, people waiting outside the locked doors of the Winnebago County Courthouse on a Sunday night.

They had chosen to watch a real-life murder trial rather than view a television program that had caused Judge Baner to schedule two unique night court sessions. Earlier he had warned jurors not to watch promotional announcements of the upcoming television movie "Fatal Vision." Now he was doing what he could to make sure the jury didn't see the actual two-part movie based on the book about Dr. Jeffrey MacDonald, the former Green Beret physician convicted of the 1979 murders of his pregnant wife and their two daughters.

Jurors had been given the option of simply being sequestered during the airing of the TV miniseries or of actually hearing testimony. They had elected to hear testimony in this trial, which was running much longer than anyone had predicted.

Spectators filled about half the courtroom when the defense lawyers entered about ten minutes after proceedings were scheduled to start. John Long joked with front-row reporters that he and Jennings were delayed because they wanted to see the first few minutes of "Fatal Vision."

Judge Baner began the session by warning that no one would

be allowed to leave once the proceedings began. Security for the rest of the courthouse was the reason, he said. In fact, the courthouse had been burglarized the week before. No one opted to leave—not even the first-grade teacher who had driven seventy-five miles from Chicago. She sat near the back of the courtroom, grading math papers.

The first evening witness would be Carolyn Bertram, Susan Hendricks's maternal grandmother, who had visited the Hendricks family just a few days before the murders. Hard-of-hearing and recently widowed, she wore a wide-brimmed ruby-red hat.

"Mrs. Bertram, are you aware of David's religious affiliation?" Long asked her.

"Well, I . . . he's a . . . yes, he's one religion . . . I mean, he belongs to one church. I belong to the other," she responded.

"That was my question," continued Long. "Do you belong to the same church he belongs to?"

"No. I am Presbyterian," she answered proudly.

"Can you please describe for us whether or not David got along well with his children?"

"Oh, yes. Beautifully."

"And when you saw them three days before this occurrence, did you have an opportunity to visit in their home?"

"Yes."

"And did you see David interact with his children in the home?"

"Well, the two girls were in school and Benjy was the only one there. And David was going to travel that afternoon, so he hugged and kissed Benjy extra before he went off to school, because daddy would not be home when Benjy got home."

"Can you tell us if you ever saw him mistreat his children at all?"

"I never heard him raise his voice to the children."

"And what about his relationship with your granddaughter, Susan. How would you describe that?"

"They were a very harmonious family. David seemed to live to do what he could for his family, and Susan seemed to live for what she could do for them. They just were so harmonious that it was like a storybook marriage."

"I see. Tell me something, Mrs. Bertram. Are you aware of David's reputation for truth and veracity in the community?"

"For what?"

"Whether or not David was a truthful person."

"Oh yes. I can't imagine him telling anything untruthful."
"If he were to testify under oath, would you believe him?"
"Oh, yes."
"Okay. Thank you."
"He's like my own kid."
The prosecution had no cross-examination.

Laverne Hendricks, who had spent many days just outside the courtroom door, occasionally watching through a window and always asking others how the trial was going, now sat in the witness box.

"Are you related to the defendant?" Hal Jennings asked her.

"He's my son," she responded, looking toward the defense table with a smile that reflected pride and an uneasy confidence.

Jennings asked Hendricks's mother about the phone call she received from David, telling her about the murders.

"I spoke with him on the telephone three times. The first call was from David to me at about eight o'clock in the morning. The next call I made to him. That was close to nine. And the third call I made to him, and that was at about three in the afternoon.

"In the first phone call, I'm not at all sure what I said. I know what David said to me, and I was so shocked and taken back that I didn't—I don't remember that real well. When I called him back was when I had assimilated this news. We talked back and forth a little bit about it, and I asked if he knew how they got in or anything. And then I told him, I said, you know we have to pray for this person or these people. I said it may be that the Lord is working in their lives in some way, and that was all I could, at the time, you know, comfort him with. And I said even though they had done this to him, that we had to pray for them, all of us, and we were all feeling this way. This is what I had talked to my other children about previous to the phone call back to David."

"Was there any discussion or statement made by you to David in that phone conversation or in a subsequent phone conversation later in the day concerning the subject of forgiveness?"

"I don't remember it in the next conversation, specifically. Actually the forgiveness part comes because of the scripture that we have known and been taught, that we are to love our enemies and do good to them that hate us. And that's what I went on when we were talking like that."

"And in your third home conversation with him, did you also attempt to offer any words of solace or comfort to him?"

"Yes. Oh, yes."

"Do you recall, Mrs. Hendricks, whether you then made any scriptural reference in thought or in passage to him?"

"Well, he had been on television and he told me some of the things he had said, and he broke down, and we talked about the fact that it was all joy and peace for Susie and the children."

Jennings had Mrs. Hendricks recall how, once police had released the Hendricks home to the family, they had checked to see if an extra house key Susan and David had kept in an electric box on the back porch was still there. It was.

Mrs. Hendricks also told Jennings that when she and Nadine Palmer inventoried and packed the contents of the house several months later, no wood stick matches were found. Jennings was hoping jurors remembered the crime-scene technician's photo of what appeared to be a match stick on the steps leading to the bedrooms. He also hoped they would remember one witness's statement that the car he saw leave the Hendricks's driveway at about nine o'clock the night of the murders sounded like a diesel engine car. Mrs. Hendricks was now driving her son's '77 Buick.

"Did you notice anything at all unusual or out of the ordinary with respect to the manner in which the car ran or the sound of the engine?" Jennings asked.

"No. It has a lovely sounding engine."

"Does it run good?"

"Very good."

"Does it make any unusual noises or sounds as far as the engine is concerned?"

"Very quiet."

"You know what a diesel sounds like?"

"Yes."

"Does that car sound anything like a diesel?"

"No."

"Would you tell me, Mrs. Hendricks, based on the time that you have spent in the past years with David and Susan, how would you describe the relationship between them?"

"I would say that they had the most wonderful relationship of any family I have ever known. They were very loving. Not, not awkwardly so. They didn't ever embarrass anybody in that way, but they would eye signal each other and let each other know what they felt about each other. I remember when we were with them in August of last year, it was on David's birthday, and she had wanted him to shave off his mustache for many, many years, and it was sort of a private joke between them. You know, if you do this, I'll do that, and so on. But anyway, he came down that morning and he had shaved off his mustache, and it meant so much to her."

Laverne Hendricks looked at her son and her tears began to flow.

"I remember him putting his arms around her and she leaned back against him, and she said, he shaved off his mustache. And then—oh, I don't know—there were countless times. On October 1st, they were visiting us, and we went to a little pageantlike thing, the Chestnut Festival, it was called. And we were walking around, and they walked around hand in hand, and the children were playing. They had an extraordinarily wonderful relationship—the whole family."

"Tell me about David and his children. How did they interact with one another, parent to children, child to father?"

"I can't say enough about them. He did everything with the children and with Susie. They all did things together. He just had to say a word to them, and they would just be right with him. It was just a wonderful family." Mrs. Hendricks shrugged her shoulders. "There are just no words to describe it. I don't say this because of what's happened, but it's true. I have never known any other couple to have a relationship like they had."

Nadine Palmer was the next witness. She called cleaning, inventorying, and packing the Hendricks home "about the most difficult job I ever did."

"Did you know prior to the death of Susie and the children that there was an extra key kept on the exterior of the house?" Jennings asked.

"Well, I heard Dave and my husband discuss it one time or other, and I don't remember just when. I didn't want to hear where it was because I didn't really want to be responsible for it. So I didn't pay a whole lot of attention. But they were discussing the reason he got and hid a key."

Jennings asked Mrs. Palmer whether she had seen her daughter take any refreshments at the baby shower they attended the night of the killings.

"Yes. She was beside me in the line and I saw her at the table picking up different things, and for some reason or another"—a note of puzzlement entered her voice—"I noticed she took a lot of cauliflower. I don't know why I would remember cauliflower, but she did. I guess maybe it's more of a new thing for refreshments than from twenty or thirty years before. But she had quite a bit of cauliflower, as well as the vegetables and cheese and things."

"Did you see her eating anything else after she had initially served herself from the refreshments?"

"Yes. I saw her put her empty plate down when we were getting ready to go, and I saw her pick up a couple of cookies because my other daughter made them, and she said, 'I have to take some more of these because Liz made them.' She liked the cookies Liz made. And she started to eat them as she left."

"Nadine, tell me of some of the things that you recall discussing there with Susan that evening in the shower. Excuse me. At the shower," Jennings corrected himself.

Normally, such a speaking error would draw a few laughs. But not this night.

"We talked about a lot of things. One was about the little boy that she and David were talking about adopting. We talked about Susan having to go to the doctor the next day. We were going to Mary Ann's house the next evening. She said, 'Don't forget, now. Dave won't be there. Did you tell Mary Ann yet?' I said, 'No, I didn't tell her yet.' But anyway she said there were a lot of things she wanted to talk about more the next evening. We talked about David going on the trip that he had planned. She said he thought maybe of leaving at four in the afternoon, but since she was going to the shower, he decided to wait till after she got home from the shower so that he could spend time with the children. And also the baby-sitter they often got was going to be at the shower.

"We were talking about a trip to St. Louis. We were going to make a trip there at Thanksgiving time to another Bible conference."

"On November 9th, do you recall, when you went down to the funeral home, did you talk to David in person there?"

"Oh, yes."

"Did you offer him any words of consolation or comfort at that time?"

"We offered each other words of consolation and comfort."

"Tell me what you told him."

"I told him that being we know of the Lord, that they are better off than in a place like earth. We know they're better off."

"Tell me, Mrs. Palmer, how you would describe the relationship between your daughter and David?"

"I have personally never known any marriage to be finer, nicer, kinder, more loving. I haven't seen anybody else that loving and kind to each other. And happy and joyful and fun-loving. I haven't."

"How would you describe David's relationship with your grandchildren, Rebekah, Grace, and Benjy?"

"He was a daddy. Just a daddy—a good daddy. The last time we were there, Becky did a little something she shouldn't have. David said, 'Now, Becky,' and he made an explanation to her. I remember that. And talked to her. Why she shouldn't have done that. The kids really adored their dad." Mrs. Palmer's narrative had the intonation of a first-grade teacher telling a story to her class. "I think one time Dave was sitting down talking to somebody, and I saw Becky, and she had a silly little grin on her face, and she backed up and backed up and backed up. All of a sudden she jumped into her daddy's lap. And then they both looked at each other, and he hugged her and they laughed."

"Was there any time that you can recall in which David was impatient or intemperate with either Susan or the children?"

"I have never heard either of them say a cross word to each other. I have never ever heard David be cross or unkind or use a bad word of any sort to anybody, let alone his children or Susie."

It was now 9:18 P.M. Jurors returned to the jury room to wait until 10 P.M. before they were released for the night.

The next day's proceedings didn't begin until 3 P.M. In its relatively short rebuttal case, the prosecution called four Bloomington policemen—each of whom testified that they never told Hendricks or anybody else that the crime scene looked like some things might have been stolen.

When the dinner hour came, the courtroom was vacated and dinner was served the jury in the courtroom. For a while, some of the jurors put on their own laughter-filled mock trial with one of the women jurors portraying Judge Baner in his seat behind the bench and another juror acting as the witness.

The jurors smiled when they saw who was to be the final prosecution rebuttal witness. His face was familiar from some eights weeks earlier. It was Dr. Michael Baden. He testified that there was no evidence that Susan Hendricks had been strangled, that the hemorrhage in the neck muscles was caused by blows from the ax.

Asked about the cut or tear in Susan Hendricks's nightgown, Dr. Baden said he could not determine how long the defect had been there or what had caused it.

"And what type of objects could cause such a defect?" Dozier asked.

"Well, a nail hook could cause such a tear—as innocent as

that—or a knife could cause such a tear. And I can't tell whether that tear has been there for days, weeks, months, or if it's a fresh happening the night of the death of Mrs. Hendricks."

"Do you have an opinion of whether the tear is consistent with having been caused by the knife that's been identified as people's exhibit number sixty-four?"

"Yes. That knife could have caused that defect."

"Likewise, other types of instruments you have indicated could have caused it?"

"Many other types of objects could have caused that defect."

"Can you be certain in your mind whether it was indeed caused by a knife?"

"No."

"And based on your examination of the autopsy photographs, the autopsy protocol, the police reports, your discussions with Dr. Romyn, and your experience and training as a forensic pathologist, do you have an opinion as to whether the injuries inflicted on the body of Susan Hendricks are consistent with having been caused by a single assailant?"

"Yes. All of the injuries found on Mrs. Hendricks could have been caused by a single assailant."

Baden also told Dozier that a study of Susan Hendricks's stomach contents indicated to him that she could have died sixty to ninety minutes after she ate at the baby shower.

In his cross-examination of Baden, Long tried to tear down the New York City medical examiner's credibility. Baden conceded that he had formed an opinion about Susan Hendricks's possible time of death only a day or two earlier.

" And I think you testified," Long continued, "the injuries that were suffered by Susan Hendricks were consistent with having been caused by one assailant. Can you state whether it is also consistent with having been caused by more than one assailant?"

"They could have been caused by many assailants."

"You examined the knife and the nightgown, is that correct?"

"Yes."

"When did you first examine these, sir?"

"This morning."

"And what facilities were made available for your examination?"

"My eyes and hands and a ruler. And my prior experience."

"And did you utilize a dissecting microscope or magnification equipment or back-lighting equipment or any laboratory equipment in your examination?"

"No."

"This examination was made by you at Mr. Dozier's request in the witness room before you testified this morning?"

"Yes."

"And is it a fact that you never saw or examined these things about which you have just given an opinion on until about 8:30 or nine o'clock this morning?"

"No, that's not a fact. I had seen photographs of the weapons previously."

"You indicated that the defect in the nightgown could have been caused by the knife hitting the material."

"I mentioned that the very tip of the knife could have caused the defect in the nightgown."

"And you refer to that defect as a 'tear.' Is it a tear or is it a cut?"

"It is really a tear. It isn't a sharp cut, and it's interesting because on the nightgown there's another area that I presume somebody has cut out—crime lab or somebody—a piece of fabric for testing, and there's a distinction between that sharp cut done by the laboratory and the irregular tear on the left shoulder of the nightgown."

"But you find it consistent with an edged instrument, don't you?"

"Yes, including a nail or a hook."

"I have just one last question, Doctor. You, as I understand it, are not here in any official capacity of your office, are you? Or are you here as a paid consultant?"

"I'm here as a private consultant, not in an official capacity, and I will bill for my time."

Dozier wasn't through with Baden quite yet. At one point he pulled the light blue nightgown from the evidence bag so that Baden could point out the tears he had examined. As Baden used the yellow "Ron Dozier for State's Attorney" ruler to point out the defects, Hendricks seemed repulsed by the sight of the blood-stained garment. He clenched his eyes.

"Dr. Baden," Dozier continued, "in response to Mr. Long's question, I believe you indicated that the injuries to the body of Susan Hendricks are likewise consistent with having been caused by many assailants. Is that correct?"

"Yes."

"Can you explain what it is then that leads you to say it is consistent with one assailant if it is also consistent with many assailants?"

"At autopsy and a forensic pathology investigation of the death, we can arrive at the minimum number of persons present in order to inflict the injuries sustained. In this instance, one individual could have caused all of the injuries sustained. There is no way the pathologist can, on the basis of the autopsy and scene investigation alone, determine if one, two, three, four, five, ten, fifteen other people were looking on, assisting, involved in a conspiracy."

"Just a few questions, Doctor," said Long. "Forensic pathologists have at their disposal other indicators which can help make a determination about the number of assailants, do they not?"

"We get a lot of different kinds of information which may be helpful."

"Will you consider information with respect to the number of fingerprints or footprints available to be helpful in this regard?"

"Yes, it can be helpful. But that gets into areas where you have to depend on other people's expertise."

"And do you think it would be proper, therefore, to take into account in this case any evidence that might happen to exist with respect to additional fingerprints that are unidentified, or footprints that don't match any of the parties in this case?"

"That would be something that could be taken into account, yes."

"Dr. Baden," Dozier asked, "in your experience as a forensic pathologist, is it unusual for you to receive reports that footprints or fingerprints have been found at the scene that don't match those of the occupants who reside there?"

"That's not unusual. Fingerprints and footprints can be in areas for years."

There would be one final witness, a witness for the defense. It was Susan Hendricks's brother, Nathan Palmer, who had gone to 313 Carl Drive with Jerry Buchanan the night the bodies were found.

"Can you tell me," Jennings asked, "directing your attention again to that time and place whether there was any conversation in the presence of the defendant, David Hendricks, which had as its subject matter the interior contents of 313 Carl Drive?"

"Yes, there was."

"Tell me who was present."

"Jerry, myself, David, and Detective O'Brien, and Brady of the coroner's office."

"What was said?"

"O'Brien made mention that David could not go into the home at the present, but after the investigation done by the police was through, they would like David to go into the house and take inventory or list anything that was missing."

"And the defendant was present at that time?"

"Yes. He had asked if he could go in and be with his family."

"Do you recall whether anyone said anything in the presence of the defendant concerning any damage to the inside of the house?"

"I believe it was O'Brien, but it could have possibly been Brady also. But I believe it was O'Brien who said that the home had been messed up or tore up or ransacked or something to those terms."

"Mr. Palmer," Murphy began, "you testified about that same conversation in the times you were here in open court earlier, did you not?"

"That's right."

"Are you now adding and indicating that there was further conversation that you now remember that you didn't testify to earlier?"

"I didn't recall that until I was asked about it."

"When was it that you were first asked about it?"

"Probably a couple weeks ago."

"And who was it that first asked you about it?"

"My mother."

"Do you remember where you were when you were first asked?"

"I was at home in Mosinee, Wisconsin."

"I presume you were asked in a phone call."

"Yes, uh-huh."

"Thank you," said Murphy. "That's all."

Testimony in the Hendricks case had ended. Judge Baner addressed the jury.

"Ladies and gentlemen, on behalf of myself and counsel, we wish to wish you a pleasant Thanksgiving holiday. Please return Monday."

Nineteen

I t was now November 27, Judge Baner's forty-eighth birthday. With the jury absent and only a few spectators in the courtroom, John Long stood before a podium to make his second appeal for Baner to enter an immediate verdict of not guilty.

Long said it wasn't being done just because it's expected when the defense ends its case.

"This motion is being made because we earnestly feel that the evidence, when even viewed in the light most favorable to the state, is such that the defendant as a matter of law cannot be found guilty beyond a reasonable doubt."

As Judge Baner took notes, Long cited a 1974 Illinois case in which the appeals court overturned the murder conviction of a woman partly because no motive was shown for why the woman would have killed her son in what was an entirely circumstantial case. Long said that in the Hendricks case, the state had been unable to show any connection between its motive theory and the actual murders.

Second, Long said, in circumstantial evidence cases, a defendant must be found not guilty if any theory of innocence seems reasonable. It had been prosecution witnesses, Long said, who testified that they couldn't identify some of the footprints and fingerprints found in the house and had failed to find a trace of blood on Hendricks or his belongings. It was the state's witness, Long said, who took a photo of the staircase in which the matchstick was found.

"Is it unreasonable to assume that anybody could have walked in a back door and left those footprints, left those fingerprints, utilized those weapons, and, in fact, if there is a third edged weapon, even walked out with one? And the only reason that blood wasn't found on the defendant, Judge, is because when they walked out of that house, they walked out with the blood on them. Is that an unreasonable hypothesis? I would suggest that it certainly is not."

Long said that in deciding the case, the jury would have to indulge in pure speculation—not legitimate inference—about why Hendricks might have murdered and how he could have done it without leaving a trace of physical evidence against himself.

Besides that, Long said, defense experts had shown that establishing a time of death based on the victims' stomach contents was unreliable.

Judge Baner had a question. Assuming that the jury accepted the state experts' opinions about the time of death, and given that Hendricks himself said he was home during that time span, how could the jury find anything but a guilty verdict?

That, Long said, would merely show that Hendricks had had the opportunity to commit the crime, not prove that he had done it. It's conceivable, he said, that the murders occurred twenty minutes after Hendricks left the house, and the state experts themselves indicated that they can't pinpoint a time of death within twenty or thirty minutes.

In response, Dozier said he intended to be brief, not wanting to give the defense a preview of his final argument to the jury.

"That carries certain risks, of course," Judge Baner said, smiling.

Dozier argued that the question of the moment was only whether the evidence as a whole, considered in a light most favorable to the state, might be enough to support a finding of guilty beyond a reasonable doubt. A possibility John Long had missed, Dozier said, was that the jury might conclude that the three children were killed long before 11 P.M. Besides, he said, the jury could find guilt beyond a reasonable doubt because of the set-up burglary, the trip to Wisconsin, and other evidence, even without certainty of the time of death.

Judge Baner said he would rule later on the request for a

directed verdict. Long was surprised and a little excited by the judge's announcement. As he returned to his seat, however, he realized that he wasn't so optimistic about the case overall. He didn't think the trial had gone particularly well for the defense, mostly because he believed a jury would have difficulty concentrating on such a lengthy case and would be likely to accept what it heard first as fact. Perhaps a directed verdict from the judge was Hendricks's most likely path to freedom. Long's attention returned to the new issues at hand as the two sides dueled and then horse-traded over the instructions that would go to the jury.

The defense had sought an instruction that would make clear to jurors the point that Long had just tried to score with Judge Baner: that the opportunity to commit a crime alone is not proof enough to convict a defendant. In other words, the expert testimony, based on stomach contents, indicating that Hendricks had not left home before the murders occurred was not proof that he committed the murders. In the end, the defense traded away that proposed jury instruction in order to get the state to accept one that was much more important to the defense.

In this instruction, the court recognized that the case against Hendricks consisted entirely of circumstantial evidence and explained that such cases require certain considerations.

"Circumstantial evidence," the instruction read, "should be considered by you together with all the other evidence in the case in arriving at your verdict. You should not find the defendant guilty unless the facts or circumstances proved exclude every reasonable theory of innocence."

With jury instructions decided, the only remaining issue was to decide what physical evidence would be given to the jury for its examination. There was little dispute. When there was disagreement over a particular item, Judge Baner would decide whether jurors would be given access to it. Ordinarily prosecutors would be eager to have jurors see photos of murder victims, but in this case the defense sought to have them submitted. Prosecutors feared overkill, that jurors might be offended by them. Long and Jennings wanted the gory photos submitted because they believed it would be hard for the jury to reconcile the violence in those photos with the loving father Hendricks seemed to be.

Judge Baner allowed those photos along with death certificates, containers of stomach contents, a Jasper Jowls stamp, a CASH Brace, balance sheets, fingerprints, Susan's diary, the ax, the butcher knife, and about two dozen other exhibits.

With the day's court work completed, the bailiff informed Judge Baner that two birthday cakes awaited him in his chambers. As the judge left the bench, he asked Hendricks whether he would like to have some.

A minute later Hendricks sat alone at the defense table, eating a piece of Judge Baner's birthday cake.

The first snowflakes of the season appeared the next morning as attorneys and more reporters than usual arrived at the courthouse for final arguments.

The courtroom was packed, and the spectator seating area took on a curious resemblance to a wedding scene in which family partisans are seated on either side of an aisle. About a dozen of Hendricks's relatives sat directly behind the defense table. At least as many members of the state's attorney's staff and Bloomington Police Department aligned themselves behind the prosecution table. Judge Baner warned those in the spectator area against causing any disturbances during the closing arguments.

The courtroom fell silent as the twelve jurors and four alternates entered. Judge Baner explained that closing arguments provided the attorneys for both sides a chance to explain "what they believe the evidence has shown. It is, however, argument and not evidence, and should be considered by you in that light only."

Brad Murphy would speak first. He began by thanking the jurors for their attentiveness, Judge Baner for providing an excellent trial atmosphere, and the defense attorneys for their participation. "All of those factors," Murphy said, "have figured in to ensure that the defendant, David Hendricks, has received a fair trial.

"You've been told before—and you'll be told again—that the defendant is presumed to be innocent of these charges. This is, of course, a rebuttable presumption. It has been rebutted in this case by the evidence. You've been told that the state has a burden of proof in this case. That burden of proof is proof beyond a reasonable doubt. We accept that burden. We don't consider that to be an unreasonable burden nor an impossible burden. It is also, however, not proof beyond all doubt."

Murphy's voice was calm, low-key, and measured. "No one in this courtroom will be asking you as jurors to possess or display any supernatural powers. All that is expected of you as jurors, as reasonable men and women, is for you to conscientiously evaluate all of this evidence, apply your own powers of logic and common sense and reason, then apply the law that is given to you by the judge to the evidence that you've heard, and thereby reach a true, a just, and a fair verdict. That, in a nutshell, is what is expected of you."

Murphy reviewed the details of Hendricks's trip to Wisconsin, including his using a fictitious license plate number on a motel registration form.

"Now that may not seem like a significant matter to you, unless and until you consider that on the witness stand the defendant indicated that he tells that lie repeatedly 'for the fun of it.'" Murphy said that Hendricks also lied to a medical technician about not having his back brace with him and to another about being on an extended vacation through the area.

The series of phone calls made by Hendricks, Murphy said, was telling.

Murphy said that Hendricks testified that his wife was to be at relatives for dinner at 5:30 P.M. "Then what reason does he have to call her at home?" Murphy asked. "He'll call relatives, to be sure. He'll even call some neighbors to get them to go next door to knock on the door. He'll call police, indicating that he suspects an accident. But when he's told by two police agencies that there have been no accidents, he's not satisfied."

Murphy said Hendricks left the Red Roof Inn, saying there was an emergency; yet he testified that when he stopped at a service station en route home to call John Cramer, he didn't think there was a problem.

"The reason the defendant called home at three o'clock and at 5:30 and called at 9 and 10 P.M. on the way home was to discover if anyone else found out what he already knew. He called to find out if the bodies had been discovered."

Murphy told the jurors that there was no record of Hendricks ever leaving for a sales trip late at night on any occasion. "Or did he leave at midnight?" Murphy asked. "In that statement, the defendant told Detective Crowe four or five different times that he left at midnight, and you heard Detective Crowe testify to that. The defendant tells you, under oath, that he left at 11 P.M."

Murphy reminded his listeners of a Bloomington policeman's late-night drive to Stevens Point, Wisconsin.

"Simple math will tell you that five hours and forty-five minutes of driving time and three stops at fifteen minutes each leave you a total travel time of six hours and thirty minutes from 313 Carl Drive to that Hardee's in Stevens Point, Wisconsin. Now what's significant about that, ladies and gentlemen, is we know what time he was at the Stevens Point Hardee's. That receipt that you are going to see is timed 7:17 in the morning. Subtraction will tell you that the defendant left at approximately 12:45 A.M. during the morning hours of November 8th, 1983.

"Consider that sales trip in light of the number of appointments that he had—which is zero. On its face, that doesn't seem to tell us much, does it, because salesmen make cold calls. I concede that. But since he had no appointments, he didn't have to leave that very Monday evening either. He could have easily left Tuesday evening. If the defendant was motivated by a desire to spend more time with his family, why does he go on a sales trip that will take him away from his family, and specifically a family dinner, on a trip that he could easily have postponed for a day because he didn't have any appointments to be anywhere at any time? He left his family under these contradictory circumstances because the time was right for him to leave his family once and for all."

Murphy recounted testimony indicating that Hendricks was seen driving away from his home just after 9 P.M. He reminded the jury that Detective Crowe became suspicious of Hendricks in his first interview with him.

"He's asked an important question, whether he locked the doors to his house prior to leaving. Which door did the defendant first tell Detective Crowe about when he answered that question there at the Cramer home? Do you recall? Did you make a note?"

Murphy read from a transcript. " 'I think I remember latching the back patio door. Front door was locked. I think it was locked. I always check it.' No, that's not unusual at all that the very first door the defendant pops up with is the door that's an apparent point of entry by some would-be burglars."

Murphy reminded the jurors of the TV interview in which Hendricks said, "they said that some things looked like some things were taken." The obvious conclusion, Murphy said, was that Hendricks gave away a detail of the crime scene "that he got from no one except by having been there himself and having set up that scene himself to make it look 'like some things looked like some things were taken.'

"The lack of physical evidence, I submit, shows only the premeditated manner in which these killings were done. The killer had planned these murders, and the killer literally executed these victims. And I submit that the evidence at the crime scene shows you not only the personality, but the identity of the killer. The scene was organized. It was so organized that this ransacking of the home was even done in a neat and orderly fashion. I submit the defendant may as well have left his fingerprint in the blood of those children because he really did leave behind at that scene much more than his wedding band on top of the dresser. He left behind ten years of a marriage that he felt that he had outgrown."

Murphy said the repeated blows to the heads of Benjamin and Grace revealed two important facts. "First, those blows represent overkill. The killer was going through great emotional upheaval and release while chopping them up. Second, the blows were deliberately and accurately delivered. There is no evidence that the pillows are chopped up, that any of the blows missed. To be sure, the killing of these children was a difficult and a bloody chore. It was an emotional event for the defendant."

Murphy warned the jurors not to make too much of the unidentified fingerprints or footwear impressions. "Those could have been made in November of 1982 or in November of 1983," he said. Murphy also warned the jurors not to be misled by perceptions of a burglary and a sales trip.

"And don't be misled by the perception that this defendant holds himself out as an upstanding, loving family man, when in reality the evidence shows that he is a man who indulges in extramarital pleasures of the flesh, and what his family doesn't know won't hurt them.

"In summary, ladies and gentlemen, I submit to you that from what evidence you've heard, only the defendant can tell us how long he pondered, planned, or fantasized the killing of his wife and kids. Only the defendant is responsible for the murders and the two subterfuge crimes that were committed at 313 Carl Drive. And you heard me right—the two subterfuge crimes. The first subterfuge crime was that the home was burglarized to mask the identity of the killer. The second is that the children were killed to mask the identity of the killer of Susan Hendricks. And lastly, Susan Hendricks was killed because she no longer fit in with the defendant's lifestyle. Thank you."

Murphy glanced at no one as he sat down. Judge Baner called a ten-minute recess.

Ron Dozier seemed confident as he began his part of the prosecution's closing argument, which he said would focus on a pair of issues: the expert estimates of the time of death and the testimony from the models.

Dozier said the defense's own experts indicated that the stomach can digest food in as few as ninety minutes for a light meal to as long as six hours for a heavy meal.

"They testified there are circumstances where it can go even beyond that," he said, "but the literature did not support that testimony. In fact the literature, in that regard, supported the testimony of the state's witness, Dr. Michael Baden, who indicated that he wouldn't be surprised to see a light meal, as in the case of Susan Hendricks's snacks at the baby shower, emptied out in an hour and a half or so. Then, if we have a range of time in which a meal normally empties from the system, why cannot we then apply common scientific principles to estimate the time of death? The answer is there is no reason why not, when you have three people whose results corroborate one another."

Dozier said that, even accepting Hendricks's version of the early evening occurrences, the children ate no later than 7:15 P.M.

"Dr. Baden, Dr. Spikes, Dr. Dwyer, Dr. Davis, Dr. Petty, Dr. Jaffe, and possibly even Dr. Zumwalt all indicated that the appearance of this vegetable material was fresh, easily identifiable, not pitted or eroded as one would expect when food is in the process of being broken down. They all agreed with its appearance. Dr. Davis, you may recall, said this stuff was so fresh appearing, he couldn't even say for sure that it had ever been in a stomach.

"On the other hand, virtually all of the starch and cheese from this pizza had been digested. That would seem to imply a period of an hour and a half or two hours. We have independent witnesses who saw these children alive at 8:15 P.M., so we at least know for sure that they could not have died before that time, and we do know they would have had to leave the bookmobile, gone back, got on their pajamas, went to bed, and apparently had fallen asleep before they were killed. So that does put the earlier period of time as perhaps around quarter till nine or nine o'clock in terms of their deaths.

"What is the far end?" Dozier left the podium and placed his arm on the edge of the jury box. "Where you put the far end determines whether or not David Hendricks killed his children and his wife, because if those children were dead before he left that house to go on this so-called sales trip to Wisconsin, David Hendricks did it. No one is going to contend to you that someone would slip in this house, ax his wife and kids to death, and sneak out without him knowing about it."

Dozier reviewed the various experts' opinions on what the outer limit might be as to when the deaths occurred. Then he challenged the idea that the three children consumed most of the pizza.

"We have a pizza that weighs one and a half pounds. Now, the defendant indicates he ate one piece, one-tenth of the pizza. This two-hundred-pound-plus man ate one piece, about 2.4 ounces of pizza. His ravenous children, despite the fact they had a snack of cake at four-thirty in the afternoon, came there and scarfed up the rest of this pizza. Now the rest of that pizza, when you subtract one-tenth, means they would have had to eat 21.6 ounces of pizza. If they divided that up equally and had three pieces apiece, that means 7.2 ounces of pizza apiece, or almost half a pound of pizza for a five-year-old, a seven-year-old, and a nine-year-old. Now I submit that's a whopping meal, plus drinks, for children of that age. So whopping and so unlikely as to be virtually, totally unworthy of belief. Half a pound, almost, apiece while the father eats 2.4 ounces.

"Now, mind you, that's assuming they split it evenly. If any one of the children ate less than his three pieces, one of the others had to account for the rest. All we have to go on is the defendant stating that they ate the whole pizza, and I submit to you that the defendant is the only one of the witnesses that testified in this case who's had the luxury of being able to sit back here and listen to the evidence against him and then tailor his testimony to best fit those circumstances. Nobody else got to do that, and I submit to you that the evidence shows that he has done that."

Dozier said the defense experts faced a dilemma. The state's experts, Dozier said, gave time-of-death estimates of roughly two to four hours without knowing how much the children had eaten.

"We didn't know what to tell them until the defendant took the stand," Dozier said, "so the state's experts were basing their opinion on the undigested appearance of the stomach contents."

But the defense experts had to somehow rationalize, Dozier said, the nearly pristine condition of the vegetables with the idea that a relatively large amount of pizza had been consumed but only a portion of it remained in the stomach.

"Well, I have said enough about stomach contents and gastric emptying. I believe that from what you heard of the testimony of all these witnesses, these children died within two to four hours after they ate that pizza. And I submit to you that everywhere it could help, the defendant is willing to maximize or minimize or whichever way it needs to go to make things look better for him, whether it's exaggerating the amount of exercise they had when he wasn't even there to see most of it, whether it's talking about running out to the car, whether it's talking about two rounds of hide-and-seek as though it somehow would prevent digestion from occurring. Or whether he's simply trying to make himself look better in some small way like indicating that when he left to get gas and left the children alone at Chuck E. Cheese, it was only at a service station across the street that he knows full well is several blocks away. He did that, I submit, not because he had an oversight, but simply because it's part of the image that this defendant has tried to maintain with other people and with you—that he is somehow better than what he really is. He simply did not want you to think that he was a poor father, a father who would leave three young children alone while he went that far to get gas."

As Dozier checked his watch, he shifted the jurors' attention to the testimony of the young women. "There are some significant discrepancies or contradictions between what those models testified to and what the defendant testified to about his activities with them. But it's obvious that the testimony of the models has internal consistency because the same things happened to so many. I think that he discovered how easy it was to get a model to take off her clothes if you converted the relationship, as he did subtly, from one of businessman/model to one of doctor/patient."

Dozier said that one of the models, Carla Webb, was the key to understanding what motivated Hendricks to kill his wife and children. "The evidence indicates that the defendant was fascinated, obsessed, with Carla Webb before he even met her. You recall Bill Ortleb testifying about him staring intently at her picture and wanting very much to get in a fitting with that person. And she was not only everything that he expected in terms of her looks, but he was sexually titillated by the fact that she would feel so at ease and comfortable standing in front of him with this beautiful body. That is when he began, he says, to feel physically attracted in a sexual way. Nevertheless, he's misreading all the signals again. Once again, Carla Webb is responding to a doctor-patient relationship—not in a sexual way as man to woman.

"But he just can't stop with Carla Webb. She has to go to practice for a play that night, and he just keeps her there. He wants her to do this and to try on this. He wants her to look at some brochures, and he has these conversations. He just can't let her out of his grasp. He admits he tried to hug her while she's there with no clothes on from the waist up, and he gets rebuffed. And he admits he said, 'I'm sorry,' or something to that effect. He admits he said, 'I'm a good Christian,' or something to that effect, and yet he totally denies that he said the words, 'My wife can't find out.'

"Why? He knows, you remember. On cross-examination, he says, 'I didn't say that. I am absolutely positive I didn't say that because I wouldn't say something like that. That's like asking for blackmail.'

"What kind of value system does that man have that he thinks that's like asking for blackmail in those circumstances? You think Carla Webb is going to say, 'Okay, fork over a couple of thousand. I'm going to run and tell your wife.' "

Dozier said it didn't seem likely that someone would make up a story about Hendricks offering to fly her to Kentucky, yet Hendricks denied it. "The reason why he denies those things, ladies and gentlemen, while admitting other things, is that it shows that David Hendricks was not just momentarily tempted by Carla Webb, but that he had every intention of pursuing that relationship. He couldn't get enough of making sure that he was going to go ahead with the photography session. He was setting her up for more fitting sessions, but he says those were going to be different. Sure they were. He simply doesn't want you to believe that it wasn't over, and that this represented a continuing pattern that had escalated to the point he was bound and determined he was going to get Carla Webb to bed. And because she rebuffed him so gently and made light of it—which for her was a way out of an uncomfortable and embarrassing situation—once again he misread the intention. He read that as an opening, as a hope for future contacts. He had every intention of getting Carla Webb to bed, and that is partly why he killed his wife and kids.

"This is a man who has been living a double life in terms of his family life and how he wanted to appear to his friends and neighbors and fellow members of the Plymouth Brethren. Yet at the same time, he's pursuing sexual relationships with these models in a hell-bent fashion, escalating right up to a few days before his wife and kids were killed."

Dozier said the idea that Hendricks was doing research for some new type of brace was a sham.

"Is he going to have a great brace that fits only beautiful, well-figured, young female persons? What about old folks and young folks and heavy folks and skinny folks and men? He would like you to believe that he was not pursuing a sexual relationship with each and every one of those models. Whether he succeeded is a different story. But with every one of them he was at least getting free looks and free feels. And if he thought any of them were responding sexually, he was quick to jump at the opportunity and turn it into a blatantly sexual escapade. And he wasn't through yet.

"It's not coincidence, ladies and gentlemen, that the most intensive sexual aggressiveness on his part with models occurred in October of 1983 with Libby Tomlinson and Carla Webb and, in fact, was continuing to occur with Carla Webb even up to the week that the wife and kids were killed."

Dozier's voice became louder.

"David Hendricks had become so boxed in and trapped by his marriage to Susan in comparison with what he wanted to be able to do with these models—the excitement, the spice that it was adding to his life—that he was no longer willing to live in that marital relationship with Susan.

"So you ask yourselves, why didn't he simply get divorced or something like that if he couldn't stand to be married to Susan any more? That's where the defendant's religious practices and his religious image come in.

"The last thing I want to do in this case is make fun of anybody's religion, and I'm not making fun of the Plymouth Brethren. Those people are good and decent folks. But they have been thoroughly fooled by this defendant to the point where they would believe, as they indicated on the stand, anything he tells them. And all this indicates how successful he has been in living this dual life."

Hendricks didn't want to give up chasing women, but he also wanted to keep his good standing with the Brethren, Dozier said. "It was going to get harder and harder as he became blatant in his sexual intentions to keep it quiet in a community the size of Bloomington, let alone what he was doing at conventions.

"The defendant also had another reason that goes deeper than that. He had been living a life in which he had created an image of almost a perfect Christian husband and father. You heard the Brethren testify to that. A wonderful relationship with his wife and kids, one we all can be envious of . . . the best marriage I ever saw . . . this is a man who never has uttered a lie from his lips . . . this is a man—and this is quotes—who never was seen either irritated or frustrated or raising his voice to his wife or his children, never said negative things about his wife or his children.

"You show me any man that's never been irritated and frustrated about his wife and children, and I will show you a man that's either a saint or a perfect individual—or he's hiding something or bottling it up. And it's not surprising when a person bottles up that kind of feeling that a tragedy results. David Hendricks created that image. He enjoyed maintaining it. And there was no way that he was going to ruin that image by asking for a divorce or admitting to the Brethren or his wife or anybody else that he was intent on getting into bed with some models.

"For David Hendricks, the only way out of this situation that would allow him to have his cake and eat it too, to continue to enjoy that image he so enjoyed and at the same time be free to pursue these sexual escapades, was to kill his wife in such a way that it would appear that someone else did it. By doing so, he would not only maintain his image, he might even enhance it with all these people feeling sorry. What a wonderful man. How well he had taken that. What a Christian attitude he's had."

Dozier's voice calmed.

"It's a shame that the kids had to go. I believe he may very well have loved his children to some extent, but they had to go because he couldn't just kill his wife and leave the children alive without that leaving some severe problems in terms of his being caught for it. Besides that, he had the ultimate religious rationalization. After all, they would be much better off there in heaven with his wife than they would be living down here on earth with the man who killed their mother.

"Ladies and gentlemen, the defense would have you believe it's just coincidence that these activities with these models occurred right before the wife and kids were killed. They would have you believe that someone just came in and killed his wife and kids while all this stuff was going on. And you know better than that.

"His two lifestyles—his apparent lifestyle and the reality underneath it—kept him on a collision course, and he had to take some action that would resolve that. And he made a cold and calculated decision to resolve that in a way that would allow him to have it all."

"Five minutes, Mr. Dozier," Judge Baner announced.

"I think the evidence clearly indicates that David Hendricks came to a fateful decision that he could kill his wife and kids and get away with it and still maintain his image. He is an intelligent man. He was capable of devising a plan to make it appear as if someone else had done it. However, he made mistakes. He was not intelligent enough to know that stomach contents can be used to estimate time of death reliably when you have three victims who ate the same things at the same time. He was not smart enough to set up a burglary scene so it looks like a real burglary.

"It's a horrible thing to think that a man would kill his wife and three kids because he wanted out of a marriage and because he wanted to keep his image intact in a community and among his religious group. No normal man would do that. But this individual is unique and is capable of doing it. And the evidence shows that he did do it, ladies and gentlemen."

Dozier's arms fell to his side. His words came slowly now.

"Little Benjy and Grace and Rebekah and Susan deserve some justice in this case. And that justice will not come until you return a verdict of guilty of murder on all four counts. I have confidence in your intelligence and your ability to reach the right decision in this case. Thank you."

After lunch, it was the defense's turn with the jury. A small line of people waited outside the courtroom for a seat to empty.

Hal Jennings would speak first. He apologized in advance to the jurors for his extensive use of notes and may have betrayed some nervousness when he said, "I'm not very good at extraneous [sic] entertainment." He reminded jurors of the oath they took.

"The entire premise of the state's case, in my judgment," he said, "has been a request—however subtly made—for you to bend and stretch the commitments you made in order to reach a collective endorsement of the state's theory. They say to you—by the effect of what they have done here—we know the defendant did these murders because if he didn't, then who did? The state's proof is that the defendant could have done these crimes. Now it is up to David Hendricks to prove to you that he did not commit these crimes. And not only that. They demand of him, in subtle form, that he, and that we, show you who did these crimes in order for David to again be a free man."

Jennings said that state officials couldn't face the prospect of letting the crime go without a solution. "It would constitute an indictment of police and prosecutors and the community and even the criminal justice system. I believe that most of the players in this drama will do anything to avoid that prospect."

Jennings urged the jurors to pay special attention to people's exhibit 96—Susan Hendricks's diary.

"Consider it in detail, study it, look at it, consider it as evidence with the same weight and significance that you would as if Susan were here to testify in this case. Susan, I believe with all my heart, would be here to testify for David along with her brothers and her sisters and her sister-in-law and her brother-in-law and grandmother and father and mother, if she were able. She would shake her head and say 'nonsense' to the state's theories about their marriage, their life, their time together, and their love for one another.

"I would ask you to look at what Susan says about her life. She corroborates much of what we have tried to show you as far as evidence is concerned to offset the state's fiction, the illusion, the sleight of hand as far as this case is concerned. I beg you to read her diary, her testament to family, home, love, and the partnership she shared with David.

"We all feel deeply that someone must be held accountable. But if this man is convicted of the murders of Susan, a loving wife, and the children in this case, then the murderer or murderers will breathe a great sigh of relief and laugh at all of us from some other place than this courtroom. The state, the police will close their file, and the search will end as far as the killers are concerned.

"I do not believe that you will accept the notion that this man murdered his children and his wife because of the moral transgression described by Carla Webb or Lee Ann Wilmoth, that he killed because of the physical pangs of sexual attraction, that moral transgression equals murder. Did David sin? Of course he did. Does that make him a killer? Nonsense!"

Jennings said he had felt bewildered for the past several weeks.

"I am used to trials. I deal in facts, proof, evidence, science. I am used to fingerprints and ballistics, eyewitnesses, documents, medical science, footprints, confessions. For weeks I have found myself dealing with nonevidence, nonfacts. I found myself answering a litany of rhetorical questions put forward by the state. 'Mr. Jennings, Mr. Long, why did the defendant lose weight? Because he was fat or because he was a murderer? Why did the defendant get a haircut? Because he had a free gift certificate to get a haircut or because it had something to do with the state's theory of murder? Why did the defendant buy new suits at Penney's? Because he needed them or because it had something to do with the state's theory of a dual lifestyle? Why did he go to Wisconsin? Why did he have an airplane? A motorcycle?'

"I have lately come to the conclusion that the reason I feel so uncomfortable with this is because I genuinely feel that I have not participated in a trial. This has been more theater than it has been a trial to serve justice. The state has come here and presented a play, not a trial. They wrote the final act first. They reached their conclusion first, and then we have the drama created to suit the final act.

"The script and the play are treated from beginning to end as a matter of science. You are told the state's scenario is based upon grave matters of science and upon the precision of science. I suggest that's part of the play. Look at this science. What's the difference here between the wizard, the soothsayer, the fortune teller who cuts out the entrails of a frog and then reads the history and future of David Hendricks by the position of those frog's entrails when dropped on a flat rock in the moonlight? Science, indeed! As far as these doctors are concerned, no tests, no lab, no evaluation, no procedures.

"What have these men of science done? They held up the olives and mushrooms to the window and they divined two hours, dead by 9:00, 99 percent certainty. This is not science. This cannot be done within the conscience of our profession.

"I think of each girl as the state asked them, 'Tell me about your contacts with David Hendricks. Tell the ladies and gentlemen of the audience how you came to be partially nude alone in the presence of this monster who ax-murdered his wife and his children.' The director taps his baton and a chorus in union says, 'I never would have been alone nude or seminude with such a horrible man if he had not tricked me, duped me, deceived me, lured me into this web.'

"But what of the missing Kim Taylor from California, who was not cast for a role in this play? We can only guess why she did not get a part. Perhaps she would have required changes in the script. The state might have to rewrite the sexual aggression theory. Perhaps it loses some of its poetic license if some female is around in 1982 who had similar sexual experiences as the girls in the summer and fall of 1983."

Now Jennings himself was reading from a script.

"Let's turn to the play itself. Act 1, as suggested, is the crime. The Hendricks family is foully murdered. David, the script reads, did it because olives, mushrooms, tomatoes, and onions can tell time. Can this be anything but pure theater?

"Did he rush the kids home from the bookmobile at 8:15, get these healthy, active children who have been whooping and playing into bedclothes, into bed, all asleep, get his weapon, kill them, clean up virtually spotless, and stroll out for a drive at 9:05? The play is the thing.

"The act goes on if you follow the state's scenario. Susan comes home after 10:35. The kids are already hacked to death. She has a cup of tea. She goes to bed with David, sets her alarm, she nods off to sleep, she never notices the kids. She detects nothing of the carnage. No sight, no smell, nothing. She does not check her kids. She does not kiss them. She goes immediately to sleep. She is then hacked to death by David as she sleeps. If you believe Doctor Baden's vegetable clock, this is done by eleven o'clock.

"Do you applaud this act? Do you feel compelled to remain for act 2? I would hope that at least half the audience would leave after the first act. But let us turn to act 2, concerning the man.

"The scenario is that David killed his family because he is a devious, cunning, evil man—made devious and cunning because of his contact with women, several of whom he lusted after. And he's made evil and violent because of his religion. The play is the thing.

"His conduct for you, for me, for any preadolescent high school student would be considered so insignificant as to be laughable. But it's elevated in this case by the playwright to a motive for murder because this man, by his history, is a good and gentle, loving, religious man."

Jennings read faster.

"All they are saying to us is this man's goodness, his life, his faith is too good to be true. The director appeals to the dark side of all of us. We're hooked if each of us will say, 'I didn't live that type of life. I got mad at my kids. I fought with my wife. I don't believe I could devote so much of my time and energy to church or family or charity. I would never go through ten years of marriage faithful to home and family, deviating only to the extent of the sexual thoughts or indiscretions which the defendant immediately fell all over himself apologizing for.'

"They have us say to ourselves, 'I could never maintain that kind of attitude as far as David Hendricks is concerned. I could never be as successful, as financially secure so young, and still maintain friends and family and faith. This guy is too good to be true. All of the Palmers, the church folk, the business associates, the neighbors, the Cramers must be duped. Nobody is that okay. Nobody is that together. I don't believe it because I couldn't do it. There must be a dark side. He isn't what he is. He is what he isn't.' The play is the thing.

"I hope that the audience that's left leaves the theater at this point. The measure of a man is what he has been. Those who know him best have tried desperately to tell you about him. Is he good or is he evil? We ask you to consider the testaments of these who know him best as opposed to those who know him least.

"I seriously, sincerely, hope that the play is over. If the audience is gone, there will be silence, and at the final curtain no applause for a final act which attempts to create a tragedy within a tragedy. If you and each of you say, 'Stop. I am a juror. This is my place, my role, my duty, I am not an audience being played to for dramatic effect or social acceptance,' then I will be satisfied.

"I hope you will say, 'I am no one's person. I am no one's fool. I am independent in my judgment, fair and considerate as to the truth, not cynical as to the importance of what we do.'

"If you are this person, a juror in search of the truth—not a player, not a critic, not simply an audience—then whatever your verdict, I shall applaud you. I believe based on what has been said here, things said, things not said, evidence heard and seen, that you will find this man innocent. I believe that you will know that this is a good man, not an evil man capable of such rage, of violence as visited upon Susan, Benjy, Grace, and Rebekah. I believe the evidence has shown that this cannot be, except in a story one's told by the prosecutor. Thank you for your time."

Jennings sat down. His voice seemed weak at the end. He appeared tired and perhaps resigned.

After a twenty-minute break, John Long took his place in front of the jury to wrap up the defense case. The two mothers, Laverne Hendricks and Nadine Palmer, now sat side by side just a few feet behind David Hendricks.

"This is a case of the gravest import," Long began. "This is a case that, for all of us, is going to be one of the most important events in our lives. It is certainly the most important event in the life of David Hendricks."

Long explained that Judge Baner would be giving the jury special instructions about this case because all of the evidence against Hendricks was circumstantial.

"He is going to tell you"—Long was almost shouting his words—"that when all of the evidence in a case is circumstantial that you should not find the defendant guilty unless the facts or circumstances proved exclude every reasonable theory of innocence. Ponder that for a moment. If, in any set of operative facts, a reasonable theory of innocence is present, as a matter of law, one cannot be found guilty beyond a reasonable doubt."

Long said much of the case centered on whether Hendricks had the opportunity to commit the murders. "That's why the whole concept of gastric contents has any importance. If everybody knew when these people were killed, we wouldn't have ten experts sitting before you talking about the same thing.

"Mr. Dozier is an excellent advocate. Mr. Dozier has an easygoing manner about the way in which he would like you to believe all of the events transpired. He would like to lead you to believe that when he talks about what their experts say that they were acting in the furtherance of science. He would have you believe that they are dealing with a scientific concept which results in enough accuracy to overcome the instructions you are going to get from the judge with regard to circumstantial evidence.

"In *Gradwohl's Legal Medicine*, you will recall people testifying, 'The rate of emptying of the stomach is so variable that it cannot be used to give any certain indications of the time of death or the time that has elapsed between the last meal and death.'

"In *The Pathology of Homicide* by Lester Adelson, you will recall the witness saying, 'The physical and chemical facets of digestion are beset by so many imponderable and uncontrollable variables *in vivo* that one cannot rely on the extent of mechanical dissolution and chemical breakdown of the gastric content to help reach a reasonable estimate as to how long the food was present in the stomach.'

"There's that word 'reasonable' again. It's a standard you are going to have to apply to determine guilt beyond a reasonable doubt. And here the experts are saying you cannot use the yardstick which the state has foisted upon you to determine any reasonable standard.

"In *The Essentials of Forensic Medicine*, it is stated that 'The foregoing,' with respect to stomach contents, 'cannot be relied upon, nor should it be relied upon as evidence which purports to fix the time of death.'

"In Taylor's *Principles and Practice of Medical Jurisprudence*: 'Most elaborate tables have been prepared of the time taken by the stomach to digest certain articles, but these are wholly unreliable.' "

Long shifted gears slightly.

"You remember kindly old Dr. Dwyer, who was here speaking with all of us, the botanist from St. Louis whose only work on the subject had been to publish a book on the various varieties of coffee plants in South America. After being clothed as an expert by the state, he indicated that through some type of magical analysis, he could take a look at gastric contents and determine whether they were fresh or not fresh, digested or not digested.

"Well, you know, I think what was overlooked in this case was precisely what this doctor did and what he had to work with, because I'm certain you will all recall with me how he was brought samples of the gastric contents straight from the autopsy room. You'll recall how carefully the coroner's office, how carefully the crime-scene people, how carefully the state's attorney's office labeled all of these vials, how everyone dutifully wrote their initials on them, how they were dated and taped. And off goes Deputy Coroner Brady to St. Louis and hands Dr. Dwyer the vials—the very vials which you saw in front of you—the very vials that if they weren't kept in the coroner's office Brady kept in his own refrigerator to make sure they weren't tampered with. And what did the good Dr. Dwyer find back on November 29th, 1983, when he examined those vials?

"He found that in Grace Hendricks, the contents of the vial were a purplish-black soup. And microscopic examination revealed ringlike masses of small cells. He couldn't tell anything. There was no doubt that it was vegetable, but it was impossible to determine the vegetable source. A purplish-black soup.

"He opens vial number 2 and what does he determine? He determines that this vial is marked as coming from Susan Hendricks, and he says in that sample no chunks of vegetable were observed. However, small white fragments of food about two milliliters in diameter were observed. These were smeared on a slide and proved to be aggregates of starch grains, probably wheat or rye. In the other two samples—one belonging to Becky, the other to Benjy, he finds gastric content resembling onions, pepper, olives, and tomato.

"And after everything was photographed, the next thing we know is they are running back to St. Louis and saying, Wait a minute! We think maybe you made a mistake. Reevaluate what you found. And on the second go-round, Dr. Dwyer now finds a veritable garden of vegetables, so identifiable he could pick them apart with his two fingers without even using microscopic examination.

"Now if I were a suspicious person—which I'm not—or the least bit cynical—which I've never been—and I had to determine whether or not based upon that evidence I could find guilt beyond a reasonable doubt for a man having murdered his wife and three children, I would ask myself whether there's something wrong with the evidence that would prohibit me from finding guilt beyond a reasonable doubt. I would ask myself whether the experts who testified in this case really had the benefit on an independent view of what really existed."

Long reminded jurors that Dr. Jaffe said there was no accurate measurement of what was taken from the four victims' stomachs during the autopsy.

"In a case, unlike anything that's ever happened in McLean County, where somebody has taken two sharp-edged instruments and literally hacked up four human beings, at autopsy where there's at one time as many as eight people milling around, the pathologist uses a four-ounce stainless steel ladle and scoops out whatever is inside the stomach. He does this without regard for the fact that these bodies have been lying in a heated environment for over thirty hours, without regard to the fact that the body fluids in the stomach would increase during that period of time, and without bothering to even put it in so much as a graduated cylinder to measure what he took out. He then, with all of this commotion going on, passes the stainless steel ladle to a layman, in one case Mr. Books, who thought he was doing right when he picked out what he thought was important, poked it into a thirty-milliliter thing, and threw the rest of it down the drain. And the other one was to our friend, the funeral director–deputy coroner, Mr. Brady, who was a little more careful. He used tweezers to pick out what he thought was important, and then he flushed the rest down the drain. I would submit to you that we have no idea what came out of those stomachs."

Next Long turned the jurors' attention to the crime scene.

"The crime-scene investigators in this case did a bang-up job, absolutely professional. And what did they find? They found evidence they presented to you in terms of its negative effect. They spent two and a half days proving something they knew didn't exist, that windows weren't broken, that there were no tool marks on the garage door, that the locks weren't picked. From day one in this trial, there's been evidence that the back door was unlocked. You could have marched the Mormon Tabernacle Choir through that back door.

"There never was a doubt that the back door was left open. Does that mean that only the defendant and the defendant alone had access to the place, or does it mean anybody could have walked in that back door?

"Another bit of negative analysis. The state would have you believe for some incredible reason that in order for a burglary to have occurred, the house had to be totally trashed, every nook, every cranny totally trashed, everything loose that had a value of more than fifty cents had to have been taken. I would suggest to you that it's not unreasonable that only certain things could have been taken. I would suggest to you that when the state had Officer Irvin tell you that he was told early on that there could have been anywhere between two and five hundred dollars missing from that house, that was just totally disregarded.

"Whenever you're trying to solve a problem, you can normally do it by two specific major methods. Number one, you can gather all of the data, analyze it, sift through it, narrow it out, and arrive at a conclusion. That's usually the best way. Number two, you can have a conclusion of what you expect it to be and then find data to support it. That's never the best way."

Long moved away from the podium and pointed to Hendricks. "Thirty-five minutes after this man was interviewed by the police officer Crowe, who had never seen a crime of this magnitude in his life and heaven forbid he ever will again, Crowe concluded this man was 'dirty.' That is Kojak talk, folks—pure midwestern, Illinois Kojak talk. The man's dirty. Not 'he's a suspect.' Not 'he's making statements inconsistent with known facts.' He's dirty. And the moment that conclusion was made, it formed a mind-set. And the moment that mind-set was jelled, all police work, all efforts stopped in looking at all of the data. They had the conclusion, and from that point the investigation turned around. They began looking for ways to bolster what they believed to be true. What people believe to be true for them is true. If you believe you are loved, you are loved. If you believe you are reviled, you are reviled. If you believe you are brilliant, well, you become a lawyer."

Long said he wanted to talk about some of the inconsistencies in the evidence.

"Number one. Is it inconsistent that Mr. Dodwell would tell us that because of the blood spatter and castoff, anybody who committed this offense would be covered with blood? Yet even with Buck Rogers laser beam analysis they were unable to find blood on anything connected with the defendant, his hair, under his fingernails, his skin, his clothing, his wristwatch, his car, anything in the car.

"I don't know how many of you happened to see the film *The French Connection*. There's a scene in it when they're looking for cocaine, and in order to find it, they literally unbolt an automobile. They have it all stripped down. They have the rocker panels off. That is what they did in this case. They removed the seats, they got into the dashboard, they removed the floor coverings, they got into the trunk. They did everything possible to find blood and they found absolutely zippo—nothing.

"You know that in that bathroom there was no blood found, save but one place. And you know that Patricia Orr and Dodwell stated that you couldn't even tell how long it had been there, and you know that in the bottom of that bathtub subsequent examination did not confirm the presence of blood.

"We're not playing games in this. This is a matter of life and death. Why is it that they would make a great show out of the fact that there were no fingerprints on the ax handle, yet totally disregard the fact that there are three identifiable but unidentified fingerprints? What type of negative reasoning can find guilt beyond a reasonable doubt when the evidence is that every Monday she cleaned her house, and they find three identifiable but unidentified footwear impressions? What they say is that the defendant is linked to the crime because the evidence isn't there, and it proves he is clever enough to have done this. I would suggest that it leads to a reasonable conclusion of innocence. Doesn't it flow logically that if you have an open house, unlocked with easy access so that anybody can get in, and you have a house that's cleaned on Mondays, but you find identifiable but unidentified fingerprints and footprints, that somebody else was in that house, that all of this could have been done by person or persons unknown?

"Of all the evidence that you heard on the stand, what solitary piece of evidence was there linking the defendant to the crime? I would suggest to you that there is no evidence, else you would have heard it."

Long said even if the jurors accept the state's negative evidence, they must ask themselves why Hendricks would have killed his wife and children.

"Well, the models have been dredged out. What evidence did the state present to show that David Hendricks was so emotionally involved and beset, so absolutely strung out on this sexual aggression, so totally engulfed in this dark side, sinful den of iniquity, that he took an ax and a knife and did this to his family?

"You know, when you actually start your work, one of the things you're going to see are blown-up photographs of what the victims looked like at the crime scene. These photos are something that for some reason the state never wanted to show you. They are photos of what type of damage is done to a small boy when he is hit in the face thirteen times with an ax!"

Long slammed his hand on the witness box. "They are the photographs of what can happen when a butcher knife is used on a young girl. They are the photographs of what happens to a mother sound asleep in her own bed when somebody goes at her with a logging ax. Over touching somebody's breast? Over the fear of a reprimand from the Plymouth Brethren? Over playing with somebody's scoliosis?

"This is the first murder case I have ever been part of in which the state hadn't wanted to show the crime-scene photos. If you can look at them and decide that action in Phoenix can cause that result in Bloomington, then so be it. But I cannot believe you will be able to do that.

"Male-female relationships are an absolute mystery to me. After handling hundreds of divorce cases, I'm not amazed by anything I hear. I'm not amazed by trapezes and ropes and clandestine meetings or by Mazola parties and big blocks of lard. I have heard it all. But let me tell you something. Not once have I heard it result in ax murder. Not once have I heard it result in two-thirds decapitation of a man's daughter with a butcher knife. Because where that exists, one would expect to find evidence of psychotic behavior.

"What has the state shown you to make you believe that the sexual aggression resulted in such an absolute internal, emotional fury that he took an ax and a knife and did the job? Did you hear anything?

"They had the temerity to stand before you and say, 'Well, he might be subject to a reprimand.' Stuff and nonsense! If it weren't an absolute life-and-death situation here, we would be laughing uproariously."

Long moved on to Hendricks's statement to the TV cameras about the possibility of a burglary. "I want you to keep in mind that there was enough hubbub about this trial to bring it two hundred miles away to be heard because everybody in Bloomington heard every single rumor. I want you to keep in mind that at the time David Hendricks made the statement to television, he had been up without sleep for over fifty hours. I want you to recall that when all of these statements were made, the family was running around trying to get some answers from the police. I want you to recall that during this whole period of time, the evidence of this case is that everybody in McLean County in any position of authority was shooting off their mouths about what, in fact, happened at 313 Carl Drive."

Dozier suddenly stood up. "Your Honor, I'm going to object to that. There's no evidence of that. It's not true."

Judge Baner had the statement read back and sustained Dozier's objection.

"I believe," Long continued, "that it has been borne out that people were holding press conferences, namely Chief Devault, and that the press conference was held during the daytime of the 9th of November. I believe it's borne out, from the testimony of Nate Palmer, that the police were talking in front of everybody at 313 Carl Drive, because he heard them say it, and there were other people present.

"The fact of the matter is that many people knew. How many people had access to that information, and how many could have told David Hendricks or asked him about whether anything was missing or about him going in to look if anything was missing?"

Long paused and gave jurors his most piercing look. His voice became little more than a whisper. "Whether you can find guilt beyond a reasonable doubt depends on whether the evidence is of sufficient quality and quantity to rule out any reasonable hypothesis of innocence. That's a very simple concept that must never be forgotten by you.

"You are going to have to do something very difficult." The room suddenly seemed very stuffy. One juror, a woman in the front row, nodded off.

"You are going to have to decide whether the state has lifted its burden in that regard. Because if you decide it has not, then you will be telling the state that they made a mistake here, that they shouldn't have shut down their investigation, that they should not have zeroed in the way they did on the basis of the evidence they had.

"You are going to have to say that the system doesn't require you to find somebody guilty of a crime. What the system requires is that if there is sufficient evidence to exclude every reasonable hypothesis of innocence, then you can find guilt beyond a reasonable doubt. That sometimes is hard to do. But that's what you all are going to have to do."

Long's voice became even softer. "Have they shown sufficient evidence to exclude the possibility of some unknown person or persons from having done this? Did they present any evidence at all to show that he was of sufficient mind to take it out on his wife and children the way those photographs are going to show he did it? If you can honestly in your hearts find that they have, so be it. That's all we're asking. I don't believe you can, not without speculation, without surmise and conjecture, without resorting to the same artifice of negative inference thinking.

"When you use the information presented from this witness box, I am certain you are going to find David Hendricks not guilty. And I am certain that you are going to send a message back—not with respect to his guilt or innocence—but with respect to the quantum of proof that this state has to have before they begin doing what they've done to David Hendricks in this case. Thank you for your kind time and attention, ladies and gentlemen."

After another fifteen-minute recess, Ron Dozier began his rebuttal by telling the jurors that a circumstantial case simply means there is no direct evidence of the defendant's guilt.

"There is no one single thing that you can point to, such as an eyewitness or a confession or something like that. But that doesn't mean that circumstantial evidence isn't evidence, because, of course, it is.

"The defense says all we've shown is that the defendant had an opportunity to commit the crime. I contend that if you accept the evidence of the experts who testified here for the state and that portion of the defense testimony which supports the state's evidence, you'll find that the defendant not only had the opportunity to commit this crime, but had the exclusive opportunity—because those children were killed when he was the only one home.

"The defense contends the state has to prove motive in this case. It is true that we believe there is a motive in this case that can be inferred from the evidence, but the state is not required to prove that the defendant had a particular motive. It is only required to prove that he committed the crime. If we can prove a motive as further evidence of why it was committed, so much the better.

"Mr. Jennings resorted to the unique device of equating the state's case with a play, that what you heard was something staged for your benefit. The only thing that was staged in this case was the burglary, and that was staged by the defendant.

"Let's consider what really happened in the investigation of this case. When the defendant returned home that night and was met there by police, certainly you do not think it was improper for police to ask him questions about his whereabouts, his family's whereabouts, when was the last time he saw them, such simple things as their names and ages, and so on. When the police officers began to get responses that to a trained officer were indicative of being dirty, that is, being untruthful or hiding something, it's natural that attention tended to focus in his direction. But I can tell you that this was a thorough police investigation in this case that followed every possible lead that anyone had. And it is not the fault of the Bloomington Police Department that the evidence kept turning back to David Hendricks."

Dozier addressed the need to get a second analysis of Grace Hendricks's stomach analysis from Dr. Dwyer.

"One of the things I hope you understand is that the state is required to basically turn over our whole investigation to the defense. We don't have the option, if we get a report back that has a mistake in it, to throw that away and say, 'Do another one because the defense is going to use this against us.' They get it all, and they love it when they find somebody made a human error, because then they can make a mountain out of a molehill and make that look like something else is going on.

"There's never been a police investigation that was perfect, that you can't find somebody who miswrote something in a report or misstated something or misheard something somewhere along the line. And one of the jobs of defense counsel—and these two guys do it as well as any I have ever seen—is to make those things look like mountains with holes in the evidence. And the reason for that is if you can do that enough times, you can turn a little doubt into reasonable doubt. Then they have done their job.

"I want to remind you that the defendant in this case was the only one that had the privilege of sitting here and hearing all the testimony and tailoring his testimony so that it could do him the least damage.

"What about the models in this case, and what does that show? Well, the defense says that the most that shows is that he's engaged in a little sexual escapade or two, touched a breast or two. But would a man like that go out and chop up his kids and wife with an ax?

"We're not trying to say that any man who goes out and is temporarily unfaithful to his wife is going to run out and kill his wife and kids. We are not dealing with any man in this case or what the ordinary person would do. We are dealing with what David Hendricks would do, and the evidence in this case indicates that he is not an ordinary man.

"The evidence in this case indicates he has spent a good portion of his adult life creating an image among his friends, neighbors, and Plymouth Brethren of being an almost perfect man, almost perfect as a Christian, as a husband, as a father. We know from our experience that such a person does not exist. And so it isn't surprising, is it, that there are flaws in this image. It isn't surprising to find that this man was leading a dual life.

"What the activities of this defendant with the models show is not that he had a temporary escapade. It shows preplanning. This whole idea about a research project and the ability with which he set up the situations and continued to pursue the situations shows that this man was totally unhappy with his sex life at home. He was seeking out sexual thrills that he was not getting at home."

Jennings spoke up from the defense table. "I am going to object for the record. There is no such evidence in the record."

"Sustained," said Judge Baner.

"I ask that the jury be instructed to disregard those two statements," Jennings said.

"The objection has been sustained," Judge Baner answered.

If Dozier had sounded impassioned, his voice now took on a sorrowful tone.

"I do not doubt for a minute that Susan Hendricks thought her husband still loved her. You will see in that diary, once again, emphasis on an almost perfect family life. All that means is that David Hendricks is an intensely private person in terms of what's really going on in his mind. He kept that secret of what he was doing with the models from his wife and everyone else. Is it because he didn't want to hurt her? Possibly. Was it because he didn't want to accept the consequence to him, the hurt that would cause him, the scorn that he might receive from his family and friends if it was discovered that he wasn't the type of person he had led them to believe?

"The fact of the matter is that what it shows with the models is that he was not done with them. If there was any evidence that he was done, that he was sorry for what he had tried to do with some of the models, it would be a different story. But the evidence in this case shows quite the opposite. It was escalating to his most serious sexual contacts which occurred right before the murders. And I submit to you that is no coincidence. He still had designs on Carla Webb, and his research wasn't through. In fact it was only beginning to get into high gear, as he was continuing to refine his techniques.

"The killing of Susan Hendricks was the only way he could get out of a marriage that had become boring to him. Husbands have killed their wives for reasons like that since antiquity. Unfortunately it happens almost with regularity."

Jennings objected, and the judge sustained the objection.

"The killing of Susan Hendricks," Dozier continued, "was the only way that David Hendricks could maintain both his image that he valued so greatly with the Plymouth Brethren and still have the freedom to pursue contacts with the models. The children had to die, too, because that was the only way it could be done and keep the suspicion away from himself. And he may genuinely have felt that under all the circumstances, they were better off.

"This crime scene was done by an intelligent man who carefully planned so there would be no direct evidence that would point to him. The defense has posited some kind of strange theory that some unknown burglar or burglars out there picked this house with the almost perfect loving couple and perfect family out of all the houses in Bloomington-Normal and happened to pick this night, the one night that he was going to leave on a business trip, and happened to pick the same lucky night that he must have forgotten to lock the back patio door. That they came in to commit a burglary, and for some reason they took the ax out of the garage and the knife out of the kitchen and went upstairs and hacked all the people to death. And then to make it look like it wasn't murder, they staged a burglary or something along that nature.

"There is no reasonable hypothesis of innocence in this case. There is no hypothesis that explains what happened here except that the defendant did it. No one else had a motive to stage this scene to be a burglary.

"This man is so organized and precise that in his office the books are lined up on the shelf to where all of them reach exactly the same point. To him, opening a bunch of drawers looked like a house had been ransacked.

"The defendant did a darn good job of hiding the evidence of the crime that would lead to him. He left nothing, except a staged burglary, because he wasn't smart enough to pull off a real burglary, and he didn't know about stomach contents. And he made two more mistakes.

"He didn't realize how good the Bloomington Police Department was in terms of the thoroughness of its investigation and the experience of the detectives in interrogating people and investigating a case."

The two mothers sitting side by side looked at each other and silently rolled their eyes.

"And lastly, I think he's made one more mistake. We have all complimented you on your intelligence and we are patronizing you to some extent. I realize that and I think you realize that. But, nevertheless, both sides did pick you in part because you appear to be intelligent people, and nothing has changed that. I think this defendant made a mistake in thinking that he would be able to pull this off at trial with the kind of testimony he gave to twelve people and four more who are as intelligent as you are.

"Your very difficult job is just about to begin. You have been here a long time. I know you are ready to go. We are tired and ready to go, too. But this is the one and only chance that there ever will be for justice to prevail in this case.

"This is the one and only time that Benjamin Hendricks and Grace Hendricks and Rebekah Hendricks and Susan Hendricks will have to have the person who committed their brutal murders brought to justice.

"I know that you will carefully consider all the evidence that you have heard over these past few weeks. I know that you will ponder this decision with every bit of common sense and intelligence that you have. I know that you care about your duties as a juror and want to reach the right decision.

"We want that, too. And, ladies and gentlemen, we are confident that you will reach the right decision. It may not be easy. But the evidence in this case does prove beyond a reasonable doubt that David Hendricks committed this crime. Thank you."

There was a slight rustle in the courtroom. Hendricks, almost symbolically, put the cap on his pen. He visually surveyed members of the jury as Judge Baner read them their instructions.

The jury listened intently, perhaps more so when the judge reached the part about circumstantial evidence. "Circumstantial evidence should be considered by you together with all other evidence in the case in arriving at your verdict. You should not find the defendant guilty unless the facts or circumstances proved exclude every reasonable theory of innocence."

The judge said the jurors' first step would be to elect a foreman. They would be given an hour to examine physical evidence in the case. Then they'd be served dinner in the courtroom. After that, he said, they would begin their deliberations. Any verdict, he said, would have to be unanimous.

At 5:02 P.M. on November 28—sixty-four days after the first of the twelve jurors had been seated, one year and twenty days since the murders were discovered—the David Hendricks case went to the jury.

Twenty

T
he six men and six women of the jury silently filed into the jury room where they had spent many hours over the previous weeks, waiting through extended delays while the attorneys wrangled over legal issues unknown and unexplained to the jurors.

In this fifteen-by-seventeen-foot space, they had read, talked, played cards, knitted, dozed, brought in their own coffeepot, and long ago adopted a unisex approach to the his-and-hers rest rooms connected to the jury room. Through the four windows on one wall, they had watched autumn take on winter's traits. And with a couple of heavy smokers in their ranks, some jurors had found this room with its eight-sided table and dozen chairs quite confining. But never so much as at this moment.

At this moment their impatience to get on with what they were chosen to do so many days ago clashed with their disinclination to really do it; their anxiousness to know if other jurors had interpreted the evidence in similar ways mingled with their apprehension about how difficult a decision could be if they held widely divergent opinions.

As the last of the jurors sat down, one of them asked if anyone wanted to be foreman.

"How about Joe?" someone asked.

The nomination was immediately endorsed by the rest. Joe Alonzo, at age forty-seven the oldest of them all and friends with all, the class clown who had instigated the mock trial during a break in one of the night sessions, would serve as jury foreman.

There was a knock on the door, and the bailiff poked her head into the room to inform jurors that the physical evidence was ready for their inspection. They would be given up to an hour to examine it. Then dinner would be served.

The courtroom was void of any other people when they entered to find a variety of items positioned on the two tables where the lawyers and Hendricks had sat during the trial. Windows on the courtroom doors had been papered over to prevent anyone from looking in.

The jurors, eager and businesslike, spread out around the tables. There was occasional quiet talk among them as they individually read through Susan Hendricks's white diary, which Hal Jennings had called to their attention. They looked at the crime-scene pictures, the vials of stomach contents, and a Chuck E. Cheese pizza, its cheese long since congealed.

"I hope they don't feed us pizza for dinner," one of the jurors joked.

Another opened the brown evidence bag containing the big blue bedspread that had partially covered Susan Hendricks's body. Several of the jurors helped lay it out to examine the size and angle of the cut or tear that had been the subject of testimony.

The jurors slowly circled the tables, looking through much of the other physical evidence they had seen or heard about weeks before: the Jasper Jowls rubber stamp, fingerprint cards, Hendricks's briefcase, a cash register receipt, some CASH Brace brochures, the brace itself and instructions for fitting it, the ax, the knife, Grace and Becky's pajamas, and more.

The hour passed quickly.

The bailiffs entered the room, quickly cleared the tables, and set up a buffet dinner for the jurors on the same tables. The jurors ate quickly. Some expressed a hope that their business could be over quickly so they wouldn't have to spend the night in a hotel. Others let it be known they wouldn't be rushed. They left their dirty plates in the courtroom and gathered around the table in the jury room.

Their discussion began slowly.

"You know, it's kind of strange," one juror volunteered, "that

David's family, Susan's family—all of them—believe that David didn't do it. They know him well and we don't. Who are we not to take their opinion?"

That engendered some debate, focused principally on the plausibility of Hendricks's trip to Wisconsin and of his seemingly unemotional statements to the police.

Some of the jurors had taken copious notes; others had taken very few. There was some dispute over what police had testified that Hendricks told them. And there was discussion about whether Susan Hendricks's kitchen calendar listed her husband's travel plans and whether the Wisconsin trip was among them. The jury would ask to see that information.

The foreman scribbled a note. "Could we get the copy of police report on David and a calendar from house?" it read.

Someone flicked a light switch which turned on a red light outside the jury room door. It was a signal to the waiting bailiff that the jury had either reached a verdict or needed help.

The time was 7:32 P.M.

After consulting with Murphy and Long by telephone, Judge Baner responded with his own note. "No," it read. "Neither have been admitted into evidence."

Even before the jurors received the judge's note, almost continuous discussion had ensued. By 8:30 they had determined that a vote on a verdict would be in order, if only to learn how divided the opinion was. Jurors wrote only one word or phrase on a piece of paper and handed it to their foreman. It seemed clear that if Hendricks was guilty of one murder, he was guilty of them all.

The foreman announced the vote. Six guilty, six not guilty.

After a couple of the jurors explained their votes, it was evident that there would be no decision that night. At nine o'clock they were bused to Rockford's Ramada Inn, where they would be sequestered for the first time in the lengthy trial.

With newspapers, radio, and television unavailable to them, and some of the jurors having trouble sleeping, a few gathered in individual rooms to play cards and talk long into the night. There was only limited discussion of the trial.

State's Attorney Dozier received a telegram from his staff back in Bloomington. It read: "May justice triumph, truth prevail."

By nine o'clock the next morning, the jurors were back around the table with renewed discussion of Hendricks's statements to police, particularly about what time police had said Hendricks told them he had departed for Wisconsin. Jurors had some conflicting information in their trial notes. They would try to get information from the trial. "Can we get a copy of the transcripts from 11-2 and 11-5, '84?" their note to Judge Baner read.

It was after ten o'clock before the judge could meet with the four attorneys and draft a response.

"No, they're not available," was the answer. Judge Baner had been inclined to tell jurors he might be able to provide some specific testimony, but all four attorneys agreed that they didn't want to open a dialogue with jurors about what might be available.

Even before jurors received Judge Baner's response, they had taken a second vote. Eight voted guilty, four not guilty.

The three women and single man who had voted not guilty discussed their reasoning. Other jurors tried to answer their doubts about Hendricks's guilt.

"My husband served on a jury one time," one of the women said. "It was just a minor case, but the judge in that case told the jury that he'd rather let a guilty man go than put an innocent person in jail. And we may not just be talking about jail here."

There was a momentary silence. Then discussion erupted again about the appearance of a burglary, about Hendricks's "no skin off my back" comment during his testimony, and then about the stomach contents. Jurors decided it would be helpful to compare the size of the vegetables on the cooked pizza with what their notes told them about the size of the vegetable fragments in the children's stomachs.

Their note to Judge Baner read "Get the pizza." Even before the judge was able to gather the attorneys together to formulate a response, the jury wrote another note.

"Can we take pieces off the pizza, and can we walk in courtroom for a ten-minute break?" It was now 11:20 A.M.

After meeting with Murphy and Long, Judge Baner answered that they would be allowed to examine the pizza in the courtroom for not longer than fifteen minutes, but that they should not remove any pieces from it. "Exhibits are provided for your inspection and observation but should not be subjected to experimentation," his response read. He assumed that the fifteen-minute period in the courtroom would satisfy jurors' desires to stretch their legs.

The jurors spent only a few moments with the pizza and a few minutes more walking around the courtroom, allowing smoke to clear from their deliberation room. By then it was time for lunch. They ate quickly. Most felt a decision was near. By one o'clock their discussions had resumed with an analysis of the times and other details of Hendricks's Wisconsin trip. They pieced it together, trying to give him the benefit of every doubt. One by one, the four jurors who had voted not guilty seemed to be swayed to the opposite side.

"It was like he was trying to cover himself with the phone calls," one of the women said. "It was like, will someone please find them in the house?"

The talk continued. Rapid-fire discussion ceased. There were prolonged silences between vocalized thoughts. Then discussion halted altogether. It was time for another vote. This time there was no paper—just an around-the-table voice vote: twelve guilty, none innocent.

Everyone sat still. No one spoke. Several jurors felt a chill. The foreman scribbled a note and flicked on the outside red light for a fifth time. He handed the note to the bailiff. It was 1:33 P.M. They had deliberated a total of five and a half hours.

It took a half hour more for Judge Baner to gather the attorneys in his chambers. He was concerned about whether the jury had reached the required multiple verdicts because the note read, "We have reached a verdict."

He sent a note back to the jury room, where silence still prevailed. "Have you reached a verdict on each of the four counts?"

While awaiting a response, Dozier informed Judge Baner and Hendricks's attorneys that if there was a guilty verdict, he would be seeking the death penalty, a matter that had been assumed by the defense from the beginning.

The jury responded that it had a verdict in each count.

Judge Baner motioned the attorneys into the courtroom. In the meantime jurors, still silent and some now visibly shaking, had signed their names to all four guilty verdicts.

Word had quickly spread that a verdict had been reached. Within five minutes every seat in the courtroom was filled. A moment later, David Hendricks, looking understandably anxious, was brought in.

His mother sat directly behind him, but behind the railing. Her son Jim sat on her right, a protecting arm around her. Next to him was Seth Palmer, then Nadine, then Liz Buchanan. About a dozen people, unable to find seats, stood in the back.

A television reporter who had hoped to flash a guilty or not guilty signal to a colleague watching through a courtroom door window was foiled when a bailiff covered the window with paper.

"For those who are present in the audience," Judge Baner said, "the courtroom doors are going to be secured. No one will be allowed to leave until the jury has left the room after the verdicts are announced. If anyone wishes to leave before that occurs, now is the time to do that." He paused briefly.

"Bring the jury in."

Slowly the jurors took their positions in front of their customary seats. All twenty-four eyes looked straight forward. None looked at Hendricks.

"Please be seated," Judge Baner said. "The matter of the People versus David Hendricks, the record will show that the defendant and all counsel are present. All twelve jurors are present and in the jury box. Now, Mr. Foreman, has the jury arrived at their verdicts?"

Joe Alonzo, seated in the second row of jurors, stood.

"Yes, they have, Your Honor."

"Would you please deliver the verdicts to the clerk."

Alonzo handed a large manila envelope to the clerk, who in turn gave it to the judge. He opened the envelope, looked at the four sheets of paper, and stole a quick look at Hendricks, who leaned forward in his chair.

"The verdicts of the jury read as follows: 'We, the jury, find the defendant, David J. Hendricks, guilty of the offense of murder of Benjamin Hendricks.' "

David Hendricks didn't move. Someone near the back of the courtroom half whispered, half shouted, "Yes!"

"That is signed by the foreman and eleven other jurors," Judge Baner continued. "Second verdict reads as follows: 'We, the jury, find the defendant, David J. Hendricks, guilty of the offense of murder of Grace Hendricks.' This is also signed by the foreman and eleven other jurors. Third verdict reads as follows: 'We, the jury, find the defendant, David J. Hendricks, guilty of the offense of murder of Rebekah Hendricks.' That is likewise signed by the foreman and eleven other jurors. Last verdict reads as follows: 'We, the jury, find the defendant, David J. Hendricks, guilty of the offense of murder of Susan Hendricks.' That is also signed by the foreman and eleven other jurors."

David Hendricks, a neutral look on his face, visually scanned the jury. Behind him, his mother sat, her head bowed. Next to her, Seth Palmer wiped tears from his eyes with one hand while his other arm extended around his mother's shoulders. Nadine Palmer, in turn, had put her arm around her daughter, Liz.

"Is there a request to poll the jury?" Judge Baner was asking.

Hal Jennings stood up. "There is, Your Honor."

The jury hadn't expected this and didn't understand what was about to happen.

"Clerk will poll the jury," Judge Baner said.

"When your name is called," the clerk said, "please stand and answer the question put to you."

In turn, the clerk called out the name of each of the jurors and asked, "Were these and are these still your verdicts?"

Each of them, perhaps more calmly and clearly than anyone, including themselves, might have expected, answered yes.

Judge Baner ordered a fifteen-minute recess. The courtroom doors swung open, and the fifteen reporters present scrambled for telephones.

Back in Bloomington, cheers erupted at the police department when news of the guilty verdict flashed over the radio.

Inside the courtroom, David Hendricks turned to see tears flowing down his mother's face. A sympathetic smile crossed his face.

Hendricks's family members, who had gathered in a remote stairwell to avoid the press during the recess, were first to return to the courtroom. Hendricks, now surrounded by four policemen, was brought back into the courtroom. He talked quietly with his mother, trying to console her, as the spectator area again filled up.

When the jurors returned, they were told by Judge Baner that their service had not yet ended and that they would have to spend the night at the hotel. He ordered the courtroom locked until the jurors had boarded their bus to their night's lodging.

Judge Baner announced that he had denied the defense's second request for a directed verdict and then informed Hendricks that he had a day and a half to decide whether he wanted Baner or the jury to decide the sentence.

Over the door to the jury room, the red light still burned.

For two and a half hours that night, Hendricks, at times

emotional, discussed the options with his attorneys. The consensus was that his best chance lay with Judge Baner. The jury, Hendricks decided, had ceased paying attention to the evidence.

When court resumed the next morning, Long announced Hendricks's decision. As jurors waited next door in the jury room, Baner quizzed the man whose life was on the line.

"Mr. Hendricks, do you understand that no action I have taken, no ruling that I've made, nor any statement I've made, should be taken to indicate my opinion as to what the penalty in this case should be?"

"I understand that, Your Honor," Hendricks responded in a calm, measured way.

Judge Baner went on to make another two dozen statements, explaining Hendricks's options, the sentencing procedure, and possible penalties, each time asking Hendricks if he understood. Each time the answer was "yes" or "I understand."

He recessed the court for five minutes to give Hendricks additional time to think about his decision, and then asked one final question.

"Mr. Hendricks, having had an additional opportunity to confer with your counsel, do you wish to persist in your earlier indication to waive your right to trial by jury as to the remaining issues in this trial?"

"Yes, I do, Your Honor."

With that, Judge Baner had the jury brought into the courtroom.

"You have been sequestered overnight to allow certain decisions to be made," Baner told the jurors. "Important decisions to be made. They have now been made. The defendant has this morning elected to waive his right to trial by jury of the remaining issues of this case. That means that your duties in this case are now concluded."

Several of the jurors glanced at each other.

Baner thanked the jurors for their service, saying there is no higher duty of American citizenship, and excused them from the courtroom.

The sentencing hearing would resume three weeks later in Bloomington.

Twenty-One

It was eight days before Christmas when Judge Baner convened a hearing into the immediate question of whether Hendricks was eligible for capital punishment.

Illinois law dictates that four criteria be considered when deciding whether the death penalty is a possible punishment for a convicted murderer. The Hendricks case obviously met at least three of them: more than one person was killed, at least one of the victims was under the age of twelve, and the convicted person was at least eighteen. The fourth factor is more subjective: was the crime a result of exceptionally brutal or heinous behavior indicative of wanton cruelty? That was the issue to be attacked by Jennings, who was now forced to argue from a position which presumed his client's guilt.

He suggested that because the children died in their sleep, because their death was instantaneous, their deaths were without suffering. "What we're talking about," Jennings told the judge, "is a case in which the state offered proof that the children saw nothing, heard nothing, felt nothing. That in fact, they were—given the horrible fact of death—mercifully killed."

Murphy responded that the killings were heinous and cruel because they were premeditated, because of the type of weapons

—380—

used, and because of the number of blows delivered to the children.

Noting the number of wounds, the number of weapons used, the nature of the weapons, the extent of physical force used, and the severity of the wounds inflicted, Judge Baner ruled the killings met all four criteria and that Hendricks was eligible for the death penalty. A hearing was scheduled for January 17 to determine if he would be put to death.

Lethal injection is the method used in executions in Illinois. The condemned person is given a complete physical examination several days before the execution date. On the day of the execution, the prison is on lock-down status, meaning all prisoners are confined to their cells. An emergency telephone line and a modular lethal injection machine are installed in the execution chamber. The inmate is offered a drug to relax him and is then escorted to the death chamber. If he is unable or unwilling to walk, he is transported on a gurney, the same gurney he will die on. A medically trained person inserts an intravenous catheter and hooks it up to the injection machine. The system, when activated by one of two persons selected as executioners, delivers in sequence variable quantities of three solutions: sodium pentathal, pancuronium bromide, and potassium chloride. Death usually occurs within a few minutes. All executions are scheduled for twelve noon.

Although Illinois's capital punishment law had been in place for seven years, and fifty-eight Illinois men had been sentenced to die, their appeals to higher courts had delayed their deaths.

Now a hearing was underway to determine whether David Hendricks would join the list of those awaiting execution.

The defense had fought to keep Dr. Richard Rappaport out of the witness box. The Chicago psychiatrist had gained some notoriety four years earlier when he testified in the trial of John Wayne Gacy, the Chicago-area man convicted of murdering thirty-three young men and boys and then burying many of them under his house. Rappaport was hired by the Hendricks defense to measure Hendricks's mental condition shortly before the trial began, specifically to see if the psychiatrist could determine whether Hendricks was psychologically capable or incapable of committing the murders. And now, in a strange turn of events, Dr. Rappaport was called by the state.

"He has a borderline personality disorder," the psychiatrist answered when Ron Dozier asked for his conclusion based on a twelve-hour examination of Hendricks over two days. "Some of the

characteristics of a borderline have to do with the individual's
expression of anger, their intensity of anger, the impulse controls,
expression of impulsive behavior, difficulties with identity—sometimes in the nature of their sexual orientation—their means of
using defense mechanisms. They tend to use primitive defense
mechanisms, such as splitting," Rappaport said.

"Such as what, sir?" Judge Baner inquired.

"Splitting. It's a method of handling anxiety by acting as if
feeling is not part of the individual. It's split off from the person's
psyche, doesn't integrate into their total being. In a person who is
splitting, they cannot tolerate the anxiety brought up by hating the
same person that they love. So they split off that feeling in their
mind."

Dozier asked Rappaport to identify the borderline characteristics he found in Hendricks.

"The first characteristic was his affect. I did not see any
evidence of intense anger. Rather, the opposite. An almost completely unemotional, affectless mood and demeanor. I still don't
know whether or not he committed this crime. I would consider the
fact that if he did, it was while he was having a brief psychotic
episode."

Rappaport had slipped off Dozier's track. Dozier tried to put
him back on. "Continue if you would, with those factors that make
up the borderline disorder you find present in Mr. Hendricks."

"The most outstanding characteristics are his flat affect and
his coldness towards the situation he was in," said Rappaport. "It's
called 'blunt affect.' "

"And your opinion as to whether or not Mr. Hendricks at this
time is a danger to others?"

"The characteristics of the borderline do not necessarily mean
he's a dangerous person. There are a lot of people who are borderline and functioning quite well in society, who are not doing things
that are dangerous."

"How is it that a person with a borderline personality can
function in society?" Dozier asked. Judge Baner had turned his
chair completely to face the witness, placing the judge's back to
Hendricks.

"Well, he has many very positive qualities and characteristics.
He's very bright and personable, aggressive, inventive. He's able to
use those abilities to deal with society and with life."

"And how would a person who has this diagnosis react under
stress?" Dozier asked.

"That's where the difficultly comes in. It's a progressive problem. Unresolved tension builds up. Acting out in the nature that this person might have done in this case usually doesn't relieve the tension. The tension mounts up again, and it could be repeated."

"Doctor, are you indicating that if a person with a borderline disorder kills once, then there's the possibility he would do it again when placed under stress?"

"Yes."

"And on what do you base that conclusion?"

"Some of my experience with people who have murdered in the past and things that I have read."

In cross-examination, Rappaport told the court that he had been unable to conclude that Hendricks was either psychologically capable or incapable of committing the murders.

Jennings asked Rappaport whether the "situational stress" he had referred to might not be a product of what Hendricks had experienced over the past fourteen months.

"I would have expected David to have had a tremendous amount of stress, based on the loss of his family, the accusation that he was the person who had caused that loss, and the anticipated penalty that might ensue, as well as the conditions under which he was living during this stressful time. And, you know, this is one of the things that affected me most. The lack of affect, the lack of signs of stress under all of these conditions, which makes me think there's something amiss."

Jennings pressed Rappaport on why his diagnosis differed sharply with other evaluations of Hendricks's mental status which found no defects.

"Psychiatrists often differ about their impressions, just as pathologists differ about their impressions," Rappaport answered. "I think I have more experience. I've had occasion to examine other murderers and have studied the subject extensively. I would say that's the basis of the difference."

Jennings wanted to know why friends and family wouldn't notice the buildup of pressure that Rappaport thought Hendricks might have experienced.

"Sometimes people don't notice the changes," Rappaport said, "because they're so subtle. For example, the pathology that he has exhibited with me is very subtle. He appears to be normal to most people."

Judge Baner had some questions of his own. He asked Dr.

Rappaport to assume that Hendricks committed the murders and to offer his opinion about Hendricks's mental state at the time.

"If he in fact did this, I could understand it as a product of tremendous stress, internal stress."

"Making the same assumption," Judge Baner continued, "have you come to the conclusion that the defendant does not suffer from a mental disease or defect that rises to the level of insanity?"

"No," Rappaport responded. "I think it's quite possible that the insanity label would apply."

"Do you believe that the defendant was exposed to any extremely unusual or overwhelming stress?"

"The primary stress, I believe, is internal. The external stress might include the thought of adopting a child, the surgery that might be needed for his wife, the previous surgery to his wife. These were the main external precipitants that I could see. Perhaps you could look at the episodes with the models as external stress. But I think it was more an internal conflict, really."

"And making the same assumption, do you believe that the murders resulted from an extreme reaction, a result of which was loss of self-control and reason overborne by intense feelings such as passion, anger, distress, grief, excessive agitation, or other similar emotions?"

"Yes."

"All right," said the judge. "You may step down, sir. Witness excused."

Jennings and Long were delighted. A witness they had sought to prevent from testifying had actually helped their case against the death penalty. The law says extreme mental or emotional stress can be considered a mitigating circumstance, arguing against the imposition of the death penalty. They decided they wouldn't even call the two psychiatrists and two psychologists they had on standby to refute Rappaport's testimony.

And Rappaport was the state's only witness.

The defense presentation began with David's mother. Hal Jennings asked her to describe her son's religious training and background.

"He was raised in what we have termed here as the Plymouth Brethren group of Christians," Laverne Hendricks began in a low-key voice, bordering on confident, a mother determined to do what she could to save her son's life. "It's a fundamentalist group of Christians. Basically, we tried to live according to the Bible, a very simple, unornate, unpretentious way of living. We live as a close family unit, all together. We brought him up in a manner which we felt was for his best benefit. We had loving within the family. We used discipline only in the form of spanking. We used the belt when we did this in the case of a serious disobedience. Other than that, there was just a very close-knit family. We took vacations together, and many of our vacations were at Bible conferences."

Jennings asked how Hendricks responded to his religious training.

"He seemed to adapt to everything very nicely. He was a very mild-mannered, well-behaved son. I have often said that he was the type of child that books are written about. Just a very easy-going boy. Very considerate and caring person."

"How would you describe the relationship between David and his father as he grew up?"

"He had a good respect for his father. His father was and is a caring person. He's a little more strict than I am in ways. But they seemed to have a good relationship. They could go out and play tennis together—which they have often done, right up until this happened. They write letters to each other all the time, even now. They share the things from the Bible together very easily."

Between questions, Mrs. Hendricks looked over at her son as only a mother does. David returned a small smile.

"Was he ever any type of disciplinary problem or social problem?"

"Absolutely none. Of all of my children, I would say he caused me personally, and my husband, too, the least amount of grievance. I would say we had the least amount of discipline action towards David of any of our children. He was always very mild-mannered, very considerate. Just a very thoughtful and sharing and caring son."

Jennings asked for Mrs. Hendricks's observations of the married life between Susan and her son.

"I have never heard David speak in any way other than kindly to Susie and to the children. I have never heard him raise his voice to any of them. I have never seen him strike any of them—even in discipline. David was an exceptional father. I would say that he put us to shame as a parent sometimes."

At the defense table, Hendricks wiped away some tears.

"He was very, very understanding and very sympathetic with his children," his mother continued. "One time Gracie locked everybody out of the van. I don't know how long it took David to open up the van, but he never once got upset with Grace. She felt very bad about having done it, but he didn't get angry with her."

Through wet eyes, Hendricks smiled at his mother. She described how her son had tried to help and console others over the past year.

"What he is going through doesn't seem to stop him from wondering how this is hurting other people," she said. "He has been concerned about his youngest brother, Danny, who has gone through some very hard times with this."

Danny was ten years old when the murders occurred and was very close to Becky, Grace, and Benjy.

Jennings asked Mrs. Hendricks to describe the grief she witnessed in David after the murders.

"I have never seen anybody as shattered as David was. When I reached the house where he was staying and I went in, he came over to me and put his arms around me. It was like I was embracing emptiness. It was just like he was absolutely empty of any feeling at all. You could tell the grief. I have never seen grief like that."

She said she didn't know whether she should write about Susie and the children in her letters to David, but that she found that he wanted her to.

"He said he wanted to hear about them because they are the only ones who really meant anything to him. He said his year of incarceration was really nothing compared to losing his family. Nothing even compares."

"Which do you feel has had more of an impact of David—his legal status and conviction, or the loss of his family?"

"Oh. No comparison. The loss of his family is everything. It's his whole life."

Brad Murphy's voice had a nervous edge as he asked his first question.

"Am I correct, Mrs. Hendricks, that David has never expressed to you any remorse for the killing of his wife and children?"

"How could he?" Mrs Hendricks answered, almost pleading. "How could he when he didn't do it?"

"Have you ever, in the time that you have ever been with David, either when he was a child or during this ordeal or since the trial, seen David angry? Even once?"

"Yes, I have seen him angry inside. I know that he was upset inside. But he never has raised his voice and struck out. He doesn't do it. He's not that type of person. He controls it. Inside. But I know when he's angry. I'm his mother."

"Did you ever see any instances when he, as a child, actually verbalized his anger?"

"Probably when he was a child, between him and his sister, Bonnie. They had their sibling rivalries."

"Would you describe your husband as a perfectionist?"

"I suppose that could be applied to him. He likes things in their proper places."

"Would you describe David as a perfectionist?"

"No. Possibly in his work habits, in his business. But not in himself. Susie was his helpmate. She was partially the making of David."

The next four defense witnesses were people who had received unsolicited donations from Hendricks's fellowship fund. All testified that Hendricks appeared to be only the administrator of the fund and sought no personal credit as the source of the money. They were followed by David's older sister Bonnie and his brother Jim. Jim Hendricks alluded to the family crisis that occurred when he decided to leave the Brethren after being barred from active participation in the meetings.

"When I made my final decision, David didn't, you know, it didn't affect him like it did my dad, really. His attitude toward me didn't really change. He was still loving, still caring."

Two more witnesses were McLean County Jail guards who said they had come to like Hendricks and never felt he was a threat.

As the hearing wore on, the courtroom slowly filled with spectators. Sitting along the back wall was Detective Charlie Crowe. And on the stand was the final witness, David Hendricks.

Under John Long's questioning, Hendricks described how he met Susie, their married life, and the development of his business. He said he first knew that his family had been killed when a relative told him. Long asked how he felt when he got the news.

"I don't recall," Hendricks said in a soft voice. "I have tried to recall for many people who have asked me. All I can recall is a kind of deadness, a numbness. There wasn't a feeling of intense anguish or horrible sorrow at the time. That came later. It's a hard feeling to describe in words, a horrible feeling. During the next day the realization of what had happened slowly came on. It really wasn't for several days that I actually, really realized what had happened."

"Can you state whether the realization culminated with the funeral services?"

"Yes. It was excruciatingly painful. I was at the grave site. There were white caskets under the canopy, and I realized that Susie and Benjy and Grace and Becky were . . ." Tears rolled down Hendricks's face. "I wasn't going to see them again. Sorry."

Long explored Hendricks's religious feelings in light of what had happened over the past year.

"My faith in the Lord has certainly helped me," Hendricks said. "But what happened to me caused me to question almost everything I have ever believed in. I went through a time when I absolutely decided that God didn't even exist, but that's long gone. I've been through some real turmoil of soul as to my beliefs."

"Today you're the last witness in an evidentiary proceeding to determine what sentence should be meted out as a result of a trial in this case," Long said. "What is your faith and the limits of it today? Have you come back to your original faith?"

"Yes. I don't think I ever lost it. I think I went through a normal grief process which made me think thoughts that I wouldn't have thought without that grief process."

"David, during the course of this trial, you've been characterized as a loner. But do you consider yourself a gregarious, outgoing person?"

"You bet."

"You were a successful salesman, were you not?"

"Oh, yeah."

"Do you consider yourself as a person who has social orientation?"

"Oh, yes. I'm very outgoing."

"When you hear yourself described as a loner, what does that mean to you?"

"Well, if they're describing me now, it means they don't know me. But it is an accurate description of me when I was a child. I could play alone for hours on end. It didn't bother me at all. I enjoyed being by myself."

"Is that the case now?"

"I'm alone now. I make the best of it, but I would much prefer to be in the company of others."

"Why do you think you may be perceived as somebody who hides or has no anger or emotion of rage?"

"Because I don't show my anger in any violent manner, either verbally or physically, ever. I get angry. I get very angry. I was probably never angrier than when Dr. Rappaport was up here, saying that I never got angry."

"David, the judge is going to be making a decision in this case, a decision based on a number of factors. One of the questions has to do with the concept of remorse. Do you feel remorse of any kind over the death of your family?"

"Yes. In my mind, I've gone through the times we spent together, you know. I have thought our life through. And every time I think of a time when one of the kids asked for some time . . ." Hendricks's voice took on a strong quiver. "And I said I was too busy or something. I think it's part of the grief process. But I have gone through that in my mind, and remorse isn't probably a fair way to characterize that. But I think I have thought about all the times I could have been a better father and husband."

"David, during the course of the trial, you took a position legally and otherwise that you were not guilty of the crimes. You underwent a ten-week trial with over a hundred thirty witnesses. As you sit here today, what is your legal position with respect to the charges of which you have been found guilty?"

A spectator sneezed.

"My legal position is that I have been convicted. In fact, I'm not guilty. I couldn't possibly do a thing like that."

"The judge is going to make a determination in this case. Would you please state to him, for my benefit, are you guilty of the murder of Susan Hendricks in your own mind or in actuality?"

"I'm not guilty in actuality."

"Are you guilty of the murder of Benjamin Hendricks?"

"No."

"Are you guilty of the murder of Rebekah Hendricks?"

"No."

"Are you guilty of the murder of Grace Hendricks?"

"Absolutely not."

"Is it your position that you're steadfastly maintaining your position of innocence?"

"Oh, of course."

The person in the courtroom who most wanted to see Hendricks put to death cross-examined him.

"To begin with a question you have been asked previously, Mr. Hendricks," Brad Murphy said, "what do you think should happen to the killer of your wife and children?"

"Who asked me that previously?" Hendricks responded, then added, "I'm not supposed to ask you questions. I don't remember being asked that previously."

"I'll answer your question if you'll answer mine," Murphy said.

"I'll answer yours without your answering mine," Hendricks responded.

"Restate the question for the witness," Judge Baner said.

Murphy did. Hendricks answered.

"I think it would depend upon whether they were in possession of their faculties. I firmly believe in the death penalty. And this may be an unusual place to say that. But I firmly believe in the death penalty in a crime like this—as heinous and horrible. If, however, they are ever found, and if it's found that they were absolutely beside themselves on drugs or for other reasons, I couldn't imagine putting somebody to death for doing something that they were not in full control of their faculties about."

"Is there anything about the crime that you know at this point that would indicate that the killer was not in full control of the faculties?"

"Yes. It's senseless. I have never seen the pictures, but I understand it's horribly grotesque. I can't imagine anybody in their right mind doing that."

"Is that what you refer to when you used the term 'heinous' nature of the offense, the grotesque nature of the injuries that were caused?"

"Yes, although any killing of a human being, in my opinion, is a heinous act. I don't care if you cleanly shoot a bullet through someone's head and it doesn't hurt them, taking a human life is a horrible thing."

"That's one of the things that causes you to believe firmly in the death penalty, isn't it—your belief in the sanctity of life?"

"Well, it tends to make me think that the death penalty should be applied very sparingly. I would think the death penalty only should be applied to someone who is so incorrigibly bad that there is no possibility of rehabilitation, and society can do nothing but suffer from that person. Otherwise I don't think the death penalty is appropriate."

"What was it about Dr. Rappaport saying that you don't get angry that made you so angry?"

"It wasn't that statement, particularly. It was his testimony in general. He misconstrued a number of things I said. I told him that I don't display my anger. I never get violent. I never display anger, or rarely."

"What do you intend to do with yourself for the rest of your life?" Murphy asked.

"I intend to have the verdict reversed on appeal if the Lord wills, then try to put my life back together—probably go into a different profession. I'm already making plans to get a degree from the U of I while I'm waiting in prison, and I'm thinking of going into law—keep as far as possible from criminal law—but going into law."

"Was it first at the grave site of your wife and children that you realized that you weren't going to see them again?"

"I'm sure I knew that intellectually before that. I remember at that time the realization really came home powerfully."

"Did you have any feelings of guilt or remorse at that time?"

"No."

"Those feelings about being a better father to them while they were here on earth with you, did those feelings only come later?"

"Yes. To anybody's eyes, as they would say, I was a model father, an excellent husband. But I knew everything. I knew all about my family life, and I knew the times when I was reading, and I would tell Becky, for instance, that no, you can't climb on my lap, I'm busy concentrating. And when you lose your loved ones like that, you go through all those things. And you think of how I could have made their life better."

"Do you really believe that you're not going to see them again?"

"I believe I will see them again. I will never enjoy the relationship of husband and father to them again. The Bible gives me no comfort that I will ever enjoy the kind of relationships I had here on earth with them."

"A couple last questions," Murphy said. "Thinking back, do you now recall where you were asked the question: 'What do you think should happen to the killer?' "

"Uh-huh. In the beginning of your questions."

"Do you now recall where you ever heard that asked of you before?"

"No."

"You don't recall during the course of that television interview you gave on Wednesday, November 9th, 1983?"

"I don't recall the exact words, but I remember, yes, I remember . . . I don't recall the interview at all. I don't even recall giving that interview. But I saw it once in Judge Baner's chambers up in Rockford. It's the only time I have ever seen that film."

"Do you recall the question being, 'What do you think should happen to the killer,' and you said you would like to see him get saved?"

"I'll take your word for it. I don't recall specifically."

"I don't have further questions."

Murphy threw his pen to his desk.

There would be a fifteen-minute recess and then the closing arguments for and against death for David Hendricks.

Murphy spoke for the state. He began by saying that he believed both the state and the defense had an appreciation for Judge Baner's "mammoth undertaking" by stepping into the case with less than two weeks' notice and then enduring a ten-week trial in a distant county.

"And now you, and you alone, have been asked to shoulder the burden of the decision of whether or not the defendant will die or live like a caged animal for his crimes."

Ron Dozier sat quietly at the prosecution table, hands folded in his lap, as Murphy said that Hendricks had shown himself to be a calculating, remorseless person, "who to this day has given us no reason to expect that he will ever be rehabilitated or changed.

"The deliberate, brutal disregard for human life. These crimes, these murders were no less than executions. These victims had no chance. Their lives were over when David Hendricks picked up that ax. That ax was a weapon of choice, showing the deliberation of the defendant. It was chosen with care for its intended purpose. It was used in a deliberate fashion. No blows appeared to miss any of the targets. To call these murders 'brutal' could well be the understatement of 1985. The force used by David Hendricks in killing his children drove their very life blood all the way across their bedroom onto walls and furniture and into closets. And that weapon that he used was calculated to inflict horrifying injuries, specifically about the face and head. Two of the victims, the two youngest, literally had their faces chopped to a state that you couldn't stand to look at them but for just a few horrifying seconds. This brutality was inflicted by the defendant, who watched with each one of the blows as that ax struck the body of his child and his wife. The bodies of his loved ones shuddered and reacted each time he struck them. And he stood there and watched as that happened on each one of those repeated blows. That viciousness—we have referred to that as 'overkill,' and I'm not sure that does justice to it—but that viciousness, particularly on Benjy and Grace Hendricks, is indicative of the most wanton cruelty that McLean County has ever experienced."

At the defense table, Hendricks was taking notes.

"These victims were no match at all for David Hendricks, even if he hadn't used a weapon. And yet he has so clearly shown his disregard for human life in other areas. He seemed to have some contempt for anything that posed an irritation to him. He lied repeatedly to prospective sales customers and to models. He lied when faced with just the minor irritation of filling out a check-in blank at the motel. But probably, first of all, he lied to himself. He convinced himself, Judge, that there were four human beings whose lives served no purpose here on earth. Very simply and grotesquely put, he reduced four human lives to blocks of wood. That's what he saw them as. Blocks of wood to be chopped on. These four people deserved to live. They didn't deserve that. And for some reason—and perhaps we haven't gotten to the very bottom of that reason yet—he thought he had the right or the authority to end lives that God had created."

Hendricks's mother, her son John, his wife, and their twenty-month-old daughter sat only a few feet from Murphy, listening. Nadine and Seth Palmer were also in the courtroom.

"The people of the State of Illinois may be the only persons in this courtroom who are standing up for the rights of the victims in this case. If that be so, that's okay. We have no hesitation in crying, even as a voice from the wilderness, when someone like this defendant shows such an utter disregard for human life. We suggest that disregard and that brutality has to be dealt with harshly. This defendant did quite a bit of calculating. He calculated where he was in this life and where really he would rather be. Then he calculated what it would take to get him where he would rather be, and then decided that the price wasn't too great to pay. But he had to surrender some things to get there. Basic things like honesty and integrity. Thank God there were miscalculations in David's calculating. He didn't calculate on Detective Charlie Crowe, who could see through his charade. A judge like Ivan Johnson who had the courage to park him in jail, awaiting trial. And for twelve jurors who had the good sense to see him for the con man that he is.

"Yet there are some things that you can't miss. This total lack of feelings, this lack of remorse, is clearly one thing that the court can consider in passing sentence."

Murphy paged through his notes, then said Hendricks was guilty of "stonewalling." "So long as David Hendricks continues to stonewall, refuses to accept the responsibility for his own actions, there is never going to be a healing of the spirit of David Hendricks, and there is never going to be a healing among those people who are family members and who lost something in the death of Susan Hendricks and those children. And in that sense, David Hendricks is making every one of those members of the Plymouth Brethren victims in this case, too. That is cruelty, Your Honor.

"I don't mean to suggest that David Hendricks hated his family. I really don't think he did. He did feel shame and guilt to the extent that he hated himself enough to kill his family. I submit this is shown by those excessive and brutal blows to Benjamin Hendricks, because those were the result of the defendant projecting his own feelings of guilt and shame on his son.

"We are not dealing with a teenaged punk who is just a wretch, an outcast who has been thrown away in society's garbage can somewhere. This is a thirty-year-old individual who has grown up, frankly, with a life of opportunity—not only physically and materially, but spiritually as well. And yet it was he who chose to throw that away. He chose that course of conduct, and I emphasize the word 'he.' There is no evidence that anybody forced, compelled, aided him, or abetted him. This defendant was the mastermind, the judge, jury, and executioner for his family. He did this alone.

"The state is now seeking justice for a lot of people. Justice for the victims. They don't have the right to life anymore, that's been taken away. But they still have a right to justice. Justice for all people, the State of Illinois, and, yeah, even justice for David Hendricks."

Murphy said the state was seeking the death penalty as a kind of self-defense for society and an affirmation of the sanctity of life. "I submit that the reality in this case is that if the court pronounces the death penalty in this case, not even the defendant, David Hendricks, will believe that the decision is unfair."

Murphy sat down and Jennings stood up.

"Your Honor," Jennings began, "I'm speaking only to the record and only to you. I do not feel at this point that it's necessary to make a speech to be quoted in the press, to change public perception. The reason I suggest to you, sir, that I'm speaking to you and to you alone and only to the record, is because of the perceptions that there have been two trials going on in this case from the beginning to the end—one being the trial of the case as presided over by Your Honor, and the other trial that goes on with respect to public opinion.

"The comments that I make may be taken as an enforcement of my client's guilt by people who do not know and understand the system. I would simply say that I do not believe personally or professionally that there has been or is now any credible evidence of this man's guilt, or that the jury verdict in this case is in any way just. I disagree with both of those premises. But the law requires that you and I now deal with the issue of life and death."

Jennings said that if Hendricks were an evil person, then it could be rationally argued that he should be put to death. But the state indirectly argued, Jennings said, that Hendricks is not evil, but emotionally sick, that he broke under tension.

"It defeats our entire system, Judge, for them to stand up and say, kill him because he was sick. You do not deter mental illness by killing somebody who is ill. You do not punish people for their acts by death if their acts were a result of an illness. That's wrong. It defeats us all. It demeans us all, and I'm opposed to it.

"You must only impose the death penalty in this case if you have an abiding conviction that this man was sane, was rational, was, well, was in fact evil. And the fact is there is no evidence to support that in this case, regardless of which side of the table you sit on. I do not believe, even in accepting the state's theory and the jury's verdict, that you can in good conscience sentence this man to death, because if I become Mr. Murphy and if I become Mr. Dozier, and if I take on the state's scenario from start to finish, there is only one explanation for saying that David Hendricks committed these acts of brutality and violence as visited upon his family. And that is that he was not at that time David Hendricks. And he was not at that time David Hendricks because of a mental illness.

"It is my personal and my abiding conviction that you, Judge, will join me in suggesting that what's right and just in this case is not the death penalty. I do not believe that David Hendricks murdered his family. I do not believe the jury's verdict was just. But above all, the death penalty is not in order because this man is not evil. By reason of his history, his family, his friends, his conduct, his relationship with Susie, his relationship with his kids, he is not an inherently evil man. He is not the devil. He is not Satan. He is not a person who kills, maims, and mutilates simply because it suits his fancy, because it fulfills an ego need, because he has no use for his family. He is not now, he has never been, he never will be that type of person. And if there is a Judeo-Christian ethic at the basis of our system and as the basis of the principles we are being asked to exercise today, then they scream at you, Judge, keep this man alive! That is all."

Now John Long would speak. Briefly, he promised.

"I am personally offended by any notion in a court of law that because a man who has continued to proclaim and affirm his innocence, will not confess to a crime which he did not commit . . ."

Judge Baner cut off Long. "This court isn't going to consider that aspect of the case, Mr. Long. That will be specifically spelled out in the finding. Lack of confession, lack of remorse is not going to be considered."

"Then I will go on to something else, Your Honor." Long explored his notes. "One does not impose the death penalty in order to affirm the sanctity of life. In order to affirm the sanctity of life, Your Honor, you should look solely at what's been presented here, as we asked the jury to look solely at what was presented to it. The motive behind this tragedy, Your Honor, was not financial gain. The motive behind this tragedy was not that the defendant was leaving his family for another woman. The motive was not for any discernible reason other than progressive sexual aggression. 'A state of mind,' says the State of Illinois, 'is what caused David Hendricks to murder his family'—in spite of the only evidence being that he never physically abused them, never publicly rebuked them, that they had a full and loving relationship, that they had not a financial worry in the world, that they were active in the community and in their church, that they participated in family projects. And because of all of that, he killed them out of a mental derangement called by the state 'progressive sexual aggression.' "

Long asked Judge Baner to consider Dr. Rappaport's statement that Hendricks has a borderline personality. "How can the state justify putting to death someone who it believes has a mental disease?" Long asked. "We are put in an absolute double-edged position on behalf of David Hendricks, because I don't believe that he is a sick man. I don't believe David Hendricks is psychotic or that he did anything to harm his family on a theory called 'progressive sexual aggression.' But the state believes it and now seeks to have him killed with that as the basis for it.

"I believe in David Hendricks's innocence. I believe that because David Hendricks could not say who did it, he was the logical suspect. And I believe he does not fall under the category prescribed by law as one who should be put to death.

"We are not going to stand before Your Honor and say that this crime was not brutal, not a heinous crime, that the possibility of the death penalty should not apply. What we are saying is that it may apply for someone else, but not for this defendant. Not for David Hendricks."

Long said that the evil characteristics attributed to Hendricks couldn't be found in him. "They won't be found except in the hysteria that grew up out of the brutality of this crime. What the state is complaining about was not born out of progressive sexual aggression. It was born out of mass hysteria, and it's only going to be after a passage of time and hopefully by further action that this man's innocence is going to be affirmed.

"In the meantime, he is entitled to life, and he is entitled to life because of his innocence and because the state has not shown any statutory basis for giving him anything but life. And for that reason, we ask the court, in reviewing the panoply of sentences which can be handed down, to choose life."

Judge Baner had been taking frequent notes during the final arguments. Now he turned to Hendricks.

"All right, Mr. Hendricks. You have a right to make a statement on your own behalf at this time. You may do that from where you are. You may stand or sit as you see fit."

Hendricks stood, a legal pad in front of him on the defense table.

"Thank you." Hendricks appeared calm, a hint of conciliation in his voice. "I don't have a lot to say, Your Honor. I wanted to take this opportunity to reaffirm again my innocence, that I could not possibly have done such a heinous, horrible thing as this. You told Mr. Long he didn't need to talk about remorse. If you will allow me, I would like to make a simple statement, and that is that I believe that remorse minus culpability equals grief, and that the state, in saying I have no remorse, is very duplicitous in their language. The evidence of grief has been abundant. It's in the psychological reports that have been tendered to Your Honor. It's, in fact, in the jail-house logs of the people who have watched me every fifteen minutes since I have been here. What I have been doing, my demeanor has been noted. The prosecution has specifically requested of them on special days, such as my children's birthdays or anniversaries, to look at me to see if I was under duress. I looked like I was grieving.

"I remember specifically being told that it was noted during Benjy's birthday. I didn't know it at the time. They have abundant evidence to my grief, to my sorrow, to the fact that I miss my family. And in spite of all that, they wish to take my life away. I find the concept incredible.

"I would like to plead for mercy, but mercy is really inappropriate in my mind because of my maintaining my innocence. I do ask for justice. I ask for righteousness, fairness, equity. I ask that the court take a look at all of the testimony that went on at the trial, all of the testimony that was given here at the sentencing, and to see if there is anything at all that shows that I am anything other than a good, average, normal, happy man.

"To say that I have never done anything wrong would be foolish. The court has seen on the stand the young ladies who have told about the worst things that I have ever done, the things that I'm the most sorry about. I feel bad about that. I feel bad about not only the violation of my personal sexual, moral code, but I feel worse about the way that I acted with a disregard to their feelings, with a disregard for respect for those young ladies. I should not have done that. They deserve more respect than I showed them. I never really realized how my conduct looked to them until I saw it through their eyes as I heard it, and I was very ashamed. I'm sorry for that. That has nothing to do with anything in this case, except that it was brought into the case.

"I do ask for the fairness of the court. I ask for righteousness, for justice. I know it's not a statutory mitigating factor, but the single biggest reason that the court should not grant death in this case is the paucity of evidence proving culpability. I am not guilty factually. I know that I'm now legally considered guilty, that I have been convicted. I understand that intellectually. But the court knows, I know, the state knows, everyone involved with this case knows, that the evidence was so very, very slim, and almost everyone was totally surprised and astonished at the verdict of those twelve people. I don't know how they possibly came to the conclusion that I was guilty beyond a reasonable doubt with no reasonable hypothesis of innocence. But they did.

"I think the court should look at it, and I respectfully request the court look at the paucity of evidence as a possible, nonstatutory, I know, mitigating factor in this case. Thank you."

David Hendricks had just completed the most important sales pitch of his life. Judge Baner finished his note-taking and looked up.

"Anything further, gentlemen?" he asked.

"No," said Murphy.

"No," said Jennings.

"That concludes today's hearing. We will resume tomorrow at 4 P.M."

Twenty-Two

More than an hour before the scheduled sentencing, a line had begun to form outside the courtroom. By 3:45 a crowd that obviously would not fit into the courtroom had gathered. All wanted to see the sentencing of the man who was arguably McLean County's best-known resident, certainly its most famous criminal.

The courtroom doors were opened. Sheriff Steve Brienen announced that members of Hendricks's family would be admitted first, then the news media, then the general public.

One by one, a dozen members of Hendricks's family were searched with a metal detector and allowed into the courtroom. Hendricks's mother smiled and apologized to the female deputy for having such a large purse and an extra bag containing her knitting. About twenty reporters filed in, and then members of the public.

By 3:57 each spectator seat was filled. Perhaps twenty persons were still outside the courtroom. They would not be allowed in. When the courtroom clock showed 4 P.M., the crowd inside became quiet.

Three minutes later, David Hendricks—dressed in one of the three business suits he wore throughout the trial—was brought in.

He started to sit at his regular seat at the far end of the defense table. But one of his attorneys, Long, silently motioned for Hendricks to sit between him and cocounsel Jennings, as if to shelter or brace him.

The bailiff intoned the familiar "all rise"—a statement that falls partway between an order and tradition. As the spectators, attorneys, and Hendricks rose, Judge Baner took his seat high upon the bench.

"The courtroom doors are about to be secured," Judge Baner said. "No one will be allowed to leave the courtroom until after the sentencing hearing is complete. If anyone wants to leave before then, they should do so now. Does anyone want to leave now?"

Nobody moved.

Judge Baner began. "The second phase hearing under chapter 38, section 9-1h has now been completed. . . ." About midway through the legalistic preamble, the judge handed the court reporter a copy of the sentencing order so she could refer to it if she wanted. Her eyes remained straight ahead as her fingers recorded the judge's words.

Then the judge began listing all the factors he considered in arriving at the sentence. Among the aggravating factors, those which might compel the death penalty: the number and ages of the victims, the brutality and wanton cruelty of the crime, the deterrent factor. Among the mitigating factors, which might dictate a lesser sentence: the fact Hendricks had no prior criminal record, that the murders resulted from specific circumstances unlikely to occur again, Hendricks's church activities, his professed beliefs, his acts of charity, history of regular employment and support of his family, his medical and intellectual abilities.

The judge said he reviewed nearly five hundred murder cases appealed to higher courts since Illinois enacted its death penalty law in 1977. He said the death penalty had been affirmed in only 4 percent of those cases and that capital punishment had never been ordered for a person who had no prior criminal record unless the murder occurred during a rape, robbery, or kidnapping. He said those facts were interesting but not enough to provide a basis for the sentence in the Hendricks case.

Hendricks made notes on a yellow legal notepad. All four attorneys watched the judge. The time for their note-taking had ended.

Judge Baner read on. "Certainly some of the cases I have studied present more grotesque and brutal deaths than does this case, and the reasons for some of those murders were equally obscure. This case, however, demonstrates an amazing and almost unbelievable disregard for human life. Not only did the family ties, but the history of a demonstrable loving relationship between the defendant and each victim, make it next to impossible for any reasonable human being to understand or to accept any reasoning behind the moments of horror that occurred at 313 Carl Drive on November 7th, 1983.

"Three beautiful children will never blossom into the individuals they could have become." A catch seemed to develop in the judge's voice. "A young mother will never know the future joys of watching and guiding the growth of those children. While these same particular circumstances are not likely to recur, the defendant's apparent total disregard for the value of these lives presents a permanent and ongoing danger to society with no reasonable basis to anticipate correction."

Tears swamped Laverne Hendricks's eyes. Her son had stopped writing. His gaze locked on the judge.

"While it is a possibility, I am not convinced that the defendant was under the influence of extreme mental or emotional disturbance at the time of each murder, and I cannot assume that he was, merely because of the senseless brutality of the murder scene.

"The jurors in this case were convinced beyond a reasonable doubt of the defendant's guilt. That decision was the result of their regular and conscientious attention to the evidence, which was capably presented in great detail and subjected to intensive cross-examination over the lengthy span of this trial. It can probably be agreed that the key factual issue in the trial was the actual time of the children's death. The proof on this issue was presented through the opinions of experts, and the factual determination relied entirely upon the relative persuasive abilities of qualified experts who differed dramatically with each other. I have already determined that the totality of the evidence was legally sufficient to reach the jury for its consideration, and this continues to be my conclusion today."

The tone of the judge's voice changed. He was moving on to another part of his considerations.

"Many prospective jurors stated during the jury selection process that they would consider the death penalty as an appropriate sentence only if they were *personally* convinced beyond a reasonable doubt of the defendant's guilt. That is the appropriate legal standard, and I also accept it as a proper moral standard. I personally believe that the defendant probably did commit these offenses, and I must emphasize that I intend no criticism of the jury or its verdicts by this sentencing order. Based upon the *evidence* admitted on trial against the defendant, I am not *personally* convinced that he has been proven guilty beyond a reasonable doubt."

Judge Baner cleared his throat. The courtroom remained otherwise silent.

"Some might say this is a distinction without a difference. However, I feel the very fabric of our justice system depends on this distinction. If the sentence issue were anything other than the most severe and irreversible sanction of death, I would disregard my own concern over the level of proof and render sentence based on the verdicts as I have done many times before in other cases."

Outside the courtroom several people pressed their faces against the small windows in the doors to the courtroom. They couldn't hear what was being said. The people inside were getting their first hint that the death penalty was not acceptable to Judge Baner in this case. He continued.

"However, as to the sanction of death, I hold the same position as do some or perhaps even all of the jurors. I cannot in good conscience apply the sanction of death unless *I* have been convinced of his guilt beyond a reasonable doubt. I have not, and mere belief is not enough."

Laverne Hendricks's hands, clenched in prayer, released. Her son sat motionless.

Judge Baner said the public, however, must be protected from Hendricks. He imposed the sentence.

"Natural life imprisonment without the right or availability of mandatory supervised release, parole, or other form of early release."

There was no visible reaction from anyone, least of all David Hendricks.

The judge said he was also fining Hendricks $44,000 and ordered him to pay the costs of the trial. He placed a lien against all property owned by Hendricks as of December 22, 1983, the date he was indicted. The numbers seemed secondary. Hendricks's life had been spared. But Judge Baner continued, saying he hoped Hendricks's substantial intellectual abilities and what appeared to be sincerely held religious beliefs could somehow benefit humanity.

"I do intend to leave with him the ability and the burden of agonizing daily for the rest of his life over his part in the waste of four innocent lives, each of whom loved him and each of whom, hopefully, never consciously learned of the brutally dark side of his nature."

For the first time since he began reading, Judge Baner looked at Hendricks.

Sheriff Brienen, who was standing at one side of the courtroom, motioned for a deputy to unlock the courtroom doors. The news media pushed past the overflow of would-be spectators outside, anxious to spread the word that David Hendricks sat passively as he learned he would not be put to death for the ax murders of his wife and three young children.

Twenty-Three

O n February 28, Hendricks completed a two-week stay at the Illinois Department of Corrections screening center in Joliet and boarded a prison bus for a six-hour trip to the Menard Correctional Center. The vehicle's southward route on Interstate 55 took him within sight of the McLean County Courthouse where, at that very moment, the inquest into the deaths of his wife and children was underway.

Under normal conditions an inquest would be held about a month after the deaths, but this one was delayed more than a year at the request of prosecutors, who had not wanted to tip their hand so soon. Now it was anticlimactic and commanded little media attention. The six-person jury's decision, that the Hendricks deaths were homicides, was presupposed. What questions the coroner's jurors did ask seemed to be posed only to satisfy their own curiosity.

The Menard Correctional Center, one of Illinois's four maximum-security prisons, was established in 1898 and sits on the bank of the Mississippi River, about an hour's drive south of St. Louis. Hendricks had been there for almost exactly a year when his case was argued before Illinois's Fourth District Appellate Court.

By mutual consent, Hendricks had parted company with his trial lawyers, Jennings and Long, and was now represented by Jon Waltz, a Northwestern University law professor, and by his business attorney, Mercer Turner.

Turner had only a nominal role in the oral arguments, focusing on the scientific evidence that helped convict Hendricks.

"All the experts agreed on one thing," he told the three-judge panel. "And that is that their opinions were based on subjective criteria. All we have is educated guesses—perhaps they could even be described as shots in the dark—as to when the children died. Expert testimony is used to provide guideposts or guidelines for a jury in a sophisticated area. In this case we believe those guideposts are very weak. And if a case is based primarily on weak guideposts, we submit, as a matter of law, reasonable doubt exists."

The bespectacled law school professor told the judges that his early remarks probably wouldn't strike them as being "very academic or fancy or legalistic."

"I speak to you as an old trial lawyer, much of my time spent as a prosecutor, when I say that the evidence in this case just doesn't feel right. On the one hand, there wasn't enough evidence of solid probative value. On the other hand, there was too much that was unfairly prejudicial. Thin on the one hand, all too heavy on the other, poisoning the well at the very onset."

Waltz took on the tone of an older uncle lecturing his nephews.

"It may not seem like something out of a law review, but the manner in which this case was tried, it seems to me, is simply not the American way. In some countries we put a person's character, his entire life on trial. And then he goes to Gorky or wherever he goes. Not here. Not this reliance on innuendo and character to distract the jurors from the basic thinness of the case on the merits."

By now, Brad Murphy had taken a job as an assistant United States attorney. Dozier would argue the appeal by himself.

"Now I will concede to you," Dozier told the appellate justices, "that it is impossible to present evidence that tends to prove a person guilty of a heinous crime that does not also reflect on the character of the accused. And I think that's one of the reasons that there is a balancing test, that the motive evidence has to be relevant and tend to prove motive, and not just something that shows a bad character."

Dozier said it was necessary to put the string of models on the stand to demonstrate a trend toward sexual aggressiveness by

Hendricks. As for the scientific evidence, Dozier said, "we proved, I believe beyond reasonable doubt, that those children were killed by eleven o'clock at night, and if so, David Hendricks had to have been the killer. He testified that the last thing he did before he left the house was kiss them all good night."

Four months later, on June 19, 1986, the three judges unanimously upheld the conviction. And because it was a unanimous decision, there was surprise when, a few months later, the Illinois Supreme Court agreed to review the case.

As written briefs were prepared for the state's highest court, the Hendricks and Palmer families joined to offer a ten-thousand-dollar reward "for information leading to the arrest and conviction of the murderer(s) of our loved ones."

A month before the supreme court was to hear oral arguments, Hendricks tried to help himself by sending the court what he called "a supplemental brief."

"Obviously, I am no scholar," he wrote; "I am simply a man badly hurt by and disappointed in the system I have always implicitly trusted. I desperately hope that system works this final time around. I am truly innocent."

Hendricks said the evidence that should have freed him was ignored by the jurors because their minds were "so overflowing with sexual-psychological theories that they simply could not think like logical people."

"I must say—as I did on the witness stand—that I am sorry for my inappropriate behavior with the models. It was ill-advised and unethical, but not 'deviate' or 'hellbent.' These were the models I used for advertising purposes. I let my active libido override my better moral judgment, true, but that is no cause for twisting indiscretion into infatuation.

"Please don't let wild speculation built on ten hours of improper conduct twist ten years of a loving marriage and a caring family life into some kind of mad, deviate, psychotic explosion of brutal murder! If you do, these murders may never be solved."

On March 12, 1987, in the ornate supreme court room just across the street from the Illinois State Capitol in Springfield, six of the seven state supreme court justices heard oral arguments. The seventh justice had excused himself from the case because of a marital connection to John Long's law firm.

Jon Waltz told the court that the issues being raised in the appeal had resulted in nearly twelve thousand appeals court decisions at the state level and nearly two thousand appellate opinions at the federal level. "This suggests to me that the time has come for a court to generate guidelines in connection with the use of prior uncharged misconduct as evidence of guilt."

Scott Graham, an assistant Illinois attorney general, represented the state, saying not all the models who testified were prejudicial against Hendricks. The real question, he said, is whether the probative value was outweighed by the prejudice.

Justice Seymour Simon asked Graham how one should weigh it.

"I think that's something that the trial court has to do in light of all the evidence," Graham answered. "And I think that once it's shown to be relevant, it becomes the defendant's burden to show that the prosecution is not entitled to admit relevant evidence because of prejudicial value, and that's simply the showing he didn't make here."

"But is that perhaps what would influence the judge to express his own doubts about the guilt during the sentencing?" Justice Simon asked.

"I believe it was just a matter that he wasn't as convinced as the jury was," Graham answered.

In his rebuttal, Waltz focused on Judge Baner's sentencing remark. "If nothing else—whatever the message to the higher court may be—it is that this was the closest of possible cases, and, this court has said it, close cases must be error-free."

Many court observers expected the Illinois Supreme Court to rule within six months, in the fall of 1987. Even by the fall of 1988 the court still had not issued an opinion.

In the meantime, the Hendricks and Palmer families, having received virtually no response to their offer of a ten-thousand-dollar reward, doubled the ante to twenty thousand dollars.

And David Hendricks had plans to remarry.

In the months before the supreme court hearing, and at the suggestion of the mother of a fellow Menard inmate, Hendricks had written to Pat Miller, divorced mother of three, telling her about himself and his case. The Toledo, Ohio, woman later visited Hendricks's parents and in August of 1987 visited Hendricks at Menard. By May of 1988, the petite, cute, and energetic brunette, four years older than Hendricks, agreed to marry him. But the Menard warden refused permission, saying that marriage could only frustrate Hendricks because there was no prospect he ever would be freed. In the meantime, Pat Miller moved with her two youngest children to a remote farmhouse about four miles from the prison and established FAITH, Inc.—Friends Against Injustice To Hendricks.

Hendricks resubmitted his request to marry five months later and was given the warden's okay. The marriage was scheduled for December 20, 1988. A few weeks later it was announced that the Illinois Supreme Court would issue its ruling in the Hendricks case on December 21. Nevertheless, the marriage went ahead as scheduled.

With Pat in a pink dress and David in his prison blues, the two were wed in a tiny prison office. Pat's two youngest children, David's parents, his sister Bonnie, and Nadine Palmer were present. Pictures were taken, kisses were exchanged, and the group was allowed an extra-long visit. And then they parted, Pat to her new home, David to his prison cell, to await the next morning's news.

The Illinois Supreme Court upheld Hendricks's conviction by a vote of four to two.

Epilogue

Some of the most dramatic moments in criminal trials occur not in the courtroom, but in the hallways outside the courtroom, where victims confront defendants, when their spouses, parents, sisters, brothers, and friends encounter each other.

That didn't happen in the Hendricks case. The victims were all dead. Their friends and family and the defendant's family and friends were all on the same side. All stood squarely behind David Hendricks. They believe their son, son-in-law, brother, brother-in-law, or friend was wrongly accused and convicted, and that freedom is still enjoyed by the guilty.

The patient reader has arrived, perhaps, at his or her own conclusions on the two central issues presented in this book: whether Hendricks is in fact guilty and whether he was proved guilty beyond a reasonable doubt. The reader may have discovered that the two are unrelievedly woven together, and that some nagging thoughts and haunting questions remain.

The prosecution suggested that Hendricks put his children to bed, waited until they were asleep, murdered them, and cleaned himself up. Then, for some reason linked to the crime, he left the home at about 9 P.M., returned to wait for his wife to come home and fall asleep, killed her, staged a burglary as best he knew how, then left on an alibi trip to Wisconsin—all the while being extremely careful to leave behind no physical evidence tying him to the crimes.

While the sequence of the killings is not critical to the state's case, it is nevertheless important to point out why such a sequence seems highly unlikely if not impossible.

The Hendricks children were seen alive, on the street, at 8:15 P.M. Any parent knows that after a night of roisterous fun, three young children are unlikely to be in their pajamas, in bed, and all soundly asleep in less than twenty minutes. And they had to be sound asleep when they died because there were no defensive wounds that would have occurred if they raised a hand or arm to protect themselves. Even if the throats of the two younger children were slit first, it would seem the resulting sound would be enough to awaken the older girl. If they were first struck by blows from the ax, the sound or the jostling motion of a mattress bearing up under the force of the ax would seem likely to awaken the second occupant of that bed.

Would Hendricks, in the absolute maximum of twenty-five minutes remaining before he was supposedly seen leaving the house at 9 P.M., be able to cleanse himself of the blood well enough not to leave a trail, put on clean clothes, and leave the house? Perhaps.

But suppose for a moment that the young man who testified he saw Hendricks leave 313 Carl Drive at 9 P.M. was wrong, that Hendricks never left the house and instead could clean up at a much more leisurely pace? Even then there are two other problems related to the state's sequence of events.

It seems very improbable that Susan Hendricks, given her nature, would have arrived home and gone to bed without first checking on the well-being of her children. And just as problematic is the fact that Becky and Benjy's hair was found on the ax. If the children were killed first, one would expect to find some of that hair transferred to either Susan or the bedspread through which she apparently was struck by the same ax. But none was found.

It seems much more likely that no matter who committed the murders, Susan was killed first. And if Susan was killed first, it is highly unlikely the children died before 11:15 P.M.

That, in turn, counters key (perhaps decisive) testimony from the prosecution's experts, notably Dr. Baden, that the children died substantially before 11:15 P.M. Even more importantly, it puts their time of death, at the earliest, much closer to the time Hendricks said he left home.

Then there are two problems with the issue of stomach contents.

If *cooked* vegetable parts were clearly visible in the children's stomachs when, according to state experts, Becky, Grace, and Benjy died some two hours after they ate, how is it that not a trace of the *raw* vegetables that Susan Hendricks consumed at about 9:15 P.M. was found in her stomach if she died about two hours later?

And why were mushrooms found in the contents of Grace's stomach? Relatives and friends say the seven-year-old was fanatical about her distaste for mushrooms, picking them out of any food item before it passed her lips. Mushrooms were clearly visible on the Chuck E. Cheese vegetarian pizza. Trial testimony disclosed that some of the stomach contents were not saved, and that a St. Louis botanist's initial examination of what he thought were Grace's stomach contents revealed only highly digested vegetable mass. Both matters may have been honest mistakes. Mistakes occur all the time in criminal investigations. But they raise the question of whether there might have been other errors in the handling of the stomach contents which were so important to this case.

Did the evidence point to David Hendricks? Or did police take a hasty, or even easy, way out and point the evidence at Hendricks?

It is hard to measure whether police focused on Hendricks as a suspect too early in their investigation. Some experienced investigators have a kind of sixth sense that guides them to a criminal even before hard evidence lays out the trail. But some of Hendricks's statements and actions shortly after the crime was discovered—statements and actions that were so important to the police and prosecution—seem in retrospect rather thin evidence.

Hendricks's response to a question from a TV reporter was seized upon by prosecutors as proof that Hendricks was responsible for the rifling of the house. "Was there anything missing in the house itself? Were you at the house itself?" the reporter had asked. Hendricks responded, "No, I was not at the house. I was never in the house, but they said some things looked like some things were taken."

In fact, in the hours before the interview took place, there had been talk of an apparent break-in. The police chief, in his morning news conference that was broadcast live on the radio, had even alluded to the possibility of a break-in. And police had even suggested to Hendricks that he might be asked to inventory the house in an effort to determine if anything was missing.

Given those circumstances, such a response to a reporter's question does not seem particularly incriminating.

And what of Hendricks's relatively calm bearing, in light of the horrendous nature of the crime? It, too, was very important to police as they concentrated on Hendricks as a suspect in the early hours of their investigation.

Could he simply have been in shock? His statement to the TV cameras less than eighteen hours after he arrived home, "Susie and my three children are much better off. . . . I know that they are with the Lord Jesus in heaven, and I am satisfied now in knowing that," was also judged inappropriate and unlikely for a person who had just learned that his whole family was wiped out. Yet it was that very type of statement that had been whispered into Hendricks's ear by consoling friends and relatives many times in the hours leading up to the interview. And it is the very type of statement one frequently hears from fundamentalist Christians when unexplained tragedy strikes. When, in May of 1988 for instance, a truck crashed into a church bus in Kentucky, killing 27 young people, one of the survivors told the press, "I'm sure they're in a better place than we are."

Hendricks *did* have the opportunity to kill his family. And if he did commit the murders, how did he do it? There is a scenario that makes more sense than the one laid out by the prosecution.

When Susan arrived home, her husband, about to depart on a business trip that would take a couple of days, made sexual advances to her, thus explaining why her clothing was rather uncharacteristically scattered about the bedroom. He enticed her into bed and told her he had a surprise for her, that she should cover her head with the bedspread so he could bring out the surprise. He reached under the bed where he had hidden the ax (thus explaining why the corner of the bedspread was found turned up at the foot of the bed) and struck her with the ax through the bedspread. Then, in an apparent emotional frenzy, he turned to his children and savagely murdered them. With some advance planning, he could have covered himself completely with a disposable medical gown, cap, and gloves, shielding himself from the splattering blood.*

The disposable clothing could have been wrapped into a neat bundle and deposited in a dumpster at a nearby hospital or, for that matter, dropped into the Illinois River as he drove over it en route to Wisconsin.

It seems such a scenario, including the ransacking of the house, could easily be accomplished in thirty minutes, putting Hendricks on the road to Wisconsin well before midnight.

There is no proof that this happened. But it could have happened whether the murders were planned days in advance, or carried out only when the opportunity presented itself.

Yet opportunity is not enough to convict a person in a completely circumstantial case. The rule of law, as the jury was instructed, is that the defendant should not be convicted unless every reasonable theory of innocence has been ruled out.

It does not seem difficult to conjure up reasonable theories of innocence—but only if one can accept the idea that the children did not die before 11:30 P.M.

Someone knowing Hendricks's business plans could have awaited his departure. On foot, he might have followed Susan's car into the garage as she came home, and then hid until Hendricks left and Susan had joined the children in sleep. Or someone or some people completely foreign to the Hendricks family could have simply happened upon an unlocked porch door. Unlikely, but possible.

Could the killings have been the product of a terrible psychotic episode by Hendricks, a period that lasted only a matter of hours?

Dr. Rappaport, who was the only psychiatrist testifying at the sentencing hearing, believed so. Yet Hendricks claims that Rappaport never administered any of the psychological tests given him by at least a half dozen other psychiatrists and psychologists—all of whom pronounced him sane and normal. Hendricks claims Rappaport instead spent the first half of a two-day conversation trying to convince him to take on an insanity defense.

Dr. Michael Campion, a psychologist from Decatur, Illinois,

*Central Illinois psychic Greta Alexander, in fact, once told detectives that she saw a person in a medical gown involved in the murders.

was among the vast majority of mental health professionals who pronounced Hendricks mentally healthy and free of significant personality and emotional impairments. He believed Hendricks was simply a victim of circumstance and even offered to have Hendricks live with him in his home for a period of adjustment after the trial if Hendricks was found not guilty.

On the other side of the scales of justice, there are some matters which seem to point the finger of guilt back in Hendricks's direction. They were not mentioned by, or at least not dwelled on, by the prosecution and involve the hours before the bodies were discovered.

The sequence of telephone calls from Wisconsin and northern Illinois seems suspect and can be construed as attempts to learn whether the bodies had been discovered or to cause them to be found.

Why, at 5:31 P.M., almost the precise moment when Susan and the children were due at the Palmer home for dinner, did Hendricks call his home? Hendricks says he didn't know what time his family was due at his brother-in-law's. That's certainly possible. But if he did know, it could simply have been an effort to learn if the bodies had been found. If not, he could continue the charade with calls to his in-laws.

When he stopped at a phone booth about a hundred miles from home and called the Cramer home, why didn't he call his own home? Or his in-laws? It would seem the natural thing to do. He hadn't tried to reach his wife at home for about two and a half hours and hadn't talked with the Palmers for at least an hour and forty-five minutes.

And why, when he was within twenty minutes of home, did he pull off to the side of the road, get out of his car and exercise for a time? He may have been tired, but it would seem the adrenaline would be flowing if he neared his home, truly anxious about the welfare of his family. Could it be that as he approached the scene of the crime, he had to pause to clear his head and think about how he would respond to the variables that might confront him in the coming minutes?

Interesting speculation. But also actions that could be entirely innocent.

Could the murders have been committed by some stranger or strangers?

The U.S. Justice Department says a third of all assaults that occur in homes happen during burglaries. Burglary carries a substantial risk of violence if a member of the household is home when the burglary occurs. Several episodes that occurred in other parts of the country at about the same time bear resemblances to the Hendricks case.

One night in June of 1983—five months before the Hendricks murders—one or more persons entered a home in Chino, California, and used a hatchet, knife, and perhaps an ice pick to murder Frank and Peggy Ryen, their daughter Jessica, and a ten-year-old neighbor, Christopher Hughes, as they slept. An eight-year-old son, Joshua, was left for dead, but survived having his throat cut and his head smashed with the hatchet.

Seven weeks later, Kevin Cooper, a black man who had escaped from a nearby medium-security prison a few days before the murders, was arrested and charged with the killings despite the fact that young Joshua had told authorities that three white or Hispanic men were responsible for the crime. Cooper was convicted on a completely circumstantial case and is now on California's death row.

One night in September of 1983—two months before the Hendricks murders—one or more persons entered a home in Fort Wayne, Indiana, and used a blunt instrument to murder Dan and Jane Osborne and their eleven-year-old son, Ben. A two-year-old daughter, Caroline, survived.

About four months later, Calvin Perry III, a young black man, was charged with the killings despite the fact that little Caroline had described her attacker as having light skin. A day later Perry apparently hanged himself in his jail cell, leaving behind notes saying, "I haven't killed nobody."

One night in January of 1984—two months after the Hendricks murders—one or more persons entered a home in Aurora, Colorado, and used a hammer to kill Bruce and Debra Bennett and their seven-year-old daughter, Melissa, as they slept. A three-year-old daughter, Vanessa, escaped death. No one has ever been charged with those killings.

In the dozen days leading up to the Bennett murders, there were three very similar cases in the Aurora area. Each time the victims were attacked with a blunt instrument, and there was no sign of forced entry into their homes. And in three of the four Colorado cases, just as in the Hendricks case, a woman's purse was found near the crime scene, its contents spilled.

There are striking similarities among all of these cases. Each occurred in low-crime residential neighborhoods near interstate highways. In each case, there was no sign of forced entry into the home, and no fingerprints were left behind. In the multiple murders, young couples and their children were victims of vicious attacks as they slept.

But there is no proof that these murders, or the Sheppelman killing that occurred in Bloomington three months after the Hendricks murders, or any of the seventeen murders that happened in Will County, Illinois, about a hundred miles north of Bloomington three and four months before the Hendricks murders, had anything to do with the Hendricks case. However, there are more serial killings, more stranger-to-stranger murders, today than ever before.

The Federal Bureau of Investigation says it used to be able to count on murder victims having some kind of relationship with the killer in 80 percent of the cases. Now the FBI figures the percentage is only 55 percent. More and more murders are committed by people who kill at random, murder for its own sake. Could the Hendricks case be one of them?

Ever since that indelible autumn morning, the Hendricks murders have weighed heavily on my mind. I respect the people who investigated and prosecuted the case. Indeed, I consider some of them friends. Yet I have come to the pleasureless conclusion that they *may* have convicted an innocent man.